Among Cultures

Among Cultures: The Challenge of Communication, Third Edition explores intercultural communication and the relationship between communication and culture, using narrative as a common and compelling thread for studying intercultural interactions. Anchored in the position that people make sense of their worlds through choosing and telling narratives to themselves and others, this text is replete with narratives and stories. Chapters address key aspects of intercultural communication, including verbal and nonverbal communication; stereotypes and bias; identity; conflict; diversity; and ethics. Using an interpretive approach to intercultural communication, the text helps students understand that although a person may appear different, his/her common sense is quite reasonable within a particular interpretive context. Resources are included to help students understand and explain the reasonableness of other cultural systems.

The text includes activities for students to complete while reading, including self-assessments and nonverbal self-knowledge tests. Reflection questions within and at the end of each chapter promote thinking and discussion on each topic. With its unique approach to studying intercultural communication via real-life narratives, this text facilitates a deep understanding of the cultural aspects of communication. In providing the narratives of others, it encourages students to tell their own stories and build a strong foundation for communicating across cultures.

New to the Third Edition:

- New chapter—"How Does Culture Impact Applied Contexts?"—explores intercultural communication as it relates to the environment, health, and technology.
- New sections on identity, silence, and terms of address as important communicative practices in intercultural settings.
- Updated sections on honorifics, key terms, social dramas and the golden approaches to ethics.

Bradford J. Hall is Head of the Department of Languages, Philosophy, and Communication Studies at Utah State University. He teaches in the areas of intercultural communication and communication theory, focusing on the link between our talk, thoughts, and actions. His research deals with issues of culture, identity, membership, conflict, and everyday conversation.

Patricia O. Covarrubias is Associate Professor in the Department of Communication and Journalism at the University of New Mexico where she teaches cultural and intercultural communication, cultural discourse analysis, global metaphors, qualitative research methods, and the ethnography of communication. Her research has been dedicated to understanding the linkages among culture, communication, and peoples' unique ways of life.

Kristin A. Kirschbaum is Associate Professor at East Carolina University, and has taught courses in health communication, intercultural communication, organizational health communication, interpersonal communication, and communication theory. Her research includes measures of communication in physician populations with structured research protocols aimed to increase collaboration and medical communication among physicians.

Third Edition

Among Cultures

The Challenge of Communication

Bradford J. Hall
Patricia O. Covarrubias
Kristin A. Kirschbaum

NEW YORK AND LONDON

Third edition published 2018
by Routledge
711 Third Avenue, New York, NY 10017

and by Routledge
2 Park Square, Milton Park, Abingdon, Oxon OX14 4RN

Routledge is an imprint of the Taylor & Francis Group, an informa business

© 2018 Taylor & Francis

The right of Bradford J. Hall, Patricia O. Covarrubias, and Kristin A. Kirschbaum to be identified as the authors of this work has been asserted by them in accordance with sections 77 and 78 of the Copyright, Designs and Patents Act 1988.

First edition published by Harcourt College Pub 2002
Second Edition published by Wadsworth Publishing 2004

Library of Congress Cataloging in Publication Data
Names: Hall, Bradford J., author. | Covarrubias, Patricia Olivia, author. | Kirschbaum, Kristin A., author.
Title: Among cultures : the challenge of communication / Bradford J. Hall, Patricia Covarrubias, and Kristin A. Kirschbaum.
Description: Third edition. | New York : Routledge, 2018.
Identifiers: LCCN 2017004574| ISBN 9781138657816 (hardback) | ISBN 9781138657823 (pbk.)
Subjects: LCSH: Intercultural communication. | Culture conflict.
Classification: LCC GN345.6 .H34 2018 | DDC 303.6—dc23
LC record available at https://lccn.loc.gov/2017004574

ISBN: 978-1-138-65781-6 (hbk)
ISBN: 978-1-138-65782-3 (pbk)
ISBN: 978-1-315-62117-3 (ebk)

Typeset in Times New Roman
by Swales & Willis Ltd, Exeter, Devon, UK

Visit the companion website: www.routledge/cw/Hall

Contents

4 How Is Culture Related to Our Identities?   100

5 Where Can We Look to Explain Verbal Misunderstandings?   130

6 Where Can We Look to Explain Nonverbal Misunderstandings?   165

9 How Can We Succeed in Our Intercultural Travels? 284

10 How Does Culture Impact Applied Contexts? 319

11 What Diversity Exists in the Study of Intercultural Communication? 353

Preface

BRAD

As I approached the writing of this third edition, I decided it would be a good idea to include co-authors that could give a fresh perspective on what had been written in the past and expand on what previous editions had covered. After making this decision, I asked two individuals who I respect both as people and scholars, Patricia Covarrubias and Kris Kirschbaum, to join me in this effort and they both graciously accepted the invitation. Their contributions have been invaluable and I have greatly appreciated working with them and their patience with me throughout this process.

This last year's elective cycle in the United States involving Hillary Clinton and Donald Trump in addition to the international struggles that are ongoing highlight the great need for cultural understanding. A lack of knowledge about and empathy for others facilitates the objectification of them that can lead us to ignore the common humanity we share, making it easy to view our social relations in terms of a competition where greed and misunderstandings rule the day. Misunderstandings all too easily lead to distrusting and hating other communities, which creates cycles of emotional, social, economic, and physical violence that injure the quality of life for us all. Although these problems are easy to see on a grand scale and may seem beyond our power to change, these grand problems are built upon the small actions and interactions that each of us engages in daily. Although it is important to work on the large problems of our day, I believe it is just as important to work on the seemingly small challenges that arise in our individual lives. I hope this book will aid you in this endeavor. Intercultural communication is an emotional experience and writing this book is an act of love and hope for the future on my part.

Intercultural Interaction: An Exercise in Serendipity

Intercultural experiences for me have always been marked by serendipity. Serendipities are unexpected finds or discoveries that eventually turn out to be both pleasant and stimulating. To me the field of intercultural communication has always been ripe with serendipities. The study of intercultural communication inherently involves exposure to different ways through which meaning is produced among and across communities. What better seed could there be to grow serendipities? When I was still very young, I was essentially planted in a field which forced interaction with many Native Americans. Some of my early experiences with this group of people were surprising, but as I sorted through them and continued the interaction, I developed not only a taste, but a love for these new perspectives. Later when I lived in Europe for a couple of years, I continued to have these surprising but stimulating experiences and was even introduced to the term serendipity, which I now use to describe them.

I suspect that for many of us it was just such serendipitous occurrences that helped our interest in culture and intercultural interactions to grow. Discovering the unexpected and then, despite any initial frustration, finding the new understanding acquired through that discovery to be sweet and stimulating can be a great motivator for cultivating those opportunities in the future.

It is my hope that each of you in your own lives and in working with this text will also harvest serendipity. For, although by its very definition we cannot control or predict its exact occurrence, we can encourage it by our involvement in and attention to a culturally diverse world. I encourage you to share with others, as I have tried to do in this book, the serendipities that occur in your own lives.

PATRICIA

As an immigrant to the United States from Mexico, for me, cultural and intercultural communication have meant much more than learning about and enacting abstract concepts and practices. Since the age of eight, my everyday life has involved confronting multiple and divergent worlds. Along the way, these worlds have clashed on occasion because the ways that some people in the United States do life was/is very different from the one I left in my original homeland. Moreover, I have had the privilege of living in and visiting several states in this country, traveling to various places around the world (Turkey, Canada, Sweden, Denmark, Spain, and Germany), and spending 18 months living and working in France. So my personal experience has meant that daily, whether in the United States or abroad, I have had to negotiate the reality that other people's lives are informed by worldviews, values, attitudes, emotions, and rules for communicating that are similar to as well as radically different from the ones with which I was raised. To give you an example, although I have lived in the United States for several decades, to this day I struggle with treating elders in the same manner as young persons. If an elder enters a room and I am sitting down I immediately stand up, and I use honorifics to address the elder rather than using a first name as is acceptable by many people here. The respectful treatment of elders is a value that was taught to me from an early age and continues to serve as a deeply felt Mexican cultural practice that I tried to pass on to my son. I am not necessarily saying that one culture is better than another; but, rather, that each culture offers a different possibility.

Intercultural Communication as Possibility

What I appreciate most about the study of cultural and intercultural communication is the fact that it offers myriad valuable, accessible, and useful possibilities for understanding one another, for developing friendships, and for enjoying peace through our cultural differences.

You and we know that cultural differences can be used as a possibility for distinguishing ourselves from others in affirming and disconfirming ways. Especially in moments of conflict, differences can bring us to assert, "I am not like you!" In extreme situations, we might use our differences to set up divisions, disenfranchisements, and oppressions at all levels of our existence. However, we also know that being aware of and understanding others' cultural differences can also serve as powerful means for achieving affirmative social ends. In moments of friendship and rapprochement we might be prompted to say, "We have more in common than I thought." One of the advantageous aspects about difference is that it can mean introducing into our lives alternative ways of speaking and not speaking, eating, dressing, managing conflict, using time, engaging nature, and making human connections, among other possibilities. Again, to give you an example, prior to my research into communicative silence, I thought that the absence of talk meant something was wrong among interactants; that communication was empty and should be filled with words—the sooner the better. Studying communicative silence has taught me a new way for appreciating it and for integrating it into my own life. Now I realize that silence can help us communicate in ways other than through words. I've learned that silence can help shape identities, and can help us construct communal connectedness and continuity. And I've learned that silence can help people protect their cherished cultures. In my college classrooms, my students are often astonished, although not always pleased, by how long I can stand in silence waiting for them to think through and respond to questions during group discussions. And I have learned to sit still and listen to the sounds nature uses to communicate. This is not a skill I developed in childhood where the clamor of Mexico City traffic was more familiar. Without question, my own life and my intercultural agility have been richly enhanced through the possibility of hearing silence differently.

It is beyond evident that our contemporary world is giving way to much painful possibility. Our planet is hosting bloody wars on every continent, routinely tolerating mass attacks on innocent civilians, generating thousands of homeless refugees, and producing countless disenfranchised people at all levels of society. Still, intercultural communication bears the promise of alternative outcomes. We have unprecedented opportunities for using our knowledge, skills, and will to shape a better world; we can do this one intercultural conversation at a time. Through the concepts, explanations, questions, suggested activities, resources, and especially the personal narratives presented in this book, we offer useful tools to help you achieve more productive intercultural relationships. It is our way of offering you a new possibility.

KRIS

Like my co-authors, I have had the good fortune to travel and live in others' countries. Those opportunities helped me recognize the wealth of diverse cultures that make each of us who we are. When I was first introduced to the study of intercultural communication in college, I was amazed! It seemed like the observations I had made throughout my life were shared and explained by others. I felt like I had discovered a new section in the library with new information to explore. I was and still am excited to travel the journey of intercultural communication.

I have also come to realize that there are multicultural influences that are regionally as well as nationally situated. I grew up in Southern California in the 1960s and 1970s. As a young person I moved with my family to the Midwest. That move produced a huge culture shock for me. Rather than sunshine and beaches, I was confronted by cold and damp weather. I was also surrounded by people with ideas and behaviors that were much more conservative than what I had experienced as a child.

I returned to Southern California in my teens and realized that even within that region there were cultural differences. In my teens and 20s I lived in a different neighborhood than where I grew up and again learned the cultural nuances of my new environment. These experiences in my early life helped me learn about being curious about differences, and keeping an open mind in order to travel the path of exploration, rather than isolation. That sense of adventure has been foundational in my studies of intercultural communication.

As an adult I lived for 10 years in three very different geographical and cultural locations. I lived and worked for three years in Abu Dhabi, one of the United Arab Emirates, three more years in Manhattan, in New York City, and another three years in the state of Quintana Roo in Mexico. In all of these locations, I learned about languages, appropriate behavior, and other features of intercultural communication that are covered in our textbook. In a nutshell, I learned the difference between assimilation and acculturation. I am a better person because of the diversity I have been so fortunate to experience in my life. I say "better" since I feel more curious than ever about different ways of thinking, acting, and communicating that I encounter on a regular basis. It is ingrained in me to say and think "how interesting" when I meet someone with different customs and different ways of approaching the world. I love the feeling of adventure I experience as I take new journeys of exploration in the world of intercultural communication.

My hope for you as a student and reader of this textbook is that you will experience that curiosity I have. I hope that you too will come to enjoy learning about new cultures, new patterns of communication, and new ways of engaging with the world and people around you. Welcome to the new section of the library!

WHAT HAS CHANGED AND WHAT HAS NOT IN THIS EDITION

The most apparent change in this edition includes a brand new chapter overviewing three specific contexts in which intercultural communication plays a vital role, including communication in and about environmental issues, healthcare, and leadership within organizational settings. Many of the conflicts in our day center around the environment, our different understandings of the environment, and how we approach issues related to our environment. The new chapter helps to reveal many of the cultural differences that can lead to misunderstanding and conflict. Healthcare is also a major area of concern for most people. There are many different approaches to gaining and maintaining good health. Understanding cultural differences in the way we approach issues surrounding healthcare is essential in helping all communities to work together for a greater good. In a world beset with problems in a wide variety of increasingly multicultural organizations, it is useful to understand different perspectives on what constitutes effective leadership. Each culture has a unique way of perceiving and enacting leadership in various organizational settings. Understanding these differences can help us function more effectively in any organizational endeavor.

In addition, there are a series of new and updated examples dealing with many of the issues that have been covered in the past. However, one thing that has not changed with the updated examples and stories is the overall narrative perspective the book adopts. This text is grounded in the idea that people make sense of their world through a process of choosing and telling narratives to themselves and others. One of the basic communicative forms through which we as humans understand our own and others' lives is narrative. By narratives we refer to any discourse which expresses actions that occur over time and are related to some point of concern. Thus, even when we are telling others about what seem like ordinary experiences in our lives, we are telling stories or narratives. We as humans are at heart storytellers. Indeed, consciously or unconsciously, we are often engaged in choosing among competing narratives. The very quality of our lives is thus inseparable from the quality of our stories.

In keeping with this belief, this text is unusually full of narratives or stories. Each chapter begins with a narrative, and a variety of narratives are interwoven throughout the text. Instead of simply giving examples, like African Americans are polychronic, we try as much as possible to share a story that illustrates this and other related concepts. We believe this is a more effective way to learn about these concepts because the stories provide not only illustrative examples, but a context upon which discussion and analysis may be based. We hope that the many narratives we include in the text encourage you to remember and be more aware of related stories in your own lives. We always love to listen to and learn from good stories, so please feel free to contact us and share any of your own stories.

OVERVIEW OF THE BOOK

The text has a variety of features that make it accessible to students. As noted above, one of the main features of the text is that it is full of narratives that can be used both as illustrations of concepts and discussion starters. The text includes various activities that students can do as part of reading the text, such as the self-assessments in terms of students' worldviews and nonverbal self-knowledge tests. The text also includes other activity ideas at the end of each chapter that are meant to provide ideas that the student or instructor may use to expand the learning process. Each student and each class may only use a few of these activities, but there are a variety of activities from which to choose. Some of them may need to be modified to better fit the individual needs of the students. The text also includes reflection questions both within the chapters and at the end of each chapter. Aside from personal reflection, these questions may be used as part of a class discussion, or students may be asked to respond in writing to one specific reflection question from each chapter.

Each of the chapter headings is phrased in a question format because learning is stimulated and aided through the asking of questions. Learning to ask quality questions is an important part of any educational process. The chapter questions come from a combination of what we feel are important questions to ask to get a solid introduction into the field of intercultural communication, and from areas with which our students have shown a particular concern over the years. For example, we have found students to be particularly interested in the ethical issues addressed in Chapter 12. To give a summary of the overall text, we briefly review each of the chapter questions and provide an idea of the way we go about answering them.

Chapter 1: What Is Meant by Intercultural Communication? There are hundreds of definitions of culture and communication in scholarly literature and just about as many struggles over which definitions are best. This is because the ability to define what is or is not covered in a concept is very powerful. Definitional work is also a very important step in our efforts to organize our knowledge in a useful and memorable way. It is very difficult to deal meaningfully with a concept if we do not at least have a rough understanding of what is meant by it. This chapter does not directly concern itself with which definitions are best. It does, however, lay an important foundation for understanding the concepts and issues that will be considered throughout the rest of the text.

Chapter 2: What Is the Relationship between Communication and Culture? Given a basic understanding of terms such as communication, culture, and intercultural, one of the next logical steps is understanding how and to what extent they connect to each other. This question also allows us to further explore some of the basic concepts in the field, such as worldviews, norms, and values, which may be considered in any specific context.

Chapter 3: How Can We Learn about Our Own and Others' Cultures? Many introductory texts do not deal with this issue, or do so very briefly. However, we feel strongly that how we learn about a topic influences what we can learn. We hope that our students will want to learn about others outside of the classroom setting and continue learning after the course is over. With this in mind, we introduce communicative forms, such as narratives and rituals, that can help us learn about others without having an advanced degree. An added benefit of this chapter is that it allows students to understand how they have been learning culture all of their lives.

Chapter 4: How Is Culture Related to Our Identities? If we cannot connect the idea of culture to ourselves, we believe it will have little lasting value in our lives. We first review what is encompassed by the term identity, including discussions of different levels of identity in our lives and the role of power in identity negotiation. We also consider the role of communication in the formation of identities and pathways that lead to our various identities.

Chapter 5: Where Can We Look to Explain Verbal Misunderstandings? The frustrations that arise from misunderstandings, even when we think we have been very clear, are at the heart of many people's desire to study intercultural communication. This chapter focuses on the issues related to verbal misunderstandings. We consider the context of our speech, the structure of our speech, and the content of our speech, providing resources for the confused and frustrated to use in sorting out what has gone wrong. We also address issues related to face maintenance during these misunderstandings. Finally, we discuss the relationship between language and thought and the implications this has for our understanding of culture.

Chapter 6: Where Can We Look to Explain Nonverbal Misunderstandings? In this chapter we focus on nonverbal communication misunderstandings. We examine not only the relationship of nonverbal and verbal communication, but also the functions of nonverbal communication in different communities. The chapter reviews research on a wide variety of different forms of nonverbal communication, including kinesics, paralanguage, proxemics, and specific items, such as food, clothes, and smell.

Chapter 7: Why Do So Many People Get Treated Poorly? It doesn't take an overly careful observer to realize that in many intercultural settings people are often treated very poorly. Some communities or types of people seem to be targeted for frequent mistreatment. This chapter tries to go beyond the usual discussions of ethnocentrism, stereotyping, and prejudice to better understand why these things exist even when people agree that they are bad. We discuss the distinctions between these three different areas in terms of their forms and functions in society. We spend more time than is usual with issues of prejudice in terms of how people justify and accept prejudice in their lives. The text deals with these areas in a way that avoids the usual defensive responses that these discussions can provoke and tries to help readers make personal discoveries and decisions about their own personal experiences with prejudice, stereotyping, and ethnocentrism.

Chapter 8: How Can We Manage Conflict in Intercultural Settings? Conflict will happen in intercultural interactions. Given that assumption, in this chapter we explore what distinguishes intercultural conflict from other forms of conflict and discuss different types of intercultural conflict. We also examine issues of fear, competition, power, and history in relation to intergroup conflicts that are so often connected to intercultural settings. Finally, we discuss and illustrate a variety of resources that people may adopt to manage intercultural conflicts in positive or mutually satisfactory ways. We conclude by considering a concept that is important to dealing positively with any form of conflict: forgiveness.

Chapter 9: How Can We Succeed in Our Intercultural Travels? Many, if not most, people will have the experience of traveling to different cultural communities at some point in their lives. This experience can be a critical incident in intercultural relations, affecting generations of people. This chapter reviews four of the major models of acculturation and how they may be used to improve our intercultural travels. We also spend some time dealing with the often difficult process of returning home from our intercultural travels.

Chapter 10: How Does Culture Impact Applied Contexts? Intercultural communication is always occurring in specific contexts that go beyond the cultural differences involved in the interaction. In this chapter we examine three specific contexts that relate to common concerns we find in the world today. First, we examine communication about the environment. Second, we explore cultural differences and implications related to healthcare. The third and final context to consider in this chapter is tied to the practice of leadership in various organizational contexts. Understanding the culturally different ways of approaching these contexts and how we may communicate in and about them provides a useful foundation for intercultural interactions in these contexts.

Chapter 11: What Diversity Exists in the Study of Intercultural Communication? This chapter begins with an overview of the three main theoretical perspectives that exist in the field of intercultural communication today: interpretive, critical, and traditional. The text as a whole is largely written from an interpretive perspective so we spend a bit more time on the critical and traditional, or social scientific, approaches. To deepen this discussion, we use research surrounding the media in intercultural settings as well as popular culture to provide examples of the different types of work and approaches that exist in the intercultural field.

Chapter 12: Can Judgments of Right and Wrong Be Made When Dealing with Other Cultures? This chapter deals with the issues of ethics and building intercultural communities. Various approaches to ethics and judgments of what is right and wrong or good and bad are discussed in detail. In addition, we propose three ethical principles which we argue are especially important in intercultural settings.

Acknowledgments

BRAD

First and foremost, I wish to again acknowledge the consistent and invaluable help of my wife Delpha. As always, she has been a source of support and strength, both emotionally and technically, without which this book would not have happened. I am grateful to my colleagues and particularly Patricia and Kris for their work and motivation in accomplishing this project. I would also like to thank the many students (too numerous to try to name here), both graduate and undergraduate, who have contributed so much to my learning over the years, many of whom have contributed specific narratives and stories of their own intercultural experiences that help bring this text to life.

PATRICIA

My deepest thanks to Brad who mentored me through his scholarship long before we met, and later as a colleague and collaborator. I thank Brad and Kris for enabling me to experience new dimensions of cultural/intercultural communication as we worked on this project. Of course, my thanks to the many students, friends, and family whose stories invigorate the materials for this book. Finally, my thanks to my teenage son, Isaac, and his richly diverse generation who continually inspire my fresh intercultural explorations.

KRISTIN

I am indebted to Brad for multiple items. First, for being such an amazing professor during my graduate school experience. He showed me how to bring scholarly material to "life." The conversations I had with Brad after I became a professor about teaching intercultural communication were equally invaluable as he helped me recapture my joy in academia through an article we co-wrote. I am also grateful to both Brad and Patricia for all that I learned from them on this project. And finally, my friends, my family, and all the students who open my eyes and continue to expand my experience of the cultures that enrich our world.

BRAD, PATRICIA, AND KRISTIN

Lastly, we all want to express our appreciation to the wonderful publishing team at Routledge and their associates. Their patience and assistance throughout the project have been invaluable. We are sure to miss some who played a major role, but we would like to thank Nicole Solano, Kristina Ryan, Colin Morgan, Kevin Selmes, Sally Evans-Darby, and any others who have worked on this project.

Chapter 1

What Is Meant by Intercultural Communication?

The humidity was so high the air had become almost visible. Sally squinted down the street at the mirages glistening off the empty road. Sighing, she turned back and studied the patient faces of the half dozen or so people waiting for the bus. Their faces, settled in matching expressions, betrayed none of the impatience that Sally herself felt. She was hot and sweaty.

Sally thought of her friends back in California.

"Women don't sweat," Karen had always said in a mocking tone, "they glow!"

Well, Sally was certainly glowing now. She had been in Western Senegal for three weeks and despite the heat and unpredictability of public transportation, she had been thoroughly enjoying her stay. Things had been happening so fast that she had hardly had time to think. Her Wolof hosts were extremely gracious, catering as best they could to her every need, but she still often found herself feeling ill at ease.

"At times I wish they weren't quite so helpful," she mused and secretly studied the faces of the Wolof around her, searching for traces of the smiles that came so readily to her host family. It was then she noticed the woman sitting on the small bus stop bench, her hands folded carefully on her lap. Sally shifted uncomfortably on her tired feet.

"If that woman were to slide just a little bit either way," she thought, "I could sit down and ease the pressure on this little toe of mine."

Gathering her courage, Sally approached the woman. She knew she didn't speak Wolof perfectly, but her many years of work on the language had allowed her to feel fairly confident in her ability to handle most simple conversations.

(continued)

(continued)

She tried to catch the woman's eye and smile as she said in the most polite Wolof she could muster, "Excuse me, please, would you mind sliding over just a bit so that I can sit down?"

The woman, seeming a bit startled, looked at Sally without any of the customary friendliness she had come to expect in her short stay in this beautiful land. Indeed, Sally felt just a bit like some unsavory specimen under observation, but the woman did slide over. Sally nodded politely and sat down. She was just wondering what sort of conversation she might strike up that would ease the awkwardness she felt after making her request of the woman next to her, when she heard the now familiar rumble of a very used double-decker bus.

"Perfect timing," she chuckled to herself and started to move with the rest toward the spot where the bus would stop.

True to most of her bus rides since arriving, the bus was already carrying what seemed to be a full load of passengers. As she waited to find her way into the bus a Wolof fellow, whom she had noticed standing right behind the bench when she had asked the woman if she would slide over, leaned toward her and said, "You know, that's not the way we do things around here."

Surprised, she followed the flow of the people into the bus and then turned around to ask just what the fellow had in mind. However, he was nowhere in sight. Obviously, he had gone to the upper deck of the bus upon entering.

"Oh, well," she sighed, "I wonder what that was all about?"[1]

FIGURE 1.1 |

Miguel Gandert

CULTURE

What Sally did not realize at that moment is that it was all about *culture*. We will come back to the incident above, but before doing so we want to explain what we mean when we use the word *culture*.

Culture has been defined in hundreds of ways over the years.[2] Each of these definitions highlights different aspects of culture, and many of the definitions even conflict with each other. The risk with so many definitions is that the definition of culture becomes so broad that it means everything, which results in it meaning nothing for practical purposes. It is important to begin our study of culture and its impact on communication by giving a few specific guidelines regarding just what is and is not being discussed when the word *culture* is used in this text.

Stop for just a moment and ask yourself, "How would I define culture to a friend interested in my study of intercultural communication?" Would you tell your friend that it has to do with values? Traditions? Food? Race? Nationality? Going to the opera? Although we believe all of these are related to culture, the last three could be misleading in terms of what culture means in this book.

If we tell our friends that we are going to do something cultured, chances are they will picture us going to the theater or a museum, for example. This use of the term culture often leads to notions of *high culture* and *low culture*. High culture includes such things as going to the ballet or other activities often associated with relative wealth and social sophistication. Low culture deals with the common activities of people from a lower economic level. In this book there is no concern for high or low culture, or some idea of people being more or less cultured. So, although attending an opera is doing something of cultural significance, so is meeting friends at the bowling alley, playing soccer, or waiting for a bus with a group of strangers.

Perhaps an even more difficult distinction is that culture is not equivalent to race, ethnicity, or nationality, even though we often use these types of labels in discussing different cultures. We will use them in this book. For a variety of reasons these differences in group memberships often parallel at least some cultural differences. However, simple group membership (based on birth, occupation, and so forth) is not really what we are dealing with. A colleague shared this experience:

> In my interviewing class I had been using an instrument called "The Dove Test," created by a Watts social worker named Adrian Dove, to illustrate the impact of environment on what people know. Mr. Dove had generated about twenty questions that lower-class blacks living in Watts could answer, but most other people could not. On the day before I intended to use the "test," I discovered that I had misplaced the answers. So I hurried over

to the office of the only African American graduate student in the program, Bailey Baker, and asked him to help me generate the correct answers. With a sly smile on his face, he asked me why I thought *he* would know them.[3]

Simply because Mr. Baker is "black" does not mean that culturally he is the same as all others that may be said to be members of the "black race." Two people may be quite culturally distinct even though they may be said to belong to the same race or have citizenship in the same country. On the other hand, two individuals who are neither from the same country nor race may, in fact, be culturally similar. This is often due in part to a shared membership in other types of communities, such as religious or professional communities. So the question is, "What are we dealing with when we consider the notion of culture?"

Culture is defined for our discussion as a *historically shared system of symbolic resources through which we make our world meaningful*. To help bring this definition alive, we will explain and give an example of each of the key terms in the definition.

System

At the core of this definition is the idea that a culture is a system. To help you get a better sense of how a system works, let us ask you to apply the mathematical system with which you are familiar to the following five problems:

1   $1 + 1 = 2$
2   $7 + 5 = 12$
3   $11 + 3 = 2$
4   $6 + 3 = 9$
5   $8 + 9 = 5$

Which of the five problems just noted are performed correctly? Most of you would probably agree that problems 1, 2, and 4 are correct and that problems 3 and 5 are wrong. Most of us gained the ability to differentiate between right and wrong with problems like these when we were quite young. However, if you were to change the system you used to look at these problems, you may realize that they are all equally true. Take a minute and look at the problems. Do you see the system that would make each of these equally true? It is a system with which we are sure you are very familiar and one you use virtually every day of your life. We'll let you think about it for a moment before explaining what system we have in mind.

We are surrounded by systems. There is the legal system, the educational system, the solar system, and the parking system at your school, to name just a few. In fact, our bodies are systems made up of various other systems, like the immune system. In short, *a system is any group of elements that are organized in such a way that the elements are able to do things they couldn't do individually*. Water and various minerals may be elements that make up the human body, but it is the way these elements are combined that gives the human body its form and ability to perform certain tasks. Although there are differences across each human body, there is enough of a consistent pattern in the way the elements are organized that we can recognize a human from a tree even though many of the basic elements are the same.

Another system is our timekeeping system. This system uses a base 12 (rather than the traditional base 10) and is commonly understood in reference to 12-hour clocks. For example, if it is 11:00 and Patricia says meet me in three hours, you know without thinking too much that she wants you to meet her at 2:00. Of course, if it is 1:00 and she says meet me in one hour, it will also be 2:00. It is this time system that we use every day that makes each of the five equations above equally true. Even though this is a common system and one easily understood, it is typically difficult to see at first if we are thinking in terms of the base-10 system we often use when we see addition and equal signs. If we had written 11:00 plus three hours equals 2:00, most people would have agreed that our equation was right to begin with.

This simple example using our time system illustrates two very important functions of any system. Systems serve to both (1) *enable* us to do things and (2) *constrain* us from doing things, whether that be finding a parking space, deciding what to eat, or deciding if something is either right or wrong. We need systems to share ideas as humans or coordinate our actions to accomplish virtually any social task. However, although systems make it possible to even have meaningful interaction with other humans, they also constrain us from seeing or understanding some of the possibilities that exist for us and others.

Let's return to the story of Sally that began this chapter. Sally was confused by the gentleman's critique of her actions. In her mind, she had been as polite as possible. The difficulty arose from Sally's assumption that there was just one system for making polite requests. The same may be said for the Wolof, who thought of Sally as rude rather than polite. In fact, there were two different systems for making polite requests operating in the opening story. The opening story is based on the experiences of Judith Irvine and prompted a discovery process that revealed some basic differences in the ways U.S. Americans[4] and Wolof go about making such requests.[5]

First, Americans tend to word requests in such a way that they focus on whether the person being asked wants to do whatever is being requested. For the Wolof this focus on the personal whims or desires of the person being addressed seems strange. If some aspect outside of the request itself needs to be the focus, the Wolof would see the demands of the social situation as more appropriate. In the case described, the situation obviously required that the woman would slide over, so there was no reason to focus on the willingness of the person being asked to slide over.

Second, the Wolof are not as comfortable with talking to strangers as Americans and do not value talk as a way to get to know a stranger in the same degree as Americans. Thus, when Sally made her request in a way that ended with a question that seemed to invite further conversation, it seemed both awkward and strange to the Wolof woman and overly forward to the Wolof man.

Finally, in the Wolof community there is an informal norm that signals the type and importance of the request. Your typical, everyday sort of request is asked in a very simple format. The syntax, or sentence structure, tends to be short and straightforward. Requests that use elaborate sentence structure, such as the "Excuse me, please, would you mind. . ." used by Sally, are reserved for those requests that are very special and important to the requester. Thus, the woman looked at Sally strangely because here was this foreigner who seemed to be indicating a desire for conversation, while almost being insulting by acting like the woman's sliding depended purely upon her good will when, in fact, it was obviously required in the situation. To top it off, she acted like this simple sliding over was some huge, important request. Perhaps she was thinking, "Foreigners, who knows what to expect from them." Irvine's research demonstrates that for Sally to have been perceived as a normal, polite person she should have just said, "Slide over."

Historically Shared

Culture refers to systems that are shared. This sharing allows members to communicate with each other in relatively efficient and effective ways. This sharing is also related to issues of identity. A shared history or tradition gives people one answer to the question, "Who am I?" This aspect of culture is illustrated in part by a story from one of our students:

The year is 1970 and the place is Texas. My grandfather is the manager for a local gas station. On a sunny afternoon, a woman drives into the station and requests that four new tires be placed on her car. Although this woman could not produce the money to pay for these tires, my grandpa gave them to her anyway on the condition that she would faithfully pay him back in small installments each week. The woman, being very grateful, agreed to this arrangement and drove away with her new tires. Weeks passed by and the woman did not return. My grandpa would occasionally see her out and ask her about the money. Her reply was always, "Oh, I don't have it with me now, but I'll get it to you next week."

Three months passed and the woman still did not repay her debt. One day the woman drove past the gas station and into a nearby parking lot. My grandpa saw the woman get out of her car and walk into a store. Immediately my grandpa rolled a car jack over to her car, lifted it up and began to remove the tires. Minutes later the woman exited the store and to her dismay saw the tires being removed.

"What are you doing with my tires?" she exclaimed.

"Actually," my grandpa stated, "these are my tires and I'm taking them back because they are not paid for."

As he bent back down to collect the remaining tires, the woman opened her purse and began to write a check. "I'm sorry ma'am, but I won't accept your check," my grandpa said firmly. The woman, looking very stressed, then dug again into her purse and produced the right amount of cash to pay off the bill. My grandfather gladly accepted the money and put the tires back onto her car.

My grandpa passed away one year after I was born so I never had the opportunity to meet him. No matter how many times I hear this story, it makes me laugh. I am astonished at how bold my grandpa was. . . I can see in my own family these values being modeled by my father and mother. Fortunately, they insisted on passing them along to their children. My grandpa may have passed away more than twenty years ago, but his memory lives in the family stories that are told.[6]

Sharing of family stories is just one way in which culture is passed along. However, this account also highlights some basic aspects of culture. As this student shares this story with siblings and other family members, a sense of who they are becomes clearer. As one student noted, family narratives are an expression of one's life. This did not have to be a *family* story, however, for it to have an influence on identity. Within a political group, nation, or some other community of people, we hear stories and get information that tells us who we are and what we act like as a group. We certainly are not bound by this knowledge, but it does teach us (often without even seeming to) what is normal and expected for people like us.

This student did not actually have to know and remember her grandpa for him to have an influence on how she thought and acted. Because this story has been retold, it is easy for her to see how her grandpa's actions have come to be reflected in her own life and the lives of her parents. Yet the cultural sharing implied in this story is not limited to family members. This story takes place within a community of people who allow and understand such actions. The experience is just one example of a pattern of actions that influence what will be seen as acceptable in the future and are themselves made understandable by decisions from the past. Culture, therefore, gives us identity building blocks and connects us with people we have never seen, be they individuals who are alive right now, who have lived before us, or will live after us.

Of course the connections that we share with one person are different from those we share with others and the nature of these connections will change over time.

We all belong to many different cultural communities, whether they are related to our families, our occupations, our nationalities, our religious or social affiliations, and so on. Although reasonably stable, these shared memberships are not static in nature. Sometimes a group of immigrants will try to *freeze* their culture in an effort not to lose it in a new land, but this practice invariably leads to surprise and often disappointment when they get a chance to return to their homeland years later.[7] Just as history is always in the process of being created in the lives we lead, so culture is always open to change. These changes are connected with what has gone before and will influence what will come in the future, but cultures are inherently in flux.

Symbolic Resources

Now that we know that culture is a *historically shared system*, we need to understand just what constitutes this system. Our cultural systems are made up of symbols that serve as resources that help us to interact with each other in meaningful ways. When we say that something is symbolic, this usually suggests that it stands for something else. If we use the word (and symbol) *tree* in a conversation, it stands for a plant in the physical world. This is a fairly easy connection to see, even though it may provide problems for understanding given the many

FIGURE 1.2 | Symbols carry powerful connotations. For example, the burning of a nation's flag often evokes emotions beyond what might be expected if just a plain piece of cloth were burned

different types of trees that exist. However, when symbols represent things that are much less tangible, such as *beauty* and *freedom*, the problems are magnified.

In the United States there has been at times quite a bit of controversy over whether it is okay to burn the U.S. American flag. Without trying to get into the merits of the various arguments surrounding this issue, it is clear that many of the problems related to this controversy are due to the symbolic nature of what is done when a flag is burned. The flag represents the United States and the principles upon which the United States as a political entity is based. Thus, burning the flag, whether it is in the U.S. or in Iran, is not simply destroying a piece of cloth. It is making a statement about a way of life. Some argue that the burning itself is symbolic of the freedoms that exist in the United States and others feel that the burning represents an effort to destroy those freedoms. Thus, symbolic acts are open to great differences of interpretation.

There are two characteristics of symbols everywhere that make these differences of opinion a natural part of our world. Symbols are *arbitrary* and *conventional*. The word *symbol* is derived from the Greek terms *bolos*, meaning to throw, and *sym*, meaning with or together. Thus, from its beginning the notion of symbol referred to something being just thrown together. The English symbol for one physical object you may be sitting upon is *chair*, the Spanish symbol for that same object is *silla*, whereas the Japanese symbol for this object we sit on is *isu*. Is one of these the real and correct symbol for that physical object and all the others wrong? Of course not. In a way, this supports the old idea that a rose smells as sweet regardless of what it is called. Because there is no necessary connection between the symbol *rose* and the physical flowers we associate with that symbol, it would smell just as sweet even if we called it "tuna."

Before going too far with this idea of symbols as arbitrary, it is crucial that we remember that symbols are also conventional. Something that is conventional is agreed upon by a group of people. The symbol *rose* is connected with a particular type of flower because a group of people have agreed that such a connection should be made and have passed down that connection. Because these connections are arbitrary, however, they can and do change over time. Think how the symbols *weed*, *gay*, *righteous*, and *bad* have changed over time because groups of people have agreed to these changes. How these types of changes occur is an interesting focus of study.

Our earlier suggestion of substituting the symbol *tuna* for the symbol *rose* probably did not seem very attractive to you. Each symbol has a multitude of connotations or informal meanings associated with it that have the power to change our perceptions. Thus, a rose by any other name (say tuna) might not immediately smell as sweet. The power of conventional meanings to influence our physical perceptions will be discussed in more detail later in the chapter, but it may interest the reader to know that the symbol *tuna* was, in fact, part of what might be viewed as a positive change in symbol use. The fish that we commonly represent with the symbol or word *tuna* used to be called *horse mackerel*. Because of the conventional meanings associated with *horse* and to a lesser extent *mackerel*, the marketing of this fish in the United States was problematic. Americans don't like to eat anything associated with horses. The use of the word *tuna* and its acceptance in representing a certain type of fish was a major part of the marketing success of what we now call tuna.

It is the conventional aspect of symbols that gives them, and culture in general, a sense of stability and consistency. Indeed, although some playing with the conventional meanings of symbols is allowed and even appreciated, if you constantly use symbols in unconventional ways, you will likely be locked up or in some other way removed from society. On the other hand, it is the arbitrariness of symbols that gives culture its dynamic and changeable quality. The fact that culture is a symbolic system gives culture both the power to change and the power over change. This ongoing tension about change is at the heart of many debates in the social sciences as scholars seek to understand these seemingly opposing characteristics of culture.

The definition of culture, however, does not simply refer to symbols, but to symbolic resources. A resource is anything that allows one to do something. Land, money, fame, athletic ability, and an attractive face can all be resources in the right setting. Symbolic resources may be tangible, such as a flag, or intangible concepts, such as freedom. The key is that these resources are both arbitrary and conventional and they help those who share them accomplish certain tasks, the most basic of which are to *share meaning* and *coordinate* multiple *actions*.

One specific task is greeting other people. One resource for greeting we have heard is the phrase, "Hey, what's up?" In England in certain settings involving royalty the phrase, "Your Eminence," is part of an appropriate greeting. These resources are each only part of a system so they are not equally appropriate at all times. Indeed, try greeting a few people today with a combination of these resources, "Hey, what's up, Your Eminence?" We suspect that you will get some responses that indicate its inappropriateness. Again, though, the setting is an important part of the overall system. Think of the different impact this greeting might have if you used it with a supervisor at work, a parent, a best friend, an unknown teenager at a mall, or the professor in your next class.

Another common resource for greeting someone in the United States is the question, "Hi, how are you?" The question serves as a way to acknowledge another person in a friendly way. It is not meant to be taken as a literal request for specific information and it is often said in passing. In fact, attempts to tell someone how you really are will usually result in confusion or frustration for all involved. This resource for greeting is not simply a matter of language, such that all English speakers share the same resources or all Spanish or Russian speakers and so on. Instead, it is the way a group of people *use* the language they have. A woman who recently moved to the United States from England told Brad that she is constantly frustrated by that question. She is torn by the sense that either she is rude in not really answering the question or the other person is rude in asking without real intent. For her, a brief comment about the weather, such as, "A bit fresh, eh?" (meaning it is quite cold) or "Lovely bit of weather, eh?" would much better accomplish the need to connect briefly with the other person.

One U.S. American realized just how frustrated so many international students are by these unfamiliar resources for doing the simple task of greeting. She shared with Brad that when she started working in Korea she was constantly asked in passing, "*Odi-ga-seyo*?" which literally means, "Where are you going?" She was confused and a bit paranoid at first. "It's none of their business," she thought, and besides no one seemed all that excited when she tried to tell them. Eventually she learned that the phrase, "Where are you going?" served much the same purpose as, "How are you?" in the United States. Instead of responding with "fine" and going on, she just needed to respond with "over there" and go on. The systems of symbolic resources we use to do simple things like greet people, go out on a date, celebrate a holiday with family, or make a request at work are all examples of culture.

Make Our World Meaningful

Now that we have a feeling for the symbolic resources that make up culture, our next concern is with what this system of resources does for us. In a broad sense it makes our lives meaningful. Although the main focus of this section will be on the idea of meaning, we do want to comment briefly on the "make our world" part of the definition. Cultures are the creation of human interaction. Culture is something we learn; we are not born with it. Any human baby can learn the culture of any community. Cultures, as noted earlier, are both stable and changing. As people discuss past issues, invent new technologies, and so forth, common understandings can and do change. Thus, as we discuss culture in this text it is important to remember that we are talking about something that can and does change, even though most of the time it is difficult to pinpoint when and where that change occurred.

The last part of this definition concerns what culture as a shared symbolic system does for us. It provides us a way to act meaningfully and a way to understand the behaviors of others as meaningful. To say that some human behavior, or any other aspect of this world, is meaningful is to assume that the significance of that behavior or object is shared. Meaning may be classified into three components: selection, organization, and evaluation.[8]

Selection

Selection refers to those things we pick out to notice. At any given time there are always many more things to notice than we actually do. This selection

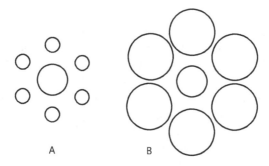

FIGURE 1.3 | Perception check

Source: *Human Behaviour: An Inventory of Scientific Findings* by Bernard Berelson and Gary A. Steiner, copyright © by Harcourt Brace and World, Inc. Reprinted by permission of the publisher.

process is learned and is often at the root of intercultural problems. Part of the problem is that humans do not always perceive things accurately. For example, in Figure 1.3, which is bigger, the middle circle in A or in B? Although to most people A looks bigger, they are the same.

However, the main challenge with the selection process in intercultural communication is that it does not involve easy right or wrong answers, but involves a difference in what is selected to notice in the first place. Each selection may be equally correct depending on the background and needs of those doing the perceiving.

Sometimes this selection process is embedded in the words we use. If we ask someone in English if it is okay if our brother comes with us, they would *know* that the person we are referring to is male and is related to the person speaking, probably through birth. However, if we make this same request in Thai, those listening will also know if that person is younger or older than the person speaking. That is because relative age is also embedded in the symbols that we would use if we were speaking Thai, just as sex is embedded in the English term "brother." The selection process can be especially difficult when what is being selected or perceived is not tangible. In Japan the emotion *amae* is a very normal and important emotion; however, there is no one-word translation in English for this concept. Efforts to translate the concept often deal with a bittersweet sense of dependency, true of some parent–child relations, but there always seems to be the sense that the definition is somehow lacking. In contrast, there is no one-word translation in Japanese for the American concept of *privacy*. The somewhat common idea that someone just needs a little privacy is a hard concept to explain clearly in Japanese. Looking at a particular relationship problem, an American may see (select out) the need for privacy, whereas the Japanese may see amae. Their different backgrounds and cultural knowledge make it very likely for certain aspects of a situation to be noticed and others to not even be recognized.

Even when the selection process appears to point toward the same thing, problems can arise. We have heard the following story passed on at various meetings associated with intercultural trainers. We do not know if it really happened or just illustrates this point well.

An intercultural specialist was conducting some training for a multi-national group and was discussing differing values. To do this he introduced a value exercise. This exercise involved pretending that you were on a sinking ship and there was only one life raft left. You had to go on it and you could only take one other person or you would all die. The other person would have to be either your mother or your wife. Thus, the problem was already selected for all the participants. Two of the participants, a British fellow and a man from Saudi Arabia, both quickly remarked that it was an easy choice. The trainer asked the Saudi who he would choose and he said that he would pick his mother, of course. The British fellow immediately complained that the wife should be the choice because as much as you loved your mother, she had lived a full life and your wife was your chosen companion throughout your future life. The Saudi disagreed, stating, "You can always get a new wife, but you only have one mother."

Both men perceived the need to make a choice between their mother and their wife, but it is obvious that the interpretations of this situation, and thus their choices, were very different. These differences were, in part, the result of organizing the concepts of mother and wife differently.

Organization

Organization refers to the connections we make between things that allow us to interpret what is going on. We understand things in reference to other things. If we were to ask you to explain what is meant by the symbol *mother*, chances are that you would talk about things like giving birth, nurturing, teaching, loving, and so forth. All of these explanations are based on relationships to other people and things. We do not know what a mother is in isolation from other concepts. The same is true for any symbol, idea, or concept. We do not know what they are except in relation to how they connect to other concepts. We referred to the symbol *chair* a bit earlier. To understand what a chair is, we need to know about the idea of sitting, how a chair compares to other furniture, and so forth.

When you encounter any situation, you are constantly making connections to understand what is going on. Stephen Barley discusses how the meanings conveyed through these connections are manipulated in many funeral homes in the United States.[9] Funeral directors are often faced with the need to help control unusual behaviors or reactions resulting from the stress related to the death of a loved one. One way of doing this is to make the funeral scenes appear more normal. For example, the dead body is treated in a way that suggests peaceful rest. Before the body is allowed to be viewed it has the mouth wired shut, the eyes stitched together, and it is laid in a coffin, the inside of which often resembles a very nice bed with a soft pillow. Because this is done the person looks like she or he is sleeping and a subtle message of peaceful rest is conveyed so that the shock of death is somewhat moderated.

Evaluation

Evaluation refers to the judgments of worth and value that are based on our interpretations. Virtually at the same moment that we select out certain elements and organize them into a meaningful situation or scenario, we will get the feeling that the actions are good or bad, right or wrong, and so forth. One effective way to start to look for cultural differences is to pay attention to the feelings of anger, annoyance, and so forth that arise when we evaluate something we see in a negative way. Indeed, Agar argues that culture itself is only really meaningful in situations where problems exist.[10] The following is an example of such a problem.

A *person from India living in the United States ran into a problem when she had an eye infection. She was told at the clinic by one doctor that she had Iritis and that she needed steroid drops. However, in going through the process to get these drops she was told by the optometrist that she simply had contact lens overuse and that she should just let it alone and that it would heal in a couple of days. Over a week later it still had not healed.*

She then visited with a friend who was in the medical profession. This friend said that it was indeed Iritis. The friend had recently seen another case just like hers. The friend, who was not officially an "eye" doctor, told her to go to a different eye doctor and get re-diagnosed. When the woman from India asked how much this might cost, she was told around 100 dollars. Because finances were tight she wondered out loud if there was any other way. Her friend told her that she could write a prescription for the drops, but would not feel comfortable doing so since that was not her official area of expertise. The Indian woman did not directly ask her friend to write the prescription because a friend would not impose that way on another friend, but she fully expected her friend to volunteer to write the prescription. The friend did not. Instead, she reiterated her advice to see another doctor.

The woman from India became frustrated and hurt; in her opinion her friend knew that she was in pain and low on funds. Her friend had the ability to cure her, but did not offer to help. The friend was following professional medical ethics, but in this woman's mind real friends did anything they could to help each other, including ignoring formal rules.

The Indian's woman's interpretation of what a friend is led her to evaluate negatively what her friend felt were very appropriate actions. In fact, she no longer considers the other person a *friend*.

See if you can pick out all three of the elements of meaning—selection, organization, and evaluation—at work in the example that follows.

The reception for the visiting officials had been going quite well, thought Fred. The food and drink were excellent and the conversations had been growing progressively livelier. Fred was interrupted from his moment of reflection by Manuel, a lecturer at a local university here in Manila. He liked Manuel. As a consultant to the Philippines Department of Education, Fred had gotten to know many of the teachers. Manuel had always seemed open and honest and a very clear thinker.

Drink in hand, Manuel nudged Fred and with a little smile quietly asked Fred who he thought was the most beautiful woman in the place.

Fred laughed a little bit, but was willing to play along, so surveying the room, he noticed a woman dressed in black standing over by the food table. He had noticed her earlier in the evening and pointed to her now.

"Who?" asked Manuel, a bit confused.

Trying not to be too obvious, Fred again pointed to the woman in black.

"Who?" Manuel asked again, now sounding a bit impatient.

Fred was amazed. How could he not see her? "That woman right there dressed in black," he exclaimed a bit louder than he had planned.

"Her?" asked Manuel in disbelief. "Why, she's just a server; I'm asking you about women!"

Feeling a bit confused and awkward, Fred stammered a little apology of some kind and quickly excused himself to go mingle with other guests. However, at the end of the evening he still felt uncomfortable about his exchange with Manuel.[11]

The situation described illustrates the three concepts of selection, organization, and evaluation just discussed. Both Fred and Manuel thought they were selecting out women, but the lower status of the woman in black made her virtually invisible to Manuel. Thus, she was unavailable to be part of a pattern that could be interpreted as beautiful women. Fred believed Manuel's interpretation that the server was not a "woman" was wrong. At the same time Fred's selection and classification of the woman in black as beautiful was also frustrating and inappropriate for Manuel.

In summary, culture is the system that encourages us to select out certain features of a social scene and make sense of the scene by showing how its elements are related, and make judgments based on the perceived worth of the pattern we discern.

Reflection Question: In what ways does the definition of culture fit or not fit with the one you had in your own mind before reading this chapter?

COMMUNICATION

For our purposes in this book, communication refers to the *generation of meaning*. This general definition follows a social constructivist perspective in which meanings are generated through the interpretive practices of humans as they work out the meanings of different messages with each other. This interpretive process goes on regardless of whether the messages are verbal or nonverbal, delivered in person or over some mass mediated pathway. Of course, the term communication is also subject to cultural nuances. In the United States, one often hears about "communication breakdowns," a "lack of communication," and the "need to communicate." These phrases generally do not convey that meaning has not been generated or that, in a dictionary sense, communication has not occurred. Instead, they mean that the type of communication that has taken place is not valued positively by those making these comments.

If a husband and wife finish a conversation by yelling at each other and blaming each other for all their problems, or a person raises an important topic with a friend and the friend just ignores it and changes the subject, many people in the world claim that there has been a lack of communication even though meaning has been generated. Tamar Katriel and Gerry Philipsen claim that for an interaction to really be considered communication, that interaction must be supportive, close, and flexible.[12] They further identify a four-step process that must be followed for it to be said in some American communities that two people have really communicated. First, one person must raise a topic that is important to him or her; second, the other person must somehow acknowledge the legitimacy of that topic; third, there must be a sharing of ideas on that topic; fourth, the people involved must end the conversation in a way that indicates they are both good people, a kind of "I'm okay, you're okay" feeling. If any one of these steps is not followed, there will be the perception that there was a lack of communication, regardless of how many meanings were generated and transmitted during the interaction. This specific form of "communication" is not equally valued across all cultures.

In spite of the many cultural differences in communication, there are two features of communication that we assume in this text are true in all cultures. Communication is interdependent and situational.

Interdependent

In much of our thinking in the West we like to imagine the world as made up of simple cause and effect types of relationships. This is reflected in the social sciences by the use of independent and dependent variables in explaining human behavior. Independent variables cause certain reactions in dependent variables. This is reflected in many models of communication. The speaker is typically seen as an independent variable who persuades, informs, or entertains the listener or dependent variable. Then when the listener becomes the speaker, to provide feedback and so forth, he or she becomes the independent variable and the roles are reversed. Much of the communication training that takes place uses this model. It assumes that if there is a problem in the interaction, one just needs to learn how to be more persuasive, more clear, or more humorous.

These models, even in allowing for feedback, often distort the communication process by ignoring the fact that people are simultaneously having an impact on each other. This impact is not so much A causing B, but A and B influencing each other's choices continually and often without conscious recognition. Even though we may have planned on giving the same lecture to two different groups, it will never really go exactly the same. Each particular interaction is different because it is interdependent or reliant on the particular people involved. The nature and direction of any communication event is always influenced by the choices of each party involved with the communication. Even if that choice is silence. This happens even in what seems like only one-way communication, like a drill sergeant giving orders. The degree of attention by the privates influences (but does not determine) the way in which the drill sergeant gives the orders.

This interdependence is important to remember because it changes how we view intercultural problems. A statement like, "She sure made me mad" is an obvious distortion and not a very useful one. Although she may have encouraged feelings of anger, one would have had to make a choice to be angry in response to her actions. At different times the exact same behaviors result in anger and sometimes in other reactions. If someone were to "flip us off" while we were driving on a freeway, we may choose to be angry, to laugh, or even to feel sorry for that person, depending on our mood and the situation. This is important to remember in intercultural communication because it means we can never just give up by laying all the blame on one party. Like the old saying, "It takes two to fight," we always have to see what we can do to help the situation, but we must never shoulder the full blame for misunderstandings. Sometimes, though, as we will see in later examples, certain parties contribute more than their equal share to the misunderstanding.

Situational

Communication, or the meanings generated in any given interaction, is always to a certain degree influenced by the situation. When we assess meaning it is always in reference to some context. Take, for example, the word phrase, "I love you, too." When a person says that to her or his mother, it has a different meaning than when the person says it to a significant other and yet a third different connotation when a person uses it with a son or daughter. Further, if a person is on the freeway and that driver we mentioned cuts the person off and shows a particular finger, the responding comment, "I love you, too," has another quite different meaning. Even though the words have remained the same, the context modifies the meanings that are generated. Because each culture organizes contextual features differently, we must always try to understand the native context.

FIGURES 1.4–1.6 | The phrase "I love you, too" can have very different meanings depending upon the situation

Reflection Question: Can we ever not communicate? What does it mean for someone to say, "There was just no communication happening in that meeting?"

INTERCULTURAL COMMUNICATION

Given the discussion up to this point, when we refer to "intercultural communication" we are referring to interactions where the *symbolic* resources, norms, *assumptions*, and expected outcomes are not shared by all the parties involved in the interaction. In the opening narrative Sally had certain expectations for how requests should be made and what to expect when one was made. However, the people she interacted with from the Wolof community had a somewhat different expectation for how to make successful requests. When we interact within our own cultural community, we share a common sense that allows meaning and coordinated action to occur in predictable ways, even when we perceive others as being disagreeable. When we interact across cultural communities, there are subtle differences in what is common sense, which may or may not interfere with our social goals. Our ability to predict or understand social outcomes has been complicated and can leave someone with an ongoing sense of uncertainty.

INTERCULTURAL COMMUNICATION AS A FIELD OF STUDY

The origins of the field of intercultural communication as it currently exists as a field of study are typically traced to the work of Edward Hall.[13] In the 1940s and 50s Hall worked for the United States' Foreign Service Institute. The goal at this point in time was to generate information regarding cultural differences that could be immediately put to practical use. Hall's book *The Silent Language* published in 1959 is typically considered the first "intercultural communication" book. Other books, including some initial textbooks for newly designed courses, were soon to follow. Of course there were earlier works that dealt with issues relevant to this area of study,[14] but they were not as influential in terms of spawning a separate academic field. Hall's work for the government was complemented by a growing interest in work related to such activities as the Peace Corps and international business. This early work was primarily concerned with very practical applications designed to help make a consumer of the research more successful in jobs that required intercultural interaction. In Chapter 11, we review the approach that grew directly from this focus as the *traditional* perspective on culture and communication.

Two other major perspectives have developed within the field of intercultural communication: *interpretive* and *critical*. The interpretive perspective is rooted in part in early ethnographic work done by Dell Hymes, who was interested in understanding the structured, distinctive ways of speaking that particular communities had developed to make sense of their lives.[15] Other researchers, such as Stuart Hall and Jürgen Habermas, began to question existing power relations and the historical structures that made these unequal power relations possible.[16] This focus was also adopted by some of the scholars working in the intercultural communication field.[17] These three perspectives—the traditional focus on practical success, the interpretive focus on understanding the other, and the critical perspective which attends to subtle forms of oppression in society—are the major perspectives currently found within the field of intercultural communication. After we have had an opportunity to gain more knowledge about basic concepts related to culture and intercultural communication, we will revisit these different perspectives in more detail in Chapter 11.

HAZARDS OF INTERCULTURAL STUDY

Finally, we want to give a couple of warnings about studying intercultural communication. It is easy to oversimplify (ignore exceptions and subtleties), overgeneralize (assume all people that share a culture are the same), and exaggerate (differences between groups of people).

Oversimplification

Edward T. Hall said that our failure to understand other cultures is often because we fail to recognize the subtleties that exist in every culture.[18] Once Brad assigned two readings in a graduate class on research methods. One dealt with research focusing on the Western Apache and the other one dealt with work done on so-called mainstream American culture. The class felt the research on the Western Apache was insightful and well done, but that the research on the mainstream American culture was merely okay and incomplete in many ways. After discussing the papers it was realized that actually the research on Americans had been done just as thoroughly as the Western Apache example (both were well done). However, because over 80 percent of the students were part of the group being studied in that project, and none of the students were Western Apache, they were able to see possible exceptions and subtle nuances in regards to the American study that they were not able to see in the one on the Western Apache. No research can completely cover every possible exception or possible nuance of meaning that exists within a culture. Remember, culture is dynamic, so even if you could understand it all at one point in time (which is highly unlikely), parts would change by the time your work was published. It is always easy to see little problems in work which examines our own cultures, but difficult to recognize these when reading research about a culture with which we are unfamiliar. Thus, we should not be shocked if we run into exceptions to something we have read about a culture.

Overgeneralization

The point about oversimplification is closely linked to our earlier caution about overgeneralizing. Instead of looking at culture per se, we are referring now to specific people. For example, simply by virtue of being native Mexican, Patricia is often expected to know about and be able to respond to questions about Mexicans in general. In the past, Anglos have been surprised to learn that she does not know how to make *tortillas* and that she does not eat *chile*. No one person is a perfect representation of a whole culture. In part, this may be because we typically are part of many different cultures. We share a system for making sense of the world with members of our family, members of our occupation, members of our church, members of groups linked to hobbies and other interests we have, and members of the regional and national community in which we live. These different systems for making sense frequently overlap, but there are differences and no one of them entirely captures the resources we have for understanding and acting in the world. So, don't be too surprised if you meet someone from a culture you have read about and that person does not act exactly as you expect. Humans are not cultural robots.

Exaggeration

Finally, we must be careful not to exaggerate the differences between cultures. If there were no differences, there would be no need for this sort of class. There are differences; however, there are also many similarities. When studying intercultural communication, it is the differences that get most of our attention. As university professors, Brad, Patricia, and Kris often have students from the United States link up with international students as conversation partners. One of the most common items they report is how surprised they were that the other person was so similar to them. Our focus on differences can at times create more anxiety than is necessary and cloud the fact that there are also always similarities. We encourage you to look for similarities as well as differences, so that as the differences arise you can appreciate how others are culturally unique in a way that adds greater meaning to your life.

BENEFITS OF INTERCULTURAL STUDY

The potential hazards just discussed are balanced by the many benefits for our study of intercultural communication. The list of reasons for engaging in this kind of study could be quite lengthy and very specific to particular situations; however, we will focus briefly on three broad and interrelated reasons.

Personal Empowerment

First, studying intercultural communication increases the *knowledge and under-standing* we have of our relationships and our world. As we come to know that there are other ways to look at what we thought was obvious, we can learn new ways to deal with old problems. Knowledge of these different perspectives gives us a broader view on our own lives and the problems we face. On the other hand, ignoring or hiding from our differences and avoiding interactions with those different from ourselves creates a comfortable, but confining, cage that limits our own growth and forewarns of further problems in the future. It is our hope that this text functions as a key to unlock any cultural cages in which we may be trapped.

Freedom from Ignorance

Second, the study of intercultural relationships increases the *freedom* we enjoy. Knowledge is power, and as our intercultural knowledge grows, we are empowered or freed in many practical ways. For example, we are freed from making choices out of ignorance. Instead we are free to make choices that allow us to act both effectively and appropriately in our daily lives. These choices may relate to the social, personal, business, or political spheres of our lives. As we learn about our differences and the sense behind them, we can escape the circle of blame and conflict to which ignorance of these differences so often leads.

Productive Relationships

Third, as we are freed from ignorance and negative attributions, we are able to build *better relationships*. Perhaps the ultimate benefit of intercultural studies is the ability to develop and maintain quality relationships with a wide variety of people. We believe that the quality of our lives and the quality of our relationships are inseparable. Culture is a valuable and basic part of everyone's life. The world is in many ways smaller than ever before because of advances in methods of transportation and communication. However, even in our local communities we have the opportunity and need to interact with people who do not share, or share only in part, our ways of making sense of the world. Lack of understanding naturally results in confusion and a variety of frustrations. As we study intercultural communication, we enlarge our awareness of how culture influences communication. That expanded awareness provides valuable resources for dealing with challenges associated with "difference" that go beyond competitive comparisons to help build communities in which we can all enjoy living.

SUMMARY

In this chapter it has been recognized that there are many different definitions of culture, but the following definition has been adopted as a working guide for this book: *Culture is a historically shared system of symbolic resources through which we make our world meaningful.* In short, culture is simply *common sense.* It affects all aspects of our lives, from the very ordinary, such as making a simple request, to the very momentous, such as how we handle the death of a loved one.

In addition, although communication is a culturally loaded term, there are two aspects of communication that are universal. All human communication is interdependent and to some degree the meanings generated in communication are always situational. Understanding these two aspects helps us deal with communication problems in constructive ways. It does this by reminding us that there is not just one way to interpret what is said and that, although all parties involved in a communication event do not have equal power, they all influence the shape and direction of that interaction. Therefore, we are not solely to blame for problems in any given interaction, but we always have a responsibility to help any interaction move in positive ways. The more power we have, the greater our responsibility.

Three hazards of studying intercultural communication were identified: oversimplification, overgeneralization, and exaggeration. These hazards do not mean that we avoid noting general tendencies or trying to identify and understand differences. Instead, awareness of these hazards can help you keep a balanced perspective during your study of this material so you can reap the benefits that such study can bring. These benefits include such things as increased knowledge and understanding, a greater freedom in our personal lives, and better-quality relationships within our local and global communities. As you read this text many other benefits of studying intercultural communication will be introduced to you and others will likely occur to you as you bring your own personal experiences to the reading of this text. We hope that your study proves to be empowering, instructive, and enjoyable, resulting in enriched human relationships.

REFLECTION QUESTIONS

1   Why is studying intercultural communication important? What types of situations may require intercultural communication?
2   Why are some communities perceived as having more culture than others? Do some communities just have more culture? Why?
3   If a culture provides a system for making sense, how many of these systems can one person use? What cultures do you belong to? How do they overlap? How are they different? How do you resolve any conflicts between these different systems?
4   If communication is interdependent, to what extent are we responsible for the outcome of any interaction in which we are involved? Think of a specific experience and think through how each of the participants influenced how it turned out.
5   What benefits can come out of interactions with those from different cultures?

ACTIVITIES

1   Have everyone in a group bring something that represents their culture and have them explain why. Discuss what culture means in our everyday life.
2   Find an international student or someone who you know comes from a different cultural background and become conversation partners. Visit informally at least once a week. Have lunch together, go out and do something together like shop, watch a sporting event or visit a museum or just sit and visit about your life and experiences. Take time to really understand the experiences the other person has had growing up in a community separate from your own. Be sure to share your own experiences as well.
3   In a group of three, take turns talking to each other for about two minutes about some topic on which you can take a stand (abortion, parking, a recent movie). When the first person talks the other people should be completely supportive and attentive. When the second person talks the others should ignore that person or act completely bored. When the third person talks, the other two should strongly disagree with whatever position that person takes. Use your experiences to discuss cultural norms as well as the notions of interdependence and context in communication.
4   Read the national news or a news magazine and see what they have to say about intercultural events. Try to find articles about the same incident from other newspapers that may come from communities quite different from your own, such as the English version of *Granma International*, *Japan Times*, or *Jerusalem Post*. How do they compare?

NOTES

1 This story is roughly based on an incident reported in J. Irvine, "How Not to Ask a Favor in Wolof," *Papers in Linguistics* 13 (1980): 3–49.

2 A. L. Kroeber and C. Kluckholn, *Culture: A Critical Review of Concepts and Definitions* (Cambridge, MA: Peabody Museum, 1952).

3 G. Friedrich, "Make Mine a Tossed Salad," *Spectra* 25 (December 1989): 3.

4 I use the term *American* here and throughout the book to refer generally to what is considered the dominant cultural group within the United States of America. We realize that there are other American countries in North America, Central America, and South America, but based on feedback from our reviewers regarding ease of reading and common use, we will be using the term *American* in this common, but very particular, manner.

5 Irvine, "Favor in Wolof."

6 L. J. Mock, "Don't Mess with Grandpa" (paper, University of New Mexico, 1997).

7 R. S. Hegde, "Translated Enactments: The Relational Configurations of the Asian Indian Immigrant Experience," in *Readings in Cultural Contexts*, ed. J. N. Martin, T. K. Nakayama, and L. A. Flores (Mountain View, CA: Mayfield Publishing, 1998), 315–22.

8 M. R. Singer, *Perception and Identity in Intercultural Communication* (Yarmouth, ME: Intercultural Press, 1998).

9 S. Barley, "Semiotics and the Study of Occupational and Organizational Culture," in *Reframing Organizational Culture*, ed. P. Frost, L. Moore, M. R. Louis, C. Lundberg, and J. Martin (Newbury Park, CA: Sage, 1991), 39–57.

10 M. Agar, "The Intercultural Frame," *International Journal of Intercultural Relations* 18 (1994): 221–37.

11 Based on one of the critical incidents related in R. Brislin, K. Cushner, C. Cherrie, and M. Yong, *Intercultural Interactions: A Practical Guide* (Beverly Hills, CA: Sage, 1986): 210–11.

12 T. Katriel and G. Philipsen, "'What We Need is Communication': 'Communication' as a Cultural Category in Some American Speech," *Communication Monographs* 48 (1981): 302–17.

13 W. Leeds-Hurwitz, "Notes in the History of Intercultural Communication: The Foreign Service Institute and the Mandate for Intercultural Training," *Quarterly Journal of Speech* 76 (1990): 262–81.

14 Some examples include G. Simmel, *The Stranger* (1908), English translation in *Introduction to the Science of Sociology*, ed. R. Park and E. Burgess (Chicago, IL: University of Chicago Press, 1921); and G. Allport, *The Nature of Prejudice* (Reading, MA: Addison-Wesley, 1954).

15 D. Hymes, "The Ethnography of Speaking," in *Anthropology and Human Behavior*, ed. T. Gladwin and W. Strurtevant (Washington D.C.: Anthropological Society of Washington, 1962): 15–53.

16 An early example of this type of perspective can be found in *Culture, Media, Language*, ed. S. Hall, D. Hobson, A. Lowe, and P. Willis (London: Hutchinson, 1980).

17 An excellent review can be found in the following article: R. T. Halualani, S. L. Mendoza, and J. A. Drzewiecka, "'Critical' Junctures in Intercultural Communication Studies: A Review," *The Review of Communication* 9 (2009): 17–35.

18 E. T. Hall, *Dance of Life: The Other Dimension of Time* (Garden City, NY: Anchor Books/Doubleday, 1983).

Chapter 2

What Is the Relationship between Communication and Culture?

Linda was in a good mood as she approached her interpersonal communication class. She had started a new job the previous week and it had been going really well. The fact that she was making almost double what she had made in her last job didn't hurt any either. Up ahead she saw Wanida coming from the other direction. Linda instantly brightened. She loved visiting with Wanida. Wanida always made her smile with the way she used English and the surprised expression she often got when she found out something new about Americans.

Wanida smiled when Linda caught her eye. Wanida liked Linda; she was so friendly. They had started having lunch together every Tuesday after class. Linda always had lots to talk about, and she was the first American who had really taken an interest in Wanida. Wanida's first few months in the United States had been a struggle. Linda had helped make the transition from Thailand to the United States a lot easier. In fact, Wanida was starting to enjoy her new life in the United States. She also seemed to be doing quite well in her classes, though she had a big test in History that next morning.

Visiting cheerfully, Wanida and Linda walked into class together.

Near the end of class their professor started talking about a research project she was working on. She explained that early next morning she needed two people to help her code some role plays she had videotaped. Professor Fresquez also indicated that because of the late notice she was willing to give each of those who helped out 20 extra credit points.

As soon as the extra credit points were mentioned, Linda knew she'd better volunteer. She had let her new job get in the way of doing a few assignments and she could really use the extra points. Linda quickly raised her hand and offered to help out. She then glanced quickly at Wanida and suggested to the professor that Wanida might also be able to help out.

Wanida felt the embarrassment of the situation and responded hesitantly, "Well, ah, I would like to, but my English may not be good and. . ." Wanida paused, hoping that it was clear that she wanted to be helpful, but that she could not do this project.

Linda was sure Wanida's English would be good enough. Besides, she would be there to help if any questions came up. The project would be a lot more fun if Wanida were there and Linda suspected that Wanida was just being typically "Asian" and being overly modest. So, as Wanida paused, Linda jumped in and reassured the teacher that Wanida's English was really very good and that she was quite capable of doing the job.

The professor turned inquisitively to Wanida and asked her, "Are you willing to help out then, Wanida?"

Wanida glanced away from the professor, but she could feel the eyes of the entire class upon her. "Yes, I will try," she responded softly, at the same time thinking of her exam the next morning.

After the professor had turned her attention elsewhere, Linda nudged Wanida and said cheerfully, "Don't worry. We'll have a good time. And we can both use the 20 points." She laughed lightly.

FIGURE 2.1 |

Miguel Gandert

(continued)

(continued)

As class ended Linda quickly gathered her things and told Wanida that she had to finish some paperwork for her new job so she couldn't do lunch today, but they should plan on lunch next Tuesday. "Besides," she said as she hurried out the door, "we'll see each other tomorrow."

The next day Linda sat staring at the video. She was tired and a bit frustrated. The room reminded her a little of a jail cell, no windows and four blank walls. The project was taking twice as long as she had expected. She was also a bit worried about Wanida. She had never showed up.

When she finally finished the project, she was close to being late for work. She rushed across campus to her car, hardly noticing anyone in her hurry. All of a sudden her eyes focused on Wanida sitting on a bench talking with another Asian student. Concerned and just a bit exasperated, she made a quick beeline to Wanida.

"Wanida, are you all right? I was worried when you didn't show up to help code. In fact, I just barely got done coding right now. What happened?"

Wanida said apologetically, "I'm sorry, I had an exam I had to go to."

Linda just stood there, somehow expecting a little more explanation and feeling the frustration grow inside her. Finally she said a bit crossly, "So, if you had an exam, why didn't you just say you couldn't help yesterday?"

Wanida just looked down and didn't say anything.

Now Linda really was upset, "Oh, just forget it." Linda forced a smile, but did not feel a bit of the smile inside. "I've got work to go to, and they're not too happy if I don't show up."

As she rushed off, Linda told herself that she didn't really mean to be hard on Wanida, but a little common courtesy on Wanida's part would have been nice. She had ended up doing twice the work for the same amount of points and hadn't gotten any of her other studying done.[1]

Why do you think Wanida and Linda are frustrated with each other? Some Americans may feel the problem was due to Wanida's lack of honesty, whereas some Thais may feel the problem is rooted in Linda's aggressiveness and lack of maturity. Social scientists who study human interaction for a living may give other explanations. For example, a psychologist may point to personality traits, a political scientist may suggest that power differences may be partially to blame, and a sociolinguist may find that tone of voice or word choice based on social class confounded the situation. There are many possible answers, but based on our discussion in Chapter 1, we can say with some confidence that no one person was entirely to blame. Both of them contributed to the frustrating situation in which they found themselves. We may also suspect that because of cultural differences, neither Linda nor Wanida really appreciated what seemed like common sense to the other.

Regardless of the explanations that people working in the different social sciences may give for the encounter described, there is a common concern for understanding the behavior or communication of the humans involved. Trying to describe accurately what happened, explain why it happened, and predict when such things will happen in the future so that we can better control what goes on in our lives are basic goals throughout the social sciences. One of the concepts used to accomplish these goals is culture. Much of the research in intercultural communication focuses on how culture influences human interaction or communication.

MANIFESTATIONS OF CULTURE

Researchers who adopt the concept of culture in an effort to explain or predict our social interactions often equate culture with one of its specific manifestations. Three common manifestations used for this purpose are *worldviews*, *values*, and *norms*. These three manifestations of culture are related to each other in many ways, but one important way in which they differ from each other is in terms of their level of abstraction. Hayakawa explains that more abstract terms are less tied to the physical world and allow for many different things to be encompassed by a term.[2] The relationship between worldviews, values, and norms is similar to the one that exists between wealth, livestock, and cows. Wealth is a very abstract term and many different things could be considered wealth, of which livestock is just one example. Worldviews are similar to wealth in that any given worldview allows for many beliefs, values, and norms. Just because two people share the same worldview does not mean they necessarily share the same values or norms. Values are less abstract than worldviews, but there is still room for great variety in understanding and expression. For example, consider the subtle variations of honesty or love in terms of both understanding and means of expression. Another example is the term *livestock* which is more specific than *wealth*, but livestock may include indications of wealth such as pigs, chickens, cows, and so forth. Finally, norms for behavior are much more concrete than worldviews or values, just as cow is more specific than livestock. Certainly there is room for individual differences across norms, but because they tend to be focused more on behavioral practices, the differences in how they are interpreted are much smaller than with worldviews or values. Like all analogies, if pushed too far, this analogy may not hold up well, but hopefully it gives you a sense of how worldviews, values, and norms are related.

The work that has been done on these three different levels of cultural expression has over the years provided many useful insights into the relationship between culture and communication. We will review each of these levels with a particular concern for how each one as a manifestation of culture influences communication.

Worldviews

Worldviews are *abstract notions about the way the world is*, thus providing a premise for what should be. By and large, worldviews are not open for challenge or debate. In fact, they are usually the premises upon which challenges and debates are conducted. Often, worldviews operate at an unconscious level, so that we are not even aware that other ways of seeing the world are either possible or legitimate. Like the air we breathe, worldviews are a vital part of who we are, but not a part we usually think much about.

Worldviews may be best thought of as answers to basic human questions, thus each of the eight worldviews discussed in this section are identified with a question and answer. The answers in each case will take the form of a continuum. A continuum implies that the answer is a matter of degree, rather than all one thing or another. For example, if we ask, "Is that water hot or cold?" it implies that it is either one or the other. However, if we view the answer as if it were on a continuum, then the answer may fall somewhere in between hot or cold and merely be warm or cool or kind of cold, all of which recognize that even such a seemingly simple question has many possible answers and that reducing the answer to two options may cause the answer to be misleading. The opportunity for misunderstanding is even more likely when we are dealing with humans and their cultural understanding than when we deal with something like water temperature. So, please keep in mind that even though the answer will identify only the two ends of the continuum, there are many possible answers along the continuum.

The eight questions and the worldviews that relate to them that we review here do not constitute an exhaustive list of all possible worldview topics. In addition, each one of these eight issues comprises only a part of a person or group's entire worldview. However, these eight areas cover a wide range of issues and deal with many of the most frequent points of difference across cultures.

Individualism/Collectivism

Our experience in reading about intercultural differences suggests that the individualism/collectivism distinction is used more often than any other concept to explain intercultural misunderstandings.[3] In answering the question of who we are, many people focus on how they are different from all those around them. They highlight unique and idiosyncratic aspects that distinguish them from others. Thus, Patricia may see herself as "Patricia" and note the many ways she feels she is different than other people she knows. Such a perspective is typical of those on the individualistic end of the continuum. Those on the collectivist end focus on their relationships with others and explain the answer in terms of shared membership in family (Covarrubias), occupation (professor or faculty member at the University of New Mexico), or other group memberships (Latina).

In the United States the individualistic approach to life can often be found in the workplace. For instance, employees turning down job transfers because they like where they currently live, employee-of-the-month programs, or expecting people to talk themselves up in a job interview are all examples of individualistic actions. Fewer individual offices or cubicles and a high priority on achieving consensus before a group meeting so as to avoid open debate and disagreement display a sense of collectivism in the Japanese workplace.

Although our worldviews tend to operate at an unconscious level, people can come to recognize differences and take these into account in intercultural settings. Take, for example, the following incident:

John was driving down the streets of Milwaukee with an international student from Saudi Arabia and started to pull into a gas station to fill up his car. The international student, Khalid, cried in a very animated way, "No, no, not here! Let's go to a different one." Surprised by his emotion, John started to pull out. At the same time John noticed that Khalid had slid down in the seat in an apparent desire not to be seen, but was watching those at the gas station very closely. Looking a bit more carefully at those already at the station, John noticed another Middle Eastern-looking man and asked if it was because he was there. Khalid nodded yes and seemed to relax as he and John merged back into the regular flow of traffic.

"What is up with that guy?" John asked.

Khalid brushed his question aside and changed the subject by asking if they were doing okay with time for the meeting John needed to make. John decided just to drop the matter and responded that they should make it just in time.

However, a few days later John was walking with Khalid over to some shops near the university when he saw what appeared to be the same fellow that Khalid had avoided at the gas station. John noted his presence to Khalid at the same time that the fellow looked over at them. The man smiled, calling out Khalid's name. They walked toward each other, kissed one another on both cheeks, and proceeded to have a friendly and lively conversation for what seemed like about 20 minutes.

After the man went on his way John couldn't resist asking Khalid again about the other day at the gas station. Khalid smiled and explained that things are different here in the U.S. If you see an American friend, you can just say, "Hi, how are you?" and keep on walking without even slowing down, but with his friends from the Middle East he needs to stop and talk for a while, no matter where he is and what he is doing. He explained further that he knew John had been in a hurry the other day and did not want to cause him to be late, so he thought it best to avoid any interaction rather than either be rude to his friend or cause John problems. John laughed as they continued down the street, remembering how he had thought Khalid had some sort of feud going with this other guy.[4]

Coming from an individualistic perspective, the idea of just briefly greeting a friend from a group we belong to and continuing on with our own plans seems like no big deal. However, these connections are much more vital to who we are from a collectivist perspective, and it is important to maintain these connections even if we are personally inconvenienced. In the example, Khalid recognized the predicament that he would face if he met his friend when he was with John, who was in a hurry to get to a meeting, and wisely avoided it. We cannot always avoid such predicaments, but if we understand what is involved in them, we can better manage them when they happen.

This difference does not mean that those who have a collectivist mindset do not have personal goals or that those who are more individualistic do not value their families or have no team spirit. It does mean that there is a subtle difference in the way we view ourselves and others and in what aspects get emphasized when group and individual needs are in conflict. Of course, at times differences are very explicit, such as in the U.S. Declaration of Independence or the Bill of Rights which explicitly protect the rights of the "individual." However, the tension between looking out for oneself and fitting in with group needs is found in every community, but an understanding of how this tension should be resolved varies across communities and can lead to a sense of frustration with others.

To get a feel for where you fit on the individualism/collectivism continuum, give yourself a score from 1 to 5 on the following set of six paired comments, with 1 equaling a greater agreement with A, 5 equaling a greater agreement with B, and 3 indicating an equal amount of agreement between the two comments.

1   A: When I think of myself, I primarily do so in terms of my family name or a social role I fill.
      B: When I think of myself, I primarily do so in terms of my first name.

2   A: It is wrong for me to put my own desires above those of other people in a group I value and to which I belong.
      B: It is wrong for me to simply go along with what a group of people want to do when I personally feel strongly that I do not want to do what they are doing.

3   A: Who I am changes depending on who I am with.
      B: I am always just "myself" regardless of who I am with.

4   A: You can learn a lot about me by watching what members of an important group to which I belong do.
      B: You can learn hardly anything about who I am simply by watching what other people in my group (family, etc.) do.

5   A: If I do what is best for the group, then in the long run each individual will be protected.

> B: If I stand up for the right for each individual to do what he or she wants, then in the long run the group will stay strong.
> 6 A: When buying a gift, I should first and foremost buy something that is appropriate for the situation and my relationship with that person.
> B: When buying a gift, I should buy something that best fits that person's individual personality or desires.
>
> Most Americans will score a 19 or higher.

Ascription/Achievement

Ascription is based on the notion that something is given to a person and does not require the person to have done something for it.[5] Perhaps the most classic example of ascription as it relates to a person's position in society is found in the traditional caste system in India. In this system each person is born into a certain role or status within society and there is no expectation that a person can or should change that position. Instead it is important to fulfill that position as best one can. Although the caste system does not have the power or legal status that it once had, there is still an awareness of it and it has a particularly large influence on inter-action in India's rural communities. Other forms of ascription may be found in family businesses where it is expected that family members will take over certain positions regardless of demonstrated ability, or where being a member of a family or graduate of a particular school provides a certain status regardless of what one has accomplished. Ascription recognizes that some rights and privileges are rightfully based on things that you personally had no control over.

Achievement is centered on the idea that one's position in society is determined by one's efforts. Achievement implies that bettering one's social position in life is not only possible, but is promoted. Many "power of positive thinking" speakers and writers rely on their audiences holding the achievement world-view. The classic example of achievement is the old American story of Abraham Lincoln who went from being a poor farm boy, growing up in a log cabin, to being the President of the United States and living in the White House. Because of a strong bias for achievement, it is hard for some Americans to see or accept the different social classes that exist in the United States and the limitations these class distinctions carry with them.

The achievement worldview also conveys a lack of respect for unearned status. In fact, people who inherit their money and social status are often presented in a negative light in the U.S. American media. In the classic Christmas film, *It's a Wonderful Life*, the hero is a person who, despite a lack of material wealth, has been kind and thoughtful to others. Due in part to financial troubles, the hero ends up despairing that he has not done any good in his life and wishes he had never been born. At the end of the film he returns from almost committing suicide to find that virtually the whole community has rallied around him and it is obvious that he is a very valued member of the community. The high regard in which he is held in his community and the audience's emotional support of this person are based on the hero's actions over the course of the film. If the hero were someone born to money and a high position within the community, but had acted in unkind and self-centered ways (which is true of the movie's villain), he would not have had the support of the community; nor would audiences feel the same kind of affection for him.

Another movie in which the difference between ascription and achievement can be seen is *The Prisoner of Zenda*. In this show the hero arrives in a small country that is having trouble with its king. The king is irresponsible and, although not a bad person, he is not portrayed as a particularly good person. His own vices allow the main villains to capture him and come close to taking over the kingdom. The hero, as it turns out, looks exactly like the king. He is recruited to help foil the plot to take over the kingdom. In the process of doing so, the hero shows himself to be a nicer and more responsible person than the real king. He is much kinder to all he meets, especially the woman who, due to an arranged marriage, is engaged to the king. At the end of the show the hero and heroine must decide whether to marry each other or to return to their roles ascribed at birth. They decide to part and live up to the roles they were ascribed to in society. When Brad has watched this movie with others, he has often heard complaints about this decision. People who have more of an achievement perspective tend to feel that the hero and heroine should have married because they love each other and that the hero, through his actions, deserved to be the king or at least to "get the girl." In contrast, he has never heard a complaint about how the hero gets all the community support and recognition in *It's a Wonderful Life*, even though his ascribed status would not indicate that he was anything special.

To get a feel for where you fit on the ascription/achievement continuum, give yourself a score from 1 to 5 on the following set of six paired comments, with 1 equaling a greater agreement with A, 5 equaling a greater agreement with B, and 3 indicating an equal amount of agreement between the two comments.

1   A: Promotions in a company should be based primarily on performance.
      B: Promotions in a company should be based primarily on seniority.
2   A: I should date anyone I want to regardless of their social, economic, or organizational background.
      B: I should only date individuals who have a social background that matches or complements my own.
3   A: I should be hired for a job because of my ability and record of past performance.

B: I should be hired for a job because I am related to or share a group membership with those who are in a position of authority.

4 A: Leadership is a skill that can be developed.

B: Leadership is something a person either has or doesn't have.

5 A: The idea of royalty and heirs to the throne and the privileges that go with it makes no sense to me.

B: The idea of royalty and heirs to the throne and the privileges that go with it seems very logical and natural to me.

6 A: I can improve my social standing by working harder.

B: I should be content with whatever social position I am born to.

Americans tend to score 17 or lower.

Egalitarian/Hierarchical

In egalitarian societies it is assumed that each person is of the same worth and value as any other, whereas in hierarchical societies the assumption is that there is natural and proper differentiation across people.[6] The egalitarian perspective assumes that every person is just as important as every other person. The hierarchical perspective sees every person as important to the extent that they complement each other's roles and a person's position of authority determines the person's relative worth. The idea of "Challenge Authority" was very popular among Bernie Sanders' supporters in the 2016 presidential primary in the United States and part of its appeal in the U.S. is that it goes against the very basis of a hierarchical community. Communities that view the world from a hierarchical perspective immediately assume that if there is a problem between a person of authority (such as a police officer) and an ordinary citizen, the person in authority is in the right. Decisions in an organizational setting should naturally be made by those in a position of authority and respect is due someone purely because of her or his position in society.

In the United States people like to think of everyone as being equal. One of the ways in which the assumption of equality is manifested is in the way Americans speak. For example, most of Brad's students call him Brad, and he is comfortable with that. It is not that people do not use formal titles, such as Professor, Doctor, and so forth, but in the United States it is very common and acceptable to call people simply by their given name rather than by a particular title. Indeed, we have seen advertisements that boast that a company will always call the customer by his or her first name. This sort of informality and general lack of concern for official titles reflects and reinforces an egalitarian perspective.

This sort of naming and informality in language contrasts sharply with many other cultures, in which a person's relative position and status are important elements in all interactions. Brad has Japanese students who feel extremely uncomfortable in addressing him by his first name and, even though they know that the class norm is to do so, they still refer to him as Hall Sensei. This difference in worldview can even show up in the language someone speaks. For example, if people are speaking Thai and refer to their brother or sister, they naturally indicate whether the person is older or younger than the person speaking. This differentiation is built into the language just as gender is built into the English terms *brother* and *sister*.

These sorts of differences may cause a variety of misunderstandings in social settings. Americans often get the feeling that Thais are not sincere because they can change from an attitude of extreme informality to one that seems marked by excessive respect when a superior enters a room. Americans may mistakenly view this as brownnosing, a slang term that refers to people pretending to be nice to get unfair advantages. Americans prefer to think of themselves as treating everyone the same. Perhaps this can best be seen in the jokes, derogatory comments, and general lack of respect that is often expressed by Americans toward the president of their country, whereas in Thailand to speak ill of the king is looked upon with extreme displeasure and would be a major social mistake.

There are other countries, however, where egalitarianism is even more pervasive than what is found in the United States—for example, Denmark. This may surprise some because Denmark has a king. However, the king is not assumed to be better than the common Dane and there are many stories that reflect this understanding. One such example follows.

A newspaperman called the Royal Lodge just before Christmas to ask the resident gamekeeper about preparation for the royal family's visit. The newspaperman found the number (which is listed in the directory) and the man who answered gave him the desired information.

"Do you have enough material?" the man finally said. "I must help my wife unpack."

Hoping to find out more information from the man he presumed was the gamekeeper, the reporter asked, "Have you been traveling?"

"Well, you are not speaking with the gamekeeper," the answer came. "This is the King. I wish you a very merry Christmas and a good article."[7]

This attitude that all should be treated the same is also reflected in many of the Danish social systems, such as healthcare. Everyone is guaranteed healthcare and there is no question of insurance or whether one has the money to pay. This equality is also reflected in economic status. One finds much greater differences between wealth and poverty in the United States than in Denmark, where the laws and popular opinion discourage such differences. In Denmark there is a concept of *Janteloven* which refers to the idea that one should not excel over others.[8] Instead, the ability to fit in with others, rather than becoming the star of some community, is seen as more socially desirable.

Americans like equality, but only in reference to some imagined starting point. This, of course, ignores the fact that everyone is always born into a historical context that affords varying degrees of advantage. Americans at times cheer for the underdog, but in the end what they truly love is a winner, and they are quick to assign star status to those who succeed. In the United States the idea of a tie in athletic events is extremely unsatisfying, but this is not the case in Denmark. In many ways, Americans relish a hierarchy as long as it is grounded in individual achievement. Danes, therefore, may be more egalitarian in terms of end results rather than initial starting points.

To get a feel for where you fit on the egalitarian/hierarchical continuum, give yourself a score from 1 to 5 on the following set of six paired comments, with 1 equaling a greater agreement with A, 5 equaling a greater agreement with B, and 3 indicating an equal amount of agreement between the two comments.

1   A: I should respect my supervisor because she or he is in a position of authority.
    B: I should respect my supervisor because of what she or he does, not because of her or his position.

2   A: Decisions made by those in upper management should not be questioned.
    B: Decisions made by those in upper management may be questioned just as much as anyone else's.

3   A: Some people should receive better schooling than others because of their position in life.
    B: Everyone should get the same educational opportunities, regardless of position or ability to pay for it.

4   A: If I play a game, I am happy if it ends in a tie or if we don't even keep score.
    B: If I play a game, I want a winner, even if that means I might lose.

5   A: I like group projects in which everyone in the group automatically gets the same score.
    B: I like for everyone to be evaluated and rewarded differently based on their own personal performances.

6   A: It is important to know the other person's status to interact with him or her appropriately.
    B: Everyone should be treated the same.

Americans tend to score 19 or higher.

Good/Evil

Some communities feel that humans are inherently good and that, if given the choice, they will choose that which is good.[9] Thus, humans are inherently trustworthy. Other communities feel that humans cannot be trusted and that they will take advantage of you given any possibility. From that viewpoint humans are naturally evil and must be kept in check with laws, precautionary measures, and diligent policing. When you next go into your bank, look at the table they have for you to write on. Are the pens chained down or are they just sitting there? What does this suggest about the bank staff's expectations? Although differences in religious belief exist at the heart of many cultural differences, they are perhaps most clearly revealed within this worldview continuum. In many Christian religions, though not all, humans are seen as inherently bad and in need of redemption. We see this in the notion of original sin and the practice of infant baptism. This orientation also appears in other religions, such as Islam which has requirements in regards to gender and dress that reflects a belief that humanity's naturally evil self will exert itself if not guarded against. On the other hand, Hinduism is built on the idea that humans are naturally good and that suffering only comes through ignorance of our real selves.[10]

This particular worldview continuum is complicated by the question of change. Can humans change their basic nature or are they always simply good or bad? Those who assume that humans cannot change tend also to believe that humans are inherently good or evil and that it is best to accept this state rather than try to change it. An example of this can be found in certain forms of Taoism. Many religions, however, are built on the idea of changing from bad to good. Most of these function from a belief that humans are inherently bad, but can be saved through a conversion process. There are exceptions. Hinduism, as already noted, assumes the inherent goodness of the person but that, due to ignorance, this goodness is often not revealed. Change, from this perspective, is a change in awareness rather than a change in nature. In addition, one of the fastest-growing Christian sects, Mormonism, assumes that people are inherently good, but that, faced with the challenges of this world, they may choose evil.[11] Within this perspective, change is a return to or an improvement on the goodness that was originally there.

To get a feel for where you fit on the good/evil continuum, give yourself a score from 1 to 5 on the following set of six paired comments, with 1 equaling a greater agreement with A, 5 equaling a greater agreement with B, and 3 indicating an equal amount of agreement between the two comments.

1   A: Children are born into sin and must be saved from this state through some cleansing process.

  B: Children are inherently innocent and good.

2 A: Without their guns police would not be respected or obeyed.

   B: Police will be respected because of their recognized authority.

3 A: One should be very careful about whom to trust and always be prepared for the worst.

   B: One is wise to be open to other people and to give them the benefit of the doubt.

4 A: Put into a position with no obvious social consequences, people tend to be selfish.

   B: Put into a position with no obvious social consequences, people tend to be thoughtful of other people.

5 A: Children are naturally selfish.

   B: Children are naturally loving.

6 A: Everyone has their price.

   B: People naturally want to do what is right.

Americans tend to score 17 or lower.

FIGURE 2.2 | Many deep-seated cultural differences are grounded in religious beliefs

Mastery/Adaptive

The mastery view of nature implies the idea that we can and sensibly should control the world around us, or in other words, "conquer the wilderness."[12] One way this worldview is manifest is an emphasis on ownership, such as owning land, water, and animals. This sense of mastery is often conveyed in subtle ways. The other day Brad was at the zoo and a bird trainer who was doing a show talked about the intelligence of the various birds. He provided as evidence of his statements the fact that some birds did what he wanted them to and some just never seemed to "learn." It left Brad wondering if the so-called stupid birds simply did not want to do what the trainer wanted even if there was a treat awaiting them. Certainly from the mastery perspective, it made sense to assume a bird was less intelligent because it did not learn its "master's" tricks.

Another way the mastery view is demonstrated is by human efforts in actively trying to change the environment through developing technology to make things easier for us (air conditioning, self-driving cars, crossbreeding of grains, and so forth). Often these sorts of things add to our physical comfort and have a natural, physical attraction.

That said, some cultures take an adaptive or harmonious attitude toward the world around them. A Native American tribe, the Chippewa, have a term, *Bimisdwin*, that refers to a type of balance in life that encourages an adaptive worldview. People with this perspective see humans less as owners and more as cohabitants of this world. Everything should be respected as having a spirit of its own, and humans should strive to adapt and blend into their environment. Examples of this worldview are evident in numerous locations around the globe. Natural mineral pools where it is possible to soak in healing waters are found throughout the United States and multiple other countries. Many forms of architecture conform to the surrounding landscapes rather than disturb the setting to suit a structure. Although not the sole cause of problems, the difference in a mastery/adaptive world view has contributed to legal battles surrounding land use, mining rights, treaty rights, and usage of waterways.[13]

To get a feel for where you fit on the mastery/adaptive continuum, give yourself a score from 1 to 5 on the following set of four paired comments, with 1 equaling a greater agreement with A, 5 equaling a greater agreement with B, and 3 indicating an equal amount of agreement between the two comments.

1   A: Owning land is a wise investment.
    B: Land cannot be owned, merely lived upon.

2   A: Crossbreeding different plants to create new and more productive crops is a good idea.
      B: One should nourish plants around you just as they nourish you.
3   A: Pioneers should be respected for conquering the wilderness.
      B: Pioneers were often reckless in the way they treated the land.
4   A: Technology makes the world a better place to live.
      B: Technology is dangerous because it separates humans from their natural environment.

Americans tend to score 11 or lower.

Social Lubricant/Information

Those who view communication as primarily a social lubricant focus on the impact even indirect messages can have on relationships and on one's self-image and public image.[14] The accuracy of the information is of less importance than the immediate social implications. Gochenour reports that when Filipinos are invited out to some event, both the inviters and invitees prefer an answer that indicates a desire and an effort to go even if the invitees know they will not attend.[15] From the social lubricant perspective communication is very powerful and potentially dangerous, and therefore it must be treated carefully and with respect. Often people within communities with such a perspective distrust those who speak too much or appear too free in their communication, because it is taken as a sign of immaturity. Those communities that focus on the information function of communication tend to see it as a neutral container that a person uses as a tool to convey her or his thoughts. Accuracy, directness, and clarity in speech are valued because of informational demands. This type of community tends to love a good speaker; indeed, public speaking as a topic of study receives more emphasis in such communities. Public speaking may also be highly valued in communities that emphasize communication as a social lubricant, but those communities tend to focus more on being poetic or the ability to have an interesting turn of phrase. The story of Linda and Wanida that began this chapter is a good example of these different attitudes. Linda was expecting and emphasizing the informational aspect of communication when she wanted Wanida to state directly whether she could help with the coding. On the other hand, Wanida was focused on the social lubricant aspect when she avoided telling the professor straight out that she would not be helping. Of course, no culture fails to see that communication has informational and social aspects to it, but the emphasis and recognition of the primary purpose of communication may be quite different across cultures.

To get a feel for where you fit on the social lubricant/information continuum, give yourself a score from 1 to 5 on the following set of four paired comments, with 1 equaling a greater agreement with A, 5 equaling a greater agreement with B, and 3 indicating an equal amount of agreement between the two comments.

1   A: You should not directly state what you believe in case there are others around who disagree.

   B: It is generally important to directly state what you believe.

2   A: It is generally best to be indirect when stating your opinion.

   B: One should be direct in one's communication to avoid misunderstanding.

3   A: I can understand why people do not tell me the complete truth and would rather they not do so than cause unpleasant feelings.

   B: I hate it when people do not tell me the complete truth.

4   A: It is important to keep the morale of your entire crew high, even if the job takes longer to complete.

   B: It is important to get the job done, even if you bother a few people along the way.

Americans tend to score 13 or higher.

High Context/Low Context

Edward Hall, who coined the terms *high* and *low context*, explains that "a high context (HC) communication or message is one in which most of the information is [already] in the person," whereas "a low context communication is just the opposite; i.e., the mass of information is vested in the explicit code."[16] This implies that a given person may engage in both high and low-context communication depending on the situation or context of the interaction. For example, you are likely to engage in more high-context communication with a very good friend than with a business associate who you only know casually. This is certainly true, but groups of people also share unspoken expectations about the proper and preferred style of communication in general. Those who fall on the high-context end of the continuum rely more on contextual cues such as background information, the social setting, relative status of those interacting, and previous experiences. Those who have more of a low-context outlook tend to emphasize the words used and the idea of just "saying it like it is." In rural communities in which there is a lot of shared information, there tends to be more of a high-context type of communication. It may only take a handshake to confirm business and a word and a look to convey many meanings rather than a contract and much explanation. The idea behind low-context communication is that the relationship or setting does not matter. What matters is that one's verbal communication is clear and informative.

Hall pointed out that one of the problems U.S. bankers had in Saudi Arabia was grounded in the difference between high- and low-context communication.[17] U.S. banks tend to be very low context. If you have ever gone to a U.S. bank for a loan, you can appreciate that everything related to that loan is carefully spelled out in print. It may not always make sense to you, but it is obvious that the bankers have carefully thought through and put into words everything related to that loan and its repayment. Your approval for that loan depends on careful credit and background checks. The Saudi banks, however, are more high context. Getting everything checked and put into words is not nearly as important as the relationship with the banker. A loan can be arranged on a handshake, without having to cover for every possible way you may default on the loan. This made the Saudi banks much faster and better able to attract the best clients. The U.S. banks were slower and could only attract those who had a reputation of a bad risk, for in a high-context system failure to fulfill an agreement has much more lasting consequences. Using their background knowledge, the Saudi banks would know immediately if you were worth the risk, whereas a U.S. bank would rely on the written contract to insure payment and even if a client had found a loophole in the past, the bank would just try to strengthen the contract.

High-context cultures rely on a lot of contextual and background information so the communication is often quick and confusing to outsiders, whereas a low-context culture's communication is more explicit. However, low-context cultures appear to allow for greater individual change and growth than high-context cultures in which a person is quickly identified and understood in a set position in society. Relationship change, both in terms of creating new relationships and dissolving old relationships and contacts, is much easier in a low-context culture.

To get a feel for where you fit on the high-context/low-context continuum, give yourself a score from 1 to 5 on the following set of six paired comments, with 1 equaling a greater agreement with A, 5 equaling a greater agreement with B, and 3 indicating an equal amount of agreement between the two comments.

1   A: If I noticed a group of empty shoes at the entrance of a new friend's house, as I entered the home I would take mine off without being asked to.

(continued)

(continued)

>   **B:**   If I noticed a group of empty shoes at the entrance to a new friend's house, I would either ask if I should take my shoes off or wait until I was asked to do so before removing my shoes.
>
> 2   **A:**   I prefer to have time on a new job to watch and listen and thoroughly learn what is expected than to have someone tell me first thing.
>
>   **B:**   When I have a new job I prefer to have my boss tell me directly and clearly what is expected of me.
>
> 3   **A:**   I prefer to live and work in a place where everybody knows everybody.
>
>   **B:**   I prefer to live in a place where I am always meeting new people and where I am allowed to live my own life without nosy neighbors.
>
> 4   **A:**   I expect people to look beyond the words I speak and consider their deeper meaning.
>
>   **B:**   I expect people to accept me for what I am and to take my words at face value.
>
> 5   **A:**   I feel insulted when people insist on explaining what I can figure out for myself.
>
>   **B:**   I appreciate it when people explain clearly what they mean.
>
> 6   **A:**   I prefer business deals to be based on a handshake and our mutually expressed agreement to follow through on the deal.
>
>   **B:**   In any business deal I am more comfortable when everything is spelled out clearly.
>
> Americans tend to score 19 or higher.

Polychronic/Monochronic

Polychronic refers to doing many things at once; monochronic is doing one thing at a time.[18] Time is viewed in a linear fashion from a monochronic perspective. Appointment times and schedules are very important. Monochronic people are likely to interrupt whatever they are doing to avoid being late for the next appointment. The polychronic view sees time, but not the clock, as important. So time matters from both perspectives, but it matters differently as it is perceived differently. In a polychronic view things such as conversations, jobs, and so forth have a time of their own and if that means that someone is late according to the clock, it is not that big of a deal. While Brad was visiting with a woman from the Navajo reservation in New Mexico, she joked about how Anglos are always amazed at how late many of the Navajo meetings get started. She thought so much concern over the clock was a waste of energy. From her perspective the scheduled time was not meant to be a rigid deadline, but a general guide for gathering. Because time is not seen as something that you only have one of, the ideas of spending time, wasting time, or killing time don't matter or even make much sense. It is relationships that matter, and if there are two things going on, that is just fine. A businessperson does not have to have calls held because she or he is in a meeting. Time has more of a circular rather than linear feel to it from a polychronic perspective.

To get a feel for where you fit on the monochronic/polychronic continuum, give yourself a score from 1 to 5 on the following set of five paired comments, with 1 equaling a greater agreement with A, 5 equaling a greater agreement with B, and 3 indicating an equal amount of agreement between the two comments.

1   A: It would be rude to keep another person waiting if you have an appointment.

      B: I don't mind waiting for someone even if we had an appointment for a certain time.

2   A: I like to use a planner to make sure I keep on schedule and get everything done I need to.

      B: I don't like to have to worry about a schedule; I prefer to let things happen as they will.

3   A: I am comfortable just greeting a friend with a quick greeting and going on with what I am doing.

      B: I expect to visit with a friend and catch up with what has been going on when I see one, even if I have something else to do then.

4   A: I can only really concentrate well on one thing at a time.

      B: I am at my best when I am doing many things at once.

5   A: I don't want someone I am visiting with to be distracted by other people or things while I am visiting with that person.

      B: I don't mind if the person I am visiting with has other things going on while I am talking with them.

Americans tend to score 17 or lower.

Think about these worldviews and how they may be reflected in the choices made by the participants in the following story which was shared with Brad a number of years ago, as well as how they are reflected in your own reactions to the participants' experiences.

Shaheed lives in the United States now, but grew up in Indonesia. There, when he was in his 20s, he met a young woman and fell in love with her. Fortunately, the woman returned his love. They discussed marriage, but wanted to act appropriately and have their families' support. Obtaining this family support was not as easy as they hoped because, even though there was no legal recognition of the caste system, there was still an informal recognition of the system and Shaheed was from a caste lower than that of the woman he loved. Acting within the culturally appropriate way, Shaheed had his mother contact the woman's mother and request a visit to discuss the potential marriage. The young woman's mother invited Shaheed's mother to tea. Before talking about the marriage at all, the woman's mother served bananas with the tea. This is something that is simply not done and Shaheed's mother understood without asking or talking about it directly that this marriage was just something that could not be done. She ended her visit and Shaheed and the woman broke off their relationship and he moved to the United States.

Shaheed was disappointed, but he understood the problem and accepted the situation. However, in part because of different worldviews, this story really bothers many Americans.

How many differences in worldviews did you recognize in this experience? We count at least five. For example, an American would have felt that the hierarchical nature of the situation that helped to establish the concern in the first place was inherently wrong. Shaheed and the woman would be seen as equals. In addition, if there were to be any differences between the two, they should have been determined by achievement, not ascribed to the individuals by birth. Third, the decision to go with what is wanted by the families or groups involved is in line with a collectivistic approach, rather than an individualistic approach which would have encouraged each person to do what was best for him or herself. Fourth, Shaheed's mother's understanding of the meaning of being served bananas at tea depended entirely upon the context, rather than the verbal message. Many Americans who hear this story worry about whether Shaheed's mother got the right message. Finally, Americans would tend to want to discuss the issue more, asking, "Why won't this work?" and trying to convince the young woman's mother that it is okay. This orientation is grounded in using communication primarily as an information source rather than a social lubricant, which Shaheed's mother did by not threatening the face of the other person or the status quo of the current relationship.

Final Thoughts on Worldviews

It is crucial to keep in mind with all of these worldviews that they are on continuums and that there are individual differences within communities (see Figure 2.3). Your family as a whole may be more collectivist in nature when compared with

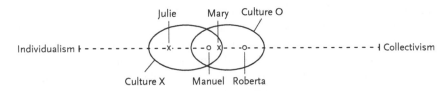

FIGURE 2.3 | The individualism/collectivism continuum

other U.S. Americans, yet U.S. Americans as a whole may be more individualistic than Mexicans. Two communities may even overlap in terms of how they fall on this continuum. Thus, a particular U.S. American may be more collectivist than a particular Mexican. Remember that these worldviews are general trends that help us to understand some confusing behaviors in another culture, but are not hard and fast rules that every member of a community follows.

In addition, because we belong to many different cultures, two people who happen to be of the same nationality may not be as culturally similar as two who share a certain occupation, economic, gender, or age status. Different settings may also affect where we fall on the collectivism/individualism continuum. How we think of ourselves when we are alone or when we are with friends, people from work, or family members may all have an influence on where we fall on the continuum. There are also different types of collectivism and individualism. Some forms of collectivism focus on membership in terms of time and generations that come before or after, and others focus on current group memberships, such as organizations in which we work or where we go to school. We may be individualistic, but do we believe that the self is something that is discovered or something that is created or achieved? Is the "true self" something that is revealed when we can do whatever we want to with no expectations placed on us, or when we are put on the spot and forced to react to a difficult situation? Or is there such a thing as a "true self"?

Cultures have different patterns of worldviews. For example, in the United States most people fall on the individualism and achievement end of those two worldviews, whereas in India people tend to fall closer to the collectivism and ascription ends of those worldview continuums. However, there is no necessary connection between individualism and achievement. Japan, for example, tends to be a highly collectivist culture, yet it is also more toward the achievement end of the continuum. Some people are surprised by the competitiveness they find in Japan, expecting collective harmony to always hold sway. The achievement, though, is more centered on the group and relative group positioning than you would find in the United States.

Finally, the potential for different patterns of worldviews often creates points of disagreement and ambiguity within a community. For example in the block-buster Avengers movie *Captain America: Civil War* that came out in 2016, the main characters disagree on the importance of hierarchy or equality in making decisions. Is the collective identity of the Avengers more important or each unique individual? Should ascribed authority or individual achievement be respected more? Do we trust individuals to be inherently good or do they need direct oversight because power inherently corrupts since humans are inherently evil? Part of the worldwide appeal of this movie was that it created tensions that could be discussed and debated across many different cultural perspectives.

Values

The worldviews discussed are also sometimes referred to as *value orientations*; however, we find it easier to keep the difference between worldviews and values in mind if we do not overlap the labels. This is especially true because the difference between values and worldviews is a subtle one. Values are grounded in specific beliefs about the way the world *should be* rather than assumptions about the way the world *is*. We may believe that people should be honest, hardworking, friendly, and ambitious, but we don't necessarily assume that they are. Regardless of whether they have the above characteristics, we may assume that all people are primarily unique and free to achieve what they will in the world. The distinction between worldviews and values gets complicated when some values and worldviews seem to overlap or deal with the same thing. For example, take the egalitarian worldview and the value of equality. We may work in an organization with a clear hierarchy and even value clear subordinate and superior roles for the purpose of accomplishing certain work-related tasks; yet, we may believe deep down that this hierarchy is a superficial and temporary creation of the workplace and that really we are all equal regardless of our particular title or position in life. On the other hand, we could value equality in certain settings, while at the same time believing that there really are differences in level of ability and worth across people based on birth and social position. Typically, though, values coincide with worldviews in more direct ways. It is important to remember, however, that people on the opposite ends of worldview continuums may still have certain values in common, and just because someone has the same worldview as someone else does not guarantee that they will share the same values.

This tension between sharing some values with members of other cultural communities while still operating from disparate valuing systems is reflected in an old debate in the social sciences known as the "culture of poverty debate."[19] One side of this debate said that those who were poor had a different culture than those who were rich and, therefore, they obviously valued things differently. Certain groups of people were claimed to value items related to material success less (hospitality as a primary value and efficiency and technology as tertiary ones) and, therefore, they were poor or had fewer material goods. From this standpoint it was assumed that they were not less successful or lazy, it was just that they valued different things than those groups who may be considered rich. Advocates of this perspective considered themselves nonjudgmental and culturally sensitive.

The other side argued that this was just a cop-out. These people claimed that some values were universal in nature. They claimed that those who were poor valued material goods just as much as those who were rich. They maintained that there was no "culture of poverty," just a lack of resources and opportunities among certain groups to gain the material goods that we all value. From this perspective, the concept of culture simply served as aspirin for the headache of injustice. These people saw themselves as true humanitarians, treating everyone just the same.

Do all people value technology and material goods the same? If we say they don't value goods like we do, is this just an excuse to avoid feeling guilty about "us" having the goods while they don't? Of course, we have presented only a simple and reduced version of the argument, but the key here is that both sides have merit. People across the world want to enjoy "good things" and we have to be careful not to assume that people who may seem very different from us do not value what we value. At the same time we have to remember that there is not a single universal value system. Therefore, our frustrations with others may be due to what is valued.

One student traveling abroad recorded the following in her diary:

They treat me like an honored guest. Ira, my "sister," even gave up her bedroom for me and slept on the couch. We always do things together, often playing cards. It seems like Ira never does anything without me. I am always included in her plans. The other evening, overwhelmed by the constant presence of other people, I retired early and left the light on so I could read for a while. After a few pages, Ira poked her head in and asked if I was okay or if I was angry, and after receiving reassurances on both accounts, if I wanted to go play cards with her and her family. Worried that I had offended her, I agreed. My American friends have all complained that the Turkish students refuse to let them alone as well.[20]

This student's desire for privacy and personal space became obvious in a setting that denied her the ability to achieve either one. Things we value, such as privacy, honesty, ambition, kindness, and so forth, are things we hold as important and desirable. Therefore, it is when we are unable to experience them that we most clearly understand what we value.

Jack Bilmes engaged in some interesting work in a Thai village that concerned the relationship between values and human action.[21] The members of the village were building a community temple, but not everything was going smoothly. Each village member had been requested to contribute a certain amount of money to the building, but only some had contributed. There was a need for more money, and the village headman was asking for more contributions from those who had already contributed. In a series of village meetings the headman was challenged by his brother regarding this decision to ask for more money from those who had already made a contribution. The brother wanted everyone to have contributed before anyone was asked to contribute more. He based his challenge on the community-held value of equity. The headman defended his decision based on the value of freedom. He argued that he could not force everyone to contribute, because each had different circumstances and the decision had to be each person's own. Others also questioned the way the earlier money had been spent, asking for a complete accounting from the person overseeing the funds. Still others came to this person's defense by noting the need for trust. In short, the values of equity, freedom, accountability, and trust were all being used in opposition to each other. All of the values were important in the village. People believed that things should be equitable and that there needed to be freedom of choice. They also felt that trust should be shown toward those in authority, and yet they still felt people should be accountable. To assume that the values caused a certain action would be to miss the point that at certain times equity was seen as more important and at other times freedom was considered more important. The values were not serving to cause behavior but rather served as resources for making sense of past actions and providing reasons for future actions.

Politicians are often looked down on in the United States because they seem to be able to make any course of action seem like it fits the values of the community. In part, this is because values are abstract concepts. The more abstract a concept, the harder it is to say with certainty that it is linked in a causal way with concrete items such as human behavior. Therefore, values are difficult to use in a predictive sense. For example, the student visiting Turkey valued privacy, yet she still chose to forgo her desire for privacy to avoid offending her host family. To deal with these sorts of challenges many researchers posit values as existing in a hierarchy. Certain values are argued to be more important for a group of people than other values.

Sitaram and Cogdell maintain that there are three levels of values: primary, secondary, and tertiary.[22] These levels highlight the fact that not all values are equal. Research has indicated that Americans, for example, have efficiency as a primary value and hospitality as a tertiary one. We are confident that you can think of examples when Americans have put efficiency over hospitality. Americans are well known in Latin America for their eagerness to get down to business rather than spending time with what the Americans perceive to be unnecessary efforts by Latin Americans to get to know the other person and develop a personal relationship. However, we suspect you have also seen situations when, for the sake of hospitality, efficiency was put aside for a time. These values are difficult to neatly categorize into levels that are consistently followed in all situations. If we read about Americans valuing efficiency over hospitality and accept that as true in all circumstances for all Americans, we may find myself misunderstanding many situations. Even with a recognition of the different levels of values, using values without understanding the particular situation and flexible ways values may be used in reference to behavior can lead to as much frustration as not being aware of value differences at all.

Norms

Part of the challenge with using values to predict behavior is that the same value may be expressed in many different ways. The expression of a given value may be reflected in a variety of different *should* and *should not* types of statements known as norms. Norms are social rules for what certain people should (prescription) and should not do (proscription). As such, they are less abstract than values. You may find many different cultural groups who value politeness, yet the norms for being polite may differ widely. Should we or should we not call acquaintances by their first names when we greet them? Should we or should we not use our hands to eat? Should we or should we not ask about someone's health or general well-being? Depending upon the community in which we find ourselves, any answer we give to these questions could be either right or wrong. The following example of how norms can vary even within the same country was shared with Kris by an associate.

Brian moved from Chicago to New Bern, North Carolina, eight months ago. He was an avid bicyclist and thoroughly enjoyed the cycling community he had in Chicago. Public transportation was bike-friendly and most of the streets were striped for bicycle lanes. There were bike racks on buses, at grocery stores, elevated train stations, and at many restaurants. Brian rode his bike to work in the Chicago "loop" where his office building had showers and other amenities that catered to cyclists. Riding a bicycle was an accepted norm in Chicago where many people commuted to work by bike, and those who did not bike were considerate of those who did.

New Bern, on the other hand, was not at all bike-friendly. Very few people cycled and those who did seemed to take their life in their hands. There was not a bicycle rack at Brian's new office building, let alone any type of facilities that would enable him to freshen up and change for work upon arrival. When Brian asked one of his new colleagues where he could find a nearby bike rack or location where he could safely keep his bicycle and possibly freshen up for work, the response was not positive. Not only was there not anything like that available, his colleague regarded him with disdain and rebuffed any further questions along the lines of cycling to work.

Brian was irritated and offended. Irritated because he found an apartment to rent based on a perfect bike route to work and back. At the time he signed the rental agreement, he considered himself very lucky. Now he wondered how he would be able to follow through with his idea. Brian was also offended because of the curt response he received from his colleague.

For the last two days Brian rode his bike to work and parked it in his office. Since there was not a sign of other bicycles on the street near his office, he preferred to keep his bike in his office rather than risk that someone might

(continued)

(continued)

steal it. Luckily the weather had been perfect so he did not worry about other facilities. But his coworkers had started to avoid and ignore him. Face-to-face communication was nonexistent and the mood in the office seemed chilly. Brian wondered what had happened to cause such discomfort among his colleagues. He now felt like an outcast, and he questioned his move to North Carolina.

What Brian did not realize was that motor vehicles were a symbol of wealth and prestige in Eastern North Carolina. Since tobacco fields had been the leading source of income for multiple generations, associated values and norms dictated that the bigger the truck or vehicle, the more prosperous you were. One of the underlying reasons that biking was not a norm was an implied association with poverty and/or legal trouble. From a cultural perspective, an individual would only ride a bicycle if they could not drive a vehicle. Therefore Brian's colleagues assumed he had huge mountains of debt or had been in trouble with the law from driving under the influence of alcohol. Fortunately one of Brian's colleagues asked him directly why he biked to work. Brian explained that he liked the exercise and ability to be outside to experience more of nature. His colleague was puzzled, but helped Brian to understand why he had been ostracized. New Bern and other parts of North Carolina are in the process of becoming much more bicycle-friendly with multiple bike racks, bike lanes, and facilities available for those who prefer to ride a bike. It could easily be said that bicycling is now much more of a norm in that part of the United States also.

There are other examples of shifting norms. In his book on U.S. American and Mexican relationships, Jack Condon points out that both cultures value honesty, but the norms governing honesty are very different.[23] Americans may allow for less than complete honesty when thanking a host or hostess for a dinner they did not enjoy or when they meet a friend who has just performed poorly in an amateur theatrical production. Mexicans, however, have a much wider range of situations when not telling the whole truth or even telling made-up stories is seen as appropriate. Often when it is claimed that people do not value the same thing, the difference is actually a reflection of different norms surrounding that value. Conflicting norms often result in negative images of the other person or group.

Jay came back from his two-month business trip in Saudi Arabia thoroughly frustrated. "I can't believe those people over there," he moaned to anyone who would listen. "You think we have problems with corruption here; you should try doing business over there. I worked my tail off trying to make contacts and it didn't do a bit of good. It turns out that the only way to make the contacts you need to get started over there is to grease the wheel with a little money to so-called middlemen, extortionists if you ask me, and to keep greasing it. And some of their habits are just downright silly. A lot of times when they eat, they all eat off of one large plate in the middle and they eat with their hands. Or hand I should say. Don't try eating with your left hand. It's considered unsanitary! If they are worried about being sanitary, why are they eating with their hand off of a group plate in the first place? And, you know, they are so backward. The women and the men don't even eat together in the same room!"

Jay was frustrated in large part because many of the norms he was used to didn't apply in Saudi Arabia, and many Saudi norms did not make sense to him. Much of the business done in Saudi Arabia depends upon *baksheesh* or a type of kickback to a middleman (and it is a man), who facilitates contacts between potential business partners.[24] The middleman is doing a service and expects to get paid for it. The more *baksheesh* the person gives, the more likely it is that the person will succeed because the middleman will be sure to treat him very well. Giving *baksheesh* is a norm in the Saudi business community. In addition, Saudis believe that God gave us multifunctional hands and that the hand is our best tool for eating. However, they are also concerned with hygiene. They reserve the left hand for cleaning themselves and use the right hand for eating. Saudis have a number of norms related to restricting male and female interaction that, within the context of their religious beliefs, make perfect sense but would be very inappropriate to most Westerners.

The point here is not to debate the relative worth of each of these norms, but to recognize that different norms lead to very different judgments about behavior.

FIGURE 2.4 |

Miguel Gandert

We have had more than one Saudi raise the use of the handkerchief as repulsive to them. "Why would you blow your nose into a piece of cloth and then stick it back into your pocket to save? It seems so dirty." Often when we encounter different or new norms, the reaction is that something is wrong. After all, we use our community norms every day to evaluate those around us. For example:

> You promised you'd call, what happened?
> I can't believe he's cheating on her!
> Johnny, is that how we ask? What's the magic word?
> I don't think a president should act that way.

Pick up a newspaper or just listen to the talk among your friends and you will soon see or hear examples of people being questioned about their behavior based on a norm. When individuals from communities with different norms interact it is only natural to find many frustrated people. It is easy for people to make judgments based on one's own norms closing the doors to many fruitful opportunities.

The question for our purposes now, though, is what is the relationship between norms and actions? Do community-specific norms cause action? Norms are often attributed great power in governing behavior. Of course, all norms are not created equal. The importance of a given norm within a community is often based on two factors: consensus and intensity. For a norm to be said to govern behavior and have an important impact in the community, it must be agreed upon in the community (consensus) and felt strongly enough about (intensity) that negative sanctions are expected and appropriate for violations of the norm. These negative sanctions may be as mild as disapproving looks or as extreme as physical punishment or expulsion from the group.

In the educational community to which we belong there is a norm against looking on someone else's paper during a test. It is called cheating, and there appears to be a high degree of consensus that cheating is wrong. The classic question is, "Would you want your doctor to have cheated on her or his exams?" In addition, to be caught cheating consistently results in negative sanctions. Based on this information, a person studying this educational system from the outside may assume that cheating is virtually nonexistent. However, in informal conversations it is hard to find someone in this system who has not either observed someone else cheating or done it to some extent themselves. Does that mean that there really is no consensus or intensity surrounding the norm of cheating? Are students and faculty just lying when they say cheating should not be done? No. We suspect it depends more on understanding the situations in which it occurs. People are masters at finding exceptions to the rule and rationalizing why in this case it is not so bad and why they are unlikely to be caught.

Swartz distinguishes between two different types of norms: guides and tokens.[25] Guides are argued to direct or govern behavior. Thus, if there is a norm in a classroom that students should raise their hands before speaking, we would expect that all students will raise their hands before speaking. In those few cases where a student does not, there will be a negative consequence for violating the norm. However, if the norm is of a token type, there is no expectation that certain behaviors will follow given a particular norm. Token norms serve a guiding function in only a loose sense. Instead, these norms merely serve to represent unity and provide a sense of community in the face of contradictory actions. Although Swartz's research with the Swahili in Africa was directed toward finding guides, he only found tokens.

We have heard people say it is the norm in the United States to shake hands when greeting someone. Does this mean that in the United States people shake hands every time they meet someone? No, it does not. Shaking hands upon greeting is a token norm that depends upon many different factors, including the social identity of the people involved, their previous relationship, the purpose of the meeting, the physical setting, and more. Listen to the talk around you, in the media and among friends, coworkers, and family, and take note of how many times norm violations of some sort are referred to. Norms obviously do not dictate behavior in a strict sense. They do provide a common ground for understanding what is going on. When different cultures are involved the common ground dissolves and all too often it is replaced by various negative judgments that function like an informal courtroom.

Reflection Question: When and to what extent are we aware of our worldviews? Values? Norms? Which do you think has more influence on our choices and actions?

TWO PERSPECTIVES ON THE CULTURE COMMUNICATION CONNECTION

Although there are many variations on these perspectives, two common perspectives on the connection between culture and communication may be termed the *monolithic force* and *reflexive force* perspectives.[26]

Monolithic Force

The monolithic force perspective is essentially borrowed from the physical sciences and has two key assumptions:

1   We can explain human behavior based on a causal model. Humans are socialized such that given the right stimulus (situation, psychological trait, etc.) humans will interact in consistent, predictable ways.
2   What we find to be true based on these causal relationships is true for entire cultural communities and has the potential to be universally true.

Culture is viewed from this perspective as the independent variable or causal force that dictates how we will interact or communicate. The three ways in which culture is given form—worldviews, values, and norms—should provide consistent resources by which a person can predict particular behaviors and actions once somebody's *culture* is known. As we have reviewed these three ways of understanding culture, it is clear that the assumptions underlying the monolithic force perspective—clear causal connection between culture and communication and a consistent application of that connection across the community—are open to question.

Reflexive Force

The reflexive force perspective is based on two very different assumptions.

Sense-Making

First, it is not assumed that the relationship between culture and communication is causal; rather, this relationship is one of *sense-making*. Worldviews, values, and norms all facilitate meaning. They help us make sense of the world around us. We use them to account for what has happened in the past, to develop a shared understanding of the present, and to plan and coordinate actions for the future. Of course, the differences across cultures in terms of norms, values, and worldviews complicate this communication process, but even when we disagree we can see that values and so forth are helping us achieve our sense of the world. Our behaviors and thoughts may not always match our norms and values, but they are always accountable to these cultural forms. If a community values kindness, you cannot guarantee that everyone will always be kind, but you can guarantee that people will use kindness as a standard by which to interpret their own and others' behavior.

Situational

Second, it is assumed in the reflexive force perspective that the relationship between cultural forms, such as worldviews and norms, and communication is *situational* rather than the same for the entire community. Just because a behavioral norm is held dear by a group, it does not mean that there is no situation in which it may be acceptably violated. A norm associated with promptness may in some, but not all, cases be superseded by a norm associated with personal hygiene. Without understanding the importance of the situation and how that can change what is appropriate or effective, we are doomed to disappointment in our intercultural interactions. If we ignore the situational nuances, then community-based norms, ways of speaking, values, and worldviews become reified into stereotypes that can distort and complicate intercultural interactions as often as enlighten and facilitate them. The best reminder of the importance of this assumption is to see how many stereotypes of groups we belong to do not hold true for us all the time, even if they do hold true for many people, including ourselves, at times.

Does this mean that concepts of worldviews, values, and norms are of no value in the study of intercultural communication? Just the opposite; all three are important aspects of each situation. Just as a community's specific values, and so forth, help that community to make sense of their world, the general concepts of values, norms, and worldviews help us to make sense of intercultural interaction. The only problem is when we overgeneralize or try to use these concepts to make people into cultural robots that act without free will and sophisticated reasoning. Brad saw a television show in which it was claimed that even the most sophisticated computers we now have are less sophisticated in terms of reasoning than an earthworm. We must be careful not to ignore the sophisticated reasoning of humans, even if it is often done unconsciously.

Culture and communication, therefore, have a reflexive relationship, each working back and influencing the other, but neither completely determining the other. Cultures have discernible patterns, but they also have an open texture to them that allows for dynamic and situational adjustments based on human needs and preferences. Culture facilitates shared meaning and coordinated action much the same way that any resource facilitates the accomplishment of some task. The meanings and actions involved with a particular interaction may become frustrating, such as in the story of Wanida and Linda, but cultural patterns can be deciphered and used to navigate communication troubles in positive ways.

SUMMARY

In this chapter we have explored three major ways in which culture is given form for understanding the relationship between culture and communication: *worldviews, values,* and *norms.* Worldviews were shown to be very abstract assumptions about the way the world *is*; values were taken to be abstract concepts that reflect what is important to or desired by a person or group. Values reflect not so much the way the world is, but the way it *should* be, the ideal. Norms were discussed as social rules that give more concrete standards for how people playing certain social roles should or should not act. These three manifestations of culture provide us with resources for making sense of intercultural interactions.

In addition, the relationship between culture and communication or human behavior has been examined. The monolithic force perspective holds that human behavior is caused by independent variables, such as culture, and that these causal relationships are consistent across communities, allowing for prediction and control. However, the causal relationship between culture and communication was shown to have problems in specific applications. Although this perspective has definite worth for initially understanding general tendencies and the reasons for cultural misunderstandings, it may lead to a distortion of the culture/communication connection.

A second perspective, reflexive force, which better fit our examples and our definitions of both culture and communication, was also discussed. This perspective views culture as a resource for communication and recognizes the importance of context and particular situations in understanding any given behavior. This perspective allows for the connection between culture and communication to be both patterned and open to change. This perspective views humans not as cultural robots, but as decision makers whose actions are accountable to social and cultural consequences.

REFLECTION QUESTIONS

1   How strong do you feel that the connection between culture and our actions is? What is the relationship between personality and culture? Which has the greater impact on us? How much can we change either one?
2   We argue that norms and values can be seen as resources for communication. They help us evaluate the past, interpret the present, and plan for the future. Can you think of examples of evaluating the past, interpreting the worth of the present, or planning for the future that do not involve implicit values and norms?
3   Can you think of your own example of how our communication has a reflexive relationship with our culture, each one influencing and changing the other?

ACTIVITIES

1   Visit with three to five people about how they are like and unlike others of their culture (however they define it). Compare the answers and write up your findings. Consider how much impact culture has on a person's actions. Do some cultures appear to have more impact on behavior than others? Why?
2   Select a list of values, such as *honesty, independence, success, beauty, friendship,* and *humor*. Discuss these with a person or persons from a different culture. Ask for examples of what is meant by these values. When are they most important? How are they achieved? Are they understood differently depending upon who is involved or the situation?

3   In a multicultural group, brainstorm different incidents that would seem to test or violate particular norms and values. Role-play how you would handle these situations. What are the differences? What types of cultures of the many cultures people share seem to be most important in influencing how they would interpret or act in a difficult situation?

4   Get together with people from different cultures and discuss time, using some of the following questions as discussion starters:

A   If you were invited to another family's house for dinner, how much later than the scheduled time would you arrive?

B   How long does a party at which dinner is served usually last?

C   If you were having a party for the students in your class, how many days in advance would you invite them?

D   How would a host indicate to a guest that it was time to leave? Would a host do this?

E   At a party or social occasion, how would you indicate that it was time for you to leave?

F   When first speaking with a date or a friend's parents, what would be an appropriate amount of time to speak to them?

G   If you had an appointment with a professor at 1:00 p.m. and arrived at 1:45 p.m., how would you expect the professor to react?

5   Individually or in a group create your own culture, along with worldviews, values, and norms that all fit together. Compare them with a friend's, or another group's. Try to role-play how each group would handle certain situations, such as a classroom, business meeting, or date.

6   Select one of your own worldviews, values, and norms. Select photos that reflect each of your selected worldviews, values, and norms. Once you have compiled the photos, examine them for the connected way they fit together or are part of a larger reflection of you as a person. Share your photos that reflect your worldviews, values, and norms with another individual or a small group of you. Note similarities and differences that help make sense of your communication choices in a greater sense.

NOTES

1   Story adapted from an incident related in K. Cushner and R. Brislin, *Intercultural Interactions: A Practical Guide*, 2nd ed. (Thousand Oaks, CA: Sage, 1996). The original story involved a Japanese young woman; however, we have had many Japanese students tell us that not mentioning the test would be atypical for a person from Japan (although the rest of the story would seem typical). In further discussions with those from Thailand, we have found this type of an "I'll try" response to be quite typical. This is also similar to what Gochenour describes about Filipinos, who traditionally will respond "I'll try" even when they know they cannot accept a particular invitation.

2 S. I. Hayakawa, *Language in Thought and Action*, 5th ed. (San Diego, CA: Harcourt Brace, 1990): 82–95.

3 G. Hofstede, *Culture's Consequences: International Differences in Work-Related Values* (Beverly Hills, CA: Sage, 1980).

4 Based on a personal experience related to Brad by Jennifer Mallory.

5 T. Parsons, *The Social System* (Glencoe, IL: Free Press, 1951).

6 Suggested by E. C. Stewart and M. J. Bennett, *American Cultural Patterns: A Cross-Cultural Perspective*, rev. ed. (Yarmouth, ME: Intercultural Press, 1991); and C. Nakane, *Japanese Society* (Berkeley, CA: University of California Press, 1970).

7 J. F. Hansen, *We Are a Little Land: Cultural Assumptions in Danish Everyday Life* (New York: Aron Press, 1970), 96.

8 M. Strange, *Culture Shock: Denmark* (Portland, OR: Graphic Arts Center, 1996).

9 F. R. Kluckhohn and F. L. Strodtbeck, *Variations in Value Orientations* (Evanston, IL: Row & Peterson, 1961).

10 H. Smith, *The Religions of Man* (New York: Harper & Row, 1965).

11 L. Richards, *A Marvelous Work and a Wonder* (Salt Lake City, UT: Deseret Book, 1976).

12 Kluckhohn and Strodtbeck, *Value Orientations*.

13 B. J. Hall, "Understanding Intercultural Conflict through an Analysis of Kernel Images and Rhetorical Images," *The International Journal of Conflict Management* 5 (1994): 62–86.

14 Suggested by P. Watzlawick, J. H. Beavin, and D. Jackson, *Pragmatics of Human Communication: A Study of Interactional Patterns, Pathologies and Paradoxes* (New York: W. W. Norton & Co., 1967).

15 T. Gochenour, *Considering Filipinos* (Yarmouth, ME: Intercultural Press, 1990).

16 E. T. Hall, *Beyond Culture* (Garden City, NY: Anchor Books/Doubleday, 1976), 91.

17 E. T. Hall, "Learning the Arabs' Silent Language," *Psychology Today* 13 (1979): 44–52.

18 E. T. Hall, *The Dance of Life: The Other Dimension of Time* (Garden City, NY: Anchor Books/Doubleday, 1983).

19 As reviewed in A. Swidler, "Culture in Action: Symbols and Strategies," *American Sociological Review* 51 (1986): 272–86.

20 J. Roberts, "Living in Turkey" (paper, University of New Mexico, 1996).

21 J. Bilmes, "Rules and Rhetoric: Negotiating the Social Order in a Thai Village," *Journal of Anthropological Research* 32 (1976): 44–57.

22 K. S. Sitaram and R. T. Cogdell, *Foundations of Intercultural Communication* (Columbus, OH: Charles E. Merrill, 1976).

23 J. C. Condon, *Good Neighbors: Communicating with the Mexicans*, 2nd ed. (Yarmouth, ME: Intercultural Press, 1997).

24 M. Bensen, "Doing Business in Saudi Arabia: A Report of Personal Interviews with Two Saudi Businessmen" (paper, University of Wisconsin-Milwaukee, 1992).

25 M. Swartz, "Culture as 'Tokens' and as 'Guides': Swahili Statements, Beliefs, and Behavior Concerning Generational Differences," *Journal of Anthropological Research* 40 (1984): 78–89.

26 A version of this distinction was first suggested to Brad by Gerry Philipsen.

Chapter 3

How Can We Learn about Our Own and Others' Cultures?

Raúl stopped as suddenly as a crawdad on a stick. Paralyzed by the sound, he didn't even dare breathe. The only movement in his whole body was his eyes' frantic searching up and down the ditch. The evening darkness was settling in and a cool breeze rustled the trees on the far side of the ditch. He shook his head, trying to get control of himself. It must have just been a trick of the wind.

"OhhhhhhhaaAhhhhhhhhh," the mournful cry rippled through the air again.

Raúl jumped without meaning to. Turning, he sprinted along the dirt road toward home. Bursting through the front door, he tried to catch his breath. He didn't hear the crackling of the fireplace or smell the roasting piñon nuts.

"I saw her!" he gasped as soon as he was able.

"You what?" his father asked, raising his eyes to meet Raúl's.

"I mean, I kind of saw her," he stumbled on, "the witch, La Llorona, I heard her. She was coming up along the arroyo near Martín's place. It was dark, but I heard her for sure."

His father looked at him intently, and his aunts and uncles had moved a little closer, looking both curious and just a bit amused. They didn't understand how close she had been. His little sister, he noted with satisfaction, hung on every word he said, her eyes seeming to have grown twice their usual size.

"Is she coming here?" whispered his little sister.

"Of course not, dear," replied papá with a little smile, "she only looks for children down by the arroyos."

Raúl, still excited, but feeling safe with his family, pleaded, "Please tell us the story again. Please."

(continued)

(continued)

FIGURE 3.1 |

Miguel Gandert

His father looked around at those present and they nodded their approval. He looked at Raúl's little sister and she echoed Raúl's "please," though with less confidence. His father smiled, took a slow breath and began.

"María was beautiful. Every young man of the village dreamed of making her his wife. María, however, knew she was beautiful and she was very proud of her beauty. She wanted nothing to do with the young men of her village. She wanted to marry the most handsome man in the world.

"One day a musician came into town. He could play the guitar and sing better than anyone in the town. Best of all, he was the most handsome man that María had ever seen. The young women of the village adored him and he obviously had an eye for the young women. Despite her grandmother's warnings, María decided to marry him. María was a vain and clever girl and she had a plan. While the rest of the young women followed him wherever he went, she blatantly ignored his efforts to get to know her. She pretended not to notice his longing gaze and the songs he sang. He became increasingly infatuated by María and soon he was openly courting her and singing her serenades in the evening. Gradually María allowed herself to notice him and eventually they were married.

"At first they were very happy; after all, they had each married the most beautiful person they knew. After a while children came and money was scarce. María's husband started drinking and staying out late and there were whispers of other women. He was often bothered by the noise the children would make and would yell at María to shut them up. Soon he started traveling more and

more often. Supposedly this was to make money for his family, but the bartenders saw more of it than his family did.

"One evening after her husband had been gone an especially long time María saw a grand carriage outside her little house. Putting away the socks she was mending, she went out to see what was going on. Her husband, dressed in very fine clothes, was leaning over their two children and telling them goodbye and that he loved them. He turned without a word to María and stepped back into the carriage where a beautiful and obviously rich young woman met him with a kiss. Together they rode off down the road.

"María was filled with anger and jealousy. With no one else around she turned on her children in a rage and, picking them up, ran to the nearest arroyo and threw them into the murky waters below. The current was swift and the children were quickly swept away. María immediately came to her senses and cried with shame, "Mis hijitos, mis hjiitos; my children, my children!" She threw herself into the water to find them. It was too late. María and her two children all drowned. But María's spirit would not give up the search and to this day she roams the ditch banks looking for her children or for other children to replace them. So you must always be careful by the arroyos, especially in the evening, or La Llorona, the weeping witch, will find you and carry you away."

The story of *La Llorona,* or the crying lady, is one of the best-known stories among children in northern New Mexico. The version of this story we have given is a combination of versions told to Brad by his students over the years. The story is explicitly told to keep children from playing in the many ditches, or *arroyos,* in the area. The ditches often flood suddenly from distant storms and can be dangerous and even fatal for those who are not careful. Patricia notes that a similar story is told in Mexico City to reinforce the importance of obeying parents. There are other messages conveyed in this story, but those will be dealt with later in the chapter.

This chapter is concerned with ways we can learn about our own and other cultures. However, it is not a traditional methods chapter that talks about interviewing, observation, and random samples; instead we focus on forms of communication that are particularly revealing in regards to a community's common sense or culture. Stories that are retold within a community make up one of these forms of communication. But before we talk about specific stories, it is important to consider some issues related to learning in general.

THE LEARNING PROCESS

There is a lot written about how humans learn and acquire knowledge. This is not the time or place to review that literature in detail, but we would like to discuss two important factors in that learning process: need and precedent.

Need

Need is at the root of all our learning. As children we have a variety of basic needs that we learn to meet as best we can. As we continue to grow, we learn how to satisfy these needs and we also develop other needs. This process of learning based on needs happens in all aspects of our lives and to some extent is a never-ending process. Although people learn different things and learn at different speeds, everyone learns to meet their needs as effectively and as appropriately as possible; effective in the sense that needs are met in ways that reasonably satisfy them and appropriate in the sense that negative consequences for meeting these needs are kept to a minimum. Learning our culture(s) helps us to coordinate our actions with others' actions and gives meaning to our individual and communal lives.

Greater, more deeply entrenched learning occurs when a greater need is felt. One complaint we have heard countless times from students about their education is that they often memorize notes and facts to pass a test or get a grade and then quickly forget it all. We believe this problem is rooted, in part, to a lack of felt need. The need to pass an exam may be real, but in many ways it is a transient and somewhat artificial need. In an effort to avoid these problems some medical schools are moving toward a model that is more needs based.[1] First-year students are not just reading and memorizing facts, they also participate in team-based learning that includes an experienced doctor. The teams learn about symptoms and treatments associated with real patient cases. The students must go out and research the information necessary to treat the various problems their patients have. Which students do you think learn the most, those who have a need to pass an exam or those who have a need to help real-life people they have met and have a responsibility to treat?

Finally, if you are taking this course or reading this book because you have plans to travel or expect to have intercultural experiences that you see as potentially challenging and beneficial, and feel a need to handle these experiences in more productive ways, you will learn a lot more than if you are just doing this to meet a university requirement that you view as only loosely connected to your overall goal. This does not mean that you will learn nothing if this reading is just part of a required course. However, you will learn more if during the course or in reading this book you grow in your awareness of your need for this material and actively reflect on the strategies you might use to produce better results with your intercultural communication.

Precedent

The second factor, precedence, deals more with the actual process of learning. A precedent is something that has gone before and provides a model for what to expect or do in the future. Our whole life is made up of creating precedence for what is to come. We learn precedence based on both direct and indirect experiences and in so doing we learn what to expect and how to act to satisfy our needs in the future. Precedent can be an extremely good thing that can help us refrain from repeating certain mistakes over and over again. However, it also has its drawbacks and can prevent us from seeing certain things as well.

Brad was at a thesis defense where he felt that precedence stood in the way of accurate perception. A Chinese graduate student was interpreting the meaning of some comments made by a Chinese informant about the Chinese nation. An American professor questioned her interpretation. He felt that she should not link the current government of China with the Chinese nation. At first what he said made sense, but as he talked about it Brad came to realize that he was operating from a mainstream American perspective which separates governing administrations, such as the Trump or Obama administrations, from the country itself. In the United States, it is perfectly normal to criticize a particular administration without feeling like you are criticizing the country itself. This separation is not as clear in China and efforts to force such an interpretation on the Chinese participant's comments made them easier for an American to appreciate, but distorted their meaning in the context of a Chinese culture. This sort of blinding can also be seen in a simple way in the math example we gave in the first chapter, in which we used a base twelve rather than a base ten to do some simple addition.

Recognizing that the use of precedence in learning can be both a help and a hindrance to learning does not change the fact that it is a necessary and inevitable part of the overall process. The question then becomes: how can we use precedence in a constructive way as we learn about our own cultures and those of others? Part of the secret to accomplishing this lies in the tensions between similarities and differences across cultures that were discussed in the first chapter. *Although this book is largely focused on differences, the recognition of similarities provides hope for real cultural learning.* Certain types of similarities become the foundation for understanding and appreciating differences. This chapter is focused on these similarities. Two common concepts in the field of intercultural communication, etic and emic, should help to explain how this tension between similarities and differences is the key to learning about culture.

Reflection Question: What is something that you feel you have really learned well (it does not have to have anything to do with school)? How did you learn it? Why do you think you learned it so well?

THE ETIC/EMIC DISTINCTION

The terms etic and emic were coined by a descriptive linguist named Kenneth Pike.[2] *Etic refers to things that cut across cultures or are universal, whereas emic refers to that which is meaningful within a particular community and is not necessarily shared across communities.* Pike argued that humans are capable of making a range of sounds. This range of possible sounds is much greater than what any one language or particular group of people make use of in their speech. The range of sounds that any human could make are etic, whereas the particular sounds and combinations of sounds that are meaningful to a specific community are emic. Sound differences that can be heard at the etic level may or may not be important at an emic level. For example, take the English words latter and ladder. At the etic level there is a difference between the double *t* and double *d* sounds. However, for some groups of English speakers there is no meaningful difference in these sounds. Speaking at a normal speed, and in the right context, we can say either one and have the other one understood. Consider the following sentences:

> Which do you want? The former one or the ladder one?
> I am always careful when I have to climb a latter.
> The more excuses you make, the matter I get.
> Why don't you take that madder up with the supervisor?

All of these sentences look a little odd because we can see the spelling, but when spoken in many areas of the United States they would sound perfectly normal. Treating the double *t* and *d* sounds as the same is an emic distinction that makes sense in some communities and not others.

The etic distinction is not limited to just sounds, but could be applied to any meaningful area of human life. In English, we call any brother of either of our parents *uncle*. However, if we were speaking Mandarin Chinese, we would use three different terms depending upon whether the person was our father's or mother's brother (*jiu*) and, if he was our father's brother, if he was younger (*shu*) or older (*bo*) than our father. Furthermore, we use the term cousin to refer to a variety of people regardless of the side of the family they are from or their age or gender. The Chinese have a term, *tangmei*, which refers to a female cousin on my father's brother's side who is younger than myself. Although such a person would be considered kin at the etic level, it is not a meaningful enough distinction (emic) within our community to have a specific term for that kin. There are, of course, changes over time in all communities of what is emically important based on need and situation.

Some use the etic and emic distinction to describe two types of research. Research that focuses on specific communities and assumes that native meanings and concepts are most important is described as emic, whereas research that privileges the researcher's labels and observations and looks for what is true across cultures is called etic. However, we believe this distinction distorts the value of Pike's work and turns the terms into fodder for political battles in the social sciences. The real value of this distinction in our opinion is understanding how the etic and emic levels can work together to help us learn about our own and other cultures. Compilations of emic observations can help create etic frameworks that in turn can be used to discover and compare emic differences and similarities across cultures. Thus, emic-level findings can help to expand and refine etic knowledge and etic frameworks can help to discover and enlighten emic concepts. Our goal currently is to understand particular cultures (emic understanding); therefore, etic frameworks will be used to aid that process.

Hymes' SPEAKING Framework: An Etic Grid

Jennifer was amazed. It was her first faculty meeting at the University of Haifa in Israel. She had taken a one-year visiting position abroad because she liked the idea of exploring life in a new country before she settled down permanently. Professor Anna Rosenblum, a young woman who was going up for tenure this year, had just stood up and verbally blasted the head of the department, Professor Adelstein. Professor Adelstein had seemed to Jennifer a stern and formidable gentleman who was not a good person to cross. Yet, here was Anna crossing him in a manner Jennifer felt bordered on rude. Didn't Anna care about her job? The way she had talked with Jennifer earlier in the week sure sounded like she wanted to get tenure and stay on at the university.

"I don't like the way this department is run," Anna had started off and from there she went on to list a variety of complaints. Jennifer kept expecting Professor Adelstein to cut Anna off and put her in her place or at least take issue with the concerns expressed. Instead, he simply acknowledged her comments and went on with business. It was not that he seemed to take Professor Rosenblum lightly, quite the opposite; he just didn't appear worried or defensive about it. Anna had sat back down next to Jennifer and Jennifer had hardly dared look at her, feeling a bit embarrassed somehow. Anna, though, had smiled slightly at her and quietly said as much to herself as to Jennifer, "Sometimes you just have to tell them dugri."[3]

One of the most frequently used etic frameworks in the study of communication and culture is an eight-part framework proposed by the linguist and anthropologist Dell Hymes.[4] He used the mnemonic device SPEAKING to help make the framework easier to remember. The framework is designed to be used to uncover and understand all of the important aspects of any type of communication act or situation, regardless of the culture. Each part of the framework is an etic concept that is potentially important in describing and understanding cultural particulars. Based on the Israeli communication scholar Tamar Katriel's work on speaking *dugri*, a form of talk easily recognized within the Sabra community of Israel,[5] we will explain and illustrate the eight parts of the Hymes framework. At the same time the sense behind Anna's actions in the faculty meeting described above should become clearer.

Scenes

The scene refers to both the physical and psychological settings in which the communication takes place. *Dugri* can be spoken in almost any physical setting; however, it has more poignancy when it is done in a public setting in which there are more people present than the speaker and the immediate listener. It is also assumed to be an unplanned situation. *Dugri* is spoken spontaneously. The psychological setting created in the speaking of dugri occurs in a dialectic between tension and bonding. It is a scene of tension because the speaker puts aside usual social expectations and expresses very direct disagreement with the other person. It is also a scene of bonding, because both the speaker's and the listener's Sabra identity is called upon and reinforced through the interaction.

Participants

The participants, or those involved in the speech act, should be characterized in the way that native members of a community characterize them, not in labels that only the researcher finds meaningful. Thus, gender, age, religion, and ethnicity may or may not be important. It may be more important that the person is a "regular," a "tightwad" or a "stranger." *Dugri* is typically only spoken by a subordinate to a superior. However, the speaking of dugri suspends traditional societal roles and the deference they imply. *Dugri* temporarily transforms that relationship to highlight the deeper common ground between the speakers, such as that they are both Sabra.

Ends

The end is the community-recognized goal(s) for engaging in the talk being studied. For example, someone listening to *dugri* talk may assume that the person is trying to negotiate a change or immediately resolve some problem; however, *dugri* is really spoken for more cathartic purposes. The speaker wants to express his or her feelings in as simple and direct a way as possible just to have them heard, not necessarily to bring about a change.

Acts (Substance and Sequence)

Acts refers to two aspects of an interaction: the act substance or topic and the act sequence or order of the interaction. The act substance, or content, refers to any important content matters that must or must not be included in the situation or type of talk under study. The sequence refers to any essential ordering within the situation or performance of the act. To speak *dugri* the content must always be in disagreement with the other person. You cannot sensibly say, "I will tell you *dugri*," and go on to agree with a person. The sequence is a simple two-part format: first, the speaker spontaneously expresses disagreement and, second, the listener accepts the criticism or disagreement without any effort to defend him or herself or to try at that time to ask question about why the person feels that way by asking questions. Remember, the goal in speaking dugri is not one of problem solution, but one of feeling expression. Responses that challenge or question in some way those feelings are inappropriate.

Keys

The key refers to the prevailing mood, tone, or atmosphere that unlocks the meaning of the act or helps a person interpret the situation. In the case of *dugri*, the mood is always an individually face-threatening one. Sincerity is expected; humor, sarcasm, or a sense of friendliness would not be appropriate. There is a sense of urgency that this feeling must be expressed now, and then business can go back to usual.

Instrumentalities

The instrumentality is the means by which the act is conveyed. This may refer to both the physical means used to perform the act and the style in which it is performed. For example, *dugri* is best spoken face-to-face. It is also done in a short, simple, direct way that may be described as almost antistyle or in other words very plain, blunt, and direct.

Norms

The norms include the should and should nots of both the production and interpretation of the act. A norm for speaking *dugri* is that you should do it directly and immediately. To wait until after a meeting and complain about something that was announced would be a direct violation of a *dugri* norm. The person should have expressed those concerns immediately and directly to the person with whom he or she disagreed. Also, *dugri* should be interpreted as an expression of trust and shared identity. Society's typical hierarchy and the social caution it promotes is temporarily put aside to allow the expression of a deep and urgent feeling. For a supervisor to hold a grudge against a subordinate for speaking *dugri* would violate a norm concerning how *dugri* should be understood.

Genres

Genre is the form in which the act may be performed, be that song, poetry, prayer, joking, story, or so forth. Certain situations or types of communication call for the use of certain forms of communication. *Dugri* is grounded in an antistyle and should be free of metaphor or indirect speech.

The SPEAKING framework is useful in that it helps a person interested in a particular type of communication act or situation to look at it from many different angles while also allowing for comparison to other communicative acts from different cultures. How, for example, is being straight with someone in the United States similar to or different from speaking *dugri*? How would brownnosing and speaking *dugri* compare? The Arab community has a form of speech known as *musayara* that involves elaborate, carefully planned speech that is very sensitive to the face needs of the other person. Regardless of their intentions, someone speaking *dugri* and someone speaking *musayara* are likely to have communication problems.[6]

Aside from using etic frameworks to understand particular acts and situations within a cultural community, there are also specific forms of communication that appear at this time to be etic or universal in themselves. One way of understanding our own and other cultures, then, is to look for these forms and try to understand the cultural codes expressed in them. Similar to the Hymes framework, these universal forms provide windows into the emic meanings of a culture. The two etic or universal forms we will review at this time are narratives and rituals.[7] Each will be discussed in some detail.

NARRATIVES

Narratives, or stories, are found in every culture. In fact, narratives are argued to be a uniquely human way of understanding the world.[8] *A narrative in its most basic sense refers to a recounting of a sequence of events that is told from a particular point of view.* Thus, a narrative is not what is happening in the here and now, but is the telling of events separate from what is currently happening. Further, a single action such as, "The father died," is not a narrative, but if we start to tell what happened before or after that event, such as, "The father died;

the son wept," we now have a narrative. Finally, a narrative always has a point of view, even when that point of view is not obvious. No one narrative can capture every possible aspect of a series of events, so what is told and how it is told inescapably express a point of view. "The father died; his heir rejoiced" tells quite a different story than the earlier narrative, even though it may be dealing with the same situation. It is important to remember that no story is told without a point of view, and, therefore, could always be told from another point of view, regardless of how much the teller tries to give just the facts.

Narratives that are particularly useful for understanding culture are ones that not only get told, but retold. We suggest no magic number concerning how many times a narrative must be retold to be culturally significant, but we do contend that narratives that are felt important enough to retell invariably carry some cultural significance. The very retelling of the narrative indicates that, at least to someone, something of value is expressed therein. This may not be a conscious recognition, but if a story has no relevance to life in general, it does not tend to be retold. From an intercultural perspective, narratives offer a means of communication by which we can better understand the worldviews, beliefs, values, dreams, norms, and feelings of others. This knowledge in turn can enable us to identify places where we can appropriately bridge our differences.

Narratives vary widely across cultures. Answers to the following questions point toward some of these differences. When is the appropriate time to tell stories? Who tells the narratives? What are appropriate story topics? Who are the appropriate audiences? How should narratives be structured?[9] In spite of

FIGURE 3.2 |

the emic differences that exist in storytelling, narratives at the etic level are essentially *actions* taken by *characters* in relation to a *problem* and the perceived *outcome* of those actions. Although they may not be obvious, careful analysis will reveal the existence of characters, problem, action, and outcome in any story. There is always some kind of character or characters in a narrative. These may or may not be human. There is also always some problem or tension that is addressed. This is true even in stories that only discuss positive things. You may tell your friend a narrative that recounts a good grade you got or a funny experience you had. It may appear at first that no problem exists; however, there is always a potential problem, such as the possibility for a poor grade, that makes the story worth sharing. Narratives that get passed along tend to deal with specific experiences with things that are general concerns for a community. There is also some action taken in relation to the problem or potential problem. Finally, the consequence or the outcome of the actions taken by the characters is presented. Often this outcome is simply implied in the tone taken by the storyteller.

Narrative Teaching Functions

Taken together, these four aspects (characters, problem, action, outcome) form a powerful teaching mechanism. We argue that all narratives teach, at least to some degree. Although there are many other ways that narratives can be categorized and understood, for the purposes of learning about our own and other cultural systems, we recommend organizing stories in terms of what they teach us. We maintain that narratives function to teach us how the world works, our place in the world, how to act in the world and how to evaluate what goes on in the world. Each of these four teaching functions encompasses two types of learning that we *need* as we go about life (see Table 3.1). We will illustrate and explain each of them.

The Way the World Works

Narratives teach us the way the world works, both at the level of general principle and at the level of particular contexts. The following narrative was reported to me as a story told in a Buddhist monastery.

TABLE 3.1 | Narrative teaching functions

Narratives teach us:

1   The way the world works (in general and in particular contexts).
2   Our place in the world (in terms of both our personal and social identities).
3   How to act in the world (both effectively and appropriately).
4   How to evaluate what goes on in the world (in terms of what is good/bad and safe/ dangerous).

There was a rich old man who died, leaving two sons. For a while the sons lived together in what was left of their father's household, but eventually they quarreled and decided to divide up their father's property and go their separate ways. Everything was divided equally, but after the settlement was finished a small packet that had been hidden by their father was discovered. Inside were two rings, one an ornate gold ring with a valuable diamond setting and the other an ordinary silver ring worth very little money.

On seeing the rings the elder brother was filled with greed. He told his younger brother that it was obvious that the diamond ring was not part of his father's earnings, but an heirloom to be passed on to the eldest member of the family through the generations. That is why it had been kept secret. The younger brother was tired of arguments, so he smiled and said, "All right, be happy with the diamond ring and I will take the silver one." Each placed his new ring on his finger, and they went their separate ways.

Now, the younger brother understood why his father had kept the diamond ring, but he was curious why he had kept the ordinary silver one. Examining it closely, he found some words engraved on it, "This will also change."

"Oh," thought the younger brother, "this is the mantra of my father," and he placed the ring back on his finger.

As time went on both brothers were faced with the ups and downs of life, but they reacted very differently. When the springs of life came, the elder brother would be elated, losing the balance of his mind. When winters would come, he would fall into deep depressions, again losing his mental balance. He became tense and unable to sleep at night. He started using sleeping pills, shock treatments and strong drugs to help him cope with his ups and downs. He was never really at peace with his life.

The younger brother also enjoyed spring when it came, but he would look at his ring and remember, "Ah, this will change." When it did, he would smile for he knew that it would. When the winters of life came, he would also look at his ring and remember, "This, too, will change." He did not despair and sure enough things would eventually change for the better. He knew that none of the ups and downs was permanent and that everything comes just to pass away. He did not lose the balance of his life and he lived both peacefully and happily.

This story carries with it a strong message that the world is always in flux. The listener is urged to accept that change, good or bad, and to enjoy life without worrying about holding on to things that will inevitably change. There are other messages in the story about the way the world works. For example, one learns that appearances can be deceiving. We wonder how many of you knew the minute that the younger brother got the ordinary, apparently less valuable ring that he would actually come out of the situation better off. This type of theme is common in quest narratives.

The second level of learning about the way the world works is in particular contexts. The following organizational narrative was told to Brad a number of years ago by a former intern with Walt Disney World Corporation.

When Michael Eisner became the CEO of the Disney Corporation he instigated the hiring of many new people. One of these new employees or "cast members" worked as a front-gatekeeper at the Magic Kingdom. I will call her Karen. Karen's job mainly consisted of letting people into the park only if they had the correct ticket.

Now, if you work for Disney, you know who the master director, Michael Eisner, is. You see his picture about 800 times going through "Traditions" [a part of new employee training], and you see it everywhere in Disney newspapers and fliers. Well, Michael Eisner and his personal entourage of three assistants approached the turnstile that Karen was at to enter the park. She felt uncertain, but she stopped all four men and said, "Mr. Eisner, I'm sorry, but I cannot let you through the gate without a ticket."

One of the assistants stepped forward and loudly exclaimed, "Do you know who this is? This is Michael Eisner, CEO of the Disney Corporation!"

Mr. Eisner immediately stopped his assistant and looking at Karen's name tag said, "Leave Karen alone, she is just doing her job. Go get us each a ticket."

The assistant hurried off to buy the tickets and Mr. Eisner assured Karen that she was doing a great job. In fact, Mr. Eisner was so impressed with the way Karen handled the situation and so unimpressed with the way his assistant handled it that he gave Karen the opportunity to be one of his assistants and demoted his current assistant. Rumor has it that Karen remained one of Mr. Eisner's assistants for many years.

Although Michael Eisner is no longer CEO of Disney, the lessons learned in this narrative have a particular context in which they are applicable. Although one may generalize what is learned, this story is commonly told to new Disney cast members and conveys a sense of how the world works within that particular organization. Whether other organizations would reward such a faithful following of the rules, especially when it relates to a superior in the organization, is left open to question. Thus, this story primarily teaches about the way the world works in the Disney Corporation, not necessarily in general.

Our Place in the World

In being taught our place in the world, we are primarily learning information related to our personal and social identities. We will discuss these two identities in greater detail in Chapter 4, but for now we will give an example of a narrative that is centered on the personal identity of the woman who shared it with Brad.

We were on our way back from a camping trip at Heron Lake when my parents decided to stop for a picnic lunch. At that time I had a little tooth that was so loose it was almost laying sideways in my mouth. To eat the pizza that we had gotten to have as a special treat for lunch was more than I could do. My dad realized that the tooth was ripe for pulling, and making a little floss lasso attempted to do so. It took some talking, though, before I would open my mouth. After much persuasion I finally did. However, just as he was getting the little floss lasso over my tooth, I let out a huge "AAAAAAHHHH," and pulled away. He then talked to me about trusting him and that it wouldn't really hurt. I again consented, but as soon as he had the lasso over my tooth and started to take up the slack I again let out an even louder "AAAAAAAHHHH!" and pulled away. This time my dad began singing me the song "Trust in Me" from Disney's Jungle Book. *This was so funny I agreed to open my mouth again. Before I even had time to reconsider the lasso was on my tooth and the tooth was out of my mouth. For an instant I was quiet. Dad said, "See, that didn't hurt. You can trust old dad." At that point I started to cry, more from the anger of being tricked than anything else.*[10]

The woman in this story relates that this story is always told when they drive by where they had that picnic lunch. Her dad, mom, or sister will bring it up. Her dad even told it to her boyfriend one time when they were all traveling that road to go snowmobiling. Since then, her husband has picked up on the story and it has become a family joke in her own family. She claims she didn't like the story at first, but she has come to see that it reflects part of her personality. As this story has now been passed on to her children, it teaches them about their mother and their grandfather. Stories that involve us or those close to us often teach us about who we are and what we are like. Are we shy? Frugal? Aggressive? Clever? In part, we learn this by the stories told about us without thinking about it.

Narratives also teach us about our social identities. Narratives that deal with members of groups we belong to and value further teach us who we are and where we fit in the world. One form of story that does this in a broad sense is a grand narrative. Grand narratives (sometimes referred to as myths) tend to deal with the supernatural and often deal with how communities or the world in general began. One such story that is well known among Vietnamese children follows.

Long ago there was a beautiful and intelligent God who ruled over the mountain ranges of the present-day North Vietnam. Her name was Au Co. One day she met the powerful and handsome God of the sea named Lac Long Quan. They immediately fell in love and got married. A few months later, Au Co was pregnant. After three years, Au Co gave birth to one hundred eggs in the same sack. The eggs hatched to give them one hundred children.

As the children grew, Lac Long Quan started to miss his home and wanted to return to the sea. Au Co felt the same and wanted to take the children back to her mountain home. They decided to split the children up. Fifty went with their father to the sea and settled along the coast and fifty went with their mother to the mountains. Many years later the population had increased and filled all of modern-day North Vietnam. The first Vietnamese dynasty, Hung Vuong, was born from these children and from then on the Vietnamese people have had the responsibility to rule this land according to the desires of their ancestors.

The person who shared this narrative with me said it was a source of great pride to him as a child. He also related that in school they would discuss this story and that he learned that he came from powerful and good ancestors and that it was important to always defend his land from any foreign invasion, Chinese, French, American, and so on. The story was a symbol of unity to him in that all Vietnamese were of one family. In this way the narrative helped him to know who he was.

All communities have these grand narratives of creation that help us understand our place in the world.[11] Some of these narratives are grounded in religion and some in other areas, such as science. If we get too caught up in whether these grand narratives are precisely "true" we can often miss the beauty and value of these stories, smugly assuming we know the truth. In our efforts to understand other cultural communities, even our own, we argue that instead of focusing on the perceived accuracy of a story, it is useful to look for the meanings these stories convey and how they help groups of people make sense of who they are.

How to Act in the World

Narratives teach us how to act both effectively and appropriately. They help us to know what is powerful and right or wrong within the context of a specific society. The following story is told by a young woman from Croatia. She learned it from her grandparents and parents.

My mother was born at the end of World War II. Her father was killed just before she was born, so my grandma took care of her alone. Grandma worked as a cook in a small restaurant and as a janitor in the building in which they lived. They lived in a small one-room apartment and all the money they had went to pay the rent and other bills. Grandma would bring leftover food from the restaurant for them to eat. Their horrible financial situation forced my mom to start working at the age of twelve. She sold souvenirs at the main square in the afternoon after going to school in the morning. Some days she was unable to sell even one thing. She learned Italian and English to help her get into the university. Because education is free in Croatia she was able to attend the university. She got a second job as a journalist. She joined the basketball team and received numerous awards in the Yugoslavian basketball league. All the while she lived in the same one-room apartment with her mother. Although her days were filled with work just to survive, she always had faith and kept a smile on her face.

She got married to my dad and they had their first child. They both worked several jobs, but they had to continue to live with my grandmother to make ends meet. They realized there was little hope for them in the town they lived in. In search of a better life, they moved four times, my mother changed jobs ten times, got two degrees, raised three children, supported my grandma, kept her faith, remained happy and was strong enough for all of us. Eventually they were able to get their own television set, car and their own house. My parents' struggle provided me with a carefree childhood. Today we have everything.

Although this story is set in Croatia, we have heard many such rags-to-riches narratives in the United States. Hard work, an optimistic attitude, and an education are positioned as the key actions necessary for success. Rather than just being told to work hard, the listener is able to visualize its importance through the outcome of the narrative.

Narratives also teach what actions are appropriate for people of various roles. Keith Basso has studied many different types of storytelling among the Western Apache.[12] The Western Apache have narratives associated with places. The name of a place is often a short description of the place and is associated with a story of what happened there; for example, "big cottonwood trees stand spreading here and there." These stories are said to "stalk" or "hunt" the members of the community, helping them to remember what is right and how they should live their lives. One such story is associated with a place called "men stand above here and there."

Long ago, a man killed a cow off the reservation. The cow belonged to a Whiteman. The man was arrested by a policeman living at Cibecue at "men stand above here and there." The policeman was an Apache. The policeman took the man to the head Army officer at Fort Apache. There, at Fort Apache, the head Army officer questioned him. "What do you want?" he said. The policeman said, "I need cartridges and food." The policeman said nothing about the man who had killed the Whiteman's cow. That night some people spoke to the policeman. "It is best to report on him," they said to him. The next day the policeman returned to the head Army officer. "Now what do you want?" he said. The policeman said, "Yesterday I was going to say HELLO and GOOD-BYE but I forgot to do it." Again he said nothing about the man he arrested. Someone was working with words on his mind. The policeman returned with the man to Cibecue. He released him at "men stand above here and there." It happened at "men stand above here and there." [13]

This narrative describes how an Apache who tried to act too much like a Whiteman was made to look stupid and laughable. The killing of the cow was not a problem. The problem was an Apache who forgot who he was and attempted to join with outsiders in trying to persecute a member of his own tribe. Basso further relates an incidence in which he saw this story used to teach.

A young Apache woman, who had recently returned home from attending a boarding school, attended a girl's puberty ceremonial with her hair rolled up in a set of pink curlers. This sort of ornamentation had been considered fashionable by her peers at the school. However, women are expected to wear their hair loose at these ceremonials and she was the only one who had not. No one said anything to her at the time. About two weeks later this young woman was at a get-together at her grandmother's home. After the meal the grandmother, who was at the ceremony, began to tell a tale. She told the tale of what happened at "men stand above here and there." The young woman left shortly after the story was over. Basso asked the grandmother if the young woman was not feeling well. "No," the grandmother replied, "I shot her with an arrow."

Two years later Basso had an opportunity to talk with the young woman and ask her about what had happened. She said that she had realized her grandmother's story was for her and that she should always act like an Apache and not try to be something else. She no longer wore those curlers and that place (and the lesson conveyed in the story associated with it) stalks her every day, reminding her how to live right. The land is crucially important for the Western Apache, in part because it reminds the people of stories that teach what is right and wrong and how to act appropriately. In this way the land is said to stalk them, shooting them with arrows that make them live right.

Some stories that are focused on what is appropriate may be much shorter, such as, *"I'm sorry, honey. I would have called, but Bill's wife was sick and I had to cover for him in the field. There was no phone around and I just didn't have time to get to one."* This type of narrative accounting is directed at the appropriateness of one's behavior and can be revealing in regards to cultural norms and to what extent they are shared and valued. Does his excuse for not calling sound legitimate to you?

How to Evaluate What Goes On in the World

There are two major dimensions along which narratives teach us to judge. First, we learn what is good and what is bad and, second, we learn to discern what is safe and what is dangerous.

The following story was told to a young woman in Sierra Leone, West Africa, by her grandmother just after the young woman had announced her plans to be married. The grandmother told her that she had shared this story with many of her cousins when they had complained to her that their husbands were not faithful and were treating them poorly.

There was a woman who lived in a large village who suspected that her husband was having an affair with another woman. She did not confront her husband, though. Instead, she went to the voodoo man to help her save her marriage. She told the voodoo man that her husband had started coming home late, wasn't interested in being intimate with her, and was often abusive to her. The woman expected the voodoo man to give her a potion she could use to help attract her husband's attention. The voodoo man said he had a potion that would make her husband faithful to her, but she must first go into the jungle and bring him the ear of a lion. The woman was shocked and scared and told the voodoo man that it was impossible to get the ear of a wild lion. But the voodoo man told her it was absolutely necessary and that he was sure she could think of ways to accomplish this task.

The woman left very disappointed and angry at the voodoo man, but she was determined to save her marriage, so she had no choice. The first time she went into the jungle she ran away when she heard the roar of the lion. The next day she took a slab of meat with her and threw it to the lion. The lion ate the meat and lay down to sleep, but the woman was still afraid to get close to the lion. She fed the lion every day for many weeks, each time getting a little bit

(continued)

(continued)

closer. Eventually she was able to get so close to the lion that she was right next to it. She was still afraid to cut off part of the ear. Instead she gradually started brushing the lion's mane while it slept. Sometimes she would pull out thorns from its mane or paw. Slowly a trust developed between her and the lion. Finally, one day she took a razor blade with her and while the lion slept she cut off the ear for the voodoo man and ran back to the village. She was excited and happy that she had accomplished her mission and went directly to the voodoo man's hut.

When she handed the Voodoo man the lion's ear, all he could do was smile at her. Finally, she demanded her potion. "There is no potion," he replied. "Go home and brush, feed, and care for your husband the way you learned to for the lion and you will find that your husband will no longer stray and you will have a happy marriage." The woman left the Voodoo man's hut very disappointed.

One of the many messages this narrative conveys is that we should not be so quick to blame others for our relational problems. It also indicates what goes into being a good wife. That which is portrayed as good and bad may differ from culture to culture. Obviously not all people will accept what has been taught in that story, because it does not fit with other previously accepted stories or their cultural system in general. If you find yourself disagreeing with aspects of a well-accepted narrative of another culture, those points of disagreement can provide clues to your own culture. If you disagree with parts of a story from your own cultural community, it is well to remember that we generally belong to many cultural groups and perhaps what is acceptable in one is not in another, creating a sense of internal tension.

Finally, there are narratives that teach people to discern what is dangerous and what is safe. The *La Llorona* narrative that begins this chapter is a kind of cautionary story that is told to children in many different cultures. It is a story that is explicitly designed to keep children away from dangerous situations, such as playing around ditches. A few other brief examples from around the world follow.

In Paraguay *there is a story known as María del Lago. A young woman named María is said to have gone with friends to ski on Lake Ypacarai. They had plenty to drink, but no life preservers. While she was skiing, waves from another boat caused her to fall. Her friends turned around to find her, but because she was not wearing a life preserver and her friends were fairly drunk they did not see her and they accidentally ran over her with the boat. Her head was cut off by the* *engine's propeller. Later all they found was her decapitated body. It is said she comes out at night looking for her head that was never found.* A line frequently used by parents when their children will be at the lake is, *"Cuidado con María del Lago* (careful with *María* of the Lake).*"*

In Russia *there are many stories about Baba Yaga, the witch of the forest. Her home is a hut that rests on chicken legs. Although she can make herself look beautiful, she has teeth of iron and loves to eat people, especially children. Her house is surrounded by a fence that is made of the bones of her victims.* The woods and marshes of Russia can be dangerous places for children to play and the thought of *Baba Yaga* has kept more than one child close to home.

In the Midwestern United States *there is the story of Katie who used to attend the now vacant high school in the town in which this is told. Katie was an All-American girl who loved everyone and especially loved her school. In the middle of her senior year she realized she was going to have to leave the friends and school she loved so much. She was very upset about this. She loved her life at school so much that she could not bear to see it end. Eventually she went up to the third story balcony of the school and in the midst of her misery she fell to her death. Now her spirit roams the hallways of her old high school even though it has been abandoned. She does not want anyone else to enter her beloved school and leave alive.* This story was passed on in part to keep kids from playing in the abandoned and potentially dangerous old school.

Interpreting Narratives

As you have read the many narratives that we have shared so far in this chapter, we are hopeful that two things have happened. First, we hope you have seen that narratives that we have labeled as performing one function actually do many others as well. Second, we hope that some of the narratives strike you as more insightful or true to the way the world is than others. We will discuss the value of these two observations in turn as they relate to our efforts at learning about culture through narratives.

None of the stories we have relayed to you serves only a single purpose, even when there appears to be a clear theme or direct purpose involved. Take, for example, the *La Llorona* narrative. Yes, children are taught that ditches are dangerous, but they are also taught about the way the world works, their place in the world, and how to act appropriately. Look back at the story of *La Llorona* and see if you can find indirect messages about pride, strangers, appearances, the responsibilities that parents and spouses have, the value of listening to your elders, and so on. The discussion of the different types of stories is meant to alert us to the many different functions that narratives serve. It is hard to learn about our place in the world without also learning about the way the world works, and when we learn how to evaluate things in the world we are also learning about how we should act. These teaching functions are not meant as a static system of categorization that allows for "correct" labeling of all stories, nor are they meant to suggest that each story should somehow fit into one and only one of the categories. Instead, these functions serve as an etic framework from which the emic meanings of the stories may be extracted, understood, and compared.

We suspect that some of the narratives may be teaching things you either question or find irrelevant. Does it trouble you that the Western Apache story didn't show much concern for the cow that was killed? "Where is the justice in that?" you may ask. Or how about the story of the wife and the lion's ear? Does this story seem just another way to keep women subservient to men? How relevant did the narrative of Au Co and the beginning of the Vietnamese people seem to you? Do you really care what the CEO of Disney does? Do we suspect that this is a narrative "planted" by some official at Disney to make Mr. Eisner look more humane and encourage the workers to follow the rules?

As powerful as stories can be, they are not without limit. One of these limits is reflected in the notion of precedence we talked about before. We accumulate stories as we grow older. Narratives that do not fit with the stories we have come to accept are typically rejected. We are not trying to say that once a story has been accepted it can never be rejected, because it can. But new stories are always evaluated based on the stories we have currently come to accept and find meaningful in our own lives.

Further, we must be able to see in the stories some point of connection to our own lives. If we perceive the narrative about Michael Eisner as just applying to Disney employees and we have no intention of ever working at Disney, we may be completely bored by the narrative. On the other hand, if we consciously or unconsciously link into the problem of what to do when a superior is breaking organizational rules, we may find the story to be interesting, relevant, and informative.

Some of the most influential stories are narratives of personal experiences that have no clear moral or lesson to be learned. It is their status as "just a story about what happened" that makes them so powerful. While people often reject direct admonitions and advice, they tend to accept without question the implicit wisdom conveyed through experiences relayed to them as an account of what happened. Narratives usually teach without our even knowing we have been taught. We encourage you to look around at the many narratives that surround you and see what they are teaching, then start to look at the narratives of other people and see what is being taught in them.

Reflection Question: What stories or narratives have had an impact on you? At home? At work? In some other organization? Why do you think they had this impact?

RITUAL

Like narratives, rituals are also a universal form of communication and examples of rituals may be found in every cultural group or community. In this introduction to the concept of ritual and its importance in understanding our own and others' cultures we will focus primarily on ritual in everyday life. In understanding and identifying rituals within any given community, we take ritual to refer to "a structured sequence of actions the correct performance of which pays homage to a sacred object."[14] As is often the case, this definition will be more meaningful and useful as it is considered in light of specific examples. Therefore, we will wait until we have given some specific examples before we try to elaborate further on the definition. Instead, we wish to begin by looking at the concept of ritual as it is commonly viewed in the United States.

(Mis)impressions about the Nature of Rituals

When we mention the term "ritual" in class, it typically evokes one or more of the following four images: (1) a form of communication that involves doing the same thing over and over; (2) communication that is essentially outdated, hypocritical, or meaningless; (3) something reserved for very specialized settings, such as religious institutions or secret organizations; and (4) something that is quite foreign to our daily lives and/or is performed by others who perhaps are perceived as not quite as sophisticated as we are. We will use each of these impressions as a foil to help explain and illustrate how ritual is a part of communal life across very distinct cultures.

Just the Same Thing Over and Over

The first notion, that ritual is simply the repetition of the same thing over and over, roughly corresponds with the "structured sequence of actions" part of the definition we gave earlier. However, viewing ritual as simply the same thing done over and over is potentially misleading. As with all of the four impressions to be considered, we will use an actual example of a ritual to help provide greater understanding of ritual communication. To begin with we will use the *keh chee* ritual as explained by Chen.[15] The *keh chee* ritual is an exchange between a host and his or her guest at a Chinese dinner table. Chen provides the following specific example:

Host:	Eat more? Come on: don't be *"keh chee"*. . . Have more food, please have more.
Guest:	No, thanks, I've eaten a lot already, really, thank you: I can't eat any more. . .

Host:	Come on, more, just a bit more. You're the most important guest tonight. . . So *"keh chee"*. . . How come eat so little?
Guest:	No, it's enough, really, really. . . I'm not being *"keh chee"*; eat more yourself. (rotating the Lazy Susan back so that the new dish is facing the host)
Host (with enthusiasm):	Come on, don't be *"keh chee,"* you can afford to eat more. . . You ate too little. Just a bit more. . . (rotating the Lazy Susan again)
Guest:	Alright, just a bit more. . . Thank you: too much food, so *"keh chee."*[16]

Keh chee may be translated as "guest spirit." Both the host and the guest may be said to have guest spirit. The guest has *keh chee* in that he or she is polite and modest about food consumption. The host has *keh chee* because he or she has provided an abundance of food. In fact, Chen notes that a successful dinner party is marked by both an abundance of food and a noisy, boisterous atmosphere. Consistent with our initial definition, the *keh chee* ritual itself, just one part of the overall dinner interaction, is marked by a structured sequence of communicative actions or moves. The first move is engaged in by the host who offers the guest more food. The guest in turn declines this offer so as not to look like a hungry pig. The host then challenges the guest's declination by finding some excuse for the guest to eat, such as, "You're so skinny, you ought to eat some more." The fourth and final move is the guest submitting to the host's offer and accepting more food. Thus, the structured sequence of actions is offer, decline, challenge, and submit. The second and third actions may be repeated before the fourth one is engaged in. This structured sequence, in accordance with the impression noted earlier, is repetitive in nature. However, this repetition is in regards to the *type* of communication, not in the sense of the same words being spoken over and over. In fact, there is room for great creativity on the part of both guest and host. Indeed, a sign of a good host is the ability to create excuses for the guest to eat more.

It has been argued that sincerity for the Chinese has more to do with correctly performing social duties than with being true to one's inner self as is typical in the West.[17] The *keh chee* ritual illustrates this very point, for to correctly engage in the ritual the guest must at some point deny his or her personal feelings. If the guest really wants more food, he or she must still initially decline, and if the guest really does not want any more, he or she must still accept more if the ritual is going to be performed sincerely.

Outdated, Hypocritical, and Meaningless

The second impression to be considered is that ritual is taken to be relatively meaningless or even hypocritical. A comment such as, "Oh, it's just a ritual," implies that one should not take it seriously, that it is just something done for the sake of appearances. The understanding of ritual aimed at in this chapter is in marked contrast to such an idea. We will draw on research from another part of the world to provide an example of how this impression distorts the concept of ritual as discussed here. In her research on communication in Colombia, Fitch discovered something she calls the *salsipuede* ritual.[18] An example of this ritual is recorded by Fitch during a wedding reception held in the home of H1 and H2. Below is the English version as presented by Fitch. It originally took place in Spanish.

G (guest):	I'm leaving.
H1:	You're leaving? Why?
G:	The little card [wedding invitation] said very clearly that [the reception would last] from 7 to 10 and now it's 10:30.
H2:	But so <u>what</u>, until five thirty (G starts to chuckle) in the morning I'll be here=
G:	=But I have to <u>go</u>=
H1:	=Hmf, that you have to go. And <u>why</u>.
G:	Because I live far away
H2:	(H2 cuts in on top of G) But that doesn't <u>matter</u>
H1:	Hmf. Says he's going. Just like (G starts to laugh again) that I'm going.
G:	But it's that I have to go catch a <u>bus</u>=
H2:	=No, no, later we'll take you
H1:	(talking over H2) Have another little drink brother.
H2:	or you can go with Alberto who lives out there and has a car.[19]

G finally agrees and stays at the party for another hour or so.

Fitch notes that given the tenacity with which H1 and H2 consistently deny G's attempts to leave, one might believe that they know G well and particularly desire his company. However, they have only just met briefly earlier that evening and have spent very little, if any, time talking with G through the rest of the time he spent at the party. In spite of the pressure to stay and the lack of interaction after the pressure has succeeded, Fitch notes that the atmosphere stayed light and friendly throughout this interaction and the evening in general.

The structured sequence of acts in this ritual include an announced intention to leave, a request for an account of why that person must leave, an account or explanation, a denial of the legitimacy of that account and a proposed alternative that would allow the guest to stay, and, finally, an agreement to stay. As with the *keh chee* ritual, some of the moves, such as the account or explanation move and denial of that account's legitimacy move, may be repeated before getting to the final agreement to stay.

Although Fitch found the *salsipuede* (leave if you can) ritual to be very common in Colombia, such an exchange could be frustrating and even very rude to someone coming from a different culture. How does one make sense of this interaction? Does the fact that the hosts did not seem to pay that much attention to G afterwards mean that their actions were hypocritical and meaningless? No, but to understand this better we need to return to the latter part of the definition of ritual given earlier, that when these structured actions are performed correctly they pay homage to some sacred object. This sacred object may be any item or ideal that is highly valued within the community in which the ritual is relevant. In other words, if the people involved in the interaction follow the steps of the ritual correctly, some ideal or cultural good is reinforced and explicitly or implicitly honored.

Fitch explains that the sacred object or ideal to which the *salsipuede* ritual is paying homage is the *vínculo* or relationship formed and celebrated during the event. This relationship or interpersonal bond is a crucial part of defining who a person is for the Colombians. It is not individual people that are so important here (or their desire to leave a party), but instead it is the connection that is formed and maintained in that situation. Fitch argues that the development and recognition of these interpersonal bonds or contacts is an important part of effectively engaging in virtually all facets of Colombian society. The point of the ritual is not that the individual's unique presence is strongly desired as much as it is that the bond created or reflected by their attendance at this social event is honored by communication that encourages a continued mutual presence.

Perhaps the meaningfulness of these rituals is best grasped when considering the consequences of not performing them correctly. Fitch reports that the few violations of this ritual (such as somebody leaving directly) were considered to be either rude or incompetent. A guest who just leaves without saying goodbye or leaves in spite of the host's efforts to get him or her to stay for a little while longer or a host who simply says, "Nice you could come, see you later," would face very negative social repercussions. Therefore, though these rituals are done routinely and often quickly, it does not mean that they're meaningless. Although it is certainly possible for a person to fulfill their part of a ritual while they privately would prefer not to, the real desire to build and maintain certain images and relationships makes their enactment anything but hypocritical.

Reserved for Specialized Settings

The third impression to be considered is that ritual is something reserved for very specialized settings, such as religious institutions or secret organizations. The last two examples may, in part, lend credence to such an idea, for these

FIGURE 3.3 |
Miguel Gandert

rituals are only done in certain social settings. One does not engage in *keh chee* every time one eats dinner in China, nor does one engage in the *salsipuede* ritual every time one parts from another person in Colombia. In addition, rituals are certainly found in both religious and secret organizations as well as other specialized settings. Virtually all religions have activities of some form which involve set steps that, when followed properly, pay homage to some form of divinity. In addition, many organizations have secret rites which would also fit the concept of ritual. However, as with the first assumption, while there may be some ways in which this assumption is correct, taken simply at face value it distorts and unnecessarily restricts the notion of ritual discussed here.

Rituals are often part of the mundane, everyday interactions of life. For example, three female Japanese students who were studying in the United States were seated at a table sharing lunch when the following exchange (translated from the original Japanese) occurred between two of the women:

A: I want you to help to organize my [essay
B: No!
(laugh) I am not a person who can give you
advice because I haven't passed the English
Proficiency Exam yet
A: (laugh) But, you are taking one of the English
classes, aren't you? English [class!

B: No! It has
nothing to do with my ability to write
English I am doing a terrible job in the
the class and (pause) I usually have to
spend three days for writing an essay like
this (laugh)

A: Come on! I have to submit this essay by
tomorrow I don't have time

B: You are so coercive! (laugh) ((serves as notice that the request will be
granted)).

This conversation is an example of what Mutsumi Noguchi and Brad term the *kenson* ritual.[20] *Kenson* is a Japanese term that may be translated as modesty. However, there are some subtle, but significant differences from what most Americans think of in terms of modesty. For example, although they both discount one's personal abilities, modesty functions more as a shield against negative attributions directed toward the individual, whereas *kenson* is more of a social glue that maintains the status quo of a relationship. This difference is reflected in the fact that one may cover oneself with clothes and be said to dress with modesty, but one can never be said to dress with *kenson*. Such an idea is nonsensical.

Hall and Noguchi's research reveals that ritualized *kenson* involves four basic steps: 1) highlighting of another's ability, 2) denial, 3) reassertion, and 4) indirect acceptance. By engaging in these four steps homage is subtly paid to the status quo of the relationship. In the case noted, there is a relatively equal relationship between two friends, although all at the table know that B is better at English than is A. However, B is aware of the implied compliment in A's request and avoids positioning herself as superior to A by engaging in *kenson*. Although, in our example, the middle steps are repeated before going to the final step, this is not necessary.

As with other rituals, however, if these steps are not followed correctly, negative social implications would arise. For example, if B just said, "Sure, I'd be glad to help," she would come across as somewhat pompous. Even if she spoke modestly (by American standards), saying, "Well I'm not that great, but I'll try," she would only be seen as expressing reluctance, not *kenson*. In addition, if A had accepted B's first refusal, she would have been seen as insensitive and would have put B in the awkward spot of seeming to be uncooperative. The *kenson* ritual requires both persons' proper participation.

Finally, and most importantly for our purposes, this ritual was done spontaneously, over a matter of seconds in an everyday setting. The young women were simply having an informal lunch together, a frequent and mundane activity. It is very unlikely that any of the individuals involved even thought about *kenson* in an explicit way while they were engaged in it. It was simply a common sort of interaction that is recognizable as a ritual only after careful analysis. Many rituals are performed without anyone even thinking about them being rituals.

Engaged in by Those Less Sophisticated Than I

This point brings us to the fourth and final assumption to be considered in this chapter, the notion that ritual is something quite foreign to our daily lives or is performed by others who perhaps are perceived as not quite as sophisticated as we are. No doubt, examples of ritual can be found in other communities besides our own, including some that we have heard labeled primitive. In fact, these are often easier to notice, because, as with the *kenson* example, many of our own rituals seem so natural and spontaneous that we never see them as such, though we notice when something has gone wrong in their performance. Even then we don't typically think something like, "Oh, he violated the *salsipuede* ritual"; we just know that the "he" in this case is rude or has some other negative characteristic.

However, if we assume that we—whatever "we" that is—are somehow above rituals, we make a serious misjudgment. To help illustrate this point let us explain a ritual that is common in the United States (and among college-educated people) and, as with the other rituals noted above, is engaged in without consciously being aware that it is even a ritual. The ritual we speak of is something Katriel and Philipsen call the *communication* ritual.[21] Violations of this ritual are often revealed in such statements as, "What we need is communication," or "There is a lack of communication here."

Katriel and Philipsen identify four communicative moves in the communication ritual that must be followed to be able to say that people really communicated. The first move is to raise some issue or concern upon which a person may take a stand. The second move involves acknowledging the legitimacy of that concern or issue as worth attending to. Third, there is a sharing of ideas on that issue or concern either from both the participants or just the initiator. The fourth and final move must in some way express the idea that "I'm okay, you're okay." This expression may be explicit or implicit. When this ritual is performed correctly, it pays homage to the inherent worth of each individual.

This is a ritual with which we suspect many of our readers will be familiar, even if they have never thought of it as a ritual. A clue to whether you share an understanding of this ritual is how you would react to violations. For example, suppose a wife says to her husband, "I'm worried about Johnny. He got in another fight today at school," and the husband responds with, "Not now, I'm in the middle of my show." Many would feel that there was a lack of communication. If this scene were typical of the husband and wife's interaction as a whole, many would feel the relationship was in trouble and would prescribe communication as a cure. Such attributions use a very culturally biased view of communication. After all, meanings were passed across people, and communication did in fact occur in what may be argued to be a very forceful manner. Furthermore, if the talk ended with the individuals blaming each other and so forth, it is likely that many would say there had been a communication breakdown, even though communication in a technical sense was going on in a very active manner. The problem is that when people don't follow the communication ritual, they are viewed from a certain cultural viewpoint as having not really communicated. Many people who might feel that they don't believe in or participate in rituals get quite offended when someone else refuses to perform the communication ritual properly.

Recognizing Rituals around Us

One may be asking how can we recognize and understand these rituals. Although a full answer to this question is beyond the scope of this chapter, we will make a couple of suggestions. One is to look for these rituals around important social events. Trice and Beyer identified events that often take place within some form of organization (business, political, religious, government, education, volunteer, family, and so forth).[22] These events include rites of passage, degradation, enhancement, integration, and termination. All of these events center around those times when someone's social role, identity, status, or power level are changed. The change may be for the better or the worse, but regardless of the direction of the change, the social relationships are altered and highlighted. Thus, one way to begin to look for rituals is to identify set times that involve some kind of relational change. This identification of recognized social change may be approached through such questions as, "Do these changes follow a certain pattern?" and "What sort of values are being honored, directly or indirectly, by change?"

However, not all rituals involve a relational *change*. Indeed, most of the examples given so far in this chapter involve more of a confirmation and recognition of existing relationships than perceived changes in a relationship. One way to start to notice such rituals is to ask yourself what you say just because you and someone else are friends, brothers, sisters, classmates, or any other social role relationship you may consider. Although the exact content may change, do you say the same types of things in a similar order in similar places? Do others in your community say similar sorts of things when they are also acting in those social roles? What do you think you get out of these exchanges? Why do you engage in them? Try to go beyond the initial surface explanations. If the pattern you discover is culturally significant, you can expect that violations of the pattern will be disturbing to one or more of those involved in the interaction.

A third way one may use to discover the rituals around us that are often taken for granted is to observe when negative attributions arise toward other people. What expectations were violated that led to the negative feelings? Perhaps it is because the other person has not been following the proper form or steps of an unspoken and culturally assumed ritual. Negative attributions can serve as a signal of where to look. Many rituals bring no attention to themselves except when their proper enactment is violated. Thus, frustrations with others provide a way to track down common rituals that otherwise would have been missed because people seemed to be just acting normally.

Reflection Question: Do you believe that rituals are truly a universal form of communication? Would our lives be better if we could eliminate rituals? Why or why not?

The Worth of Rituals

One question that often comes up in a discussion of rituals is, "Why don't people just be open and get to the point?" If a person wants more food, that person should just say so, and if a person does not want more food that the person should be open about that as well. Rituals may seem very inefficient, a sort of cultural fluff that would be better put behind us. We will try to illustrate the importance of rituals by reviewing a ritual Brad learned and participated in while still a youth.

When I was very young, we moved across the country to within walking distance of my mother's parents' home. Around the age of seven or eight I started helping out around my grandparents' place by mowing, weeding, and doing other yard work. After one of these initial efforts, my grandmother gave me some money for my help. Quite excited about this turn of events, I told my mother about the money, but she was not as excited as I. "Didn't you tell her no?" she asked. My uncomfortable silence was answer enough. She then tried to explain to me about fixed income and helping out just because we were family, and that I should not be taking my grandparents' money for helping.

So, the next time I helped out and was offered money, I told my grandmother, "No thanks, I was just happy to help out." My grandmother insisted on paying me. Finally, after going back and forth a bit she stuffed the money into my pocket and told me to get an ice-cream or something. Worried that my mother would find out (she always seemed to), I explained what had happened to me. Instead of being upset, she noted that at least I had tried. I quickly learned that if I communicated

(continued)

(continued)

in the right way, said no at first and indicated that I just wanted to help out, it was okay to get the money (which I wanted), but that if I did not communicate appropriately, the same activity, taking the money, was not acceptable.

Some might assume that Brad was actually learning how to manipulate people and that it would have been better if he had just taken the money without the ritual. We disagree with this, because as time went on Brad found himself *wanting* to help out and not get the money. At certain times he could accomplish this by doing the act secretly or leaving before the ritual could be enacted, for once the ritual was started, a violation never created the same good feelings. This development of the right feelings was an important part of his cultural education. It was part of the development of his cultural competence. Brad was being taught about important values within his community, such as respect and gratitude. Rituals may seem to be very ineffective ways to accomplish certain immediate tasks, but what is sometimes forgotten is that the primary tasks being accomplished are to affirm and reaffirm certain types of relationships and to teach values that are important in a particular cultural community.

Rituals are a vital part of any community not only because they teach people what is good, and provide, as we have noted, a way to create and maintain important social relationships, but they also serve a cohesive function for the larger community in general. With all the rituals noted thus far, people who are engaged in them do not consciously think, "I am engaging in a ritual." Yet they still routinely follow a structured series of acts, the correct performance of which pays homage to some cultural good or ideal. So, even though certain aspects of the content may vary and there is a sense of spontaneity, if someone violates the proper form, it is immediately noted and has negative implications for the social standing of the violator. In this way rituals work to bind communities of people together, even in very individualistic cultures. Recognizing and understanding these rituals within our own and other communities provides one way to better appreciate and understand that which is significant in other cultures. We will cover two other ways that we may learn about cultural differences, social dramas, and attending to key words or terms that have particular significance within a community.

SOCIAL DRAMAS

Another window into cultural differences can be found in what may be referred to as a "social drama." Social dramas are a process through which potential violations of community-accepted social norms are publicly recognized and managed.[23] The processes of identifying and challenging misbehavior as well as the public efforts to redress or manage these normative violations are ideal sites for seeing the power of culture at work. Turner identified four component parts in a social drama: a breach or violation of some social norm or value; the crisis or public recognition of the violation which typically constitutes a challenge; attempts to redress the challenge; and finally some sort of assessment of the efforts to remedy the problem and the subsequent resolution, either resulting in the person being reintegrated into the good graces of the community or being seen as no longer an acceptable member of the community.[24] These social dramas are always grounded in cultural norms for both interpreting and producing action. Examining the sense displayed in the social challenge, response, and public assessment embedded in these dramas provides an insight into the system of resources a community uses for making sense of symbolic action.

The social or public nature of these dramas implies that these occur at the community level, but the size and nature of the community vary. Sally Hastings reported on a social drama that occurred within a community as small as a group of Asian Indian graduate students at a university in the northeast United States.[25] The action in question was related to an article written by an Indian student for the college newspaper that was critical of India. The action was publicly addressed in a satirical skit at an India Night event put on by the Indian Student Association. The event revealed two contrasting rules that distinguished this community from traditional U.S. American college communities. One was the importance of being true to "who you are" in terms of staying loyal to your group membership, rather than just doing your own thing. The second focused on the importance of being interdependent, rather than independence in terms of relationships. Both rules highlighted specific ways that the worldview of collectivism may be played out in specific practices and expectations, thus providing insight into an Asian Indian community's communicative practices for anyone interested in observing.

Another example that is at a larger community level was centered on comments made by Donald Sterling, the former owner of the Los Angeles Clippers, a basketball team in the National Basketball Association (NBA). In 2014 a tape surfaced in which Sterling was heard to make extremely negative comments toward "blacks," including telling his girlfriend at the time to not be seen with them at games. The outcry related to these comments was immediate and loud and resulted in Sterling being banned from the NBA, even though he was an owner in that league. The public discourse related to this incident is informative in terms of cultural norms and meanings. His comments violated norms grounded in equality and human dignity. In the United States, the values of equality and communication that demonstrates explicit respect for the worth of all individuals, regardless of skin color, are strongly held.

In the public discourse we heard related to this issue, no one challenged those norms. However, there were those who debated Sterling being banned on one of two fronts; one was tied to freedom of speech and the other was tied to rights of privacy, both of which are important normative values in the United States as well. The freedom of speech arguments came and went quickly in the news we listened to. Most indicated that Sterling was free to say what he wanted, but the public and the NBA were also free to react as they wanted. The thinking here was that we are free to say what we want, but so are those who wish to criticize the behavior in question. The stronger argument, in terms of the legal proceedings, was the privacy argument. Many commentators decried what was said, supporting the norms of equality and respect for all racial groups, while still wondering if this sets a bad precedent in terms of rights of privacy. The recording apparently was made in his living room without his knowledge. The battle then became the right to have disagreeable opinions in private versus the right to have them in public. Even though it was said in private, the assessment so far indicates that Sterling, in his role as owner of a public team and an employer of individuals from many different races, is still responsible for these comments and the comments suggest a larger issue that someone in this public role is accountable for. In this case Sterling made the situation worse by taking part in a national interview and focusing more on attacking others than on apologizing for his actions. In the end Sterling sold the team (under pressure) and is no longer a member of that community. There is much more that could be written related to this case, but our hope in mentioning it is simply to illustrate how these social dramas serve as windows into cultures. Many of these same values were also played out in the political arena as Donald Trump and Hillary Clinton took contrasting viewpoints on how to handle problems facing the United States in the election that culminated in Trump's win in 2016. Paying attention to what becomes a social drama and how these dramas are played out in the public helps us to better understand the values and norms of a given cultural community.

By the time you read this, the social drama we have referenced will be a thing of the past, but there will be current dramas going on in your community and in other cultural communities. If you want to learn about a culture, pay attention to what is being challenged publicly and how these challenges are being responded to or how the violations are redressed, and note the public assessment of the whole process. The public assessment is particularly important as it often reveals cultural divisions within a political or national boundary and different assessments are often tied to one's membership within a cultural community. For example, recently Russia and the Ukraine have been at odds with each other in terms of political control. We know individuals who have lived in the Ukraine, but come from different backgrounds, some pro-Russian and another pro-Western Ukraine. Their assessments of the social drama being played out in the Ukraine are very different from each other and can provide insights into some cultural differences in terms of values of different cultural communities within the same national boundary.

KEY TERMS

Attending to the key terms or key words that people use is another way of understanding what is going on culturally. Key terms are words or phrases that have particular importance or significance within a community. The specific meanings people give to the key terms they use give clues as to the ideas, beliefs, values, goals, attitudes, feelings, and aspirations held by the particular group. This notion can be better understood if we consider that outside of a particular community the same word can have different meanings. Further, the frequency with which a term is used gives clues about the importance and intensity the concept holds for the community members.

For example, in today's Facebook community, the terms "wall," "timeline," "friend," "unfriend," and "post" hold special meanings to users. Outside of the Facebook context the term "wall" might mean a barrier made of concrete, brick, or stone and not the virtual space within a social networking site. On Facebook a "timeline" serves as space for users to post photos, images, and stories that represent their values, feelings, and aspirations. A timeline in another context may refer to a chart indicating when assignments or tasks are due. In the context of the broadcast news industry, terms such as "breaking news" and "news bulletin" are used to justify the interruption of scheduled programming and/or to bring urgency to a significant, unexpected, developing event that is being covered live. In contentious political discourses about immigration key terms that surface consistently are "documented" vs. "undocumented" and "legal" vs. "illegal." And in the context of healthcare in contemporary debates in the U.S. the word "affordable" can be considered a key term. To make healthcare accessible to all citizens, on March 23, 2010, President Obama signed into law what is called the Patient Protection and Affordable Care Act (PPACA). The term "affordable" highlights a cultural premise that all citizens should have access to medical insurance.

The work of Boromisza-Habashi offers an example of the broad impact that arguments over the meaning of a single key term can bring about.[26] He demonstrates how different sociopolitical groups in Hungary interpreted the term *gyűlöletbeszéd* or "hate speech" in contrasting ways that led to unproductive results. He argues that the term *gyűlöletbeszéd* was the subject of heated debate in Hungary between the years 2000 and 2006 in arguments about what did and did not count as public discourse. Boromisza-Habashi claims that continued political disagreement about what the term *gyűlöletbeszéd* meant unified some people and factionalized others, thus dealing redressive action about a social ill that many people agreed existed.

In her work with Mexican construction workers in the port city of Veracruz, Covarrubias found that the workers routinely invoked two terms to describe their ideal types of interpersonal relationships—*confianza* and *respeto*.[27] *Confianza* is shown to be a complex blend of trust, confidence, familiarity, and confidentiality that is best achieved via through uses of the pronoun *tú* [informal "you"]. *Respeto*, best achieved via uses of the pronoun *usted* [formal "you"], is shown to mean respect, but with an added emotional intensity that is not necessarily part of a universal definition for respect. Further, the two key terms *confianza* and *respeto* are also shown to play an important part in workers achieving the types of interpersonal relationships that, in turn, help them construct networks of cooperation that are fundamental to the completion of their work-related tasks.

In the work of Katriel and Philipsen, the term "communication" has a very different meaning than the definition one would find in a dictionary.[28] Studying the speaking patterns of middle-class white Americans, the authors defined "communication" as close, open, and supportive speech. Further, they found that according to their study participants, relationships were formed not by "mere talk," but, rather, in and through "real communication" wherein people can come to know one another as individuals. The key terms here then point to uses of "communication" as a means for constructing fruitful interpersonal relationships. We can see, then, that the term "communication" is contingent on a particular sociocultural context and not on a universal meaning.

SUMMARY

This chapter has focused on how we can come to learn about our own cultures and those of others. Two vital aspects related to learning in general, need and precedent, were identified. Humans tend to learn best when there is a felt need. The process of learning is mediated by precedence. We are constantly testing new information or perspectives against what we already know and understand. This process has its advantages and disadvantages, but it is similar in form to the etic/emic distinction talked about by linguists and others interested in intercultural communication.

The etic/emic distinction suggests a way to understand and compare different cultures. Items that can be said to be potentially relevant for all people are etic, whereas the items that are meaningful to a specific community, regardless of their meaning to other groups, are emic. Emic observations can help to create etic frameworks. These etic frameworks can in turn help us to discover and compare the emic meanings across communities. One of the most common of these frameworks is Hymes' SPEAKING framework. This framework provides a way to articulate what is important in any given speech situation or in the performance of any recognized communicative act.

In addition to frameworks, there are certain forms of communication that may be said to be etic or universal in nature. One such form is the narrative. All human communities have narratives. These narratives, or stories, help humans to make sense of their world and share their experiences. Narratives are inescapably teachers. Whether there is an explicit moral to the story or not, there is always teaching going on. Four major areas that these narratives teach us about are: the way the world works, our place in the world, how to act in the world, and how to evaluate the world around us. Looking at what stories teach about these four areas can help us understand our own and other cultures.

A second universal form of communication discussed in this chapter is ritual. Rituals are structured sequences of action that pay homage to some cultural ideal. Rituals are not meaningless, routine exercises that take place only in specialized settings and are performed by people less sophisticated than ourselves. Instead, rituals are part of our everyday lives. They provide a way for us to confirm our common identity with those around us and learn about those values and relationships that are important in our cultural communities. Paying attention to the rituals involved with life changes or to the frustrations we feel when everyday rituals are not followed can help us to learn and understand what is important in a culture.

Finally, we reviewed how social drama and key terms or words provide a window into what is perceived as important within a cultural community. Social dramas are performed on a communal stage and involve a challenge grounded in a purported breach of normative behavior. Efforts then are often taken to redress or in some cases repair the breach and in any case there is a public or social assessment that has consequences for the membership of those involved in the violation of cultural norms. The talk that revolves around this process is inherently revealing in terms of what norms and values are important within the particular worldviews of a cultural community.

REFLECTION QUESTIONS

1   What role do you feel *need* and *precedent* play in your own learning process?
2   What other teaching functions do stories have in addition to the ones we note in this chapter?
3   What differences are there between narratives that appear to just relay what happened and those that seem to be created to explicitly teach a message?
4   We argue that rituals teach and reaffirm important cultural values. What specific values are being taught in your community through the enactment of rituals?

ACTIVITIES

1   Select either a named type of talk (flirt, gossip, introductions, trash talk, and so forth) or a specific situation (eating out, a funeral, the classroom, Thanksgiving dinner, and so forth) within a community to which you belong. Use Hymes' SPEAKING framework to describe what is culturally understood and important about this type of talk or situation. Select what appears to be a similar type of talk or situation from a different cultural community, and see what differences and similarities you can find.

2   Gather common folk stories from a culture different from your own. Analyze them in terms of the four parts of a narrative. What types of characters are there, and what types of problems do these characters face? What actions do these characters take? How successful are they? Do some problems and characters show up over and over again?

3   Visit with students from other cultures about narratives they remember from their home culture. Using the teaching functions overviewed in Table 3.1, talk about what is being taught in these narratives.

4   Select a narrative from your own culture that is retold (a bedtime story, a favorite family incident, a story from work that is told to all the new employees, etc.) and consider what is taught in that narrative. Imagine that different people (or characters in the story) are telling the same story. How would the story and what is taught change if your boss or an ex-employee told it? If your father or your sister told it? If Cinderella or the stepmother told it?

5   Interview people about what they think of when they think of rituals. How does this compare to the typical reactions discussed in this chapter? Or: brainstorm with members of your own community all the rituals in which you participate, even everyday ones. Identify which are the most important to you. Why? How do you feel when they are violated?

NOTES

1   A. Sanoff, "Hotbed of Innovation," *U.S. News and World Report*, March 18, 1996, 72.
2   K. Pike, *Phonemics* (Ann Arbor, MI: University of Michigan Press, 1947); and K. L. Pike, "Etic and Emic Standpoints for the Description of Behavior," in *Communication and Culture: Readings in the Codes of Human Interaction*, ed. A. Smith (New York: Holt, Rinehart & Winston, 1966), 152–63.
3   Adapted from an experience reported in T. Katriel, *Talking Straight: 'Dugri' Speech in Israeli Sabra Culture* (New York: Cambridge University Press, 1986).
4   D. Hymes, "Models of the Interaction of Language and Social Life," in *Directions in Sociolinguistics: The Ethnography of Communication*, ed. J. J. Gumperz and D. Hymes (New York: Holt, Rinehart & Winston, 1972), 35–71.
5   Katriel, *Talking Straight*.
6   Y. Griefat and T. Katriel, "Life Demands *Musayara*: Communication and Culture among Arabs in Israel," in *Language, Communication and Culture*: *Current Directions*, ed. S. Ting-Toomey and F. Korzenny (Newbury Park, CA: Sage, 1989), 121–38.

7 G. Philipsen, "The Prospect for Cultural Communication," in *Communication Theory: Eastern and Western Perspectives*, ed. D. L. Kincaid (San Diego, CA: Academic Press, 1987), 245–54.

8 W. R. Fisher, *Human Communication as Narration: Toward a Philosophy of Reason, Value and Action* (Columbia, SC: University of South Carolina Press, 1987).

9 K. H. Basso, "'Stalking with Stories': Names, Places, and Moral Narratives among the Western Apache," in *Western Apache Language and Culture*, ed. K. H. Basso (Tucson, AZ: University of Arizona Press, 1990); E. Stone, "Family Ground Rules," in *Making Connections: Readings in Relational Communication*, 2nd ed., ed. K. M. Galvin and P. J. Cooper (Los Angeles, CA: Roxbury, 2000), 49–67; and R. Scollon and S. Scollon, *Narrative, Literacy and Face in Interethnic Communication* (Norwood, NJ: Ablex, 1981).

10 J. Quintana, "The Tooth" (paper, University of New Mexico, 1998).

11 C. Grant, *Myths We Live By* (Ottawa, Canada: University of Ottawa Press, 1998).

12 Basso, "Stalking with Stories."

13 Basso, "Stalking with Stories," 119–20.

14 Philipsen, "Prospect," 250. See also E. Rothenbuhler, *Ritual Communication: From Everyday Conversation to Mediated Ceremony* (Thousand Oaks, CA: Sage Publications, 1998).

15 V. Chen, "*Mein Tze* at the Chinese Dinner Table: A Study of Interactional Accomplishment," *Research on Language and Social Interaction* 24 (1990/1): 109–40.

16 Chen, "*Mein Tze*," 109.

17 L. Stover and T. Stover, *China: An Anthropological Perspective* (Pacific Palisades, CA: Goodyear Publishing Company, 1976).

18 K. Fitch, "A Ritual for Attempting Leave-Taking in Colombia," *Research on Language and Social Interaction* 24 (1990/1): 209–24.

19 Fitch, "Leave-Taking," 210.

20 B. J. Hall and M. Noguchi, "Engaging in *Kenson*: An Extended Case Study of One Form of 'Common' Sense," *Human Relations* 48 (1995): 1129–47; example dialogue is from p. 1131.

21 T. Katriel and G. Philipsen, "'What We Need Is Communication': 'Communication' as a Cultural Category in Some American Speech," *Communication Monographs* 48 (1981): 302–17.

22 H. Trice and J. Beyer, "Studying Organizational Cultures through Rites and Ceremonials," *Academy of Management Review* 9 (1984): 663–9.

23 G. Philipsen, "A Theory of Speech Codes," in *Developing Communication Theories*, ed. G. Philipsen and T. Albrecht (Albany, NY: State University of New York, 1997), 119–56.

24 V. Turner, *The Anthropology of Performance* (New York: PAJ Publications, 1988).

25 S. O. Hastings, "Social Drama as a Site for the Communal Construction and Management of Asian Indian 'Stranger' Identity," *Research on Language and Social Interaction* 34 (3) (2001): 309–35.

26 D. Boromisza-Habashi, *Speaking Hatefully: Culture, Communication, and Political Action in Hungary* (University Park, PA: Penn State University Press, 2013).

27 P. Covarrubias, *Culture, Communication, and Cooperation: Interpersonal Relations and Pronominal Address in a Mexican Organization* (Lanham, MD: Rowman & Littlefield, 2002).

28 T. Katriel and G. Philipsen, "'What We Need Is Communication': 'Communication' as a Cultural Category in Some American Speech," *Communication Monographs* 48 (1981): 301–17.

Chapter 4

How Is Culture Related to Our Identities?

Van slumped back into the big, overly soft couch staring at a Sports Illustrated *magazine. He was only partly paying attention to the article on the decline of the 49ers. He was also watching with amusement as his friend Jimmy razzed the young Ute woman who worked here at the Native American Students Center.*

She had been straightening up the newspapers and Jimmy had started complaining about the number and type of selections available. She had just laughed and suggested he write the governor. "You Kiowa have such a way with words I'm sure he would come down here personally to restock our shelves for us. While you're at it you might ask him to bring lunch, perhaps some roast puppy and dumplings you Kiowas are so fond of."

"I would," Jimmy responded without missing a beat, "but I know you Utes prefer collie. Besides Van over here thinks you're too skinny already to be missing any meals."

Van glanced up from the magazine, grinning. The young woman looked over at him laughing lightly. Jimmy continued, "You notice he always hogs that big, soft couch. It reminds him of his last girlfriend. Though that couch looks mighty puny compared to her."

Van joined in the fun, "Yeah, she was real comfortable, but like a lot of Navajo she had a one-track mind when it came to food. I used to call her in the morning before we were to meet at school, and I'd ask her what she had for breakfast."

The Ute woman laughed, "Mutton Honey."

"You knew her too?" Van laughed. "You're so smart maybe you can explain to me why Jimmy here is known as the best buffalo snagger this side of the Mississippi."

"Old Jimmy comes from a family of buffalo snaggers, eh?" joked another young Native American man who had just walked into the room. The room immediately grew quiet.

FIGURE 4.1 |

Miguel Gandert

"Yeah, thought we may go hunting this weekend," Jimmy said in a more reserved way addressing the newcomer, Larry. "You a big buffalo hunter?"

Jimmy and Van were not that familiar with Larry and, the few times they had met, Larry seemed to try too hard. The feeling in the room had definitely changed when he entered.

"Oh, I've done my share of hunting in my day, but I'm too busy with school and work right now." Larry paused. No one said anything and the young Ute woman excused herself to go finish some business.

"Yeah, I got an awful lot going on." Larry spread the comment out slowly and looked a bit sorry for himself.

"So what's been going on?" asked Jimmy.

"Been pretty busy working for one thing. I've been commissioned by this rich white woman back East to make a peyote fan. She's seen some of the other work I do. Likes it a lot. She's paying me a lot of money to do it."

Van looked back at his article on the 49ers. Jimmy nodded really slowly and responded quietly, "That sounds pretty good. There is always somebody who'll pay money."

"Just got to have the connections," Larry said, obviously proud that he had those connections.

The conversation died out and pretty soon Larry left the center.

(continued)

(continued)

> *Van turned to Jimmy, "You knew he was just bullshitting about making that fan. Why didn't you say something?"*
>
> *Jimmy laughed a little, "Yeah, I knew he was bullshitting. He has probably never even seen a peyote fan. If you knew, why didn't you say something?"*
>
> *Van just grinned and leaned back further into the overstuffed couch.*
>
> *Walking over to a stack of newspapers, Jimmy said out loud, but almost to himself, "I don't know why that guy tries to act like he's an Indian. He doesn't even know how."*[1]

The interaction described above is rich with identity markers. Drawing from work by Steven Pratt and D. L. Weider, we will explain just a few of these. The initial interaction between the woman, Jimmy, and Van is an example of razzing. Razzing is a common form of verbal sparring that is enjoyable to Indian interactants and displays their *Indianness*. By *Indianness*, we are not referring to whether the person can legally claim to be a Native American, but instead whether she or he is a recognizable *Indian* among other Indians. This identity is important at many powwows and other pan-Indian events. Pratt and Weider's work indicates that, although there are many tribal differences, there are also certain communicative patterns used at pan-Indian events that are associated with being an Indian. The teasing ritual of razzing is one of these. Razzing may seem too harsh to some who may be offended by its content and it is viewed among Indians as a distinctly Indian type of humor. Razzing often involves either shame stories where someone's mistakes are exaggerated, or jokes about tribal memberships using stereotypes in humorous ways. Razzing evolves out of specific situations and people are expected to take and give the teasing without getting offended. There are limitations, though. Razzing should not reference family members, or be engaged in with a person much older than yourself. Larry entered and immediately brought Jimmy's family into the interaction. Obviously he did not really know how to participate in the razzing.

Although Larry is Native American, in the minds of Van and Jimmy his communicative behaviors demonstrate that he is not a *real* Indian. He is uncomfortable with silence and brags about making the fan for a lot of money. His communication should be more modest. Jimmy and Van respond appropriately to Larry, though, by not challenging him directly about his boast and, thereby, continue to demonstrate their own *Indianness* just as the razzing had done previously. We have only scratched the surface of how the above incident both displayed and created an Indian identity, but we will refer to the example again as we discuss different elements of identity.

IDENTITY

Identity, *or the image by which we recognize ourselves and others*, is an important part of every interaction. Identities are markers of who we are, allowing ourselves and others to be recognized and interacted with in meaningful ways. Identities carry with them powerful expectations for behavior. The meaning various identities have in our lives is grounded in the interplay between similarities and differences. We have both personal and social identities, each connected to different relational rights and responsibilities that can vary across cultures. One of the ways in which cultures function to make sense of the world for us is through our understanding of different identities and what to expect in relation to these identities. Some identities, such as *pearly queen, best boy*, and *shaman*, are very community specific; other identities, like *mother* and *father*, cut across many cultures even though the expectations that constitute them may vary. Identities empower us and also imply social expectations for both ourselves and others, the violation of which can have serious consequences for our identities. Identities are a social creation and can change over time and through interaction.[2] In this chapter, we will explore the impact of identities on intercultural communication by discussing the difference between personal and social identities and the fundamental role of similarities and differences in understanding these forms of identity, the nature of expectations created by identities, the relationship between identity and communication, and the pathways people take to establish and recognize particular identities.

Social and Personal Identities

Each of us has two types of identity that, depending upon the context, may or may not be salient in our interactions with others. We have a personal identity and a social identity. Personal identity refers to our perception of ourselves and others as unique, idiosyncratic individuals, distinct from all others. Often these identities are centered on characteristics we associate with ourselves, such as being stubborn, friendly, or open-minded. Social identity refers to the perceived role or communal memberships we and others have. Roles, such as student/ teacher, boss/employee, parent/child, customer/salesperson, imply an identity that is grounded in particular tasks and relationships to other people in terms of their roles. Communal memberships tend to be quite broad in nature and are often resilient to change. They are typically associated with large-scale communities, such as nationality, ethnicity, gender, or religious or political affiliation. Indianness, which we read about in the incident that led off this chapter, is an example of a social identity. Personal and social identities are often combined at any given point and we all interact with others based on multiple identities.

For example, during a study abroad experience Kristin could be seen as a respectful American student in one setting and an assertive, female intern in another.

Identity always involves a tension between similarities and differences. Similarity and difference are at the very heart of identity, and identity really exists only in the interplay between similarity and difference.[3] Any identity or combination of identities that a person may adopt or have, such as mother, client, acquaintance, stranger, Asian, or Spanish, implies something shared with others (similarity). At the same time, our identities imply differences as well. Expectations involved with being a stranger are different, at least in part, than the expectations involved with other identities. If Patricia claims any of the above identities as her own, she is highlighting a similarity that distinguishes her from others who do not share that identity (difference). Even to claim a very broad identity, such as being human, brings attention to what humans share (similarity) and what separates them from nonhumans (difference). In addition, difference always implies a higher-level similarity. The difference between Catholic, Baptist, and Hindu makes sense only in relation to the fact that they are all religions (similarity). A Catholic identity does not distinguish a person from females, but it does from Baptists and Hindus.

Perhaps you are asking, what about my own personal identity or my understanding of who I am as a unique individual? You may think this is surely grounded only in difference. It is what distinguishes me from all those around me and, in spite of what other identities we share, it gives a unique expression to those identities. We would not argue with the importance and role that differences play in these unique or personal identities. However, we maintain that similarity is essential for these identities as well. Similarity is essential in two ways for these types of identities.

One way that similarity is necessary is related to the concepts we use to think about ourselves and what makes us unique. Are you outgoing, shy, easily angered, patient, witty, sensitive, or all of these combined, depending on the context? All of those characteristics through which you see your unique self are used by others to make themselves feel unique as well. We are not saying that you are not unique, but to understand your uniqueness you will use concepts that others also use to view themselves as unique. Some people are very good at using generic descriptions to convince other people that they understand their unique situation. Part of what makes this possible is our shared use of concepts to understand our individual selves.

The other reason that similarity is essential is that our unique personal identity only becomes a factor socially when we share a larger group membership with others. If I am the only American among a group of people, it may make me unique at one level, but at another it prevents others from seeing my personal self. The same can be true for virtually any other social identity associated with a group.

FIGURE 4.2 |
Miguel Gandert

"As the only *female* in the group, what do you think?"
"John, how do *African Americans* feel about this issue?"
"Let's ask our *Hindu* student in the back his opinion."

These kinds of comments discourage us from being able to really see the other's personal identity in the same way that I may see someone else's identity who is "just one of us." When Brad was young, there was a French girl whose family moved into the school district and she was in his class. For a long time she was just "the French girl." Her personal identity and uniqueness were obscured by a blatant social identity difference. Over time, he and others were able to get to know "Natalie" as a person, but it was really only after she had at one level become one of them, sharing a social identity in the class. Until we share a group membership or identity, our personal identities are of little social significance. It is in the context of similarity that difference can be seen, just as it is in a context of difference that we see what we share with others.

Reflection Question: We argue that both similarity and difference are at the heart of all identities. Do you agree or disagree? Why or why not?

In any given relationship or setting there are many different identities, both personal and social, that can be drawn upon and created in our interactions. These identities imply certain rights and responsibilities in the relationship and thus are intimately connected with power. Think about the different types of identity and the power each conveys in the following account taken from the travel memoirs of Sarah Streed.[4]

No matter what threats I uttered, or what vigilance I gave to catching the offenders, the majority of the students cheated on tests, exams, and homework assignments. I understood that the Moroccan school system fostered this temptation, because only an educated person could hope to get one of the few available jobs, even with some palm-greasing. But I also felt that if I couldn't give each student an accurate grade, I might as well not teach. For the sake of academic integrity alone, I had to grade according to knowledge and merit, rather than according to which student was the most cunning in his efforts to avoid an accurate grade.

At the end of the semester, I gave the final exam, graded it and then averaged out semester grades. During class, I called each student up to my desk to show the final grade. Grades were calculated on a scale of one to 20. A Moroccan saying has it that 20 is for the Prophet Mohammed, 19 for the King, 18 for the best student, and so on, all the way down to zero, with the "moyenne," or average passing grade, being ten.

I called Hamid, a well-dressed student, up to my desk. His final grade was a number eight. He was extremely upset.

"But look," I showed him the line of figures in my gradebook. "These are all your scores, and they average out to an eight."

"You can't give me a below-average grade," he said to me, genuinely shocked. "My father is the richest man in this town."

"This will be your grade," I said. "It's the grade you deserve. Now leave."

After school, he and a friend were waiting. They followed me back to my apartment chanting, "Miss, Miss, please change the grade, just to a ten, just to the average, please." I never said a word, just shut the door in their faces.

The next morning I was organizing my materials in the classroom, waiting for the bell, when I noticed another teacher of English, a young Moroccan man I had seen at teachers' meetings, beckoning to me from the hall.

"Sarah," he said, "I understand you are going to give Hamid a below-passing grade."

"It's an accurate grade," I said.

"Oh, I'm sure it is," he said. "It's just that his father is the wealthiest man in our town, and his father doesn't want him to get low marks."

"I don't care what his father wants," I said.

"There's just one more thing," the teacher said, visibly embarrassed, "I share a house with Hamid's brother. I've been sent by the family, to you as a fellow teacher, to change his grade."

Suddenly I understood. I had passed his house. It was a nice little bungalow with a yard—much more than a teacher could afford.

"Please," he said, appealing to me directly. "Will you change his grade?"

"No," I said, and walked back in the classroom.

I ignored the whispering and walked up to the blackboard. I was very angry, but determined not to show it to the students, all of whom by now knew what was happening.

"Turn in your books to page 23," I said.

After school Nadia [a Moroccan friend and fellow teacher] came to my apartment. Her family lived in a village a one-hour bus ride away, so on the days when she had classes back to back she spent the nights with me. I told her about the incident. She wasn't surprised.

"It's very difficult Sarah," she said, "to fight against the corruption . . ."

[The next day] Nadia came over about suppertime.

"Sarah," she said as I let her in, "you'll never believe what happened with Hamid's grade." Her voice was shaking with anger. "Sometimes I cannot stand it. I was in the salon marking my grades, when the History teacher came in—you know her, she's very wealthy and is friends with the 'moudir'[principal]. Well, she began marking her grades and she came to Hamid's name, who is a student of hers in History. She told us that she had been instructed to add five points onto his History grade to make up for his English grade. So she gave him a '17' in History, instead of the '12' he was supposed to get."

It was hopeless.

"Oh Nadia," I said. "Don't you be upset. It's too bad but it's my problem."

"But that's just it," Nadia said, "I told her she shouldn't change the grade— that it was too corrupt, even here in Morocco—and another teacher who was listening, sneered at me and said, 'Do you think you are in the United States or something?'"

We ate our dinner in silence and listened to the street noises coming through the open window. All I could think was that Hamid had won; when his grades were averaged together, he would do fine, because his History grade would make up for the English one. He had swerved around me and was speeding down the path of academic success without obstacle.[5]

Many different identities are intertwined in important ways in this experience. At a personal identity level Sarah feels she is an honest person; patient, but firm; a person who stands for what is right. At a social identity level she is a teacher and must be true to that role. Her understanding of that role as reflected in her comment, "If I couldn't give each student an accurate grade, I might as well not teach," is also tied to the norms of another social identity, being an American. In her mind, these identities give her the right to exercise certain types of power. Yet, some of her identities (American, female) are a point of opposition for many around her who may perceive her as assuming a condescending and superior attitude. The good and noble personal identity of Sarah is only seen by her friend. The friend identity seems to hold power with others regardless of her communal identity. Identities tied to wealth and personal connections are acknowledged, accepted, and respected by many of the Moroccans, but are seen as inappropriately powerful by Sarah. The different identities and the conflicting views of the power and expectations associated with each of them make it a difficult situation to resolve in ways in which all parties will be satisfied that what is best has been done. Some issues involved in this experience will be revisited when we discuss ethics in Chapter 12, but for now we hope you can see how the different forms and levels of identity and the cultural differences in how they are understood by each individual in the interaction complicate the situation.

The experience described also illustrates how different forms of identity may be operating at the same time (Sarah, the American teacher). This multilayered enactment of identities was also captured in a story told to Brad by one of his students who is Navajo and engaged to be married to a young man from the Zia Pueblo. She and her boyfriend, we'll call her Robin and him Bruce, were at her home. Robin's relatives were asking her lots of questions about the baby they planned to have. Robin answered the best she could for both of them. After a while Bruce asked Robin's relatives why they kept asking her all the important questions about the baby's future. Her relatives explained that in the Navajo tradition, the woman was the key decision maker. Bruce then joked, "Her? Why would I let her make such big decisions about our future? She can't even decide what to wear in the mornings." Instead of seeing any humor, Robin's relatives saw only disrespect, and later her aunts pulled her aside and warned her to get Bruce straightened out or drop him.

Robin's communal social identity implied different expectations for her social identity between her and her future husband. We also see a very different understanding of the power of men's identities and women's identities between the Navajo and Zia Pueblo cultures. However, at a personal level, the student indicated that Bruce's response was not a big concern to her. This was probably because of the frame that her relationship role, developed over time with Bruce, gave to the situation. This example also reminds us not to overgeneralize; although all those involved were Native Americans, there was still room for cultural misunderstanding and different expectations related to identity.

Identity is a term that refers to many possibilities at any given time. Dolores Tanno talks about her struggles with identity in terms of the communal identities of Spanish, Mexican American, Latina, and Chicana.[6] She describes how she went through stages of her life where she connected with each of these identities. Her discussion reads like a progressive journey, and at the end she recognizes that each of these identities is important and valid depending upon the situation. With her family in northern New Mexico, her Spanish identity is important; as she strives to balance different cultures in her life, she is Mexican American; her efforts to connect with an even broader community highlight her Latina identity; and in situations in which political empowerment is important, her Chicana identity comes to the fore. Of course, she has many other identities at different levels.

All of these identities are important in understanding our lives and the lives of others. The identity or identities that are salient depend on the context, such as where we are, who we are with, and what we wish to accomplish, but the identities we enact have the power to change the situation. Each identity choice interacts with other situational factors to create perceptions of rights and responsibilities that both empower and disempower ourselves and others.

Expectations Related to Ourselves and Others

Any identity we associate with ourselves or others always involves a set of expectations. These expectations are connected to our verbal and nonverbal communication patterns and are the very substance of the identity. One way of identifying these communicative expectations is to consider them in regards to the role we play at any given time in relation to those around us.

Role Expectations

Although the term role is often used synonymously with the term identity, it carries with it implications that do not fit the full definition of identity. The term role is borrowed from the theater and the specific parts the actors and actresses play in a show. A role is something one puts on and takes off depending upon the needs of the situation. Therefore, a role is the part people play in the ongoing storylines of life. These parts or roles are recognized as relevant only in certain situations. Our role as teachers is not one we always play, but when we are playing it we do so by engaging in a range of actions associated with that role in our community.

The identity of *Indian* referenced in the above example was treated as a role that someone may or may not choose to play. To successfully play this role, and thereby be identified as a real *Indian*, one must demonstrate the ability to *razz*, to be quiet and modest at appropriate times, and to maintain harmony in face-to-face interactions. One role with which you are familiar is that of teacher. I am sure that, as a student, you realize that there are many different types of teachers.

Most of what distinguishes these types for you is related to what makes a teacher good or bad, effective or ineffective. These expectations about the teacher identity can vary widely across cultural communities. Often these expectations are simply taken for granted. Some of these expectations are culturally necessary for someone to be considered a teacher at all. Usually the things that are essential to being a teacher are fewer than what goes into making a *good* teacher and often operate at an unconscious or implicit level.

Brad had this idea of implicit expectations brought home to him in a powerful way when he was an undergraduate college student, as the following example illustrates.

I signed up to take a summer statistics course. I did not know the professor and as it turned out, neither did anyone else in the class. The professor was new to the university, and I suspect was in his early thirties. On the first day of class we all struggled into class with the enthusiasm typical of those attending required statistics courses. Virtually all the students were there by five minutes past the scheduled starting time, but no teacher had arrived. We waited in relative silence for about five minutes and then people started wondering out loud where the teacher was. The department office was on the other side of campus and no one wanted to walk over there to find out what the problem was and, besides, he may just be a bit late this first day. Five more minutes passed. People started making comments about teachers in general and this teacher in particular. There were complaints about how they expect you to be on time, but excuse them for being late. Someone asked, "What is he?"

"Huh?" I wondered. I was informed that you were expected to wait longer depending on whether the teacher was a full, associate, or assistant professor.

This started another brief discussion in class about the whole educational system and soon it was more than 20 minutes past the scheduled starting time. People finally started to get up and with disgust in their voices declare that they had had enough and that they would just come back the next class. Just as the first ones were at the door and I had stood to leave, a fellow dressed informally stood up and said to everyone, "I'll be your teacher."

People laughed and started to leave. But the fellow asked them to come back and, standing at the chalkboard, wrote the teacher's name, his, on the board. He also pulled out of his little bag a stack of papers that he declared were syllabi. The class was still standing, unsure how to take this student who had just declared himself to be the teacher. I was trying to remember if earlier I had said anything rude about the teacher within earshot of this fellow who now seemed to be changing before my eyes. It turned out that the fellow was indeed our statistics teacher, but it wasn't until near the end of the second class period that I felt very comfortable with the idea. He never really explained why he had taken on the identity of student for so long, but he proved to be an excellent statistics teacher.

You may be thinking, well, he was the teacher all along. We argue differently. We argue that it was not until he started to enact teacher communication practices, such as addressing everyone from the front of the classroom, handing out syllabi, and discussing assignments, that he became the teacher. From the university administration's standpoint he was the teacher all along. After all, he had done the right things in interacting with them, signing his contract, going to the classroom, and so on, but if he had never changed from his initial student communication patterns in the classroom, he would not have filled the role of teacher. In addition, unless he continued to enact the teacher identity at the university, soon no one would have seen him as a teacher.

There are, of course, cultural differences in terms of what is expected from a teacher or other identities. Most of these expectations go beyond whether one is a teacher or some other identity and deal with the quality of teacher or type of person you are. Do teachers allow students to speak out in class? Do teachers ask questions, tell stories, or just state facts? What types of relationships are appropriate between a teacher and a student? In Brazil teachers are often very friendly and informal with their students, and it is fine for a student to pat them on the back and generally be very informal in their interactions compared to what is expected in the United States. However, in Japan the teacher is expected to act in a much more formal way than is found in the United States.[7]

Students also have different expectations associated with them. Should they look directly into the eyes of a teacher who is speaking to them? Should they jump in and help another student answer a question? Should they always raise their hands before talking? Should they disagree with a teacher? Should they stand in respect when addressing a teacher? Differences in the expectations associated with identities do not always result in a person not being identified as a certain type of person, but they can still lead to confusion and problems.

I miss China; things are so strange here. My teacher does not teach, he just asks some questions and then everyone starts talking about whatever they want. What kind of a class is this? I didn't come here to learn about the personal feelings of these Americans. Why can't they wait until the end of the lecture to ask their questions? When the teacher does start to explain something, people just interrupt him and give their own ideas. Even more confusing, the teacher just listens to them all and acts like what they have to say is important even when it is obviously not even on the topic of today's readings. The teacher says he wants participation. I take notes and listen respectfully, but this doesn't seem to be what is wanted. What kind of a class is this?

We have heard comments like the above from more than one international student as they tried to adjust to the American classroom. Given the setting, who initiates the discussion, hands out the reading assignments, and so forth, there is no real confusion about who is the teacher and who are the students, but there is still a lot of confusion about what is the appropriate or effective enactment of the teacher and student identities.

Language Expectations

One of the most powerful expectations that forms our identities is the very language we speak. Consider the following example

---

"Oh, so do you speak Spanish?"

The question hangs in the air, as it always does, for I am often asked this question. I am introducing myself at the campus Latina group. I had come believing that everyone was going to be open and accepting. I mean, we were all Latinas, right? Puzzled by the pause, I could see the doubt of my membership grow in the eyes of those around me. Suddenly I began to justify my "Latinaness." I have taken classes, I have a grandmother who is fluent, I have a strong interest in my Mexican American heritage, and so on. As the list grew I glanced at the woman who had asked the question, the oh-so-knowing look on the face of "mi compañera." She had written me off the minute I had drawn a guilty breath. She was an expert, and she knew how to weed out fakes.

It seems like such an easy question, like some standardized form and all I had to do was check a box "yes" or check a box "no." When I am asked this question I immediately feel like one of those people on Sesame Street when they play the "One of these Latinas is not like the other. . ." game. I am, of course, the one out of place.[8]

Some years ago when Brad was teaching in Wisconsin, the university there had Richard Rodríguez, a well-known Hispanic author, come and speak. When Brad visited with the woman who helped coordinate these types of presentations, she mentioned to him that she had been amazed by the negative reaction of many members of the Hispanic community. She had never had a guest come who had created such an uproar and protest from any group either within or without the university. Intrigued, Brad went to the presentation and asked some questions. Many felt that Rodríguez had betrayed his Hispanic identity by what he wrote about, by his stance on many issues, including bilingual education, and by his focus on an American rather than Hispanic identity. In reading Rodríguez's autobiography, Brad found a telling incident where, at the encouragement of a nun, his parents agreed to speak only English with him and his siblings, in the home or otherwise. He states that the following scene, recorded in his book, was "inevitable":

One Saturday morning I entered the kitchen where my parents were talking in Spanish. I did not realize that they were talking in Spanish however until, at the moment they saw me, I heard their voices change to speak English. Those "gringo" sounds they uttered startled me. Pushed me away. In that moment of trivial misunderstanding and profound insight, I felt my throat twisted by unsounded grief. I turned quickly and left the room. But I had no place to escape to with Spanish.[9]

Although there is much else that happens and Rodríguez eventually comes to feel that his learning English was crucial to his personal success, it seems to us as we read Rodríguez's account that an identity as well as a language was lost at that period of his life. He would argue that one was found as well and that his most important identities were not lost. In any case, the importance of language in our perceptions of identity is supported by a considerable body of research.[10]

What language, dialect, or jargon do people have to speak to be considered a member in the groups to which you belong? Our identities are invariably interwoven with our ability to communicate in expected ways. What these ways are can often be the point of heated debate. In many parts of the United States a controversy surrounding "English only" and *American* identity has received a lot of attention. Communicative competencies carry with them much power at all levels of social interaction.

COMMUNICATION'S RELATIONSHIP TO IDENTITY

Our communication is connected to our identity in two ways. It both *reflects* our identity and is *constitutive* of it. For many people the idea that our communication is a reflection of our identity is nothing new. We work from this assumption in much of our everyday lives. If we know you are a teacher, a Democrat, a senior citizen, an American, an introvert, a woman, a friend, a Baptist, a coach, or any other of the many possible identities that a person may have, we feel we know you better and have an idea of what to expect from you. Of course, this supposed knowledge is based on stereotypes (which we will discuss in detail in Chapter 7) and may be wrong, but that does not change the feeling we have that we know you better as we discover different identities that you may be said to be.

Reflective

If we say that we can *identify* something or someone, it implies that we are familiar enough with that thing or person to recognize and distinguish them from others. Identity labels, like the ones noted in the previous paragraph, are part of our culture or system for making sense of the world. Although their accuracy may be debated, every culture provides labels for people so that members can recognize them and have an idea of what to expect from them. This expectation is based on the common idea that people's actions will *reflect* their identity. This perspective assumes that identities are something we have or are and that they are generally stable and consistent. Our communication naturally reflects our identities just as a mirror reflects the physical item in front of it.

We often use the idea of reflection when we try to figure out why someone has done something. Does knowing that someone is Japanese or a conservative or a salesperson explain his or her behavior to you? You may have heard or used comments such as, "Well, what can you expect of a [fill in the identity label of your choice]?" or "Remember, she is a [identity label]." This everyday sort of mental process is also found in much of the research done on intercultural communication, albeit based on systematic sampling. Researchers ask people questions, such as what gender they are or what nationality they belong to, so that they can make claims about females or Germans, for example. If people did not accept that communication is a reflection of our identities, such claims would have little value. Based on a variety of research, many Japanese are known to avoid telling people "no" in situations in which Americans would typically expect a direct "yes" or "no."[11] We consciously adjust what we listen for if we are working with a person from Japan as opposed to someone from the United States. We are confident that there have been times when knowledge about a person's identity, such as this person is Japanese, has helped us connect better with the other person and avoid potential problems.

Still, you will do well to remember that the assumption that our actions or communication are simply a reflection of our identities can lead to both misunderstanding and to seeing what we want or expect to see, regardless of what has physically occurred. Gwendolyn Gong's experience as a self-identified *Mississippi Chinese* with a well-intentioned, but misguided, colleague illustrates this process.[12]

"We ought to have lunch. What's your schedule?" my colleague inquired.

"I've already eaten. Plus, I've got so much work to finish in my office today. Sorry that I can't join you while you eat." I was uncomfortable, yet truthful.

"What'd ya eat? Betcha had egg rolls, eh? Gong, you're always eatin' egg rolls—at least you used to. Remember when you first came here years ago? I couldn't believe it—a Chinese, teaching English—with a Southern accent, too. I used to share an office with a fellow named Joe, who'd eat tacos and avocados all the time, and then I'd see you across the hall, eatin' egg rolls. Right, Gong? Don't ya remember?"

"Well, no, I really don't remember, but I suppose it's true," I replied, trying to go along with my colleague. . . my voice trailing off, diminishing with every syllable.[13]

The colleague's memory does not match Gong's, but it does fit with expectations she has about what Gong, as a Chinese, would eat all the time.

Constitutive

The second way that communication is connected to identity is that it *constitutes* identity. This idea tends to be more difficult for students to remember or understand than the idea of communication reflecting our identities. At least within the United States we are used to thinking of ourselves (identities) as reasonably stable, independent entities that provide a foundation for our communicative choices. The idea that communication constitutes identity turns our usual thinking around and can be difficult to appreciate. However, we can see examples of this kind of thinking in everyday life as well.

Brad was standing in line at the grocery store the other day when he heard one woman say to another with some feeling, "She's no mother." This somewhat unusual comment in that setting caught his attention, and he listened a bit more to what was going on. It quickly became clear that she was referring to a woman on the front of a tabloid magazine on display near the checkout area. From what he was able to gather, the woman who was no mother was the female biological parent of a child that was the center of a court case. This woman had "deserted" her child many years ago, never communicating with her, and now that some good things were happening for the child this woman wanted to come back and take custody of the child and reassert her identity of mother. The woman in the grocery store was not seriously doubting the biological connection between that woman and child, but she was questioning whether the woman's actions qualified her as a "mother." It was the woman's actions that disqualified her from being a mother in the mind of this other person. We suspect that if the lady at the grocery store had been asked about the woman when the child was first born, she would not have said she was "no mother." However, her later communicative actions (or lack of them) put her *motherhood* in a cultural sense in doubt. The idea of communicative actions constituting our identities presents identity not as a static thing but as a process, an ongoing achievement that is much more fluid than we may normally think.

Identity from this perspective is something we *do* rather than something we inherently *are*. Right now you are *doing* an identity, perhaps *diligent student*. If you quit reading this and call up someone you know to go out and do something fun with you, you may be doing *friend*. Of course, we are not limited to doing one identity at a time. A person may do friend and student and many more identities at the same time, but often one will be primary. This perspective views a person as moving from one identity to another in an ongoing flow directed by our own communicative choices and the context in which we find ourselves.

Communication constituting our identities may be understood in part through a cooking analogy. Our identities may be compared to many different food items, such as cakes, cookies, and casseroles. Our communication in this analogy would be the ingredients that go into the cake or other item. Certain ingredients may be perceived as essential for a cake, such as flour, water, eggs, sugar, and salt, whereas others are perceived as essential for certain types of cakes, such as chocolate. The quantity of certain ingredients and other types of ingredients may be seen as important only to improve the quality of the cake. Although there may be great differences among what kinds of cakes there are and the quality of their taste, people can generally identify a cake from a cookie. This is true even though many of the same ingredients are used. In the same way, certain kinds of communication are associated with certain identities. The way the communication or ingredients are organized and shaped makes a big difference to the outcome. There are many different identities that may be created through our communication.

A person may think of the identity labels that exist within any culture as a recipe that tells people how to recognize or create these identities. In the example that opens this chapter, Van and Jimmy could both tell that the person bragging about making a peyote fan was not a *real* Indian. Others who do not share their cultural recipe for how to communicate like a real Indian may be offended by Jimmy and Van's verdict. You may have felt a stronger sense of this offense in the story of the woman who felt that her *Latina* identity was challenged because she could not speak fluent Spanish. However, the offense does not change the fact that identities are constituted in our communication. Instead, the offense usually indicates an outsider perspective and an area of cultural difference.

One issue that arises when we think about communication constituting identity is, whose identity is authentic? And who gets to decide whose is authentic? We have students who get very offended by the idea that someone had the nerve to refer to a person who by birth is a Native American as "not a real Indian." They want everyone to be accepted as what they want to be regardless of their communication. However, if we really want to understand how identity functions within a culture, it is hard to ignore the constitutive role communication plays.

The power of this relationship between communication and identity is shown in the following experience.

As a black female, one might assume that my race allowed me easy access and acceptance from other people of color. That is far from the truth. What I encountered instead was that, since I did not speak the popular slang, I was somehow pretending to be something I was not. Somehow I was perceived as trying to be "white." I shall never forget my first day of public high school. I had begged my parents to allow me to attend what I considered a "real" school. For most of my education I had been attending private Catholic schools in the heart of the downtown financial district. This afforded me a fine education, but also was the source of my naiveté. I remember being approached by two black girls who seemed wholly interested in me and where I was from. As soon as I opened my mouth and began to talk, I was shut down. There was no longer the sincere interest in the new "black girl." I was transformed into an object of ridicule. I was asked questions that came across as, "Who in the hell do you think you are?" and "Isn't there a 'real' black person in your family somewhere?" They started calling me "chocolate milk" and "Eskimo pie." I had not met their expectations and, until I could, I could never really be black.[14]

Although we may say that identities are constituted by our communication, it is obvious from the preceding example that we cannot simply choose at any moment what our identity will be regardless of the context. First, we often do not share the recipe for certain identities with others even if we belong to the same ethnicity, gender, or nationality. Understanding this can help us avoid some of the broad assumptions made about groups of people based on the reflective way of thinking. Second, as we learned in the very first chapter, all meaning in communication is to some extent situational. Thus, the context mediates what identities we can choose. Sometimes things one may have no control over, such as age or skin color, are seen as essential parts of how one communicates an identity. Children often point out the limits of identity choice when they remind each other, "You're not my mom or dad." Even though one of the siblings may enact part of the communicative patterns expected of parents, there are certain contextual features that do not allow them to pull off that identity successfully.

The purpose of reviewing the reflective and constitutive perspectives on communication and identity is not to decide which is best. Both have limitations. We cannot just constitute any identity we may want to at any time we may want to. However, the static view of our communication simply reflecting our identities may create distorted expectations and encourage us to miss the way identities are used and understood in practice. Instead, we encourage you to be open to both perspectives. As you try to make sense of who you and who others are at any given time and how to deal with intercultural problems that arise from discrepancies associated with these identities, remember that communication both reflects and constitutes identity. This dual realization can help you overcome the problems associated with either perspective used in isolation.

PATHWAYS TO IDENTITY

Although there are many possible identities a person may claim or be associated with, there are two basic pathways people travel in the establishment of identity: *avowal* and *ascription*. These pathways to identity are differentiated by whether it is the person in question who primarily establishes an identity or whether the person's identity is primarily established by others. We use the term *primarily* here to remind us that although these two pathways to identity may be very different and lead to very different identities, the establishment of identity always involves input from both ourselves and others. These two pathways do not operate in some form of vacuum, but they are still distinct enough that they are worth considering separately.

Avowal

Through our actions we assert or avow certain identities to ourselves. We travel the avowal pathway when *we try to fit ourselves into our idea of what is allowed and expected of the identities we envision for ourselves.* This avowal can be at both conscious and unconscious levels as well as done both verbally and nonverbally, and it is not always done willingly. We may not be happy with an identity we assign to ourselves, but we still find ourselves acting in ways that support such an identity. As we avow certain identities, we encourage others to treat us in ways that support those identities. These may be only passing identities, such as responsible citizen. Brad remembers reading in a newspaper many years ago about a person who left the following note on a car they had just run into in a parking lot. "Hi, people are watching me so I am writing this note so that they think I am leaving my name and insurance information for you. But I'm not." It was signed *The Wrecker*. We are certainly not encouraging this sort of deceit, but it does display the power of acting out a certain identity. Unless there is an obvious reason for people not to accept that identity, people will tend to treat you according to the expectations associated with the identity you avow.

Part of the challenge interculturally is that identity expectations surrounding certain roles don't always match; thus, attempts to avow certain identities can cause confusion and hard feelings. A woman from India who attended college in the United States and now teaches here relates how even very basic identities, such as what a *woman* is, can be a point of confusion.

After spending many years in the U.S. and discovering feminism, I returned home one summer and found I was very frustrated by the way language was used about women in India, such as the frequent use of the term girl. Every time someone would refer to me as a girl, I would correct them, saying I was a "woman." That behavior puzzled most people. I found it also made me a bit uncomfortable, too. There was just something about it that didn't sound quite right, but I couldn't put my finger on it. The crunch came one day when a guest at our house referred to a friend of my mother's as "that woman." My mother immediately corrected him and said it was lady, not woman. He apologized and said he hadn't meant to call her a woman. It was obvious I was missing something and I asked about what was meant by the words woman, girl, and lady.

It was explained to me that the word girl has a youthful connotation and was complimentary in nature and was appropriate to be used with any female younger than yourself. It was common for females in their mid-forties and above to still be called girl. The word lady is used as a way to show respect toward a female in the sense that she is not common, comes from a good family, and is worthy of respect. Woman has a very different connotation to it. The word has garnered the connotation of common, old, almost of suspect character, and sexually questionable. I also learned the words boy, gentleman, and man have taken on similar cultural connotations in India as the words for females. After that episode I stopped insisting that I be referred to as woman at home. However, I did make a point of referring to all the men I knew as boys.[15]

Even though two communities may share the same word for an identity, it does not mean that identity and the expectations implied by it are the same in those communities. To see oneself as a woman or as a lady can have very different implications for the way one chooses to act, depending upon whether one is working from an American or Indian cultural system. These sorts of problems can also haunt uninformed translations and create misunderstanding even when everyone involved is well intentioned.

Often we avow identities at an unconscious level. We just see ourselves as acting naturally, given the situation. Recent writings on identity have pointed out that one of the most extreme cases of identity taken for granted is that of *whiteness*.[16] This is particularly true in the United States, but it is true in some other areas of the world as well. Often those who are white don't see themselves as having any ethnicity or cultural identity in the way that other minority groups do. They see themselves as just sort of a generic middle ground, an unquestioned norm to which all others may be compared. In the U.S. they may even wonder why we can't just all be Americans. They don't realize that many American traditions are intertwined with their white ethnicity and that often what is heard by other communities when such comments are made is, "Why can't we just all be white?" Because of their dominant position in society for so many years, it is hard for many white Americans to see themselves as an ethnic group in the same sense that black, Asian, and Latina/o Americans are perceived as such. Whites often enjoy certain privileges in society without realizing it. For example, white art, history, and literature are often seen as the "classics" and ethnic art, history, and literature as folklore or folk art. Because white people do not consciously see their privileges and expectations, it is harder for them than for those of other identities to recognize the advantages that white people enjoy. However, as population and power shifts occur, the awareness of whiteness increases. Typically this awareness is generated out of a sense of competition and a need to protect traditional privileges. Certainly there have been white groups who have been discriminated against (such as the Irish and Italians) and not all white individuals are in a position of power. However, it does provide an excellent example of how an identity that others see people avowing may be completely taken for granted by those enacting the identity. Perhaps the unconscious confidence and assumption of one's place in the world is one of the expectations tied to this identity.

Ascription

The second pathway to identity is ascription. *Ascription refers to the process of having an identity assigned to you by others.* The concept of ascription was contrasted with achievement in our discussion of worldviews in Chapter 2 because an ascribed identity is something given rather than achieved. We may hope that an identity we avow will also be ascribed to us by others, but this is not always the case. Because our expectations about what behaviors are associated with which identities vary cross-culturally, we may end up with an ascribed identity that we never expected. The ascription process involves both the reactive and proactive fitting of an identity with a particular person or group.

Reactive

The reactive practice of ascription is typically used to explain past and present behaviors or to predict future actions. In his report of what happened in Chicago to a new director at a settlement house for boys, noted ethnographer Gerry Philipsen offers an interesting example of how ascribing a culturally identity

FIGURE 4.3 | Covarrubias family photo. What does it say about identity?

to someone leads to attributing motives.[17] The new director tried to deal with the unruly and defiant boys by reasoning with them and getting them involved with group decision-making. The approach was not successful. A man from the neighborhood had observed these efforts and was perplexed by the director's obvious refusal to do what was perceived as normal and appropriate, to him and others, and punish these boys physically. The neighborhood man assured the director that he would have his and the parents' full backing in physical punishment, thus assigning the director to the role of cautious outsider. However, the director still did not adopt the physical approach. The neighborhood man thought that perhaps the director was homosexual. The director, however, was married so that identity was discounted. The man then reasoned that physical discipline was against the rules and that the director was simply a very law-abiding citizen. The rule explanation was also eventually discounted and the man came upon a final attribution that stuck. He told the director, "You're a saint. That's what you are." Whatever the director was, he was not just a *normal* director to the man and the man had to somehow understand the identity of this director. If our attributions based on the expectations associated with a particular identity do not hold up in practice, we will search for an identity whose expectations can be aligned with observed actions.

Because certain types of actors or identities are associated with certain communicative actions, we naturally try to make sense of what we see others do through the ascription of certain identities. However, identity ascriptions are not always straightforward and clear.

Andy was surprised and confused. José just didn't seem himself anymore. The last couple of days he was always busy. Andy and José both worked at a small school in New Zealand. He had come over from Australia and José from the Philippines. Both new to the area, they had struck up a friendship, had had many good conversations over the last two semesters, and frequently ate dinner together.

Andy tried to remember when the problem seemed to have started. He had first noticed it Wednesday afternoon after the faculty meeting. He and José were supposed to meet for dinner as they often did, but when Andy had mentioned something about it José had just said, "I have too much to do to get my presentation ready," and rushed off. Andy had felt a strain in their relationship ever since.

He thought back to the meeting. The main agenda of the day had been Andy's presentation on the mathematics curriculum. Things had gone smoothly. So smoothly in fact that they had had time to have José discuss a few ideas he had been thinking about for the science curriculum presentation he was scheduled to give the coming week. That had also gone fine, even though José had been a bit tense. Andy had asked a few questions that José obviously hadn't thought too much about yet and he had felt pleased that he could help sharpen his friend's thinking before it came time for the formal presentation.

Was José jealous? José had always been a supportive friend, so that idea didn't feel right. He shook his head as he walked by one of the veteran teachers at the school, Margaret Potter. Maybe something had happened earlier in the day, bad news from home, perhaps?

Margaret walked by Andy who hardly seemed to even notice her as she said, "Hi." A few moments later she saw José in the copier room. His "hello" also seemed a bit distracted. She had noticed that José and Andy, who were usually together during breaks laughing and talking, had seemed at odds with each other the last few days. Concerned, she asked José, "What's going on with you and Andy? You seem to be avoiding each other. I thought you were friends."

José looked down, "I thought we were, too. But you were at the meeting last Wednesday." José shrugged and left the room.

Margaret watched him go when it hit her. She needed to talk with Andy. She had worked in the Philippines for almost 10 years before coming to New Zealand to teach six years ago. She should have seen it at the time, but she had gotten used to things here. José had been asked to comment briefly on some of his curriculum ideas since they had finished with Andy's presentation early. José had been a bit hesitant and when he had commented on a few things, Andy had jumped in with some very direct, but insightful questions. No doubt they would force José to think through some of the issues before he had to actually give his presentation, but it had put him on the spot in front of the whole faculty. She knew Filipinos were very sensitive about being put on the spot publicly like that. Friends just didn't do that to each other, even if it would be helpful in the long run. José had obviously been deeply hurt by what would seem like a betrayal by Andy.[18]

Andy was confused because the idea of jealousy, which fit the situation, didn't seem to fit his perception of José as a friend. José was deeply hurt because Andy's public questioning of him was obviously something a friend would not do, thus the ascription of friend no longer fit. Yet Margaret was able to start to understand part of the problems based on the Australian and Filipino identities of Andy and José. The key issue in this incident is not who was right or wrong, but to see that from whatever position we are in, direct participant or third-party observer, we use identities (friend, José, nationality, etc.) in understanding the actions of those around us.

Proactive

Proactive ascription goes beyond just assigning an identity in an effort to understand others; it can also lead to us to treat others in ways that pressure them to take up certain identities. In this way we may try to create the social world we perceive by encouraging others to act in ways that fit with our notions of the world and who others are. Michael Agar, in discussing his work with helping to resolve problems between Mexican and American coworkers, commented that he felt the biggest problems arose out of what the people supposedly knew about each other.[19] They each expected the other to fit a strict Mexican or American identity and treated them accordingly. Expectations of large-scale groups like these are often misleading in particulars, and treating people as if they are a problem about to happen tends to lead to problems happening.

Amy Tan expresses her frustration with the proactive ascription that happens with the Chinese in the United States, even though some may consider it a positive trait.[20] She feels that the image of the Chinese as always polite and obliging robs them of a range of emotions and may limit their ability to lead in certain situations. She further notes that she has witnessed tourists who come to Chinatown expecting self-effacing shopkeepers to admit that their goods are not worth the price and to lower it and get quite upset if they do not. Yet the tourist would not be shocked or upset if a Caucasian shopkeeper in San Francisco was uninterested in bartering over price.

One area in which this proactive ascription has created many challenges is intercultural communication between dominant group members and minorities. Minorities in any community are typically seen as outsiders or, at best, marginal members of the community. As such, they are often placed into a negative role, defined by dominant group members as less than desirable and often of suspect character. These pressures and feelings are often very subtle, but they are very real. One of Brad's graduate students who is African American told him that on more than one occasion she has had white friends or good acquaintances tell her, "I don't consider you black." She wonders exactly what that means. Is she supposed to be flattered or relieved? The implication is obvious. There are negative characteristics that these *friends* associate with the identity of being *black* and somehow she has shown herself to be above those negative expectations. What the friends probably considered a personal compliment serves as a backhanded insult to her and to millions of other people.

Growing up in a society in which one is considered a minority tends to create a foundation of negative expectations and ascription that often forces one to resist in various ways. Henri Tajfel and John Turner proposed something called the Social Identity Theory that in part addresses this concern.[21] They argue that social identities are made sense of in comparison to other relevant identities. They also maintain that faced with a negative social identity, such as is often subtly attributed to minorities, people will react in one of three general ways.

1   They may agree with the negative expectations associated with the minority group and seek as much as possible to join the dominant group and distance themselves from their home community. Brad saw this in an experience shared with him by a Native American student who explained that he often felt uncomfortable in classes with other Native Americans. Afraid that they would say something stupid that would reflect badly upon him, he hoped they would just be quiet and he would cringe when another Native American would raise her or his hand in class. In a similar vein a young

woman, who acknowledged that she was Hispanic, expressed that she hated being in classes with what she called gung ho Hispanics. She didn't want to be associated with people that she felt blamed all their misfortunes on their ethnicity. She felt that too many Hispanic people were seeking special privileges, and she didn't want to be perceived as a whiner; she just wanted to be an *American*. Regardless of your feelings toward these two cases, they illustrate an awareness that negative attributions exist in society toward an identity that the people involved could claim. Both express a desire not to be connected with these negative attributions and a desire just to blend in with the dominant group. Because this reaction is one that fits easily with dominant group perceptions, those who choose this path are often rewarded by the dominant group and are viewed as sincere people who simply want everyone to be equal. The danger is that it reinforces the idea that there is really something wrong with those who identify with a minority identity, and it may lead people away from valuable cultural traditions.

2   Minorities may directly fight those in a majority or dominant position. The response is one of direct conflict. "You try to put me down and I'll put you down even more." We have been in situations where we have heard members of a minority group verbally rip apart members of the dominant group. Often these situations are characterized by a sense that we are the "victims," and the dominant group is an oppressor that can never be forgiven. Anything that is associated with the dominant group in this reaction is considered inherently bad and must always be resisted. The danger here is that it creates a vicious circle of combat from which there is no hope of escaping.

3   Minorities may also try to change the comparison points that have in some way led to the perceived negative identity. One way this may be done is to revalue factors that are seen as negative in the dominant society. These factors could include language, dialect, other ways of communicating, religious beliefs, basic values, or anything else associated with the group identity. This is a perspective that does not accept the negative associations that are often subtly associated with their minority status, but instead of trying to tear down the other, they try to show the value of their own. One of the quickest examples of this is revealed in the phrase, *Black is beautiful*, that became a kind of theme for the African American community many years ago. Another way to change comparison points is to use a different point of comparison. For example, we may acknowledge that the dominant group has some values or skills that our group could learn from, but at the same time recognize that our home community has many values and skills that the dominant group would do well to learn. Of course, efforts to change a dominant way of thinking, and maintaining this change in the face of numerous social pressures, are very difficult and time-consuming.

The options suggested in the Social Identity Theory are helpful in the sense that they encourage us to think about how we want to deal with identity struggles that naturally arise in communities. The first two options are both questionable because they imply a win/lose mentality. Either the minority group has to lose, accepting their inferiority and trying to assimilate into a new identity, or the dominant group has to lose by being eternally guilty and viewed as unable to relate to and converse authentically with the other groups. The final option, although difficult to enact, is a win/win option that is worth the extra effort it takes.

Reflection Question: Do you think the Social Identity Theory has covered all the possible responses to the subtle negative expectations that are so often cast upon minority groups?

One of our main concerns with the theory is that it can be interpreted as placing the whole responsibility for what happens with minority/dominant group relationships on the minority group. The theory, of course, is written in a descriptive rather than prescriptive manner, but we think it is important to consider the dominant group members' actions in this situation. Unless members of the dominant group are willing to acknowledge the structural and often unseen negative associations that minority groups face, true change will not take place. If dominant group members' reactions to minority groups are either to ignore them or are centered in cycles of blaming themselves or the minority group, little good can be done. Instead, dominant groups must be willing to expect and learn about the good in others. Dominant group members must resist the desire always to be in charge, trying to fix things for other communities. The minority group members themselves are the best ones to deal with problems they may face, especially if treated with respect and not ascribed characteristics that are inherently incompetent or bad.

Much of the discussion of ascription thus far has focused on the dangers or negative aspects associated with this consequence of identity. It can, however, have many positive outcomes as well. We have heard many stories over the years in which someone improved their life and felt better about themselves and others because someone believed in them and treated them as if they were someone important. Whether it is for good or bad, however, ascription is not something we can avoid. Hopefully it is something we can be more aware of and turn to our and others' benefit.

SUMMARY

In this chapter we have defined identity as *the image by which we recognize ourselves and others*. We note that each of us has both a personal and a social identity. Our personal identity is our understanding of ourselves as unique, idiosyncratic individuals. Our social identity is tied to the roles we play in society and our group memberships ranging from occupations to gender to ethnicity and nationality, to various other communities with which we affiliate. The meanings these various identities have in our lives are grounded in the interplay between similarities and differences. Though not always explicit in nature, self and other identification involves a process of constant comparison with other individuals and groups, and it is in the perceived similarities and differences that we are able to make sense of much of our lives. Our identities also impact the relative power we have in an interaction or the rights and responsibilities in a given relationship.

Regardless of the identity we take upon ourselves or that which we associate with another person, we have certain expectations that are perceived as natural for that type of person. These expectations have implications in terms of the relative power or rights and responsibilities we have in a given relationship. The expectations we have center on how we should act, how we should feel, and how we should think. When these expectations are not met, internal and external conflict often follows.

We reviewed two main perspectives. One was that our communication is a reflection of our identities. The other was that our communication constitutes our identities. Both of these perspectives are insufficient by themselves, but taken together they provide a way to understand many of the problems that arise out of identity concerns and conflicts.

We also discussed two pathways to establishing our social identities: avowal and ascription. Identities provide models for our own lives, such that we choose to act in particular ways so we can avow certain identities. The avowal of certain identities allows us to accomplish various goals in our relationships and life in general. Second, we ascribe certain identities to others, or they to us, to help explain why people act the way they do and create a world that fits our present understanding. Reactive ascription is used to help create new understanding of who others are and their role in the world, whereas proactive ascription focuses on how we encourage others to adopt certain identities and thereby act in certain expected ways.

Culture and identity are intimately related and, if we want to understand our own and others' cultures, we must have an understanding of what identities are important in a particular culture, how they are maintained, where and when they are salient, and why they are connected to all of our communication encounters.

REFLECTION QUESTIONS

1   Which idea seems more accurate based on your own experiences, that communication constitutes our identities or that it reflects our identities? What examples can you think of to back up your opinion?

2   Some of the examples used in this chapter indicate that some people discount another person's identity based on their communication. Do you think this is valid? Why?

3   Are there other options than those described in the Social Identity Theory for dealing with an unsatisfactory identity? What are they?

4   What are your impressions of a *white* identity? How does it relate to minority identities?

5   Which level of identity has the greatest impact on how you see yourself and what you choose to do?

ACTIVITIES

1   Make a list of 15 of your identities. Which are the most important to you? Why? What expectations do you think your culture shares about these different identities? How do these identities influence the way you communicate? Do any of them put conflicting pressures on you to act in different ways? How do you resolve these conflicts? If possible, discuss these issues with a group. This process is particularly useful if you can discuss these expectations with an individual or group of individuals from a different culture to see which expectations are similar and which are different.

2   Individually or with a small group, rent a video about or observe people in a new setting. How quickly can you pinpoint five of their identities? What is their most important identity based on your observations? How did you come up with your answers? What evidence can you supply to support your claims? If you are with a group, how much agreement is there across group members?

3   Select an identity that you would say you do not have and act as if you have it for a complete day. Write a summary of your experiences, your feelings, and the reactions of others during the day.

4   Select an identity you have for each of the three levels of identity discussed in the chapter and then identify examples of how each of these identities are established through both the avowal and ascription processes.

NOTES

1   This story and the explanation afterwards are based on S. B. Pratt, "Razzing: Ritualized Uses of Humor as a Form of Identification among American Indians," in *Communication and Identity across Cultures*, ed. D. Tanno and A. González (Thousand Oaks, CA: Sage, 1998), 56–79; and D. L. Weider and S. B. Pratt, "On Being a Recognizable Indian among Indians," in *Cultural Communication and Intercultural Contact*, ed. D. Carbaugh (Hillsdale, NJ: Lawrence Erlbaum Associates, 1990), 45–64.

2 K. Tracy and J. S. Robles, *Everyday Talk: Building and Reflecting Identities*, 2nd ed. (New York: The Guilford Press, 2013).

3 R. Jenkins, *Social Identity* (London: Routledge, 1996); and C. Serino, "The Personal-Social Interplay: Social-Cognitive Prospects on Identity and Self-Other Comparison," in *Social Identity: International Perspectives*, ed. S. Worchel, J. F. Morales, D. Paez, and J. Deschamps (London: Sage, 1998), 24–43.

4 S. Streed, "A Moroccan Memoir," in *The House on Via Gombito*, 2nd ed., ed. M. Sprengnether and C. W. Truesdale (Minneapolis, MN: New Rivers Press, 1997), 63–99.

5 Streed, S. "Moroccan Memoir," 87–9.

6 D. Tanno, "Names, Narratives, and the Evolution of Ethnic Identity," in *Our Voices: Essays in Culture, Ethnicity, and Communication*, 3rd ed., ed. A. Gonzalez, M. Houston, and V. Chen (Los Angeles: Roxbury, 2000), 25–28.

7 B. Finkelstein, A. E. Imamura, and J. J. Tobin, *Transcending Stereotypes: Discovering Japanese Culture and Education* (Yarmouth, ME: Intercultural Press, 1991).

8 M. Timko, "Se Habla Español?" (paper, University of New Mexico, 1997).

9 R. Rodriguez, *Hunger of Memory: The Education of Richard Rodriguez* (Toronto, Canada: Bantam, 1982), 21–2.

10 Y. Tsuda, *Language Inequality and Distortion in Intercultural Communication: A Critical Theory Approach* (Amsterdam, the Netherlands: John Benjamins, 1986).

11 B. J. Hall and M. Noguchi, "Engaging in *Kenson*: An Extended Case Study of One Form of 'Common' Sense," *Human Relations* 48 (1995): 1129–47; and J. C. Condon, *With Respect to the Japanese: A Guide for Americans* (Yarmouth, ME: Intercultural Press, 1984).

12 G. Gong, "When Mississippi Chinese Talk," in *Our Voices: Essays in Culture, Ethnicity, and Communication*, 3rd ed., ed. A. Gonzalez, M. Houston, and V. Chen (Los Angeles: Roxbury, 2000), 84–91.

13 Gong, "Mississippi Chinese," 87.

14 M. Aiken, "Labels and Identity: Reflections of an African American" (paper, University of New Mexico, 1997).

15 S. Malhotra, "The Power in Kernel Images" (paper, University of New Mexico, 1997).

16 T. K. Nakayama and J. N. Martin, eds., *Whiteness: The Communication of Social Identity* (Thousand Oaks, CA: Sage, 1999).

17 G. Philipsen, "Speaking 'Like a Man' in Teamsterville: Culture Patterns of Role Enactment in an Urban Neighborhood," *Quarterly Journal of Speech* 61 (1975): 13–22.

18 Story adapted from an incident related in K. Cushner and R. Brislin, *Intercultural Interactions: A Practical Guide*, 2nd ed. (Thousand Oaks, CA: Sage, 1996).

19 M. Agar, "The Intercultural Frame," *International Journal of Intercultural Relations* 18 (1994): 221–37.

20 A. Tan, "The Language of Discretion," in *Language Awareness*, 6th ed., ed. P. Eschholz, A. Rosa, and V. Clark (New York: St. Martins Press, 1994), 352–9.

21 H. Tajfel and J. Turner, "The Social Identity Theory of Intergroup Behavior," in *The Psychology of Intergroup Relations*, ed. S. Worchel and W. G. Austin (Chicago, IL: Nelson-Hall, 1986).

Chapter 5

Where Can We Look to Explain Verbal Misunderstandings?

Mallory wasn't sure what she was feeling. She was leaving Japan after some four years of teaching, and her emotions were anything but clear. One of her fellow teachers, Fred, a young man from Canada, was helping her with her luggage. She couldn't help laughing as she glanced at Fred. She remembered when she had first heard about Fred's appointment to come teach in Japan just over three years ago.

It had already been an exhausting day. The activities Mallory had planned to help her students understand American culture had not gone very well. Sometimes it was just hard to get the kind of participation she needed for the points she wanted to cover to really become clear. But she couldn't complain too much. She had known the activity was risky when she decided to try it. Mallory had already been teaching in Japan for a year and was getting a good idea of what would work and what wouldn't. Still, sometimes she just had to try something different. It was probably more for herself than for her students.

"Oh well," Mallory sighed and headed to the faculty room. Upon opening the door, she was immediately greeted by a sight that took her mind off her struggles in the classroom. Gathered around an old oak table in the back of the room was a large group of teachers. Their voices filled the room with a feeling of shock and displeasure.

"What could be causing this commotion?" she wondered, walking over to the table. Suddenly one of the teachers turned to her and thrust some papers at her.

"What is this?" he demanded.

Mallory took the papers and started to read. It was the application of Fred Saberhagen, a new English teacher from Canada. He had been recruited by a Canadian organization that was working for the school to help find native English speakers to come and work in Japan. He would be arriving in two weeks and the school had just been forwarded his application.

"Is this man serious?" The teacher who had given her the papers in the first place pointed to a section that asked in bold letters, "What Makes You A Strong Candidate For This Position?"

Mallory started to read what Fred Saberhagen had written. It was nothing that would have surprised too many people back home in the United States. Fred basically had listed the many reasons he felt qualified for this position. He had been the student body president of his high school. He had remained active in leadership positions throughout his college career. He noted that he had graduated in the top 5 percent of his college class. He described some of his experiences in athletics; he was obviously a talented athlete. He noted numerous awards and scholarships he had won related to both his academic and athletic abilities. He went on to describe how culturally sensitive he was, citing some successful multicultural experiences that he had during his college years and his ability to adapt to new and difficult situations. As Mallory read the application, she was impressed. He seemed like a well-balanced and accomplished individual who would likely be able to deal with the ambiguities and challenges he would face during his time in Japan. Still feeling confused, she stopped reading and began to listen to the comments that still flowed around her. It was clear from each new comment and the wave of agreement that followed it that Fred was seen as egotistical and lacking any sensitivity.

"He is very proud of himself."

"Canadians must be worse than Americans."

"How could someone be so rude and still be hired?"

"This man thinks much of himself. I doubt he will work out here."

There it was, the fear that underlay many of the comments being made. Mallory understood. Fred's "boasting" of his abilities created the image of a person so full of his own ego that true teamwork, at least the kind that was the foundation for so many Japanese organizations, did not seem possible.

She tried to explain to her colleagues that for Fred to get this job in Canada he had to "sell" himself and express his strengths in ways that seem out of place in Japan and inconsistent with the values of the Japanese culture. "He will likely be an excellent teacher and team player," she reassured them, hoping it was true.

Her colleagues seemed slightly relieved and even amused that this type of talk would be expected or desired. However, there had still been a feeling of concern and that feeling continued for some time to come. Fred had been a pleasant surprise, though. He had adapted well and became one of the most respected gaijin, or foreigners at the school.[1]

FIGURE 5.1 |

Miguel Gandert

Misunderstandings of the kind described above are common in intercultural interactions. None of the interactants was looking for trouble. In fact, the goals of the new Canadian teacher and the goals of the Japanese school administrators and current teachers were complementary. Even so, misunderstanding occurred and negative attributions were starting to be made. The Japanese teachers were obviously disappointed in the conduct of their future colleague and, if Fred could have seen their reaction, he probably would have been equally amazed and concerned. Of course, there are many times when people do not enter into communication with the best of intentions. These sorts of situations will be discussed in detail in Chapters 7 and 8. For our purposes in this chapter, we will consider situations of misunderstanding in which those involved initially want things to work out, but still face problems.

The experience conveyed in the story above had a happy ending in real life, but not all intercultural misunderstandings end up that way. Sociolinguist John Gumperz conducted an extensive research project in England that dealt with cultural misunderstandings or examples of what he called "cross-talk."[2] The interactions he studied were from a variety of ordinary situations that were important to those involved. One of the situations studied was job interviews between English employers and East Asian applicants. These interviews frequently backfired due to cultural differences, and employers lost well-qualified applicants and applicants lost jobs they desired and for which they were well suited. One of the most glaring differences was the East Asian tendency to present their own abilities in indirect and modest ways. The English employers were looking for an approach that involved a more direct selling of oneself and one's abilities. Gumperz and his associates recognized that many of these examples of *cross-talk* are grounded in different conventions related to our verbal communication.

Understanding what is appropriate to say in a given context (such as a job interview) and how to interpret what is said in a given context is part of our cultural knowledge. Members of different cultures often share many of these contextual understandings; however, this is not always the case. Considering our assumptions at a contextual level is one useful place to start as we try to understand why what we said was not understood the way we meant it.

VERBAL COMMUNICATION AND CONTEXT

Meaningful verbal communication is inescapably linked with the context in which we perceive it to be taking place. In fact, humans tend to learn the meanings of words not from a dictionary, but from their use in context. If you go golfing for the first time and hit the ball a couple of times so that it turns sharply to the right, one of your partners may comment on your *slice*. You may thus pick up that in golf when you hit the ball and it turns like that it is called a slice. The next time you go golfing you work hard to stop this from happening, but now you find the ball turns sharply to the left. Wanting to show off your newly acquired knowledge, you say to your partner "I just can't get rid of my slice." Your more experienced partner may then look at you a bit strangely and say, "What do you mean? You're hooking the ball every time." Now you realize that a slice is when the ball turns to the right and a hook is when it turns to the left.[3] Thus, you are gradually learning the cultural knowledge necessary to talk like a golfer. This process of learning the cultural knowledge necessary to engage in meaningful communication by attending to how language is used in practice is something that begins very early in our lives.

When we talk to others it is natural to assume that they will understand what we say in the way we intend; after all, we understand what we mean. However, what seems sensible and clear within one cultural context may seem very inappropriate and confusing in another. The philosopher H. P. Grice argues that our knowledge of the context in which an utterance is made is crucial to understanding that utterance's meaning.[4] He noted that if we were to only take the literal (or denotative) meaning of a given verbal comment, we would often be misunderstood and/or seen as rude. Instead we learn to understand the connotative or implied meaning by taking into account the context in which the utterance is made.

When a person asks us a question such as "Is there salt down there?" or "Do you have a watch on?" we would not simply answer "Yes" and then go on with our other business as the literal interpretation of the question would suggest we do. Instead, we would be more likely simply to hand them a salt shaker or say something like, "Just past four o'clock." That is because, given the general context in which we would expect to hear such questions, we would realize that the person wanted more than just to know if salt was at one end of the table or if we were wearing a watch. Of course, it is also easy to make contextual changes that would alter the nature of how a person might reply. For example, Brad was shoveling snow off a sidewalk with some friends the other day and applying rock salt on the icy spots. In this case, he may respond to the salt question with a "Got it covered" comment that would be very confusing in the dinner table context. Or Brad may be at a party where some contest needs to be timed and be asked if he is wearing a watch, in which case he may say something like, "I'm sorry, mine doesn't show seconds," again a reply that would be confusing if the question had been asked of him by a stranger on the street. Patricia's mom had a friend accompany her to a doctor's visit (long ago) and when the doctor told her to "swallow" the interpreter friend translated it from the dictionary as "golondrina." My mother sat stupefied. "Golondrina!!!" The friend and the doctor got more frustrated by the minute. It wasn't until Patricia's mother got home to look up the word "swallow" that she realized the friend had been translating the word for the bird, swallow vs. the verb "tragar."

Contextual Frames

Grice further suggests that humans tend to talk in ways that are required or expected given the type of talk exchange in which we perceive ourselves to be involved.[5] Even if we are being unkind or are engaged in conflict or deceit, our talk can still be seen as cooperating or fitting in with the situation. These situations or recognized talk exchanges may be thought of as frames that help provide meaning and order to our communication with others.[6] These may include such things as interviews, dinner, greetings, dating, teasing, attending church, selling a product, or just sitting around visiting with friends. There are hundreds upon hundreds of frames with which we are familiar, without even consciously thinking about it. Just like a picture frame directs our attention to what is inside and limits what else we will pay attention to, contextual frames guide us to see things in certain ways and make it difficult to notice other things that may be going on.

Frames are an essential part of understanding the context of any given situation. The same behavior may have very different connotations depending on the frame. We can stand up at a football game and yell, "Come on, you wimps, kill that sucker," and, although a few people may think we are getting too involved in the game, it is a comment that is quickly forgotten and not worried about.

However, if we stand up and yell the same thing in a courtroom, it is received in a very different way. Thus, frames are a crucial part of changing our behaviors into meaningful actions, such as cheers, threats, or cries of encouragement.

Of course, the existence of one frame does not eliminate the possibility of other frames, as one type of talk or frame may be embedded within another. In other words, we may engage in gossip in the middle of a business meeting (both are known types of talk that serve to frame what is happening at a given time). Cultural communities share expectations about who engages in different types of talk, where, when, and why, as well as what is and is not appropriate given a particular frame. Neither these expectations nor many of the frames themselves are culturally universal. For those interested in intercultural misunderstanding, there are three types of expectations associated with framed or recognized types of talk that are important to keep in mind. First, frames provide an assumption that certain communicative actions will be engaged in. Second, frames evoke and assume the legitimacy of certain informal rules. Third, frames assume and imply certain identities.

Frames and Expected Forms of Communication

A while back Brad was on the Navajo reservation for some training in relation to their peace-maker court, a form of mediation that is based on traditional Navajo concepts of conflict management. At the beginning of one of the meetings, those attending were asked to introduce themselves. Those who were with him on the visit, mostly graduate students, all took turns introducing themselves, as did Brad. Each of those there gave somewhat similar introductions, explaining our position at the university and our interest in or reason for attending this meeting. After we were done, the Navajos present introduced themselves, not in terms of their direct connection with this meeting as we had, but rather by identifying and briefly talking about the maternal clan to which they belonged within the Navajo tribe and then finally briefly noting their paternal clan. It was then explained to us that Navajos are always seen as part of their mother's clan and that talk framed as an introduction should begin with that identification.

If we had been in Japan for a similar "training" meeting, the introduction frame would have assumed bows and the exchange of business cards. Brad would have been wise to present and receive the business card with care (perhaps even doing so with two hands). He should take time to read the card and keep it in front of him for further reference. If he simply grabbed the card without really looking at it and jammed it in a pocket somewhere, noting that he would find one for the other person later, he would have presented a very poor picture of myself and his respect for the Japanese colleagues in the room. Introductions of some form are a common frame found in all cultures, but the assumptions associated with them can vary greatly.

Anna Mindess relates how different assumptions about what is involved in introduction in deaf culture and what she calls "mainstream American culture" were first brought to her attention.[7] She was working on a book related to the deaf community and desired Dr. Thomas Holcomb, a highly respected deaf educator, to serve as a consultant. She went to his office for the first time and introduced herself to him. In her own words she explains what happened.

I told him about the book project, explained who the publisher would be, and asked if he would be interested in working with me. He answered with a cool "Perhaps," and asked to read some of my completed chapters.

It was only after we had started to work together that I became aware of the error that I had committed. While discussing definitions of culture, Tom proposed that we use Carol Padden's definition. I agreed and casually mentioned that I knew Carol Padden because she had been one of my thesis advisors. "You know Carol Padden! Why didn't you tell me before?" Tom demanded. I remember feeling perplexed because he seemed to think I owed him the information. Finally, because I know how significant introductions are in the deaf culture, I made the connection. "You mean I should have told you that the first day we met in your office?" I ventured. "Yes!" came the strong reply.[8]

Further research by Mindess confirmed that introductions should include mentioning the names of important people she knew that the other person might know. This type of name-dropping introduction felt uncomfortable to her, but was both expected and desired within the deaf community.

Introductions are just one example of a frame about which people of different cultures have different assumptions. For example, the incident that began this chapter is marked by different assumptions about how best to present oneself when applying for a job and what employers are interested in seeing demonstrated. Thus, when faced with a cultural misunderstanding one way to approach it is to try to understand what type of frame the people perceive and what the assumptions associated with that frame are for the cultures involved.

Frames Evoking and Assuming Informal Rules

Many of the expectations that help us make sense of particular behaviors within the context of a particular frame are best understood as rules. In other words, each frame could be studied as a series of should and should not statements. Related to the initial story, the Japanese teachers felt Fred should not have been so direct in his self-praise. He should have acknowledged the help of others and noted his good fortune and the circumstances that had allowed him to be in the position he was now in. Because such expectations tend to be thought of in terms of rules, reactions to violations of these rules tend to be negative. After all, something that violates a rule is not just seen as different, but as wrong. However, these rules are rarely written down and are generally taken for granted.

There are different consequences for violating the rules that are associated with a particular type of talk. One consequence is that people are not even able to engage in that kind of talk. For example, if one person tried to frame the talk as gossip by saying, "Did you hear what Mary did the other day?" and another person responded with, "I like Mary and it is none of our business what she did," interest in another's affairs has not been expressed and, thus, a basic rule for engaging in gossip has been violated. This rule is so basic that without following it gossip talk may either cease or never have occurred.

A second, and more common, consequence of violating the rules is the sense that the violator is wrong, incompetent, or bad in some way. At least to some extent, this can happen along with the first consequence, such that someone might feel the person who refused to engage in gossip to be hypocritical and self-righteous. Typically, however, our reactions are similar to those of the Japanese teachers in the opening experience. We identify the person as intentionally rude in some way or unintentionally incompetent. In many homes of Spanish heritage in northern New Mexico it is just assumed that when a person goes by for a visit she or he will be fed no matter what time of the day it is. To either not offer to feed or to refuse to be fed is an indication that either you dislike the other person and are, therefore, intentionally being offensive, or that you have not been raised right and, therefore, are socially ungracious, although not maliciously so. In either case your violation is not simply different, but wrong.

In the United States, an informal rule in relation to help-giving is to give help when asked, but if not asked, don't intrude. If a person needs help, it is assumed they will ask. An international student from Lebanon with whom Brad worked closely on a variety of projects was frustrated by this rule and frequently found himself being reprimanded for violating it. He was always looking around to see how he could help others who worked with him at his part-time job at the University and was consistently told to mind his own business and to let others do their own work. Sometimes, however, situations arise that blatantly indicate a need for help. In these cases Americans will offer help, but if that offer is declined, Americans are quick to "respect the other person's privacy and independence" and leave them alone. These sorts of rules are quite different in many other parts of the world where the rule is don't bother other people, but help when you see a need to help. The assumption in many places is that people will not want to intrude so they won't ask and may even decline the offer of help, but if you see the need, you should insist on helping. This difference is at the heart of one Chinese man's story of frustration.

One day I was carrying some very heavy parcels in the Student Union building. Other people asked, "Do you need help?" and I would say, "No thanks," wanting to be polite. If they were Chinese, they would have insisted on helping me and the outcome would be that they would help carry my parcels and I would say thank you many times. But Americans, after hearing my initial reply would just go away and leave me. Over time I have learned to frankly say my feelings and ask for help, but I still feel very rude.

Violating the rules governing these norms is always uncomfortable and can be a very difficult adjustment. Take, for instance, a very broad frame, *dating*. The rules surrounding dating or interactions related to developing relationships are different in New Zealand than in the United States. This difference proved to be a source of confusion and frustration for one young woman who came from New Zealand to the United States to study at a university. The idea of casually dating another person (or maybe even dating different people during the same time period) one-on-one was both amazing and uncomfortable to her. In talking with a roommate about this, her roommate just laughed and told her about a phone conversation she had just barely finished. It went something like this (the roommate is referred to as Rachael):

Rachael: Hi?
Matthew: Hi, Rachael. It's Matt. What are you up to?
Rachael: Well, I'm just getting ready to go to a movie with Blake, a guy
              I just met in my biology class. Why? What are you doing?
Matthew: Well, I was going to see if you wanted to go get some dinner.
Rachael: Well, I can't tonight.
Matthew: That's okay, how about tomorrow?
Rachael: Sure, that sounds great.

The young woman knew that such a conversation would probably not occur in New Zealand and if it did, Rachael would soon have a very bad name. In New Zealand, one-on-one dating is not done until you are very serious about each other and have gone out together in groups of friends many times. Rachael obviously didn't know Blake all that well, yet she was willing to go out with him alone, and her relationship with Matthew couldn't be very serious, but she was going to go out with him alone as well. In New Zealand, rules for the development of these types of relationships require group invitations and allow for one-on-one dating only after the couple are very serious and planning a long-term relationship. This young woman from New Zealand noted that even television in New Zealand portrayed romance as always growing out of group settings. This is quite different than in the United States, where many young people would not even consider it a date if a whole group of friends were going out together for some activity. When Brad visited with this young woman about this, she indicated that she was trying to adapt to American ways of doing things but was finding it hard, especially because of her sense that only a "tramp" would date that way. This feeling that her actions would place her into an undesirable social identity leads right into the third aspect related to frames which we will now discuss.

Frames Evoking and Assuming Identities

In Chapter 4 identities were discussed as involving sets of expectations. In addition, identities are part of the expectations associated with various frames. Only certain types of people can legitimately engage in certain types of talk. And certain types of talk require certain types of identities. It is hard to have a parent–teacher conference without either a parent or a teacher present. For many a wedding implies a bride and a groom. For others those identities are not necessary. Sometimes identities are built in to our understanding of a type of talk, such as with an invitation, that assumes in the very definition that one must take on the role of inviter and another the role of invitee if the frame is to be recognized.

One frame that illustrates this general point is *dlodilchi* [dlow (as in flow) - dill - chee], a form of greeting among Navajo families. Willink discusses *dlodilchi* as a challenge that creates laughter.[9] *Dlodilchi* is often done between uncles and nephews, aunts and nephews, grandparents and grandsons, and other extended family members, such as in-laws. The teasing that makes up *dlodilchi* is not done in a malicious way, and it is not done in front of strangers. Willink provides the following example:

Uncle: Hello, in-law. My other in-law, Jim Begay, doesn't come empty handed. He drives the latest model car. Where is the elk? My in-law Jim Begay brings me elk meat he hunted and killed himself.

Nephew: Hello, Uncle. Oh yeah, I can out do that shrunken up old man. He doesn't even know how to shoot a gun straight he is so nearsighted. The elk will probably be a few feet away, ready to charge him. I always see him down the road with his thumb out in his patched up shirt and jeans. Where are you going uncle?[10]

Willink maintains that the uncle is not only saying hello, but he is saying hello "nephew" and is challenging his nephew to be the best he can be. The nephew responds to each of the humorous challenges and demonstrates that he is a good nephew. Willink discusses his own participation in such events and even recalls hearing family members discuss beforehand how to handle the expected *dlodilchi* or teasing from an in-law. He also provides examples of how this greeting can be used to let other people know about things they should be doing for the older family member. In this way *dlodilchi* is used to teach and maintain relationships in a positive, humorous way.

As we try to use the notion of frames in understanding communication across cultures it is important to remember that violations of the implicit rules for communicating within a frame tend to cause negative reactions. Some of these negative reactions are tied to the identities that are implied in the frame that makes sense of our talk.

Although treated separately here for the purposes of illustration, the three frames focusing on context, communicative act, and identity typically are interwoven in our daily experiences, such as in the following example shared by Xiaoshen Jin.

The [Chinese] secretary has a new boss today. He is an American. Now it is already 6:00 pm, time to go home. But she goes to her boss's office before she takes off and asks him, "Is there anything else I can do? If not I will take off now." To her surprise, he says, "Thanks for asking. Yes. Could you help me translate this document?" She takes the document without saying anything and goes back to her seat to work on it. The next day, 6:00 again, the secretary takes her pretty purse and goes to her American boss and says, "I take off now. Bye." He smiles and says, "Bye. Have a good day."

Why does the secretary go to her boss's office before she leaves? It is because she wants to be polite. Does she ask for more work to do before she leaves? No. She absolutely does not. Then what does her question mean? This is not a question, this is just the Chinese way to say "bye" to him. Now we see why she is surprised when she gets extra work from the boss and has to work overtime. Her American boss did not understand her "meta-message." They are not com-municating at the same level. However, the Chinese secretary is a smart girl. She starts to learn to talk more directly, like her American boss.

On the contrary, if we postulate the Chinese secretary doesn't change the way she says "bye" to her boss and keeps doing it every day, her boss will sooner or later get confused and question why his Chinese secretary always asks for more overtime work instead of going home after work. Is there a problem with her? Do the Chinese only live to work and have no social life?

In this example you can see how the context (the end of a work day), the forms of communication (for saying goodbye), and identities involved (boss and sec-retary) intermingled to create a potentially confusing and frustrating situation.

Reflection Question: Can you think of any conflicts you have had with another person that turned out to be a consequence of each of you framing the situation differently?

VERBAL COMMUNICATION: STRUCTURE AND CONTENT

Verbal communication refers to our use of words, either written or spoken. In an effort to explain the meaning of words, particularly when words are not taken literally, Grice proposed four maxims for verbal communication.[11] These maxims maintain that our speech should be of the right *quality* (accurate and true), the right *quantity* (neither too much nor too little), *relevant* (given the purpose of the conversation), and performed in an *appropriate* manner (clear). These maxims are not intended to be used as descriptions of what actually happens; instead they are to be used as clues for why people sometimes take things that are said to mean something different than the literal definition of what is said. For instance, if Patricia were to write a letter of recommendation that only said, "I can honestly say he is very punctual," there is a good chance that the prospective employers will read the recommendation as negative, although being punctual is a positive trait. Because Patricia violated the maxim of quantity and said too little for the purpose of this type of talk they would suspect that she was just avoiding writing things that would be negative. Grice argues that to understand how these maxims work, a person must have a variety of types of information. For our present purposes, the culture of the speakers and listeners is a crucial part of that information. Because cultures vary, the way that these maxims would be understood by members of different cultures would also vary. We will review each of these four maxims and how the verbal content and structure implied by them may be a source of cultural misunderstanding.

Quality

Sometimes our students have the opportunity to be one-on-one partners with students who have come from other countries. Recently one of these students related the following to Brad after class.

I took Shang (from China) with me and some other friends to a party last night. Anyway, you know how in Seinfeld *the character Elaine always says "get out" to mean "no way" or "you're kidding," like she is amazed or in disbelief. Well, I have a friend who does the same thing. Anyway, Shang started telling us about how she had gone skydiving as a little girl. My friend in excitement cried out, "Get out!" Shang looked confused and then, thinking she had offended us, went over and started gathering up her stuff. It wasn't until she was almost out the door before we figured out what had happened and convinced her it was okay to stay.*

The student wanted to make sure Brad knew what had happened in case he heard about Shang's upset and was concerned. However, the misunderstanding was cleared up and it simply became a point of humor, not upset.

Quality implies that things that are said are assumed to be true and accurate. In a previous chapter we discussed that different cultures have different views of what it means to be honest. Sometimes desires to be kind or helpful are seen as being more "true" than simply stating in an explicit way what we think we know or how we feel at a given moment. We will not take the time to go back into detail on these types of differences; instead, we will focus on another important practice related to this maxim, the use of idioms. Idioms are simply statements that are not strictly *true*, but their meaning is understood by a group of people. If you ask what happened to Martha and Kristin says, "She *kicked the bucket*," it does not mean in her community that she literally did this; it means she died. Just like the student's friend did not literally mean that Shang should get out of the apartment. Idioms are common in all cultures with which we are familiar, but when used in intercultural settings they can create a lot of confusion.

Idioms

One potential area of misunderstanding related to idioms is when to use them and with whom. For example, Kristin would not use the *kick the bucket* idiom in just any setting or with just any person. If you are talking with your grandmother and going to tell her about someone who has died, you may use what is often perceived as a gentler idiom and say the person has *passed away*. Understanding the context of when an idiom is appropriate or sensible is part of our cultural knowledge.

Another challenge is that some idioms are so common that we hardly even realize they are idioms, such as "What's up?" in the United States. Americans are not really trying to find out what is above them. They know that such a phrase is simply a greeting that commonly means "I notice you and I am interested in you." Mr. Tuffaha from Jordan shared with Brad that during his visit to the United States that he was consistently left perplexed by this statement. He said, "At first I thought they were asking, 'What is the matter with you?' and that I must look sick or sad or something. So, I tried to always smile when people were coming near, but still they said, 'What's up?'" Some idioms become virtually institutionalized within a community, last for centuries, and may spread with time to other communities. Others (like the "get out" example) are more like popular slang and come and go in a relatively short period of time.

In the United States, a person may be talking to someone about a career change that she thinks is good and make the comment, "A rolling stone gathers no moss." In this setting, she would not really be commenting on literal rocks and moss, but would be implying that change is good and that the person is like the rolling stone. After all, who would want moss growing on them? However, in Japan, this same saying can convey a very different meaning.[12] Moss has a very positive connotation in Japan and this idiomatic saying conveys a negative image, not a positive one. This idiomatic saying contains not an admonition for change, but a warning that too much change does not allow people to develop important relationships and continuity in their lives. In this particular instance many Japanese are aware of the Western meaning related to that idiom and its use would not create a problem. Thus, using the same idiom may create a problem in one intercultural situation and not in another.

Idioms exist in every language and can cause confusion regardless of the language being learned. In Russia we could hear about someone "soaping someone's neck" and be left quite confused. This idiom is similar to one in English about "raking someone over the coals."[13] Or perhaps you are in Spain trying to learn Spanish and someone says, "*Yo tengo una tía que toca la guitarra*" (I have an aunt who plays the guitar). Such a phrase may leave us quite confused or trying to comment about the person's aunt in a positive way. However, this phrase as an idiom functions to say "So that's news?" or to tell someone that their previous comment did not really apply to the general point of the conversation.[14]

Even when people share the same language, they do not necessarily share the same ways of speaking. Idioms are one example of this. When Brad was in England he lived with an English family for almost a year. Early on during his stay he needed a suit and had one made for him. When he showed it off to the family he was staying with, the wife said, "That don't look half good." Brad was taken aback for a moment and the wife, seeing this, explained that it meant that the suit looked good on him. He was used to that type of meaning being conveyed by the phrase, "That doesn't look half bad." Which is better, not being half bad or half good? Does it matter? Another example from Brad's stay in England was that "tabling" a topic meant that it was about to be talked about rather than the meaning he was used to, that the topic would be discussed at a later time. Another example is the common meanings of the word *homely* in India and the United States. In India homely is used to describe a woman who has good domestic skills, and it is a positive term often used in personal ads placed in the newspaper.[15] However, in the United States the term has a negative connotation about the person's appearance and would not likely be found in such ads. So what is the true and accurate use of the phrase "let's table the topic" or the word "homely"? In addition, idiomatic differences are often found within different regions of the same country. In any case, the content of our speech is not always as straightforward as we may believe. Certain phrases or sayings become commonly known and understood within communities with meanings that are not literally tied to the meanings of the words used and thus complicate intercultural interactions.

Quantity

Marianne was not surprised. Her husband, an Armenian from Lebanon, had just finished telling about what to him was a most amazing and amusing incident that had just happened on the bus. It was her husband's first visit to Sweden, Marianne's native country. Her husband and some of his extended family had come with her to visit the land of her youth. Her husband was still shaking his head. He and his relatives had been on the bus in Stockholm and were visiting with each other, talking and having fun, when all of a sudden a Swedish guy had turned around with a stern look on his face, put a finger to his lips and said, "Sshh!" His whole family had been shocked into silence.

Silence

The quantity of speech maxim indicates that there is a proper amount of talk for different circumstances. A person may be seen to talk too much or too little. In many communities in Sweden, Finland, and Denmark, knowing when to be silent is a treasured attribute. Too much talk is seen in a negative light and not respected. One should have a sense of quietness about oneself. Most people in the United States, even ones who think of themselves as quiet and reserved, find that they are very talkative compared to the expectations of quietness within these communities. When it is appropriate to talk and the amount of talk expected are often unconscious differences across many communities.[16]

Elaborated and Restricted Codes

Basil Bernstein suggested that our speech patterns vary along a continuum between what he calls *elaborated* and *restricted* codes.[17] Similar in nature to Edward Hall's notions of high and low context discussed in Chapter 2, elaborated speech relies on the explicit verbal expression to carry the meaning of a comment to the listeners, whereas restricted codes rely on past knowledge and more implicit aspects of the situation to convey their meaning. Every culture may be seen to encourage either an elaborated or restricted code depending upon the situation and needs of the moment. However, these situations and needs often do not match, resulting in a variety of misunderstandings and offenses. As we consider the impact of verbal communication on a misunderstanding, we cannot simply look at differences in meaning. We must also consider the amount of verbal interaction involved and the expectations others have concerning that amount.

Relevance

Relevance implies that what one has said connects and is meaningful in some way to either what has been previously said or to the purpose of the interaction in general. Thus, certain types of questions about age, marital status, or how much money one makes may seem overly personal or irrelevant to some North Americans when traveling abroad, but they are very relevant to the members of the community in which they are traveling. What members of one community feel is relevant is not always the same as what those from another community feel is relevant. There are many ways that relevance may manifest itself in our talk. We will give a few examples of real experiences and then discuss the different ways relevance or the perceived lack of relevance influenced the communication.

Forms of Address

Gerald was uncomfortable. He had been excited to leave his homeland of Sierra Leone to come study in the United States, but some things about school in the U.S. were just plain weird. For example, his teachers all wanted to be called by their first names. His chemistry teacher, Dr. William Avery, insisted on being called Bill and he was older than Gerald's father! This man had a wonderful reputation in the field and surely he deserved to be referred to with respect. Gerald had tried the first half dozen times to call him Dr. Avery, but the teacher wouldn't even respond until he started calling him Bill. Gerald wanted to give his professor the respect he deserved, but the professor just felt that Gerald was being difficult.

Questions and Answers

Mary Allen was intrigued. She had never had an opportunity to interview a person from Japan for a position with the firm. It had happened somewhat unexpectedly, due to some new international connections and the need to find someone who could relate to international experiences and could also speak Japanese. Ms. Goshima had been strongly recommended by a friend, and Mary was looking forward to hearing about her experiences. After a few brief pleasantries, Mary said, "So tell me about one of your greatest success stories." Ms. Goshima paused and then began, "I have worked with many good people. . ." She went on to discuss some of the positive abilities of these people when Mary interrupted her and said with a smile, "Yes, I am sure they were wonderful, but what about you?" Ms. Goshima paused even longer and then began again, "It was indeed an honor to work with them. I have learned a lot and I wish I had learned even more. I try, but sometimes I am a bit slow. I hope my work was not too much of a disappointment for them. . ." As Ms. Goshima went on Mary quit really paying attention. "What is wrong with this woman?" she thought. "If this is her greatest success story, she is obviously not right for this firm."

Manner

Grice's maxim on manner is mainly concerned with being clear or lucid given the demands of the situation. Although almost all that has been discussed up to this point is related to improving clarity, we believe this maxim is best considered in terms of the language used. One of the most obvious barriers to intercultural communication exists when those interacting do not share the same language. There are basically two things to do when you are faced with this problem. First, find a good interpreter and, second, start learning the other person's language.

There are many examples in business of poor translations, due to translations that are too literal or because the fact that words may have multiple meanings is ignored. For example, Bud Lite beer's slogan "Delicious, less filling" came out in Spanish as "Filling, less delicious." Kentucky Fried Chicken's motto, "finger lickin' good," came out in Chinese as "eat your fingers off." These mistranslations occur during translations into English as well, such as the dentist in Hong Kong who advertised, "Teeth extracted by the latest Methodists," or the English sign in a French shop window that read, "We sell dresses for street walking."

A good interpreter does more than translate the literal meaning of the message. The interpreter must translate the cultural meaning so that misunderstandings are avoided and the communication is effective and as appropriate as possible. Sometimes this affects the length of each response in ways that may seem odd to those unfamiliar with both languages. Some of these challenges are illustrated in the exchange below between a doctor in the United States, a Vietnamese patient, and their interpreter.

> Doctor to patient in English: Are you married?
>
> Interpreter to patient in Vietnamese: This doctor asks if you are married. She does not mean to insult you. In America a woman can have a baby without being married. It is not a shameful matter. Please do not be offended.
>
> Patient to interpreter in Vietnamese: I do not understand. In my country this would bring great shame to my parents. My husband would be very angry if he heard this question. It shows him no respect.
>
> Interpreter to doctor in English: She says she is married.[18]

The idea of a doctor finding out if someone is married may seem like a simple exchange that should have little difficulty being accomplished, yet the language and cultural differences can make it and many other exchanges rife with potential misunderstanding.

The second step we suggested was learning the other language. This, of course, is much easier said in a sentence than actually done. One challenge with learning another community's language is the negative perceptions (real or imagined) that native speakers may develop about the second-language learner. Someone may be a very intelligent person and have much to contribute and share with others, but if that person is just learning a language, it is very difficult to find words to express insights and share feelings. Nishiyama notes that many Japanese businesspeople or students who come to the United States speak what may be considered by native English speakers to be a substandard English.[19] This type of perception can occur regardless of the languages or cultures involved. Discomfort with the second language often results in speaking behaviors that come across as overly cautious or annoying to the native speaker.

However, it has been our experience that any sincere effort at learning another's language, even in small amounts, is appreciated. This is generally true even with the French, who have a reputation of being particularly zealous about their language and the way that it is used. We have heard many Americans complain about how rude the French are. However, listening to their stories reveals that they usually expected the French to adapt to their English. Given the long history of tension and competition between the French and the English, we wonder if the French would really get a better reception among the English if they were visiting in England and trying to manage with just French. We know we have heard in the United States more than one person complain about people who were trying to get by here without learning English. Platt, who has studied French culture for years, notes that negative experiences with the French tend to happen when no effort at learning their language is made.[20] She further maintains that if someone does insult your efforts at speaking French, it is usually done in fun and you should feel free to joke back. For those who still feel they have problems getting help in France, she suggests five magic words of the French language that she claims will virtually always have a positive impact: *Excusez-moi de vous déranger, monsieur (or madame),.* . . (Excuse me for disturbing you, sir [or madam],. . .). The key is to remember that language is the foundation of verbal communication and the more we expand our language skills, the greater our ability to engage in clear communication and to understand problems that arise from unclear language or mistranslations.

Code-Switching

Another practice that is connected to language and the manner in which people speak is what is known as *code-switching*. Code-switching happens when one switches which code or formal language one is speaking. At times this is done in different situations, such that in one setting (dealing with the government or at school, for example) people may speak English and then at another place (perhaps at home or with a group of friends) speak a different language, such as

Spanish. Sometimes the topic will have an impact on language choice. For some people, certain topics just seem to need to be discussed in a certain language. Code-switching is also done within a single setting or topic of conversation. It may be done within a single conversation or sentence. Often code-switching is done to either converge or diverge from those around the speaker. Switching to one's home language, even for just a moment or two, can remind those you are talking with about a shared identity or an identity that is not shared. When both languages are not shared by all of the participants code-switching can often create a sense of separation and antagonism in those who feel intentionally left out. However, those speaking the other language may not realize the sense of separation or desire to exclude the others, but may be focused on the content they are expressing. These issues should be kept in mind when code-switching is done and misunderstandings occur.

Reflection Question: How do you feel when someone is speaking to others around you in a language you cannot understand?

Gratuitous Concurrence

Finally in regards to manner, we should mention *gratuitous concurrence*, a concept identified by Liberman.[21] Gratuitous concurrence occurs when people do not understand each other due to language troubles, but for the sake of the conversation agree with the other and try to fill in appropriate answers even when they are unsure of the correct meaning. When Brad first landed in England he had this difficulty with a customs person. He knew the other person was speaking English, but the West Indian accent on top of English versus American way of speaking English left him completely baffled. Yet he nodded when it seemed he should and tried to fit in with what was needed. Brad got through customs, but he never did understand a single thing the fellow said.

Liberman gives two examples that further illustrate this process:

Robin: Are you studying Greek right now?
Miguel: It's very interesting.
Robin: Did you study Greek?
Miguel: Yes.

Actually, Miguel was neither studying Greek nor was he sure what Robin was saying, but he was able to try to keep the conversation moving in a positive way. A second example given by Liberman is of a much more dangerous nature. A Vietnamese immigrant visited an all-night pharmacy to get a doctor's prescription for sleeping pills and painkillers filled. When asked if he understood the directions, he just smiled and nodded, knowing some reply was wanted, but not understanding the question or the directions.[22]

We all have experiences in which we miss something in a conversation and just sort of play along until we can catch up. The problem when different cultures and languages are involved is that we often never do catch up. We have frequently had students in the United States find out that gratuitous concurrence was at the center of a missed appointment with one of their international conversation partners. They thought the person was agreeing with them, only to find out later that the person had not really understood, but hated to keep asking questions so just acted agreeable without ever really understanding what had been asked of them. One of the reasons people engage in gratuitous concurrence is to save *face*. Face refers to the public image that each person desires to create and maintain. Admitting that one does not understand, particularly on a repeated basis, can be very face threatening.

The four maxims of quality, quantity, relevance, and manner help us to detect what sort of cultural differences in verbal communication may lead to these difficulties. These four maxims are neither exclusive nor exhaustive. Careful consideration of them will show that certain problems related to one maxim may overlap with another maxim and you may discover challenges that the maxims did not clearly cover. However, as with the contextual assumptions, the maxims do provide a suggestive and useful resource for us to use when looking for answers to intercultural interactions where there are problems in terms of verbal communication.

TERMS OF ADDRESS

In every human society, people use one or more verbal symbolic resources for pointing specifically to someone; that is, for indicating a particular person other than ourselves. Symbolic resources can include: birth names, nicknames, clan affiliations, pronouns, occupational, educational and other honorific titles, terms of endearment or offense, or neutral terms. Importantly, these resources for pointing to another or terms of address not only allow us to signal a particular other, but they also enable us to express our relationships with others. For example, in using a term of endearment such as "dear" or "sweetheart," the speaker conveys affection directly to a particular person. Moreover, by the very uttering of a given address term the speaker makes known his or her social relationship with the hearer. That is, people express what Covarrubias calls the "relational alignment" between interactants in a given context. As we will see below, terms of address communicate our socio-cultural values, attitudes, feelings, and emotions about ourselves in relation to one another. José shares this story about a situation he experienced with address practices:

After finishing my M.A. degree in the United States, I returned to my native Ecuador. Shortly after my return I interviewed for a job at one of our universities. Soon into the interview I noticed that my interviewer, who was the academic human resources manager, started looking very disapprovingly at me. At that moment I felt embarrassed when I suddenly realized that I'd been addressing her by her first name. I don't know what happened to me because I know how one is supposed to address someone in a formal situation in my country! Maybe I got used to the more casual first name basis that is so common in the U.S. All I know is that I could hear myself saying to her, "So, Martha, what would be my work responsibilities?" and "Martha, what do you think about a new course?" And "Martha...." I felt I was being disrespectful. To this day I believe that I made a terrible impression on my interviewer because of the way I called her by her first name. And, no, I did not get the job.

In other situations, several of our U.S. students reported that when their parents reprimand them, the expected address to the male parent or caregiver is "Sir" or "Ma'am" to the female parent or caregiver. And our Asian students have taught us that in Mainland China, Taiwan, Singapore, and other Chinese-speaking societies honorific address terms such as *san* following the family name is expected when speaking with people of higher social ranks.

Reflection Question: Can you relate to the examples above? Have you ever addressed someone in a way that based on the person's reaction you realized that just broke a social rule? How did you recover from the social breach? What were the social consequences of the breach?

Looking into the ways that people across the world address one another can give us invaluable information about culture because the rules informing address practices directly are linked to a given society's worldview. Terms of address enable people to express different kinds of relational alignments. These alignments can be based on power and solidarity,[23] status and intimacy,[24] or *confianza* [trust, interpersonal closeness, and confidentiality] and *respeto* [respect].[25]

Pronouns

In contemporary English in the U.S. and other Anglophone societies, the pronoun *you* generally is the only term available for addressing one other person. However, this was not always the case as "thou" and "thee" were once used. Seventeenth-century Quakers in the U.S., prompted by socio-cultural beliefs about equality and humility in interpersonal relationships, opted for a preference for using "thou."[26] "Thou" had been used by working-class people to signify "you." And "thou" also was used as a means for expressing intimacy, as when addressing God. During the thirteenth century, the pronoun "you," which had been used in the plural, started to be used as a more formal singular "you." "You" in the singular was used by people of higher economic means when addressing each other. And "you" was used by persons of lower social status to persons of higher social status, such as servants to masters and children to parents, with "thou" used in return. So, we can see that an intentional move was made to use communication resources to express the flattening of the social hierarchy by evolving into the use of a one-term "you" for addressing one other person.

A different situation occurs in other communities. Several languages spoken around the world including Spanish, French, German, Italian, and Russian incorporate pronominal resources that enable communicators to choose different ways of saying "you" to one other person. For example, in Spanish, communicators can choose between *tú* (informal "you") and *usted* (formal "you"), and sometimes *vos* (informal "you") (i.e., in Argentina). French communicators can opt for *tu* (informal "you") or *vous* (formal "you"), while German interactants may choose between *du* (informal "you") and *Sie* (formal "you").

Covarrubias explained that in her native Mexico address forms not only are socially important and consequential, but they can be very complicated.[27] Using the conversation of construction workers in the port city of Veracruz, she showed how the workers used the Mexican Spanish address pronouns *tú* and *usted* to shape their interpersonal networks in 21 different ways, which they, in turn, used to create networks of workplace cooperation. The workers used both *tú* and *usted*, even within the same utterance and speaking to the same person to creatively construct relationships based on friendship, closeness, affection, and playfulness as well as relationships based on respect, admiration, fear, and formality. In ways perhaps surprising to outsiders, workers sometimes used the formal *usted* to underscore closeness and the familiar *tú* to highlight hostility. Covarrubias noted that in the Veracruz community, as in other Mexican societies, knowing how to address people bears significant social consequences not only for the specific communicators but also for their families. Using address forms appropriately provides audible evidence to hearers that a person was raised with the proper rules of politeness. If, on the basis of polite and respectful speech, a person is deemed to be *bien educado* [well bred, polite], then social and professional opportunities are more likely to come their way because showing oneself to be polite not only gains positive face to the speakers as well as to their immediate and extended families, but it also opens doors of opportunity that otherwise might be closed. Conversely, failure to use address pronouns in culturally appropriate ways a speaker might be evaluated as being *mal educado* [not well bred; impolite], causing speakers and their extended families to lose face.

So, ever vigilant of *el "qué* dirán" [What will others say?], which is a Mexican version of "face," workers said they were careful with their speech "*para no regarla*" [so as not to blow it]; in other words, so as not to lose face.

Honorifics

Honorific titles are used as means for giving face to people by acknowledging their social standing in a given community and according them respect and esteem. Honorifics can be based on age, marital status, gender, education, occupation, education, or other social designation. For example, in U.S. societies some married woman like to use the title Mrs. In Italy, a man holding a professional title may be addressed as, '*Ingegnere*' instead of '*Signore*' [Mister]. In many Latino communities the terms '*Don*' + first name or '*Doña*' + first name are used to express respect for elders. Our Indonesian colleague, Sonia, tells us:

The term "Ibu" or "Mother" is used to formally address women between the ages of mid-30s and 60s. For women older than 60, the term used is "Oma," the Dutch term for "grandma." My cousins address me as "Cici," the Chinese term for elder sister, and I address my older female cousins in the same way. I like being addressed as "elder sister" because there's a sense of respect, responsibility, and kinship. Same goes for men: "Bapak" or "Pak" which is the formal Indonesian term of address for males. It means "Father." Since we're Chinese, many of my brothers' and my dad's employees (we own a motorcycle spare parts distribution company) refer to them as "Koko" or "Ko" meaning elder brother.

The use of occupational, educational, and other titles are important in many cultural contexts. For example, in everyday U.S. life, there are many situations where using occupational titles is optional. It is generally acceptable for a college student to address an instructor as "Professor"; however, it is not unusual for professors to invite students to call them by their first name. This practice has proven to be somewhat problematic for some of our international students who come from societies where the use of formal titles is more expected. They have told us that the more casual U.S. address practices sometimes makes them feel uncomfortable because they seem disrespectful, especially in interactions involving interactants of unequal social status. Calling professors by their first name, to them, suggests that everyone loses face—the speaker for being disrespectful and the hearer for being disrespected.

But it is important to remember that making large generalizations can be inadequate and that address practices, like all communication, depend on context. Even in the U.S. there are circumstances where occupational titles are the preferred practice. Some examples would be military, religious, and medical contexts. Military personnel traditionally are addressed by their rank (i.e., general, sergeant, private). Catholic priests are traditionally addressed as "Father," Protestant ministers as "Pastor" or "Reverend," Islamic worship leaders as "Imam," and Jewish religious leader as "Rabbi." In the medical profession, physicians generally are addressed as "Doctor," and in aviation, the pilot of a plane may be called "Captain."

In the U.S. address preferences also vary according to ethnic groupings. Collins and Moore explained that given the historical, political, and sociological context of slavery and racism in the U.S., many African Americans, especially members of older generations, prefer the more formal titles of Mr., Mrs., Miss, and Dr., especially during first meetings.[28] A common practice during slavery was the withholding of assigned names as a means to demoralize and humiliate the enslaved persons. Today, a history of racism continues to prompt many African Americans to feel invisible or disrespected and thus the more formal forms are preferred over the use of first names or nicknames until relationships are developed and permissions for different address forms are granted. The authors note that via the use of titles and by avoiding the use of first names or nicknames, the hearer is offered respect and dignity. Recognition of honorific titles extend respect and dignity within intercultural communication.

In traditional Chinese communities, the cultural imperative calls for interactants to maintain face and give face by using occupational titles in formal contexts to address one another. Angela, a Chinese native who works for a Western firm in China and who also has worked in the United States, explains that these address forms are still practiced in contemporary China, but adds that intercultural adaptations are common especially for non-Chinese organizational workers.

We use these forms of address automatically and without second thought. This is how we were taught by our parents, and this is the practice by everyone. This practice goes way back to the traditional Chinese culture of respect. We show respect to people who are social seniors—seniors in age, seniors in ranking, and seniors in professions. Teachers are in a highly respected profession. No matter who the parents are, they being a company's president, they still show tremendous respect to their child's teachers. A teacher can criticize a parent who might hold a very senior role in a company or in government organizations. Being a doctor is also a very respected profession due to the knowledge and power that doctors have. Doctors have to go through 7–8 years' training to earn the title. They have special knowledge in areas that ordinary people do not have. In a way, doctors "control" someone's life or death. And a company president is

(continued)

(continued)

respected because of his rank and the power associated in a company. A person with president's title is perceived as successful. In a society where hierarchy is still practiced, being a company president is respected and admired. Because of the power, status, and knowledge associated in these roles, we grow up calling them by their professional title plus their last name. For example, we say: Doctor Wang (王医生), teacher Zhang (张老师) or president Zhou (周总). If I do not follow these social rules, I will be perceived as not educated and not respectful. The doctor, the teacher, or the president will not be happy about me and they might think I am not educated. But, over the past 14 years, with foreign invest-ment and China's opening to the outside world, we started not calling company presidents by their titles in Western companies. We call these senior-ranking people by their first name. But this phenomenon only happens in Western com-panies in China. The state-owned companies and private Chinese-run companies still follow the traditional rules. If you follow the traditional rules, you give both yourself face (because you show respect and you are seen as educated) and the counterpart face too.

In this section, we have broached an important and ever-present communication phenomenon, terms of address. We have discussed what terms of address are, key forms of address, and what people achieve in and through their use, par-ticularly as it pertains to the concept of face. We have underscored that when it comes to address forms, it is important to keep in mind that practices vary sig-nificantly across cultures, and that there are always consequences—positive and negative—that result from their enactments. We showed that breaching the rules for enacting personal address can result in the loss of face and other potentially damaging outcomes. We also showed that using address forms productively can result in the construction of respect, dignity, *confianza*, friendship, and kinship for ourselves and for others.

Reflection Question: Think about a nickname that you allow only certain people to call you based on their relationship with you. Try to figure out why that is. What does the nickname sug-gest to you when used by other than the person you allow to use it?

FACE CONSIDERATIONS

An additional concept that can be very useful when seeking to deal with the problems that arise out of these verbal misunderstandings is the concept of face noted earlier. Face considerations are particularly important when considering how to address another person. Brown and Levinson identify two kinds of face.[29] One is called positive face and it is focused on our desires to be accepted and recognized as a valuable member of a community. Words of praise or other indications of our acceptance all attend to our positive face needs. A second type of face is called negative face, not because it is bad, but because it is essentially the opposite of the other type, just like a film negative is the opposite of the actual picture. This form of face values autonomy and allowing a person to do and accomplish what they wish to do. Comments that respect another's independence and freedom to choose reflect this type of face. When and how these different forms of face are emphasized vary across cultural communities, but they are always there.

When seeking to clear up misunderstandings it is important to consider how our efforts may impact the various faces of those involved in the misunderstanding. Take for example two counter-posed claims reported by one team of researchers discussing differences between black and white language styles:[30] A black woman telling her white conversation partner, "You are so naive," and a white woman telling her black conversation partner, "You are so selfish." The roots of this problem were linked to different language styles. In comparison the black style emphasized the feelings of the speaker and the need to speak directly and assertively (which was seen as selfish), whereas the white style focused more on the sensitivities of the listener and the need to be accommodating and indirect (which was as being naive). However, once the misunderstanding occurs there is more to handling the situation than just pointing out the existence of two conversational styles. Each person's face has been threatened in the misunderstanding and the challenge that is created is to come up with communication strategies that will help both individuals preserve face. These strategies must take into account the cultural differences in terms of how direct or indirect to be with verbal communication.

DIRECT/INDIRECT COMMUNICATION

Zodenek raised his hand. The question "What aspect of communication has caused you the greatest difficulty in the United States?" had been put to his small group of multicultural conversational partners. After his experience at lunch the answer was fresh on his mind. "I come from Albania and like many Eastern European students I have trouble with all the 'thank yous' and 'pleases' I hear all the time. In my country saying 'please' and 'thank you' is not a polite thing. It is considered ironic and puts the other person into the position of a servant.

(continued)

(continued)

If we do say it, it is done in a very low and humble way so as not to create offense. Here I hear it all the time and it annoys me. People also seem annoyed that I am not always saying 'thank you.' At lunch today I was standing in line to get food and when it was my turn I said, "Hamburger and French fries," and the person beside me added "please." I didn't feel embarrassed or anything. Just real angry at him. I wish people would keep their pleases to themselves.

Although there are many things going on in these examples, one of the sources of the frustration and misunderstandings that occurred was different notions of what was verbally relevant. In the first example, Gerald felt that Professor Avery's age and accomplishments made his social position relevant and thus the term *Doctor* was the only sensible way to refer to him. For Professor Avery, it was his personal identity as Bill that was important and relevant to the situation and the fact that he had a Ph.D. was so irrelevant that he would not even recognize efforts to include acknowledgment of it into verbal communication. In the second example, Mary was expecting a much more direct response to her question. Ms. Goshima, however, was uncomfortable with the question and felt her response should be very indirect and establish a proper sense of modesty before revealing the answer to the question. If Mary had been more patient, she would have eventually heard the answer to her question, but she was not really paying attention when it finally came because she felt that Ms. Goshima's comments weren't really relevant to her query. In the last example, the Americans that Zodenek was dealing with all felt that expressions such as *please* and *thank you* were very relevant to any situation in which a person was either asking for something or being helped in some way. Zodenek felt that these expressions were not needed in these types of situations.

One of Patricia's friends, José Castro Sotomayor, shared the following experiences of how the level of directness in e-mail communication created very different impressions in different countries.

I am from Ecuador, South America, and I did my Master's in the United States. The last semester of my M.A., I had the opportunity to teach an undergraduate class. My advisor told me to contact her if I had questions about the material and the way the class should be taught. My e-mails were something like this:
    Dear Jennifer,
    I hope you are having a good day.
    I was wondering if you could help me with. . .
    Then, I asked my question or ask for advice and finished:

I really appreciate your help in this matter.

Have a good day,

I signed with my full name and my position.

After several e-mails, she called me into her office. When I got there she politely said: José, I have a lot of e-mails to read during the day. So please, if you need to ask me something just ask. *Tell me what you need in one sentence, and I will help you. That is my job. You are not asking for a favor.*

I got the message and started writing short, concise, and to-the-point e-mails. The communication between us greatly improved, and she appreciated my diligence and efficiency.

After finishing my studies, I moved to Colombia, where I worked for a university coordinating research projects. One of my responsibilities was to organize meetings, ask for reports, and foster new ideas for future projects. In the name of the efficiency I had learned, my e-mails looked like this:

Good morning Lorena,

I need the financial report on Tuesday. There is a meeting on Thursday, and I need to read it in advanced.

Thank you

One afternoon, the Dean of the Faculty I was working for called me into his office. Before the meeting ended, he said: You are doing a good job coordinating the team, but you could be more polite in your e-mails. People think you are distant, even rude.

Thus, I shifted again. My coworkers appreciated my "good mood" as well as my swiftly response, which I had learned during my grad studies. Now, depending on whom I am writing to, I choose the style of my e-mail, because I always want to be polite.

Of course, what counts as politeness and being sensitive to other's face can also vary culturally.

Later I started working at a company that was fully online. This was my first time working in a team spread in several countries and meeting with coworkers only through Skype. The work schedule was flexible, which I liked. However, the way the company kept control of the work was new for me.

One morning I received a call from my boss. He told me that I was "wasting time." I did not understand what he meant by that, so I asked "Why?" He said: "You don't have to write a letter thanking us every time we do something for you or the team. We know you are thankful for it."

I don't know if online companies work this way. Perhaps I need more time to get used to the way online work is done.

Technology often complicates the way we receive much of the verbal communication we use because it lacks some of the nonverbal cues for understanding that we will discuss in Chapter 6. The directness or indirectness with which we communicate is culturally based, just as the ways that people express respect and consideration toward others. Verbal communication is, of course, a direct manifestation of the language we speak. Thus, the relationship between our language and our thoughts is an important area to consider if we want to fully cover the challenges of verbal communication in an intercultural setting.

LANGUAGE AND THOUGHT

Language is often equated with culture, such that if a person or group loses the ability to speak a traditional language, they may be viewed as having lost their culture. Indeed, each culture may be said to have its own unique language, whether this language is formally recognized as a distinct linguistic variety, such as Spanish and Italian, or simply involves different dialects or ways of using the same formal language. These language differences do not merely reflect different cultures, but actually help to create our expectations for the world and our understanding of how we relate with each other. For example, the Japanese have a term for a particularly bittersweet type of relational emotion involving dependency called *amae*. Do people who speak only English, a language that has no equivalent word in its lexicon, develop this type of relational emotion?

Britta Limary, a German who married a Lao while living in the United States, explained how language can make a difference in how we perceive the world.[31] This is a useful example, because it ties back to our discussion of terms of address. In the Lao language great stress is put on addressing people correctly according to one's familiarity with that person and to the age, social status, family relationship, and gender of those involved in the conversation. For each aspect of "I" and "you" a different address or term (27 in all) is used depending upon the speaking situation. There are different "I's" and "you's" when speaking to officials, children, older people, intimate family members, and so forth. In German addressing people has only one form of "I" and two forms of "you" (formal and informal, depending on the person's status). In English, however, there is essentially only one form of "I" and one form of "you." The Lao language reflects the idea that individuals do not exist in and of themselves, but rather are defined by their relationships to others which create life spaces for themselves and others. These life spaces are created and maintained through language. It is difficult to grasp the Lao meaning of "I" and "you" in English because the language does not structure the world in the same way.

Dealing with these language differences can be emotionally exhausting and mentally challenging, as Martha's experience illustrates.

Martha's parents had arrived in Japan from the United States three days ago. Martha had been excited to show off Japan to her parents and looked forward to being their personal tour guide. Now she only felt exhausted. The constant pressure of keeping her parents entertained and informed, while simultaneously maintaining positive relationships with the Japanese she came in contact with, was tiring. Perhaps the hardest part of all was the constant switching back and forth between Japanese and English. When she talked with her parents or others in English she tended to be quite expressive and very direct in her feelings, but when she started speaking Japanese she felt less emotional and rarely stated her points or feelings directly. Instead, she found herself actively using metaphors and being very concerned about the other person's social position. That night as she lay in bed trying to make sense of her jumbled emotions, she screamed in her head, "Ahh! I'm becoming schizophrenic."[32]

Martha is beginning to understand just how powerful language is in shaping our world and influencing our behavior.

Reflection Question: Is there anything that is meaningful to you that you find difficult putting into words?

Sapir-Whorf Hypothesis

One of the most frequently used ideas to understand the role of language in our thoughts and actions is the Sapir-Whorf Hypothesis.[33] The strong version of this hypothesis states that *language unconsciously determines how we perceive the world*. Thus, the limits of our language become the limits of our world. Our actions are connected to our language because we are assumed to act based on our perceptions of the world and these perceptions are determined by our language.

Research has brought into question a number of issues related to the linguistic determinism suggested by this strong version of the Sapir-Whorf Hypothesis. For example, one group of researchers examined the perceptual process among French-speaking, Wolof-speaking, and bilingual children.[34] Sets of three pictures were given to the children, and they were asked to categorize which two were most alike and explain why. Each set of three contained two that were alike in color, two that were alike in form, and two that were alike in function. The Wolof language uses the same term for the colors orange and red and it does not contain a single term for the color blue. Based on the Sapir-Whorf Hypothesis, it would be expected that the Wolof-speaking children would tend to categorize the pictures based on form and function, rather than color differences that were not salient in their language. This did not happen. The French-speaking and bilingual children slightly favored form and function categories and the Wolof children significantly categorized their pictures more often based on color. The fact that the Wolof language does not have certain color words did not mean that the Wolof speakers could not perceive the color differences.

Roger Brown argues that although language and thought are closely related, it is a need-based relationship rather than a causal one that exists between them.[35] He argues that humans categorize their world by using language based on their needs. He uses Whorf's famous, but questionable, example of the Eskimos' many terms for snow to help make his point.[36] Although the Eskimo may have more terms for snow than the typical English speaker, it does not mean that an English speaker does not or cannot perceive these differences if there is a need. For example, English-speaking skiers have many more terms for snow than an English speaker who does not have a lot of experience with snow. Typically the more serious the skier, the more terms for snow the person has. Certainly access to these terms encourages a person to make sense of snow differently than would a person who has no such vocabulary, but the lack of vocabulary is not a perceptual wall that cannot be crossed.

In any profession or area of knowledge, from plumbing to philosophy, a language is developed that facilitates shared meaning and coordinated action based on the needs of those involved; however, as vitally important as this language is, it does not completely dictate what can be perceived. This is true with cultures as well. The language system used by a culture is inescapably tied to the perceptual system, but it does not create a static system that locks its members into a view of the world that cannot be changed.

It is important to remember that language is one example of the symbols we discussed in the first chapter as resources for making sense. Even though symbols are powerful and conventional, they are also arbitrary and dynamic. Language is inherently ambiguous. If we say, "The man is at the door," what does that mean? Is the person inside or outside the house? How close is he to the door? Does it mean the same thing to say, "The taxi is at the door"? Being "at" the door does not always mean the same thing. The difference in meaning relies on our knowledge of concepts like taxi and man and in what context it is "sensible" to find each of them "at the door."[37] Because language is ambiguous and the meaning of specific language use, such as our "I love you, too" example in the first chapter, is always in part shaped by the situation in which it is found, language does not provide a solid base from which to consistently predict human behavior. Similar to worldviews, values, and norms discussed in Chapter 2, language provides a resource through which we make sense of our world and deal with the situations we encounter each day.

SUMMARY

In this chapter we have discussed two major areas to consider when intercultural misunderstanding occurs in verbal communication. These areas serve as resources in our efforts to discover how it is that people with good intentions may still misunderstand what we feel we stated so clearly. The first of these was contextual assumptions, with particular concern for the frame or type of talk we see ourselves participating in. We are almost always involved in some culturally recognizable type of activity that frames what is expected and sensible. This form of framing helps us to make sense of specific actions that tend to be assumed or taken for granted in a particular culture, evokes and assumes informal social rules, and both relies on and implies certain social identities. By paying attention to these expectations associated with frames, we can attune ourselves to see cultural differences that are otherwise easily missed.

The second area was the verbal structure and content of our communication. Although there are many different aspects related to the way we use language, we used Grice's four conversational maxims to review many of these important differences. The maxim of quality allowed us to examine idioms and other language habits that cause confusion. The quantity maxim highlighted the different amounts of speech expected by certain cultures in particular circumstances. Grice's relevance maxim allowed us to look at expectancies related to forms of address, question asking, and the degree of directness used by the interactants. The manner maxim brought our attention to issues of translation and code-switching. In addition, the common, but potentially dangerous, concept of gratuitous concurrence was discussed. Considering these maxims and the need to attend to individuals face needs is important in our efforts to understand and manage verbal misunderstandings.

We discussed one of the key areas of study related to intercultural communication differences in regards to verbal communication, terms of address. We reviewed what terms of address are, key forms of address, and what people achieve in and through their use, particularly as it pertains to the concept of face. We have underscored that when it comes to address forms, it is important to keep in mind that practices vary significantly across cultures, and that there are always consequences—positive and negative—that result from their enactments.

Finally, language as the basis of verbal communication was discussed as an important influence on our thoughts and actions. The Sapir-Whorf Hypothesis was reviewed, and the importance of understanding the communicative needs of a community as well as the ambiguous nature of language for making sense of this influence was reviewed and illustrated.

REFLECTION QUESTIONS

1   Two different levels of misunderstanding are contextual assumptions and verbal communication. Based on your own observations, which of these do you feel creates the most problems in intercultural settings? Why? How easy is it to separate these in actual practice?

2   How large do you believe the influence of language to be on our lives? What impact has learning other languages had on your thought process?

3   What examples can you think of where people have violated the maxims suggested by Grice? How has their violation impacted the way you understood their message?

4   Can you think of an example of gratuitous concurrence in your own life? Have you ever just nodded in agreement with someone whom you could not understand due to language difficulties because you didn't want to keep asking the person what he or she had said? What was the outcome?

ACTIVITIES

1   Make a list of all the terms of address that were used by your family as you were growing up. What were your parents or caregivers trying to teach you through the use of these address forms? Compare and contrast this list with your classmates and note similarities and differences in beliefs about power, solidarity, status, intimacy, *respeto*, and *confianza*.

2   Select a frame or named type of talk from your community, such as gossip, flirting, teasing, eating a family dinner, attending class or an interview, then try to discover all of the assumptions about communication related to the frame. What are the informal rules that a person is expected to follow related to that frame? What types of people can or cannot participate in this kind of frame? Find someone from a different culture and compare what you found about your frame with a similar frame from their culture. Discuss how these similarities and differences may create misunderstandings.

3   Try to translate a poem or song into another language without missing any of the subtle meanings that exist in its native language. How easy was this task? What made it easy or difficult?

4   One-on-one or in a small group have a discussion with a person or persons from a different culture about some of the areas discussed in this chapter. Some question ideas include:

> What is a common greeting among friends? Family members? Business associates?

> What are some common expressions conveyed through gestures?

When should titles, such as Dr., Professor, Miss, Ms., Mr., Mrs., and so forth, be used? When should these titles not be used?

What are some differences between how family members talk as compared to business associates or friends?

How would a host indicate that it was time for a guest to leave? Or, how would the guest indicate that he or she needed to leave?

NOTES

1 Adapted from K. Speakman, "Understanding Cultural Differences" (paper, University of New Mexico, 1997).
2 J. Gumperz, *Discourse Strategies* (Cambridge, MA: Cambridge University Press, 1982).
3 This example assumes the player is right-handed. The directions for what is a slice and a hook would be reversed if you are left-handed like Brad.
4 H. P. Grice, "Logic and Conversation," in *Syntax and Semantics: Vol. 3 Speech Acts*, ed. P. Cole and J. Morgan (New York: Academic Press, 1975), 41–58.
5 Grice, "Logic and Conversation," 50.
6 E. Goffman, *Frame Analysis: An Essay on the Organization of Experience* (New York: Harper & Row, 1974).
7 A. Mindess, "Your Polite Is Different than My Polite," *Views* 11 (1998): 11.
8 Mindess, "Polite," 11.
9 R. Willink, "*Dlodilchi*" (paper, University of New Mexico, 1996).
10 Willink, "*Dlodilchi*," 4–5.
11 Grice, "Logic and Conversation."
12 Y. Iwaki, "Comparing Japanese and American Proverbs" (paper, University of New Mexico, 1997).
13 L. S. Gray and D. Georgeoliani, *Guide to Russian Idioms* (Lincolnwood, IL: Passport Books, 1997).
14 R. H. Pierson, *Guia de Modismos Españoles* (Lincolnwood, IL: Passport Books, 1985).
15 E. M. Rogers and T. M. Steinfatt, *Intercultural Communication* (Prospect Heights, IL: Waveland Press, 1999).
16 C. Braithwaite, "Communicative Silence: A Cross-Cultural Study of Basso's Hypothesis," in *Cultural Communication and Intercultural Contact*, ed. D. Carbaugh (Hillsdale, NJ: Lawrence Erlbaum Associates, 1990), 321–7.
17 B. Bernstein, "Elaborated and Restricted Codes: Their Social Origins and Some Consequences," *American Anthropologist* 66 (1964): 55–69.
18 N. Katalanos, "When Yes Means No: Verbal and Nonverbal Communication of Southeast Asian Refugees in the New Mexico Health Care System" (master's thesis, University of New Mexico, 1994), 14.
19 K. Nishiyama, *Doing Business with Japan: Successful Strategies for Intercultural Communication* (Honolulu, HI: University of Hawaii Press, 2000).
20 P. Platt, *French or Foe*, 2nd ed. (London: Culture Crossings, Ltd., 1998).
21 K. B. Liberman, "The Hermeneutics of Intercultural Communication," *Anthropological Linguistics* 26 (1984): 53–83; quoted material is from page 62.
22 For related research see P. Geist, "Communicating Health and Understanding in the Borderlands of Co-cultures," in *Intercultural Communication: A Reader*, 9th ed., ed. L. A. Samovar and R. E. Porter (New York: Wadsworth Publishing, 2000), 341–54.

23 R. Brown and A. Gilman, "The Pronouns of Power and Solidarity," in *Style in Language*, ed. Thomas A Sebeok (Cambridge, MA: MIT Press, 1960), 253–76.

24 R. Brown and M. Ford, "Address in American English," *The Journal of Abnormal and Social Psychology* 62 (2) (1961): 375–85.

25 P. Covarrubias, *Culture, Communication, and Cooperation: Interpersonal Relations and Pronominal Address in a Mexican Organization* (Boulder, CO: Rowman and Littlefield, 2002).

26 R. Bauman, *Let Your Words Be Few: Symbolism of Speaking and Silence Among Seventeenth-Century Quakers* (New York: Cambridge University Press, 1983).

27 P. Covarrubias, "Culture. . .".

28 W. L. Collins and S. Moore, "Cross-Cultural Differences in Preferred Forms of Address: Implications for Work with African American Adults," *Advances in Social Work 5* (2) (2004): 163–71.

29 P. Brown and S. Levinson, "Universals in Language Use: Politeness Phenomenon," in *Questions and Politeness: Strategies in Social Interaction*, ed. E. Goody (Cambridge MA: Cambridge University Press, 1978), 56–289.

30 M. L. Hecht, R. L. Jackson II, and S. A. Ribeau, *African American Communication: Exploring Identity and Culture*, 2nd ed. (Mahwah, NJ: Lawrence Erlbaum Associates, 2003).

31 B. Limary, "Language and Culture" (paper, University of New Mexico, 1997).

32 Based on personal communication with K. Speakman, 1997.

33 E. Sapir, "Conceptual Categories in Primitive Languages," *Science* 74 (1931): 578; and B. L. Whorf, "A Linguistic Consideration of Thinking in Primitive Communities," in *Language in Culture and Society: A Reader in Linguistics and Anthropology*, ed. D. Hymes (New York: Harper & Row, 1964), 129–41.

34 C. M. Eastman, *Aspects of Language and Culture* (Novato, CA: Chandler & Sharp, 1985), 26.

35 R. Brown, *Words and Things* (Glencoe, IL: The Free Press, 1958).

36 The well-known Eskimo example has come under question in recent times from other sources; see G. Pullum, "The Great Eskimo Vocabulary Hoax," in *Language Awareness*, 7th ed., ed. P. Eschholz, A. Rosa, and V. Clark (New York: St. Martin's Press, 1997), 128–39.

37 R. Scollon and S. W. Scollon, *Intercultural Communication: A Discourse Approach* (Malden, MA: Blackwell, 2000).

Chapter 6

Where Can We Look to Explain Nonverbal Misunderstandings?

Lynn was in Japan for the second half of her study abroad experience. It was the first time she had ever traveled outside the United States. In fact, it was the first time she had been outside of her own state. During her journey she had experienced many adjustments in the way she communicated with others. Her journey began in Italy where she lived and studied for five weeks. Her first days in Italy were very disorienting. Verbal differences were definitely an initial shock for her. Before her studies abroad, Lynn took an introductory Italian class to help her communicate. However, once she arrived in Italy she realized there was more to communication in Italy than knowledge of words. She quickly learned to accentuate her spoken words with various gestures to have simple interactions with others and ask questions. She still chuckled when she remembered her second day in Italy when she asked a waiter for ice in her water. She didn't know the word for ice cubes so she crossed her arms and shivered then pointed to her water glass, hoping that would convey she wanted something cold (an ice cube) in her glass. The waiter eventually brought her a few ice cubes, but the interaction was comical. Lynn also learned that ice was not commonly added to beverages in Italy and she grew to enjoy beverages as they were served.

Another big adjustment for Lynn in Italy was how affectionate Italians were in public. She was not used to seeing that kind of intimacy in markets, on sidewalks, and in train stations. She noticed people holding hands, embracing, and lovingly stroking or touching each other. Welcomes seemed to include kissing and prolonged hugging. In fact, everywhere she went people seemed to crowd her.

(continued)

(continued)

They stood so close! She remembered her first train ride. She had entered the train and chosen a seat with empty seats on both sides of her. As the train stopped and more people entered those two empty seats quickly filled with others. At one stop, someone even squeezed in between her and the person in the seat next to her. No one else seemed to find it problematic, so she shrugged it off as she realized that she was used to more personal space than was common in Italy. As she spent more time in Italy she noticed that tables were closer to each other in cafes and restaurants, and that as Italians gathered in parks and other common gathering spots, they often sat and stood very close to one another. She grew to enjoy the closeness and to feel the warmth conveyed through that type of close proximity with others.

Now Lynn was in Japan for the second five-week segment of her study abroad experience. She had arrived in Tokyo the day before and was greeted at the airport by others in her group who spoke English. She instantly felt at ease. Today was the morning of her second day in Japan and she set out to find a park she heard was particularly beautiful. She had a train map and knew which stop she would exit to reach the park. As she boarded her first train, she noticed that the train was relatively empty. She also noticed a woman who was older than she but looked friendly so she sat in the seat next to her. She instantly felt the woman stiffen and the few others in the train car seemed to become somehow uncomfortable. As the train stopped at the next station, Lynn noticed the people who boarded glanced at her with an odd look before taking their seats at a more remote location within

FIGURE 6.1 |

the train car. The woman Lynn sat next to did not relax her posture, nor did she look at Lynn with a nod or smile. These were all gestures Lynn had become used to experiencing as she rode trains around Italy. She had also learned to sit next to people that she would be more comfortable pressed up against as more passengers crowded onto the trains. However, the woman she sat next to on this train in Japan sat very still and never acknowledged her presence. After three stops, the woman very stiffly stood and departed the train without a glance.

What Lynn experienced on her first train ride in Japan was how communication codes for proximity differed from Japan to Italy. Her experiences in Italy taught her unspoken codes of communication that helped her navigate a new country and make sense of others' behavior. Although Lynn was unaccustomed to the closeness with which Italians communicated when she first arrived in Italy, she became more comfortable and grew to enjoy the closeness. Lynn quickly realized during her first train experience in Japan that proximity communicated different meaning in Japan. Lynn would eventually learn new communication codes for her study abroad experience in this new location.

Use of space and touch are forms of nonverbal communication. Gestures that help to accent our spoken language are another form of nonverbal communication. As you will learn in this chapter, nonverbal communication is closely tied to culture. There are many forms of cultural nonverbal communication that are mostly governed by informal norms or unwritten rules. The key is flexibility, appreciation, and realization that violations of nonverbal codes and norms are readily recognized.

Lynn's experiences traveling illustrate one reason why it is so difficult for anyone socialized in one culture to be more like those of another culture. Not only do we have different ways of verbally expressing ourselves, we also have many unconscious nonverbal behaviors that carry different meanings in different communities. In Chapter 5 we referred to work by Gumperz on the difficulties that Asians had with job interviews in England. Although many of these difficulties were, as noted, based on different verbal communication styles, different nonverbal conventions (such as voice intonations, turn-taking norms, and eye contact) further complicated the situation. Nonverbal communication is an additional resource in our search to find out why the messages we intend to convey often end up conveying something quite unexpected.

ROLES OF NONVERBAL COMMUNICATION

Nonverbal communication is a very broad concept. This is not too surprising given that its very name stresses more what it is *not* than what it is. Thus, everything around us that influences communication or conveys some sort of message to us but is not the actual words of our language is nonverbal. It doesn't take long to realize that this covers a lot of material. Although we will not dedicate an entire section to this issue, it is important to remember that nonverbal as well as verbal communication is inescapably connected to the context in which it occurs. For example, the meanings of a wink while flirting, sharing a secret, standing in front of a mirror, or being interrogated by the police are all quite different and have as much or more to do with the context of the situation as with the actual act of winking. Thus, as you read about various aspects of nonverbal communication, never lose sight of the importance of context in actual interaction.

To help us become familiar with this broad topic area, we will organize our discussion around three major types of nonverbal communication—kinesics, proxemics, and paralanguage–as well as considering a few other miscellaneous types of nonverbal communication. Before proceeding with a discussion of each of these areas, however, we think it is useful to review six roles nonverbal communication have *in relation to verbal communication*. These roles are consistently discussed by those who have spent their lives studying nonverbal communication.[1] The six roles are as follows:

Repetition

Nonverbal communication often reinforces what is also being conveyed in the verbal code. Patricia may say that she wants to remember two major points and hold up two fingers, thus repeating and reinforcing her verbal message. The sports referee who both calls out and signals the type of foul that has just been committed is another example. By repeating the verbal message nonverbally there is a better chance that the message will be clear to the audience.

Contradiction

Although nonverbal messages often repeat and thus support our verbal messages, they may also contradict them. Kris may say the words "I am happy," but the tone of her voice and the look on her face may contradict that message. It is often claimed that when nonverbal messages contradict verbal ones, the nonverbal messages have more credibility and power. This is because the nonverbal messages seem harder to manipulate consciously.

Substitution

Certain types of messages and forms of information require verbal communication to get the meaning across, but many do not. A simple gesture may convey the message that someone did a good or a lousy job. A touch may convey sympathy. These nonverbal ways of expression do not require any verbal communication to get their meaning across and in that sense can be viewed as substituting for a verbal message.

Accentuation

Sometimes nonverbal cues do much more than just repeat a verbal message. They emphasize it and bring increased meaning to what has been said. If a teacher uses the words, "Please don't talk in class," you get a certain understanding, but if the teacher slams a group of books down as she yells those words staring right at you from only a foot away, you get a different message, an accented message.

Complementary

Nonverbal messages also complement and in part modify our verbal messages. For example, a hushed voice as you tell someone you love them; the stern facial expression as you express your anger; the shoulder pads and helmet you wear as you talk about being part of a football team. This complementary redundancy helps us to communicate effectively.

Regulation

Nonverbal communication also helps us to regulate the flow of verbal communication. Brad may indicate who is to speak next simply by changing who he is looking at. A nod of the head may encourage someone to continue or stop what they are doing. In this way nonverbal communication shapes and changes the flow of a conversation.

Although we have separated verbal and nonverbal communication for the purposes of discussion and analysis, most of our communication inherently involves both, and we need to remember how intimately these two types of communication are related. Looking at verbal and nonverbal communication individually may help us understand the source of certain intercultural difficulties, but in the long run we will understand intercultural communication better when we consider both and their relationship to each other. Remembering that the role nonverbal communication plays can best be understood in relation to verbal communication and that all verbal communication (that we are aware of) is accompanied by some form of nonverbal communication is critical to a full understanding of what is going on in any interaction. Thus, nonverbal communication is a critical and consistent part of all intercultural communication.

FORMS OF NONVERBAL COMMUNICATION

Kinesics

Kinesics refers to the study of body movements, such as facial expressions and gestures, as a means of communication. These sorts of nonverbal behaviors tend to be learned at an early age and operate at an unconscious level, making it very difficult to always be aware of what we are doing. However, we notice differences in others and make attributions about them based on these differences. We will review some factors related to facial expressions first and then move to a discussion of body gestures.

Facial Expressions

One very important part of facial expressions is the eyes. In Korea they have a term, *nunch'i*, that means to communicate with the eyes and refers to a type of intuitive communication that occurs without verbal communication.[2] Eye contact has been the source of many cultural misunderstandings. If children are listening to a parent or an adult, such as a teacher, should they look at the person directly or should they cast their eyes down to show respect? Many white communities within the United States and Europe and certain Arab cultures expect the child or subordinate to look at the person in a superior position when he or she is talking, yet for many Latino, Native American, Mexican, African, and Asian cultures, to look directly at the superior would be a sign of defiance and lack of respect.

Smiling is common around the world and may seem like a fairly simple facial expression, but the situation in which it occurs can be a source of great misunderstanding, as the following two experiences demonstrate. The first is related by a Chinese woman.

After living in the United States for more than a year I am still puzzled by the fact that Americans can treat things so lightly. For example, after hearing my unpleasant experience, Americans might say, "That is too bad," with a smile on their face. I felt offended when I first saw the smile. I thought to myself, "How come this person is not sympathizing with me at all? He or she can laugh at my misfortune!" What puzzled me more was that Americans talk about their own miserable experiences in a light way as well. One American woman casually told me about a vacation saying, "After my dad passed away, my mother and I needed a break. He had been sick for years," and she smiled. I was shocked by her way of expressing relief. I decided Americans are very selfish and heartless because they could not have a serious face when they should be expressing sympathy or sorrow.[3]

The following took place in a doctor's office in the United States.

The elderly Vietnamese lady sat in the laboratory waiting to have her blood drawn. She had just been told she might have an aortic aneurysm. She would need a series of tests to rule out this condition.

As she sat there, her smile grew broader.

The [American] lab technician turned to the health provider, and said, "She always smiles when I draw her blood. I think she trusts me."[4]

Both of these examples illustrate how a smile can be misunderstood. It is likely the Americans in the first example are trying to be encouraging and not let their own problems weigh down someone else. The Vietnamese woman's smile in the second example is a smile of stoic self-protection rather than an indication of trust or liking. These examples also remind us of something else. Just because the women in the two examples are both from *Asian* cultures does not mean that they share the same nonverbal types of reactions. In some Asian cultures a smile may indicate embarrassment or nervousness, but in others it may just be seen as a lack of seriousness, and in all cases it is important to consider the situation.

In spite of the many cultural differences that exist in nonverbal communication and facial expressions, one of the most interesting and well-supported findings concerning nonverbal communication has to do with similarities. Paul Ekman and associates have conducted research on the facial expression of emotions for over 30 years and, based on that research, there appear to be six basic emotions—sadness, happiness, anger, surprise, disgust, and fear—that are visually expressed in universal ways.[5] Two other emotions, interest and shame, have also received some support in terms of the universality of their expression.[6] This support has been generated in such diverse countries as Germany, Greece, Japan, Scotland, Sumatra, China, Italy, Turkey, Brazil, Argentina, the United States, and more. There is also evidence that not only can people recognize these various emotions around the world, but there is agreement about the level of emotional intensity expressed. Go to Figure 6.2 and examine the photographs. Can you identify which of the six emotions noted above as having universal facial expressions the person is trying to convey? The answers are at the end of the chapter.

Try to match which of the following six emotions (disgust, fear, surprise, anger, happiness, and sadness) is being conveyed in the following facial expressions. See the end of the chapter for answers. How much impact would it make in your ability to interpret the emotional expression if you knew these people personally or knew the context?

FIGURE 6.2 | Emotion recognition test

One interesting follow-up study to the early work done on the universality of facial expressions found that situational factors make a big difference in the emotions that are perceived.[7] Researchers found that when people were simply shown pictures of the various emotions and asked to identify them, there was a high degree of agreement on which emotion was which. This supports the other claims of universality. However, when the pictures were accompanied by descriptions of the situation the people were in, differences in interpretation arose. It appears that, although certain expressions in isolation have similar meanings around the world, culture makes a difference when situational factors are considered. Depending on who is present, where people are, the issues involved, and other situational factors, members of different cultures may suppress or modify the expression of certain emotions. In addition, the situation affects what emotions are even seen as reasonable to feel at a given time.

Reflection Question: How universal do you think emotions are?

Body Movements

Aside from facial expressions, kinesics refers to a wide variety of body movements and gestures. Trying to keep all of these differences in mind can prove challenging. One child development specialist from the United States, whom we will call Sue, recently found that out while visiting in Thailand.

Sue decided, impromptu, to go visit a private preschool she had noticed while staying in Had Yai. So, without an appointment (not really a good idea), she stopped in and in broken Thai mixed with English explained her desire to tour the school. The woman in the office graciously agreed to show her around. Sue was aware that rank and relative position are important in Thailand and so when she met a monk or someone older than herself she tried to be especially respectful. She was also aware that one way to show this respect was through a traditional greeting in Thailand known as "wai." The hands are pressed together as if in prayer, and the head is bowed. The higher the hands and the lower the bow, the more respectful is the greeting. As Sue was leaving she said the customary, "Sawadii-ka!" and simultaneously waied to the teachers and to the director. As she turned to leave, she looked over at a group of children who were around four or five years old and in unison they chorused "Goodbye!" Completely delighted, she spontaneously waied with a deep bow. The children's mouths fell open and the teachers exchanged disapproving glances. Everyone seemed in a state of shock and a feeling of tension had filled the room. Sue, unsure how to handle the situation, immediately left.

Sue knew how to *wai* and she knew that bowing was generally important in the Thai culture, but, as is so easy to do in a new environment, she forgot to consider the context. When one bows and how low one bows all depend upon the relational context. Relational hierarchy is very important in Thailand. Sue's deferential actions may have been appropriate in certain settings, but given her status of elder visitor such actions directed toward the children were extremely confusing and uncomfortable for the students and teachers alike.

There are hundreds of differences in kinesics across cultural communities and it is not practical to try to review these here. Instead, to help you get a feel for some of these differences, we ask you to take the following 10-question quiz.[8] It provides a sampling of the sorts of differences in kinesics to be found across cultures and will give you an idea of how aware and knowledgeable you are of these differences.

For questions 1 and 2 match the country with the meaning typically associated with the gesture.

1   The thumb and forefinger are held together in a circle while the rest of the fingers are outstretched.

   A   Spain   ___Zero
   B   Japan   ___Money
   C   United States ___Vulgar insult
   D   France   ___ Okay

2   Known as the *fig*, the fist is held up with the thumb stuck in between and through the forefinger and middle finger.

   A   Ukraine   ___Nothing, you will get nothing
   B   Brazil   ___Obscene expression
   C   Guatemala   ___Good luck
   D   Malta   ___Got your nose

3   You are at the theater in Denmark and have to squeeze by people who are already seated. To avoid insult you should enter the row facing the people so that your back is to the stage rather than to those you are crossing in front of.

   True or False

4   In which of these countries would it be rude to touch someone's head, such as to pat the head of a child (more than one may apply)?

   A   India
   B   Thailand

C   Germany

D   Uruguay

5   In Russia the thumbs-up sign used in the U.S. would mean:

A   You are crazy

B   Approval

C   I don't know

D   Obscene insult

6   In which country or countries would I beckon someone to come here by turning my palm down and waving my fingers back and forth?

A   Peru

B   Portugal

C   Philippines

D   Japan

7   Which of the following would <u>not</u> be an insult in Egypt (you may choose more than one)?

A   Handing a person a drink with your right hand

B   Sitting so that the sole of your shoe is shown to the other person

C   The thumbs-up gesture

D   Pointing with the forefinger toward another person

8   In England raising the forefinger and the middle finger in the shape of a "V" always means victory and is seen as a positive gesture.

True or False

9   In Norway using a lot of gestures is seen as a sign of immaturity and, when possible, people should keep their hands in their pockets while talking.

True or False

10 Wagging the head from side to side to indicate "no" is true for which of these countries?

A   Greece

B   Turkey

C   Japan

As with the table of faces, the answers to this quiz are found at the end of the chapter. We encourage you to check how you did. If you got eight or more correct, you are an intercultural whiz. Most people are familiar with only a few of the many differences in gesture and meaning. Our quiz focuses on general national differences, but if we started to look at differences by region, occupations, religious or social groups, and so on, many more differences could be noted.

It is virtually impossible to memorize all the differences, especially because over time the meanings change. Instead of trying to memorize all kinesic differences around the world, we suggest that you get books that deal with these differences or talk with people who are familiar with them and try to learn some of the important differences between your own culture and the particular culture of the community with whom you will be interacting. Knowing how to get out of a crowded row of people in a theater in Denmark probably will not be much help if you are going on a business trip to Mexico.

Still, even when a person is aware of a relevant difference, it can be very hard to remember to put this knowledge into practice, because many of our gestures are done quickly and without conscious thought. In the earlier example, Sue knew what was culturally appropriate, but forgot to put it into practice because of her feeling at a given moment. However, when you are able to recognize what you did wrong you are in a much better position to explain the misunderstanding to those around you and move forward in a positive way with the interaction in which you are involved. In general, people are willing to forgive (even if they don't appreciate) intercultural mistakes when they understand why they happened.

Five Functions

Our kinesic behaviors are typically seen as fulfilling five major functions.[9] Each of these functions are briefly noted here:

Emblems

Emblems are gestures that convey a precise verbal meaning that is associated with them. In this way emblems may substitute for what would otherwise be said verbally, such as waving goodbye. In Italy we may express our disregard for another simply by flicking our fingers out forward from under our chins. In the United States the thumbs-up sign and the circling of the forefinger and thumb in the okay sign are quite common emblems. Of course, as the quiz above indicates, such emblems are not universal. Although many emblems involve the hands, not all do. Consider a wrinkled nose to indicate that you don't like something.

Illustrators

Illustrators are intentional gestures that are meant to help clarify or support a verbal point or message, such as pointing to an object that is being discussed.

A gesture that in some instances functions as an emblem substituting for the verbal message may at other times function as an illustrator supporting the verbal message. Although some cultural communities, such as France and Italy, have become quite famous for their extensive use of illustrators, these nonverbal cues can be found throughout the world, and their use can help clarify verbal messages.

Affect Displays

Affect displays are generally linked to people's facial expressions and serve to express emotion. Often these cues appear to be more spontaneous than thought out or consciously intended as emblems or illustrators. Thus, a person may subtly, yet visually, express disappointment even while stating how happy she or he is. Generally, affect displays that contradict the verbal message are viewed as more truly reflecting a person's feelings. Thus, some people work very hard in international negotiations to eliminate or carefully control any affect displays.

Regulators

Regulators are those nonverbal cues that help to coordinate turn-taking and other interactional tasks. These tend to happen quickly and routinely, without much conscious thought. They may be found in the quick movement of the eyes or eyebrows, in a nod of the head, or through a change in how one's body is posed (leaning backward or forward). Scollon and Scollon demonstrate how generally unconscious differences in these regulators often lead Anglo-Canadians to dominate conversations with Athabaskan Native Americans with whom they interact, even when they don't want to.[10] For example, the Anglos have a shorter pause time between turns, leading them to jump into a conversation before the Athabaskans expect them to or to not give the Athabaskans time to respond before moving on in the conversation.

Adaptors

Adaptors are assumed to be largely involuntary actions that provide a valuable source of information about what a person is really feeling. Adaptors include things like a quick flick of the hand to straighten one's hair, scratching oneself, or dabbing at a tear. These types of nonverbal actions are thought to help one adjust to a situation, rather than to communicate a message purposefully. Police have been known to note that when lying, persons will often play with an object in their hand.[11] How reliable interpretations based on these types of nonverbal cues are is open to debate.

Proxemics

It was hard for Sam to concentrate on what Martín was saying. Martín was visiting from Chile and English was not his native language, but that was not the problem. Sam was all too aware of Martín's hand resting on his arm. He tried to ignore it, but he felt like people passing by were staring at them. He didn't want people getting the wrong impression. They wouldn't know Martín was from Chile and, even if they did, it was one thing to give someone a friendly pat, but quite another to just stand there holding the other guy's arm, occasionally rubbing it. It just wasn't natural. He had tried to disengage from Martín through some purposeful gestures and stepping back slightly, but Martín persisted and Sam always ended up with Martín's hand on him again. Sam had been asked by his supervisor to help with transportation for Martín during his stay in the United States and he didn't want to offend Martín.

Now what was that? Martín had just asked a question and he hadn't really been listening. He pretended not to have heard right and asked that Martín repeat the question. Martín apologized for his poor English and started again. Sam knew he must look foolish. If only Martín would just mellow out on the touching thing; he wasn't that bad a guy.

Space

Proxemics is the study of our use of space, both in our interactions with others and with objects in our environment. As with other nonverbal aspects of our communication, our use of space is largely done without consciously thinking about it. Edward Hall, whose work on proxemics helped to bring the importance of studying intercultural communication to the attention of people throughout the world, identified four different spatial zones of interpersonal communication: Intimate, personal, social, and public.[12]

The intimate space (contact to 18 inches) is reserved for those who have a very close relationship, such as a parent and child or two lovers. If a situation forces people without such a relationship this close, they often make up for it by distancing themselves in other nonverbal ways, such as averting their gaze or minimizing any gestures. The personal space (1½–4 feet) is where most casual conversations between friends and acquaintances occur. The social space (4–12 feet) is used by strangers when possible or people in certain types of business interactions.

Public space (12–25 feet) is generally reserved for formal meetings or addresses, such as a politician talking to her constituents or a teacher lecturing to his class.

Hall's work and that of others has shown these distances to be culturally specific. In Saudi Arabia, for example, people generally tend to stand much closer than people in the United States. There is even a common derogatory saying that refers to the person who "withholds his breath from others." Although this is not an attitude you will find in most mouthwash commercials in the United States, in much of the Arab world it is desirable to stand close enough to the persons with whom you're interacting so as to smell their breath. At times Americans and Arabs may seem to be playing a game of chase while talking with each other. The American backs up every so often and the Arab soon closes back in. In Egypt this desire to be near others is also reflected in public places. When entering a nearly empty bus or theater an Egyptian will go sit next to the other person already there whether or not she or he wanted to converse with the other person. While this example references an Egyptian cultural practice, recall the example from the beginning of the chapter about the train in Japan. There are, of course, differences within the United States in terms of space as well. Harvey reported that over 90 percent of Navajos who move from home to attend a U.S. university experience space violation in terms of people standing too close.[13]

Touch

Although Sam's experience with Martín was complicated by their different ideas about spacing, a major problem for Sam was the actual touching. Touching is important in all human development[14] and it is the focus of the study referred to as *haptics*. It is important to keep in mind that factors related to who touches whom, when, where, and how are all connected to our cultural upbringing. Research has shown that touching in public places occurs much more frequently in countries such as Venezuela and Italy than it does in the United States.[15] In countries such as Japan and England touching in public is even less frequent than in the United States.

One situational factor in touching in virtually all cultures is that of gender. In Malaysia and many other communities men and women do not touch (hug, hold hands, or so forth) in public, except for perhaps a brief handshake. This is true even if they are married or are each other's significant other. However, same-sex touching is very common. Men and women may hug or link arms or hold hands as they walk with members of the same sex. Such touching is not a sign of any intimacy beyond simple friendship. Some years back, Egypt banned all Columbia Pictures in part because of a Columbia production that had many nonverbal inaccuracies in it, such as showing the Egyptian president publicly kissing his wife—a completely unacceptable act.[16]

Paying attention to the role of space and touching in intercultural interactions can illuminate many cultural misunderstandings. Being aware of these differences in the use of space will not eliminate all feelings of discomfort, but it can help us avoid making negative attributions about others based on those feelings of discomfort.

Reflection Question: How much space do you need as you interact with others? What types of situational factors make a difference in this answer? How do you defend your "own personal space" when it is threatened?

Paralanguage

Para references that which goes alongside of or in combination with something else. Thus, paralanguage deals with that which directly accompanies our verbal communication, such as rate, accent, pitch, laughter, volume, and turn-taking cues. We cannot speak without engaging in paralanguage as well. For example, all of us speak with an accent or a distinctive dialect.[17] Even those who speak the standard form of a language such as English have an accent. After all, "standard English" is not the same in the United States as it is in England or in Australia. The pronunciation guides found in dictionaries are only institutionalized accents. Our accents can cause communication problems in two ways. First, if we are unfamiliar with an accent, it is often hard for us to understand what is said. The extra work required to listen to someone with an unfamiliar accent may result in our giving up and not really paying attention or judging the person as deficient in some way. One frequent concern we have heard expressed by college students in the United States is in regards to the accents of international teaching assistants. The teaching assistants are typically very well qualified in terms of knowledge, but their accents can force students to have to work much harder at understanding what is being talked about. If the course is important or difficult for the student, he or she is likely to become very frustrated if the teacher is hard to understand. In turn, the teaching assistants are aware of their communication limitations and also become very frustrated. These types of situations often require considerable patience and perhaps making use of office hours to help clarify concepts that were unclear. The second problem arises because our accents often tell others about the community in which we were raised and are often associated with the stereotypes linked to that community for good or bad.

Kris remembers when she moved to North Carolina from New Mexico. She had difficulty navigating the strong southern accents at first, but didn't realize how she adapted until she had a friend visit her after she had lived in North Carolina for about eight months. Kris and her friend entered a store and shopped while chatting with the store owner. As they left the store, Kris's friend remarked, "I didn't understand a word he said!" Kris realized in that moment that she had become accustomed to the accent and was at ease with the communication patterns associated with a southern style of speaking.

Kris has another friend who was born in raised in North Carolina and moved to California. The recently transplanted friend had a blind date recently. He told Kris that the date went well until the end when the woman told him she had enjoyed the evening and was pleasantly surprised to find out he wasn't that dumb after all. When Kris's friend asked what she meant, the woman replied, "Well when you first started talking I figured you were a dumb country bumpkin." Although we will discuss these issues in more detail in a later chapter, the stereotypes we associate with certain accents often lead us to see only those things we expect to see and hear.

How we say something has a large impact on how others understand it. We have talked with Japanese students who thought a particular American was angry because of how loud and fast they were speaking, when actually the American was just positively excited about what he or she was speaking about. The other evening Brad was reminded of the impact of how we say things when he saw a television commercial he had seen in the past. It shows a group of young guys visiting over the phone, but the only word used is "dude." Each time the word is used it conveys a different emotion, such as surprise, disbelief, anger, liking, curiosity, and so forth. The verbal code may hold steady, but thanks to different intonations many different meanings were conveyed. Have you ever heard someone say one thing, but mean something quite different? How did you know this? We suspect paralinguistics had something to do with it.

In the United States, African Americans and whites often run into difficulty due to different nonverbal ways of communicating related to paralinguistic cues.[18] African Americans tend to be more dynamic, intense, and emotional in the way they express things. Differences in volume or pitch are neither inherently good nor bad, but they are often attributed as such by listeners whose own practices differ from what they are hearing. Many white Americans see African Americans as loud, pushy, and aggressive to the point of being out of control. Many African Americans see white people as too controlled, hypocritical, and lacking real feeling. Often these negative attributions are grounded in paralinguistic differences. Kochman argues that these differences are due in part to African Americans' emphasis on feelings and white Americans' emphasis on sensitivities. He relates the following experience of Joan McCarty to help illustrate his point.[19]

McCarty was attending a play. It was a comedy and she was enjoying it immensely and laughing heartily. Partway through the play a white woman turned to her and said, "You are really outrageous!" McCarty was hurt by the

(continued)

(continued)

remark and asked the woman what was wrong. The woman replied, "You are laughing so loud. I mean, come on! It's funny, but. . ." McCarty was amazed—it was a comedy, after all. In thinking about it she decided the woman wanted her to feel the laughter, but not express it.

The white woman wanted McCarty to be "thoughtful" of the sensitivities of those around her (including herself), whereas McCarty was more concerned with allowing herself and others to express their feelings freely. There is not a right or wrong here, just a difference in style or expression. We need to remember that often our frustrations have less to do with *what* is being said than with *how* it is being said. Of course, this is a good time to remember that these types of differences between white Americans and African Americans (or other large groups) are just tendencies and can differ by region and individual. For example, we have known many very expressive white Americans and many reserved and soft-spoken African Americans, yet we have also observed on occasion misunderstandings arise from just the differences discussed by Kochman.

Reflection Question: What, if any, public displays of emotion do you think are appropriate? When? With whom? How?

Turn-taking cues are another aspect of paralinguistic communication that can cause frustration. We have had more than one Native American student tell us how easy it is for them to be left out of small-group discussions with other groups of Americans because the turn-taking cues and timing are different from what they are used to. However, Americans can also find themselves overwhelmed by the speed of turn-taking. Wolfgang reports that even Americans who speak fluent Portuguese frequently get cut off in mid-sentence and interrupted.[20] In Portugal such fast-paced conversation is a sign of interest, and the conversations that move along at what may be seen as a normal pace in the United States are seen as cold and boring. This is similar to Carroll's finding regarding the value for active engagement in conversations generally expected by many French speakers that is often seen as "interruptions" rather than "contributions" by mainstream Americans.[21]

Paralanguage is always closely involved with language, but in certain tonal languages it is unrealistic to separate them because the intonations used are part of the language. Thai provides an excellent case example.[22] In Thai the same word may have very different meanings depending on context and upon whether the tone is high, low, rising, falling, or mid-level. For example, Mai mai mai maai mai (spoken with the proper tones) translates to "New wood won't burn will it?" Also, yung with a middle tone means "mosquito" whereas yung with a falling tone means "to bother." Thus, yung yung may mean "mosquitos are bothersome" or "mosquitos are bothering me." Finally, yaa (low tone) means "don't," yaa (middle tone) means "medicine," and yaa (falling tone) means "grass." Thus, yaa thaan (eat) yaa might mean "don't eat the grass" or "don't eat the medicine" depending upon your tone. Worse yet, if you really mix things up, it might mean "grass eat medicine"; or in translation to a Thai who hears it from a foreigner "Hi, I'm a dumb foreigner who can't speak Thai to save my life."

Silence

Before talking about some usages of silence across cultures, it is important to discuss what silence is. Defining silence is much harder than it might seem because there are so many forms of silence. Also, one cannot think about silence without simultaneously thinking about its counterpart, sound. We need one occurrence to define the other. For instance, when you think of silence, do images of the stillness and absence of sound you experience in the presence of nature—mountains, open sky, a sandy beach, or a descending sun—come to mind? Or, does silence mean the gaps of sound between words or musical notes, or the hush just before a concert begins? Does silence mean the suppression of spoken words during yoga, tai chi, qi gong, or meditation? Is the silence you are thinking about imposed by someone else or is it freely chosen? Or is it accompanied by other communication actions, such as listening? To further complicate the drafting of possible definitions, Patricia's son, Isaac, reminded her with good-humored boasting that he can communicate for hours in silence with his friends. It took her a while to figure out that by "silence," he meant sending text messages! Thus, taking into consideration the increasing complexities of defining silence, which now are enhanced by contemporary technology, *we define silence as the refraining from using verbal, oral, or sound systems in interaction.*

Recalling Grice's maxims from Chapter 5, the quantity of speech maxim indicates that there is a proper amount of talk for different circumstances. A person may be seen to talk too much or too little. In many communities in Sweden, Finland, and Denmark, knowing when to use silence is a treasured attribute. One should have a sense of quietness about oneself and too much talk is seen in a negative light. On the other hand, many people in the United States find quietness, or "shyness," something that needs to be overcome. The goal here is to make us conscious of the existence of variance across communities. Being aware of the diversity of meanings silence can imply is helpful in understanding moments when misinterpretations and misunderstandings can occur. By isolating such moments, we can take appropriate steps to foster more beneficial outcomes.

One way to examine intercultural similarities and differences about silence is through the widescreen lens of what commonly is referred to as Western cultural perspectives vs. non-Western (sometimes called Eastern) cultural perspectives. In Western cultural perspectives silence is often approached as "consumptive" or as negative, unproductive, and empty interactional spaces that should be filled with words. For example, many of our American students have told us that being in silence makes them feel awkward, nervous, uncomfortable, embarrassed, and self-conscious. Bruneau notes that "[i]n intercultural relations in many Asian countries, Americans become uncertain and feel awkward in a general atmosphere of silence with the uses of longer communicative silences" (p. 78).[23] In our own teaching experience, when students are asked to sit in silence, invariably within a couple of minutes someone starts laughing, fidgeting, looking around, finding the floor or ceiling a fascinating object to stare at, or breaking the silence with, "Can we talk now?" In contrast, non-Western approaches often treat silence as "generative," as positive, productive, creative, and fruitful interactional spaces wherein people make their lives meaningful.

Some time ago, Patricia was a guest at a summer social gathering at the California home of her friend, John. She explains:

The party was held in John's beautiful backyard, a space large enough to show-case a huge swimming pool, multiple barbecues, patio furniture, and lots of lush greenery. The pool area was bordered by tall hedges and rows of thickly padded lounge chairs. When I saw this part of the yard I could not resist the indulgence of sitting unobtrusively and alone on one of the lounge chairs to enjoy the scenery and quiet peace. I'd been in this mini paradise for about 15 minutes when John discovered me, and with a tone of irony said, "Well, Miss Communication! Come and communicate with the guests! Go talk!" Pointing me to the party-goers, I clearly understood that he thought I was acting inhospitably and that he meant for me to immediately join the group and engage in communication, which for him meant to talk. Feeling embarrassed and scolded, I quickly rose from my cushioned post and rushed to join the group, wondering what I would say to people I'd never seen before.

Social scenes as the one described above can be seen as fundamentally cultural moments. Based on his cultural framework, John was proceeding from his distinctive understanding of how social things should go at a garden party and what silence meant in this setting. For John, as a host, the particular type of social gathering activated a contextual frame with set expectations and rules about how one should act communicatively. What counted as a party, for him, was grounded on the belief that a party meant a social gathering wherein invited guests should interact by engaging each other in talk. Sitting alone on a lounge chair was outside of that symbolic frame. Apparently others shared in that knowledge of expected behaviors at a garden party as, to the best of Patricia's awareness, she was the only person in a group of some 40 people who was outside of the activity of group conversation.

From John's reaction, Patricia could infer various assumptions about what for him (and others) constituted appropriate communicative behavior at this particular social scene. The following informal rules of engagement appear to have been activated: Rule 1: Persons attending a party should gather with each other and not isolate themselves from other partygoers; Rule 2: Partygoers should communicate with one another; Rule 3: Communication means talking or conversing; Rule 4: A scholar of human communication should know that communication means talking (this rule was conveyed more by the tone of reprimand from the party host than by the content of the utterance); Rule 5: When a social rule is breached, the rule violator should be sanctioned. To Patricia, the sanctioning was performed by the use of the biting label, "Miss Communication." Clearly, the expectation in the social scene was that at garden parties guests should interact with one another via talking. This situation exemplifies how within the briefest, expected and unexpected, and most mundane human interactions, our everyday life is composed of real-time moments that are deeply cultural, poignantly felt, and sharply consequential. In recalling the social scene above, Patricia is also reminded of an American Indian woman who once described an interpersonal situation that was different from the one she experienced in John's backyard.

In this case, Myrna, a Salish woman, described interaction that was routine at the home of her grandparents when she was a young child. Myrna recalls that a longtime family friend would come to the house for a visit. The friend and the grandparents would sit in the living room in silence and at the end of three hours the guest would rise and announce that he was leaving. Of this experience Myrna says, "and that's the world I grew up in."[24] As Myrna explains, in her particular Salish world much of a visit to friends could and did occur in silence. This is not to say that interaction was absent, for indeed interaction occurred. It did not occur, however, through abundant talk, but rather through abundant silence. We cannot help but wonder how a gathering might have proceeded if Patricia's friend John and Myrna's grandparents and visitor had been guests at each other's homes.

The above illustrations point to different perspectives about silence and what people across communities see themselves doing in and through silence. As we have seen, in one worldview interaction is something that can and should occur via talking. In another worldview interaction is treated as something that can and should happen in silence. Although much attention has been given to how humans artfully deploy spoken words to create an array of worldviews, silence merits at least equal consideration. In fact, it is precisely the sharp contrasts for enacting and interpreting silence that render this aspect of human interaction a uniquely rich site for understanding intercultural similarities and differences.

Silence and Socio-Cultural Identities

One of the many social outcomes people can achieve within silence is the creation of identities. Identity here is seen as produced within particular socio-cultural contexts. For example, Patricia sees herself as a shy, sometimes funny, optimistic, and hardworking and committed single mother who is a university professor. However, how she sees herself is a composite of her personal attributes plus many cultural influences, such as her native Mexican upbringing, *familismo* or notions about the role of family in everyday life, Mexican Spanish as her language of origin, Catholic traditions, what she was taught about when to speak and when to be silent, how to behave as girl who was *bien educada* [well mannered].

Various scholars have produced empirical work on the topic of silence in the everyday lives of American Indian groups. Working with American Indian college students, Covarrubias and Windchief explained how students in a Pacific Northwest university put silence into action to achieve three powerful outcomes in the service of their communities. These outcomes included using silence to particularize, perpetuate, and protect culture. Specifically, students said they used silence to particularize their cultures by contrasting their communication patterns to non-Indian groups, particularly dominant U.S. white society. Study participants explained that silence, for example, served as a means for expressing respect for others' turns for speaking. They added that these moments of silence often are misinterpreted by "white people" as an unwillingness to participate in discussion. However, for the Native interlocutors, silence reinforced their social identity. As Connie, a Yaqui participant put it, "It's being true to myself and who I am."[25]

The college students also explained how they used silence purposefully to perpetuate or extend the life of their cultures across generations. By replicating the practice of silence the American Indians could and did contribute to helping their culture last, endure, and survive. Salena, a Crow woman, explicated that she valued the silent practices she learned from her father as she was growing up, adding that she now models those preferred practices for her own children. Students also said that they used silence to protect their respective Native cultures from outside encroachment. In other words, they purposefully maintained reticence about cultural knowledge to protect collective ownership of that sacred and intellectual wisdom. By not talking about such matters, specifically to "the Whiteman" or "white people" as they put it, they were able to prevent unauthorized outsiders from inappropriately tampering with various forms of their traditional ways of life. By enacting silence they could secure culturally informed spiritual ceremonies, uses of medical plants, and indigenous innovations. Students said that they and other members of their communities could preserve their sacred cultural ways simply by exercising silence about them.

Cultural differences in terms of silence can also be reflected within a family. See if you have observed something similar to the experience shared by Sarah, one of our students.

Terminal illness in any culture is a difficult experience. When my father was diagnosed with cancer over ten years ago, I found myself in a constant state of negotiating silences. My paternal side of the family responded to the illness through silence: they never discussed the diagnosis, the illness, or the chemotherapy. To them, being surrounded by silence allowed the "normal" state of things to continue. When I was with this part of my family I found myself adhering to their unspoken code—ignore it, do not discuss it, and it will cease to exist. Because nobody ever talked about things, I assumed it was not okay to talk. So I copied their code for communicating by emulating it.

However, my maternal side of the family opted for a very different approach. In their way, the assumption was that if you weren't talking about a situation, then you weren't doing well. So, when I clammed up, they would probe until I opened up and talked about what I was thinking and feeling. We openly discussed the treatment, their emotions, and my father's wellbeing. Silence to them was not an option. As a girl of 11 years, I found myself caught between two family cultures, learning to negotiate silence in contradictory ways with members of my own family. When I was with my father's family, which includes several medical doctors, I did not talk about my dad's illness. When I was with my mother's family, we talked about it openly. My father's reaction was someplace in between—he discussed things factually, but not emotionally. He didn't discuss feelings, but only the facts.

My dad lived with the cancer for six years. It was not until his illness was officially labeled as "terminal" that his family acted like they accepted that he was sick. So, they condensed seven years of discussion into three months when he was finally diagnosed as terminal. They started to visit more and call more often. All of this was very confusing to me. However, I did learn to survive in two different cultures, two sets of very different expectations, and two opposing ways of communicating. I guess you could say that from a young age I learned to adapt and conform to my environment and to different ways for communicating in that environment. Nevertheless, all this was very confusing for me, to say the least. Deep down I preferred discussing my dad's illness. After my dad's

(continued)

(continued)

death we fell out of touch with that part of the family. His family stopped calling, they didn't visit anymore. They cut off all social support. Only one of my five uncles came to my high school graduation.

Exploring the ways of silence of other cultural groups, Carbaugh, Berry, and Nurmikari-Berry explored culturally grounded enactments of silence in the Finnish community. The authors write that for many Finns quietude or *hiljaisuus* comprises a "natural way of being."[26] This natural way of being refers to the idea of a person being undisturbed in one's thoughts; of being contemplative and being thoughtful. From a Finnish vantage point, being contemplative and attentive to one's thoughts is seen as positive because contemplativeness is viewed as favorable for a person's overall wellbeing. In this natural way of being, then, it is accepted and acceptable to maintain quietude during social interaction. It is not evaluated as an act of inhospitableness as it might be in another cultural context. From a Finnish worldview, one can be silent and still show consideration for others. In fact, quietude is a way of demonstrating consideration and respect for others even within the course of a group visit. A study participant who came from a culture where talking was privileged over silence summarized his experience with Finnish quietude within social scenes this way: "We have come to enjoy these moments immensely, alone in our thoughts for awhile, able to be calm and quiet with others, together, for several minutes on end."[27]

Silence and Social Relationships

As we humans are able to use speech as a means for creating, maintaining, and adjusting our interpersonal relationships, we also can use silence to achieve similar social ends. We can and do use silence to configure our relationships with one significant other or with diverse types of groups. Speaking generally and bearing in mind that all communication to some degree is dependent on its context, Japanese communities, among others, have been shown to value silence more positively than talk.[28] Some of the reasons for this include face-saving concerns and concerns for building relationships on the basis of interpersonal harmony.

In another example, members of Italian-American Mafia-type organizations are able to establish particular types of social relationships by honoring the code of silence or *omertà*. Through the shared precept of *omertà*, which prescribes withholding information from persons in official political or administrative authority, members can express solidarity, complicity, and loyalty to one another.

Religious groupings offer other examples. In some Christian milieux silence constitutes a core precept as well as a core practice of worship. A case in point is Quaker forms of worship. An example of the way silence serves as a powerful medium for activating Quaker principles comes from, Geneviève, Patricia's friend of more than 40 years. She describes how silence performed in the act of "centering down" offers an opportunity to demonstrate one's skill in communicating with God, as well as creating a link between parishioners or "the Meeting," not only with God, but also with each other:

As a life-long member of the Society of Friends, commonly known as Quakers, I have had several instances where I communicated with other members of the congregation without the use of words, through silence.

I remember what happened one Sunday morning during our "Communion after the manner of Friends" when parishioners or "the Meeting" engage in what we call "centering down," which in the context of Quaker worship is a time to quiet oneself and sit in silence until someone feels that God, through the Spirit of God, is prompting them to speak. That Sunday I sensed strongly that I should go to the piano, turn to a hymn, and sit silently without starting to play. Instantly, someone requested that I play what turned out to be the very song I had spontaneously turned to. The meeting sang as I played the song and when they finished, I quietly returned to my pew.

Another time, as my husband was seated at the back of the sanctuary and I was in the front I felt strongly that he should rise and speak on a certain subject, and he did precisely that. We had not previously discussed this subject, nor had I ever urged him to speak about it.

I feel that the Quaker practice of "centering down" allows me to clean my mind of extraneous thoughts and makes me more receptive to the feelings and needs of people around me. Silence allows the heart to speak. Silence connects us to God and to each other in deeper ways.

Silence and Conflict

Silence can also act as a way to express or sidestep conflict, frustration, and pain. Perhaps in your own life you have engaged in "the silent treatment" as means for creating or responding to antagonism. Or, maybe you have opted for silence rather than engaging in an argument with someone whose emotions seemed out of control. Perhaps someone exercised silence with you as a strategy for avoiding confrontation. Possibly there have been times in your life when your frustration was such that silence was the only way of calming yourself or someone else. We probably have all known moments when the pain we were experiencing was beyond words, and silence was our only comfort. Further, misinterpreting silence can lead to catastrophe. Saville-Troike recounts an incident involving Egyptian pilots who radioed Cypriot air traffic controllers of their intent to land. The Greek personnel responded with silence, intending to communicate refusal. The Egyptians, however, interpreted the silence as assent. The outcome was the tragic loss of life.[29]

In his landmark study of Western Apache silences, Basso (1970) explains six specific socially ambiguous situations wherein individuals refrain from speech. These include: (1) when meeting strangers, (2) during courtship, (3) when greeting those returning from a long absence, (4) while getting cussed out, (5) during mourning, and (6) during ceremonials.[30] What these different situations have in common is that each involves uncertainty and unpredictability in social situations where the status of participants is ambiguous and where role expectations may have shifted. Silence, then, is the preferred communication behavior until individuals have a better sense of the social situation. For instance, when meeting strangers, silence is opted for within group situations. Once the individuals have a clearer sense of the other person, then they proceed to speak. In courtship, Western Apache young people get to know each other better by getting a sense of each other, rather than by talking. When relatives that one has not seen for a long time return or when college students return home after a long absence, silence is preferred, again, until people get a sense for each other and listen to what has happened to the returning relative. When extreme anger has been expressed, silence is preferred by the person being vented at, for what would be the point of trying to speak to someone experiencing unrestrained emotions? Silence is also enacted during times of mourning to express respect to those who have lost a loved one. And silence is preferred during healing ceremonies, as healing requires quietude. In all of these situations we can see that silence serves as a communicative strategy for responding to one another with care and sensitivity until greater interpersonal certainty can be established. Via careful observation and mindful listening, possible interactional conflict, at least ideally, is averted. For example, consider this experience shared by Heidi, a professional mediator.

In mediation training we are taught to embrace silence. Initially it doesn't feel like a natural fit, as mediation is all about effective communication. However, over the last ten years I have grown to appreciate the power of silence as not only a calming tool, but also as another way to communicate without the need for the spoken word. The use of silence often allows the participants time to reflect, connect, and ultimately move forward toward resolution.

As we sat down in my small but comfortable conference room the lines were immediately drawn; the husband on my left with his attorney and the wife to my right with hers. I took my place at the head of my large oval mahogany conference table. Waters and snacks acted as a barrier in the middle. I could tell this was going to be a contentious one as the air in the room was electric and thick with anger and tension. It had taken me three months rather than my usual few weeks to get this particular couple and their respective attorneys to the table.

My gut instinct was on the mark; barely five minutes into the mediation things turned ugly, accusations and insults began to fly. . . largely fueled by the husband's attorney. As a professional mediator, I am trained to know that I set the tone of my mediations. A large part of my job is to "model" the behavior I would like my clients to emulate. Thus, as the situation escalated, I knew it was time to take back my mediation and regain control of the room. In doing so, I politely asked both attorneys if they would please step outside and sit it my waiting area, so I could work with the parties on my own. Fortunately they both agreed and left peacefully. The minute I closed the conference room door, "Jeff" and "Sue" quickly picked up where their attorneys left off. I sat quietly and let the couple vent. After another ten minutes or so, the couple suddenly realized my silence, the arguing faded and each looked at me quizzically. I continued to sit, hands folded in front of me on the table, saying nothing for another moment. I then looked up at each of them purposefully before I spoke. In a quiet but firm voice, I said, "You each have a choice." Jeff and Sue stared at me, listening.

"You can either continue to argue and ruin the mediation, which you should understand will be your only chance at having actual control and decision-making power over your own divorce (i.e., assets, debts, parenting plan). Or, you can go to trial, which, knowing your judge's massive case load and docket schedule, won't be till next August (it was now only September) and he will decide your case. And quite honestly you may or may not like what he decides. Or, should you choose to work together here today, we may actually be able wrap up your divorce, allowing you the opportunity to walk out of here and begin to move forward with your lives. It's your decision. . . just know that either way, both your attorneys and I get paid for today. I'll give you a few minutes to think about it."

So, we sat in silence, I looked down, feigning ambivalence. My clients looked down in contemplation. As the minutes passed I began to feel the tension in the air slowly dissipate, I finally looked up at my clients and could see the physical change in their body language reflecting the sense of calm which now enveloped the room. As I searched their faces, I noticed Jeff and Sue actually looking at each other (without anger), and I knew this was the moment. They were ready to move forward.

Using the power of silence gave my clients the time to reflect on what was important to them, their children, the home which needed to be sold, and even their dogs. In the silence, Jeff and Sue were able to embrace their anger and frustration and then let it go. Over the next three hours, we were able to work through what needed to get done (without the attorneys present) and complete their entire divorce. We were even able to work out a timeshare plan for the family dogs!

To help mitigate the many problems people must deal with due to intercultural communication differences, it is useful to focus on silence as a symbolic form within which we make sense of our world. The goal is not to erase our sociocultural differences but to understand how we as communities make sense of our world through what we share in common and what makes us distinctive. It is possible to bridge at least some of the differences that can cause rifts among us through the thoughtful use of silence.

Reflection Question: Are there times in your life when you communicate with others via unspoken means (perhaps with a sweetheart or someone you have known for a long time)?

OTHER FORMS OF NONVERBAL COMMUNICATION

There are many other types of nonverbal cues that communicate to us as we go about our daily lives. Some of these are found in the way we use the physical world in terms of our living environment, the clothes we wear, and the food we eat. Other aspects include things such as smell and our relationship with or use of time. All of these types of differences can create confusion or misimpressions for a person interacting with those of a different culture. We will briefly consider each of them.

Living Environment

The environment in which we live and the way we as people adjust to that environment is a large topic and we can only scratch the surface in our discussion here. How we build, organize, and decorate our homes, schools, places of worship, and businesses are all part of our culture. What do certain colors and designs represent? What artifacts created by humans do we feel are important and what are we comfortable around? We have a colleague who complained after a recent trip to China that she could hardly stand all the bare walls in the places she lived. Pictures and other decorations on walls just seemed common sense to her, and she had a hard time understanding why these things weren't important to the Chinese.

Another clear example of these differences can be found in the workplace. Although differences can exist based on occupation-related cultures, Germans and Americans tend to prefer and operate in workplaces that are divided into separate offices, allowing for personal privacy. Even here, however, there are differences in that Germans tend to keep their doors closed at all times unless there is a particular need to have them open, whereas Americans more often keep their doors open unless there is an increased need for privacy. In contrast, it is very common in Japan to find everyone in a single large room that is not divided into private offices. This allows for greater collaboration and a sense of togetherness. This, of course, does not mean that everyone is equal; as a general rule, the farther one is from the entrance, the higher one is in the hierarchy of the organization.

Clothes

The clothes we wear and the personal accessories we use, studied under *objectics or artifactics*, can also be points of misunderstanding. Different cultures have a tendency to prefer different colors and levels of brightness in clothing. Cultures also vary in terms of the amount and type of clothing that should be worn. In many Arab cultures the lack of clothing worn by Americans, especially women, in public places is obscene. In the United States it seems that any

FIGURE 6.3 | Our dress says so much about who we are

excuse to dress "down" is taken. There are dress-down Fridays at work, and in general casual dress is seen as desirable. In Spain there is a tendency to dress "up."[31] Fashion, appearance, and quality tailored clothing is important. In Spain it is said that only the teenagers and vacationers dress as relaxed as Americans do on a regular basis.[32]

Food

How taste is used to communicate is studied under *gustorics* and food certainly serves as means for communication as well as another major source of intercultural conflict and frustration. What we eat and how we prepare it is an essential part of who we are as a people. Seaweed may be a great source of protein, but most Americans don't have the taste for it that Japanese do. Other cultures are shocked that Americans eat cows or that they eat corn-on-the-cob, which in China is purely a food for swine. There is a memorable tale told of a rich American couple who were traveling abroad with their beloved pet poodle.[33] They took the poodle with them everywhere until one day disaster struck at a fancy restaurant in Indonesia. There, due to language differences, they struggled to make their orders clear. Thinking they had finally gotten through, they also indicated nonverbally that they would like something for their dog. The waiter nodded in understanding and picked up their poodle and took her away. Thinking that their beloved dog was just being taken to a separate place to be fed, they nodded and thanked the waiter. The next time they saw their poodle was when with pride the waiter lifted off the cover of their meal as they were about to be served. Their poodle was definitely well done. We don't know if this actually occurred, but it may have, as the following true but different experience illustrates.

Joe was happy. He had been teaching English in China for almost a year now and he was finally starting to really adjust to the many cultural differences he had found. His students seemed to enjoy his teaching as well. In fact, things were going so well that in honor of his birthday his students were going to take him out to eat at a better class of restaurant than he could typically afford. His students handled everything, including ordering the meal. As Joe ate, visited, and laughed with his students, he noticed how good his meal was. He was particularly enjoying the meat. He wasn't sure what it was, but it was much more tender and flavorful than what he had gotten used to in China. As the meal continued, his curiosity got the best of him and he asked one of his students what this delicious meat was. "Dog," came the reply. All of a sudden it didn't taste quite as good.

Although food differences are part of any intercultural travels, some locations have become renowned for the importance they place on food. It is likely that wherever you live certain foods will be seen as important. When Brad tells people that he lived in Wisconsin they often say, "Oh, beer and brats, eh?" Patricia lives in New Mexico and the well-known state question was, "Red or green?" which refers to which type of *chile* you want. Indeed, to fail to serve *chile* at a social gathering in New Mexico is often seen as unusual or the mark of an outsider. We also tend to think of other communities in terms of the food they eat. One of Brad's daughters had an Italian teacher who recounts her trips to Italy solely around what and where she ate. Indeed, one Italian traveler in extolling the virtues of traveling to France rather than England stated, "France: a land with a thousand sauces and only one religion; England: a land with a thousand versions of religion and only one sauce."[34] Brad remembers being amazed when he first went to England to find out that they really only had one kind of salad dressing available to buy at the store.

Oftentimes food differences are not quite as dramatic as the examples given above and may have more to do with the way something is cooked. For example, one of our graduate students from Texas recalls when she asked to make a meal for her fiancé's family who were from Cuba. She knew they loved beans because they ate them often and, although their beans were a bit too much for her with all the vinegar and such they used, she knew what she called a great "Mex-Tex" bean recipe that would really show them what beans could taste like. She spent all day cooking at her mother-in-law's place and, despite the worried looks that she got from various in-laws, she was sure her beans would be a big success. Alas, the beans were barely tasted by the whole family, and there was an awkwardness throughout the rest of the evening. She came to realize that, although her own family and her future husband's family both loved beans, they were very different foods after they had been prepared. Given the above examples, it is easy to understand why people returning from a trip abroad often are most excited about getting back to foods they know and love.

Smell

Closely related to food is the impact of smell on intercultural relations. The study of smells and how they are perceived is studied under *olfactics*. While living in England, Brad had a number of acquaintances from Pakistan and on more than one occasion was privileged to visit with them in their different homes. Without exception, as he entered he was always struck by the smell of these homes. Due to different cooking practices, the homes had a smell he was not used to. In fact, all homes, people, and places do have a smell, but some grow so familiar that they do not seem to have an odor at all. However, we have noticed that part of what makes visits back to our childhood home so enjoyable are the familiar smells and the good memories they invoke. We consciously notice them now when we visit because we are no longer surrounded by them. In Japan the sense of smell is very important. There is even a common game, usually played by young women, where they have to match smells correctly with different types of flowers.

Time

Last, but certainly not least, we come to uses and perceptions of time or *chrone-mics* as a nonverbal part of communication. Time can also connect to food, among other everyday activities. How long does one take to eat? When do we eat? In Spain people typically do not eat the evening meal until sometime between 9:00 and 11:00 p.m. Time, of course, affects all aspects of our lives. If Kris arrives to a business meeting 20 minutes late, that certainly communicates something; but what it communicates depends in great part on the culture to which she belongs. In Singapore or Norway it would be considered very offensive to be late, whereas in Bolivia or Saudi Arabia it would not be a major problem. Similar ideas about time are reflected in regards to social activities as well. It would almost be considered pushy to arrive less than an hour late to a social party in Mexico, but to be so late in Finland would be very insulting. It is always a good idea to find out early on what the other culture's attitude about time is.

There are various ways that scholars have tried to categorize the different approaches to time that are found across the world. One of those that we discussed in Chapter 2 is the difference between *polychronic* and *monochronic* orientations to time.[35] Cultures with a polychronic perspective see time in a circular way, allow for multiple things to be done at once, and emphasize the natural time involved in the completion of activities. Those who have a more monochronic perspective see time as linear, emphasize schedules and doing one thing at a time, and prioritize the clock in daily activities. These different ways of thinking about time create some of the most common and frustrating misunderstandings as people of all cultures travel on either business or pleasure.

Another way time may vary across cultures is whether the community has a past, present, or future orientation. Places as different as China and England both highly value tradition and learning from the past. Many Latin American communities are more focused on the present and living for the moment. The United States is generally more of a future-oriented community, emphasizing planning and looking forward to change. Of course, these orientations are broad tendencies and the past, present, and future are valued in varying degrees in all communities.

Time can also be related to seasonal differences. For example, certain stories are not told until wintertime in many Native American communities, Muslims fast between sunrise and sunset at the time of Ramadan, and summer is not a good time to conduct serious business in many Scandinavian countries.

Reflection Question: What are important *times* in your community?

INTERCULTURAL LISTENING AND NONVERBAL COMMUNICATION

Thomlison defines intercultural listening as the process of receiving, attending to, and assigning meanings that are influenced by cultural differences.[36] Certainly listening, just as context, is important in both verbal and nonverbal communication. We chose to cover this topic here because many listening problems occur because we focus entirely on *hearing* the words and forget that attending to nonverbal cues is just as important if we want to *listen* effectively in intercultural settings.

Although the way we listen can be a very personal thing, there are also general cultural tendencies in regards to listening that can create misunderstandings. One common one is the use of eye contact. Eye contact and other eye behaviors and movements comprise the study referred to as *oculesics*. In some cultures eye contact is seen as evidence that real listening is going on, whereas in others direct eye contact may be seen as a sign of disrespect and deviance, indicating that the person is not really listening. Asante and Davis argue that in the United States there are different listening response patterns between many African Americans and whites.[37] They maintain that whites focus more on the nonverbals, such as eye contact, and that African Americans tend to include more of an interactive verbal response that Smitherman refers to as *call* and *response*.[38] Asante and Davis go on to explain that these differences often lead members of each group to feel the other is not really listening or is rude.[39]

Copeland Griggs, Inc., have produced an intercultural training film that depicts various scenarios that have occurred in different parts of the world.[40] In one scenario a U.S. American on business in Mexico is shown waiting impatiently at a small restaurant. It is obvious that the person he is waiting for is quite late according to the clock. When the person finally arrives, he visits with others at the restaurant and generally shows himself to be little concerned with time, even though he does say that he is sorry he is late. In the video the

Mexican gives the U.S. American many cues indicating that he wants to get to know the person better before doing business, but the U.S. American is so busy and concerned with the business end and trying to convince the Mexican that he should buy his products that he does not notice what the Mexican appears to be saying. Typically when we show this video, those watching react very negatively toward the U.S. American because it seems so obvious that he is missing what is really being communicated. However, it is our experience that it is much easier to see these shortcomings in others or in videos than when we are actually involved in the situation. There is a good chance that the American has another appointment already set up and is in Mexico on a tight schedule. In his interest with the task at hand and the situational demands of the context it is quite natural for him to miss the many cues to which he needs to be attending to listen effectively.

Each of the different types of nonverbal messages we have discussed in this chapter, kinesics, proxemics, paralanguage, environment, dress, food, touch (haptics), smell (olfactics), eye behaviors (oculesics), and time (chronemics), all send messages that we often assume we understand without ever really thinking about them actively. We spend much of our communication time listening to others, but often this listening has more to do with hearing and sounds and making assumptions than with really understanding the messages conveyed. In our own culture these assumptions and lazy listening habits can often be enough to get us through most situations. However, in intercultural interactions this sort of listening often results in problems. It becomes more important to attend to the nonverbal communication around us and to attune ourselves physically to what is being communicated. We also need to be prepared to take a bit more time with interactions and avoid the urge to speed things up by planning our next message while the other person is still speaking because we assume we already know what is going to be said. It is our hope that the discussion of various types of nonverbal communication will increase your awareness of things to attend to when you want to listen actively to others from different cultures.

SUMMARY

In this chapter we have discussed another source of intercultural misunderstanding, even when all involved have goodwill and desire to interact in positive ways: nonverbal communication. Nonverbal communication was shown to play six major communicative roles that are closely related to our verbal communication. Although we separate verbal and nonverbal communication for the purposes of discussion and analysis, it is important to recognize that it is difficult in practice to separate these areas. In addition, as with verbal communication, the meanings associated with nonverbal communication are interdependent with the context in which they occur.

We discussed three main types of nonverbal communication, beginning with kinesics. Kinesics deals with the movement of the body and our facial expressions. These movements and expressions function as emblems, illustrators, affect displays, regulators, and adaptors in our interactions with others. Second, we reviewed work done with proxemics, or items related to space or—in the case of touch, lack of space. Third, different elements related to paralanguage, the nonverbal cues that go alongside of all verbal communication, were reviewed. Indeed, intonations that are usually classified as paralanguage may be seen as part of languages and have a profound impact on the meaning of an utterance.

We have addressed another important source for possible intercultural misunderstandings—silence. We have shown that contrasting cultural premises about silence shape people's cultures, their identities, and their relationships. We have seen how Western approaches tend to view silence as consumptive, or as an emptiness that should be filled. And, conversely, other cultural approaches treat silence as generative, productive, and as a natural way to be. We have shown how peoples of diverse societies use silence to express their personal, social, and communal identities. We have also demonstrated that people use silence to shape interpersonal relationships, and even to manifest and mitigate conflict.

Various other nonverbal aspects (such as use of our physical environment, clothes, food, smell, eye movement, and time) were also considered. As with the other nonverbal aspects, what is seen as good or appropriate is not universal and we need to be able to recognize the legitimacy of other ways of doing things. A key part of this recognition is taking the time to really listen. Listening itself may be manifest differently among different cultures, but we can likely all improve our abilities to listen to the entire communication process.

Nonverbal communication is an area ripe with potential misunderstanding. When the fruits of our intercultural interactions seem to be conflict and misunderstanding, it would do us well to carefully consider our often unconscious nonverbal behaviors. Often a little sensitivity and care in this area allows us to harvest intercultural interactions that are much more productive for everyone involved.

REFLECTION QUESTIONS

1   In the last two chapters, you have read about verbal and nonverbal misunderstandings. Based on your own observations, which of these do you think creates the most problems in intercultural settings? Why? How easy is it to separate these in actual practice?

2 Do you agree that certain emotions appear to be expressed facially in similar ways around the world? Are there other nonverbal aspects that seem universal to you?

3 What foods are important to your cultural community? Why do you think this is the case? What kinds of memories are associated with these foods? Does the way food is prepared make a difference in your community?

4 What differences in how people seem to listen have you noticed among different groups? How might these differences in listening styles create problems?

5 Think of adages or sayings that you grew up with in your childhood home. For example, did you hear, "Silence is golden, speech is silver," "A child should be seen and not heard," "Speak up!," "*Si tacuisses, philosophus manisses*" [If you had kept quiet, you would have remained a philosopher], or "*Hablando se entiende la gente*" [It is through speaking that people can understand one another]? How do you think those beliefs affect what you think about silence today and your interactions with others?

ACTIVITIES

1 Do your own facial expression test using the 12 pictures found in this book. Get people from three or four different cultures to see if they can tell what emotion the person in the picture was trying to convey. How much agreement was there?

2 Test certain nonverbal assumptions in your own culture. For example, to test space, go into an area of the library that is almost deserted. Go up and sit at a table where there is only one person and sit right next to that person and start studying. Or go into an eating area and sit down at a table with just one person there. The less crowded the area, the better. Observe the other person's reactions. After a little time of observation explain what you are doing and ask them about their initial reactions. Be careful in the types of things that you choose to test that you do not create a real threatening situation for yourself or others.

3 With a small group of fellow students research another culture and the way they handle certain situations (both verbally and nonverbally). Based on that information, put together a series of skits that illustrate cultural differences between various cultures. Perform these skits for your class and see if they can pick up on the areas of potential misunderstanding.

4 Find a partner and sit together knee to knee without breaking eye contact. Experience what it is like to sit in silence. Discuss with your partner and later the full class what the silence felt like and if you experienced an urge to speak.

ANSWERS TO FIGURE 6.2 FACIAL EXPRESSION TEST

A: Disgust

B: Fear

C: Happiness

D: Sadness

E: Surprise

F: Anger

G: Fear

H: Happiness

I: Sadness

J: Disgust

K: Anger

L: Surprise

ANSWERS TO INTERCULTURAL KINESIC CUES QUIZ

1 A. Spain=Vulgar insult; B. Japan=Money; C. United States=Okay; D. France=Zero.

2 A. Ukraine=Nothing, you will get nothing (a gesture often used toward children who are asking for too much); B. Brazil=Good luck; C. Guatemala=Obscene expression (the fig gesture often has negative sexual connotations, especially in many European countries); D. Malta=Got your nose (again a gesture often directed toward children).

3 True; it is rude to turn your back to those sitting in your row.

4 A. India and B. Thailand. Although certain individuals in the other countries may not be that fond of a head pat, it is not a serious social faux pas.

5 B. Approval, the same as in the United States. However, there are many places where this gesture is an extreme insult, such as in many Middle Eastern countries or in Australia where it means "up yours."

6 All of them. The United States is one of the few countries in which one beckons for others to come with the palm held upward. This sort of beckoning (palm up), especially when done with only one finger, is only used toward animals in many countries.

7 A. Handing the person a drink with the right hand. If this had been done with a "left" hand it would have been insulting, because the left hand is reserved for performing more unsanitary tasks.

8 False. It only means victory when the hand is positioned so that the palm is facing toward other people. If the "V" sign is given, but done with the back of the hand toward the other person, it is a crude and insulting gesture that means "up yours." We have seen U.S. American speakers listing off a series

of points that inadvertently give this gesture to their English audience as they talk about their second point. This usually results in a bit of discomfort and shaking of heads at "stupid Americans."

9 False. Although it is true that a lot of gesturing is associated with immaturity, it is rude to keep your hands in your pockets while talking.

10 C. Japan. In Greece "no" is indicated with a single quick nod upward and in Turkey it is indicated by raising the eyebrows, tilting the head back, and slightly squinting all in one brief movement. The side-to-side shake of the head means no in Japan, just as it does in the United States.

NOTES

1 P. Ekman, "Communication through Nonverbal Behavior: A Source of Information about an Interpersonal Relationship," in *Affect, Cognition, and Personality*, ed. S. Tompkins and C. Izard (New York: Springer, 1965); and M. L. Hickson III and D. W. Stacks, *Nonverbal Communication: Studies and Applications* (Dubuque, IA: Wm. C. Brown, 1985).

2 J. H. Robinson, "Communication in Korea: Playing Things by Eye," in *Intercultural Communication: A Reader*, 9th ed., ed. L. A. Samovar and R. E. Porter (Belmont, CA: Wadsworth Publishing, 2000), 74–81.

3 J. Yin, "Comparing Cultures: China and the United States" (paper, University of New Mexico, 1999), 32.

4 N. Katalanos, "When Yes Means No: Verbal and Nonverbal Communication of Southeast Asian Refugees in the New Mexico Health Care System" (master's thesis, University of New Mexico, 1994).

5 P. Ekman and W. V. Friesen, *Unmasking the Face* (Englewood Cliffs, NJ: Prentice-Hall, 1975); and P. Ekman and W. V. Friesen, "Universals and Cultural Differences in the Judgments of Facial Expressions of Emotion," *Journal of Personality and Social Psychology* 53 (1987): 712–17.

6 C. Izard, "Cross-Cultural Perspectives on Emotion and Emotion Communication," in *Handbook of Cross-Cultural Psychology*, Vol. 3, ed. H. Triandis and W. Lonner (Boston, MA: Allyn & Bacon, 1980), 185–222.

7 As reported in L. L. Barker, *Communication*, 5th ed. (Englewood Cliffs, NJ: Prentice-Hall, 1990).

8 Information for the quiz came from personal experience and various books; two of the better ones for this kind of information are: T. Morrison, W. A. Conaway, and G. A. Borden, *Kiss, Bow, or Shake Hands: How to Do Business in Sixty Countries* (Holbrook, MA: Bob Adams, 1994); and R. E. Axtell, *Gestures: The Do's and Taboos of Body Language around the World* (New York: John Wiley & Sons, 1991). Also see *Culturgrams*, a series of newsletters for over a hundred countries published by the David M. Kennedy Center for International Studies at Brigham Young University.

9 D. G. Leathers, *Successful Nonverbal Communication: Principles and Applications* (New York: Macmillan, 1986).

10 R. Scollon and S. B. Scollon, *Narrative, Literacy, and Face in Interethnic Communication* (Norwood, NJ: Ablex, 1981).

11 Leathers, *Nonverbal Communication*.

12 E. T. Hall, *The Hidden Dimension* (Garden City, NY: Anchor Books/Doubleday, 1966).

13 C. Harvey, "Nonverbal Behaviors: Differences in Cultures—Navajo and UNM Cultures" (paper, University of New Mexico, 1996).

14 J. K. Burgoon, D. B. Buller, and W. G. Woodall, *Nonverbal Communication: The Unspoken Dialogue*, 2nd ed. (New York: McGraw-Hill, 1996).

15 O. M. Watson, *Proxemic Behavior: A Cross-Cultural Study* (The Hague: Mouton, 1970).

16 D. A. Ricks, *Blunders in International Business* (Cambridge, MA: Blackwell, 1993).

17 We use the terms accent and dialect in similar ways here, but technically speaking dialect is a broader term that does not just refer to pronunciation styles, but includes word choice and grammar as well.

18 M. L. Hecht, M. J. Collier, and S. A. Ribeau, *African American Communication: Ethnic Identity and Cultural Interpretation* (Newbury Park, CA: Sage, 1993); and T. Kochman, "Force Fields in Black and White Communication," in *Cultural Communication and Intercultural Contact*, ed. D. Carbaugh (Hillsdale, NJ: Lawrence Erlbaum Associates, 1990), 193–217.

19 Kochman, "Force Fields," 195.

20 A. Wolfgang, *Everybody's Guide to People Watching* (Yarmouth, ME: Intercultural Press, 1995).

21 R. Carroll, *Cultural Misunderstandings: The French-American Experience* (Chicago: University of Chicago Press, 1990).

22 These examples of Thai language come from a colleague, Spencer Lee, who has lived and worked in Thailand for many years.

23 T. J. Bruneau, "How Americans Use Silence and Silences to Communicate," *China Media Research* 4 (2) (2008): 77–85.

24 P. Covarrubias, P., "(Un)biased in Western Theory: Generative Silence in American Indian Communication," *Communication Monographs* 74 (2) (2007): 265–71.

25 P. Covarrubias and S. Windchief, "Silences in Stewardship: Some American Indian College Students' Examples," *The Howard Journal of Communications* 20 (4) (2009): 333–352.

26 D. Carbaugh, M. Berry, and M. Nurmikari-Berry, "Coding Personhood through Cultural Terms and Practices: Silence and Quietude as a Finnish 'Natural Way of Being'," *Journal of Language and Social Psychology* 25 (3) (2006): 203–20.

27 Carbaugh, Berry, and Nurmikari-Berry, "Coding Personhood through Cultural Terms and Practices."

28 I. Nakane, "Silence and Politeness in Intercultural Communication in University Seminars," *Journal of Pragmatics* 38 (2006): 1811–35.

29 M. Saville-Troike, "The Place of Silence in an Integrated Theory of Communication," in *Perspectives in Silence*, ed. Deborah Tannen and Muriel Saville-Troike (Norwood, NJ: Ablex Publishing Corporation, 1985), 3–18.

30 K. Basso, "'To Give Up on Words': Silence in Western Apache Culture," *Southwestern Journal of Anthropology* 26 (1970): 213–30.

31 H. Wattley-Ames, *Spain Is Different*, 2nd ed. (Yarmouth, ME: Intercultural Press, 1999).

32 Wattley-Ames, *Spain Is Different*.

33 Found in D. A. Ricks, *Blunders in International Business* (Cambridge, MA: Blackwell Business, 1993).

34 V. Guy and J. Mattock, *The International Business Book* (Lincolnwood, IL: NTC Business Books, 1995).

35 E. T. Hall, *Beyond Culture* (Garden City, NY: Anchor Books/Doubleday, 1976).

36 D. Thomlison, "Intercultural Listening," in *Listening in Everyday Life*, ed. M. Purdy and D. Borisoff (Lanham, MD: University Press of American, 1997).

37 M. K. Asante and A. Davis, "Encounters in the Interracial Workplace," in *Handbook of International and Intercultural Communication*, ed. M. K. Asante and W. B. Gudykunst (Newbury Park, CA: Sage, 1989), 374–91.

38 G. Smitherman, *Black Talk: Words and Phrases from the Hood to the Amen Corner*, rev. ed. (Boston, MA: Houghton Mifflin, 2000).

39 Asante and Davis, *Handbook*.

40 L. Copeland (Producer), L. Griggs (Executive Producer), and I. Saraf (Director), *Going International: Managing the Overseas Assignment* (San Francisco, CA: Copeland Griggs Productions, 1983). Film.

Chapter 7

Why Do So Many People Get Treated Poorly?

Vanessa's brother had called that morning from California. After visiting about family, school, and her plans after graduation, he asked her if she had heard on the news about the cops beating some illegal aliens the other day.

"Yeah, it reminds me of those cops from the recent shooting."

"Those cops in California are so racist they just beat the snot out of anybody they don't like."

"Well, I guess you guys over there have plenty of wetbacks for them to beat," she said. Then, trying to lighten things up, she joked, "Lucky you didn't get mistaken for one, playing all that 'beanerball' like all the other wetbacks."

Her brother laughed softly. He didn't really like being associated with the term wetback and changed the topic.

"So how did it go at the used car place? Did you get a fair trade on your old car?"

"Well, the guy tried to Jew me down, but I held firm and I think it worked out okay."

"It doesn't surprise me, sis. Most women don't have a head for business, but you always were quite the Indian trader when we were young."

"Hey now, who wanted to be the lawyer of the family?" Vanessa laughed.

After a little more joking, the conversation ended and Vanessa turned to her computer. She usually went online around this time of day before she had to go to work. Today she was feeling quite excited about it. She had spent the last four days talking online with a guy named Adrian who she had learned was attending another university about two hours away. She had been in a chatroom when all of a sudden she had gotten an instant message from some guy named Adrian. She had hesitated at first, but she replied and they had

(continued)

(continued)

had a great visit. He had found her accidentally because he had just sent out a general message of "hi" to anyone logged in on a university account at her university. Since then, they had talked every day and things had gotten better every day. He was funny and talking with him seemed to make her whole day go better. She had been a bit worried about the contact and hadn't given out much information about herself, but she had been relieved when she had made some calls and found out he was a real student where he said he was. She hoped he wasn't just some dumb jock, though.

She was in luck—he was also online and soon they were visiting as usual. Later in the conversation she mentioned that she was Catholic and would be going to Mass that weekend. He wrote back and said his parents were devout Hindu, but he really wasn't into religion.

"Hindu?" she thought and asked a few more probing questions. It turned out that his parents were first-generation immigrants from India.

"India?" she had wondered aloud. "Isn't that somewhere over by Japan or was it Saudi Arabia?" This didn't sound so good. She continued to think about what she knew of people from India. "Hmmm, they don't eat cows, they are small in stature, they talk funny like that convenience store clerk on the 'Simpsons' and they're terribly sexist. After all, their women always have to be covered in robes and veils. Weird."

About then she noticed that he was asking about maybe getting together sometime to meet. A few moments ago that would have sounded exciting

FIGURE 7.1 |

and a bit romantic, but with an "Indian"? All of a sudden her interest just seeped away.

"No, I don't think that is a good idea," she said. "I don't believe in relationships that get started online." She felt a bit guilty, but she knew she wouldn't be having any more chats with Adrian.

Soon it was time for Vanessa to head out to work. She hopped in her car and headed to the mall where she worked in a clothing store. As she drove by the museum downtown she noticed what seemed like a hundred little Japanese guys streaming out of the door. She groaned silently.

"They are everywhere," she thought.

It reminded her of the trip she and two of her friends had saved for and finally took to Australia two summers ago. They were tight on money and had stayed in hostels. Unfortunately, so had countless groups of Japanese. They had tried to be nice about it at first, but the Japanese were just impossible. They were loud and pushy and always seemed to be up too early and noisy at night, and she had thought Japanese were supposed to be quiet and polite. She and her friends had not been able to get away from them. There was always another group everywhere they went.

Vanessa paused in her remembrances as she came to a stoplight and noticed an old homeless guy sitting over on the sidewalk. Carefully, so as not to look obvious, she reached over and locked her other car door. You just never knew with people like that.

Walking into the mall, she passed a group of guys wearing baggy jeans. She didn't look over at them. She knew their type and didn't want any problems. She'd had a friend back in high school that had gotten beaten up by guys like this.

"Jerks, I wish they'd get a real job instead of hanging around here, but I guess they've got all the money they want from selling coke to the little kids from their neighborhood. Why get a real job?"

Vanessa was relieved to get into work. She smiled and waved at John, one of her coworkers. After clocking in, she ran into Tiffany, her section manager. Vanessa forced herself to be nice. Tiffany was a real ditz, a typical blonde, and she hated having her as a supervisor. She still couldn't believe that Tiffany had gotten the promotion over her; she had been there as long as Tiffany and wasn't nearly as dense. But Tiffany just had to wiggle her little blonde head and Matt, the store's main manager, was at her beck and call.

"Men! They're all alike."

Her thoughts were disturbed by an announcement over the store intercom.

"Call on line four," the voice said.

She hated that. It was the store's new code meaning that someone black had entered the store and all the sales staff were to be particularly watchful for shoplifting. It had seemed so prejudiced to her when the policy had been

(continued)

(continued)

explained to her and she really wasn't that sort of person. But it did seem that they had a lot of problems with black people shoplifting and some of them just couldn't be trusted. She'd had this black woman in the other day claiming she'd bought something here and wanting a full refund, and when she had tried to explain that they didn't even carry that item in the store, the woman had started yelling about her rights and Vanessa being prejudiced. It had been so embarrassing. If these people didn't want a bad reputation, then they should act decently.

It reminded her of her last job as a waitress. All the waitresses had a code for when Native Americans came in. They were such awful tippers no one wanted to serve them. No wonder they didn't always get the best of service. Vanessa sighed. It was going to be another one of those days.

Because there are well over a dozen instances of stereotyping, ethnocentrism, or prejudice in this story about Vanessa it may seem unrealistic. However, these types of things and many more are going on in the world every single day. This opening story combines many different, but real, incidents and thoughts that students have told us about over the years. Sometimes students have heard so many lectures about the evils of prejudice that they tune out, yet stereotyping, ethnocentrism, and prejudice are still some of the major obstacles in intercultural relations, and it is important that we better understand how and why these creep into our daily lives. These are real challenges that can be found all around us. We have done some research in this area and these sorts of problems seem to be found everywhere there are groups of people. It is not just a problem for groups that have come to have a reputation for being prejudiced. Individuals from any background or group can develop prejudice toward other groups, even toward groups they believe are prejudiced toward them. It is so often a vicious circle of blame and justification.

Although the United States has had more than its share of problems with these challenges to getting along, they can be found throughout the world. Sometimes we are told that a particular country, such as Morocco, Switzerland, Japan, Panama, and others, doesn't really have prejudice like they do in the United States. Invariably we will later, through observation, reading, and especially talking with other people from that particular place, learn that, in fact, they do have such problems there and that those making the claims have either lived a very sheltered life or have become so used to the particular prejudices afflicting their part of the world that they fail to see them. Usually they do not belong to a group that is typically a target for prejudice in that community, so it may be easy for them to miss the problems. The groups targeted may be different, but these are worldwide problems.

We will discuss each of these particular challenges—stereotypes, ethnocentrism, and prejudice—in some detail. Hopefully, as you read this chapter, you will think about how these issues may be affecting your own life and not just focus on "others" who have the "real" problem with this and how much you wish they could read this chapter.

STEREOTYPES

Stereotypes are attributions that cover up individual differences and ascribe certain characteristics to an entire group of people. Some writers treat stereotyping as simply a less severe version of prejudice. As such, stereotypes are often seen as the forerunners of prejudice and, when our stereotypes become strong enough, they turn into prejudice. Although we recognize a certain logic in this thinking, we believe it confuses distinctions between stereotypes and prejudice in ways that lose some of the value that each concept has for helping us to understand and deal with the world in which we live. These distinctions will become clearer as we discuss prejudice and another related concept, ethnocentrism. However, we want to lay the foundation for this distinction by first considering the very roots of stereotyping: categorization and the human desire to understand and make sense of the world around us.

Categorization

When we categorize the world around us, what are we doing? We are putting things together that are perceived to match in some way and simultaneously separating those things from other concepts or objects in the world. A category highlights what two or more things have in common in contrast to other things that do not have this commonality. We categorize all the time. We know what cars, rocks, shovels, relatives, poisons, schools, blouses, and musical instruments are. These things are categories that highlight some point or points of similarity that makes the categories recognizable and useful in our efforts to interact with each other. There are many different levels of categorization; therefore, even though we know certain things are musical instruments, we can also recognize that within that category there are such things as wind instruments, percussion instruments, string instruments, and brass instruments. Within each one of these types of instrument categories are further divisions and categories. This sort of layered categorization can be found in virtually everything around us. Our world is a very complex environment, and categorization makes it possible for us to manage and, at least in part, understand it.

Categorization is the fundamental quality of conscious human thought.[1] We could not think as we now do without categorizing things. Knowledge would be impossible, as there would be no basis for carrying information from one experience to another experience. We can drive a new car without any difficulty because we categorize and know what a key, steering wheel, gas pedal, and so forth are. We don't have to learn it anew each time. Another example is zippers. We know how they work in general and don't have to rediscover how to use a zipper each time we encounter a new one. Examples of this kind are endless. Our language inherently assumes categories. We know what letters are and what are not letters. We know basically what words mean within a particular language and what they do not mean.

We have spent some time emphasizing the basic role of categories and categorization to our human existence, for without this process society could not exist as we now know it. Categories are crucial to all of humanity and that will not change.

Humans have demonstrated a great desire to learn about their world. We want to understand what is going on around us and we do this in part through the use of categories. The knowledge and categories that have been generated by different human communities may in some cases be very different, but every human community has generated knowledge of various types that they use to live every day of their lives.

Fundamental Attribution Error

Obviously, one of the things we as humans want to understand is other humans. So how do we do this? We categorize what they do based on some perceived similarity. Statements such as those that follow reflect this process:

> Women are good listeners.
> Men are often aggressive.
> Be careful around people who dress like that.
> Oh, I get why he was so polite. He's from Japan.
> Well, you shouldn't be surprised by that kind of behavior. She's a lawyer.

The minute we categorize people and attribute any behavior, belief, or feeling to that category, we have *stereotyped* them. We have put them together in a way that focuses on a similarity (real or imagined) and provides an explanation (accurate or inaccurate) for behavior. Simultaneously, we are for that moment masking or ignoring for all practical purposes the differences that exist between the humans placed in that category.

Stereotyping involves an extension of a form of reasoning that has been labeled the fundamental attribution error because it is so common around the world.[2] The fundamental attribution error may occur when either we or someone else has done something that needs to be explained. This form of reasoning is particularly strong when action is perceived as negative or strange. Specifically, if someone else does some questionable act, such as trip, yell in anger, or refuses to share what they have, we tend to attribute that action to that particular person's inner disposition or personality. He or she is seen as clumsy, hotheaded, or stingy. On the other hand, if we do the same thing, we tend to emphasize situational influences. We note that someone moved a skate to a place it shouldn't be so, of course, we tripped; we have had a bad day and our reaction of yelling in anger is really just an expression of frustration about all of those things that have been done to us throughout the day; or we know that we can't give part of what we have away right now because we are saving it for another, more important time. This does not mean that the opposite never occurs. Sometimes we are surprised by someone's actions and blame it on the situation, or at times we fail at something and in turn think of ourselves as losers; however, the general tendency among humans appears to be the process captured by the fundamental attribution error.

The connection between this thought process and stereotyping is made when the other person we are observing is seen as belonging to a different category from us. In this situation people not only feel that the questionable act is a stable part of that person's personality, but associate that type of action with the entire category to which that person is seen as belonging. If we hear a woman say something negative about another person at work, we may silently conclude, "Women are such gossipers, always looking to backstab someone else." If the person who had said the same thing was a man, he would "know" better than to make such an attribution because he is a man. So, instead, he would either take the situation into account or pick another category that he does not share with the other person as a way to explain that behavior, such that he is French, homosexual, or communist. We all belong to many categories, so there are always many from which to choose. In the example of the woman who made the negative comment about a coworker, we might as well have selected some other category, such as Mexican American or secretary, or whatever category of person came to mind in that situation. Which category comes to mind depends in part on the previous stereotypes we have developed. Stereotypes have been shown to have a great impact on what we perceive and what, through the process of avowal and altercasting, we are likely to encourage in others.[3] Using the example we started with in the previous paragraph, we may have the stereotypes that secretaries gossip, secretaries are women, and women gossip. If it turns out that the person who spoke about others was a woman and a secretary, we would have confirming proof in our own minds that our stereotype was true. Alas, noticing other women secretaries who did not do that would probably not change our stereotype; it may only make us think of those other women as exceptions to the rule. If it turned out that the woman who gossiped was a scientist and we don't typically think of scientists as gossipers, we would probably only connect her gender with the gossip. On the other hand, if the person who spoke that way turned out to be a male secretary, we may simply attribute the gossip to his secretary identity. In this way stereotypes tend to reinforce themselves in our minds by predisposing us to expect and look for certain things.

We don't learn all, or even necessarily most, of our stereotypes from personal experience, though. We also learn stereotypes from our family, friends, co-workers, and the mass media. Part of the indirect learning process of stereotypes is similar to what we just described because we tend to assume that the stereotypes we hear from others, particularly when we trust those others, are based on personal experiences, and they are then also given credence. Stereotypes that we learn through others are accepted before we have any personal "proof." However, given the power of stereotypes to attune our way of thinking, we can often find such so-called proof.

Five Points of Variance

Stereotypes vary along five major dimensions: *direction, intensity, specificity, consensus and accuracy.*[4]

Direction

Direction refers to whether the stereotype is positive or negative. Some stereotypes, such as those people are *lazy*, *rude*, and *dumb*, are obviously negative. Others stereotypes, such as those people are hardworking, polite, and smart, appear to be positive. However, when we focus on a rather narrow aspect of any one person, even positive-sounding stereotypes can become negative. Tan laments that the stereotype of Chinese as always very polite gives people the idea that they can't take a strong leadership role.[5] In the same way, stereotypes of African Americans as athletic may prevent some from seeing the intelligence and hard work that goes into athletic achievements. Or the idea that Japanese are very smart in mathematics may create problems for those who are not. Because stereotypes limit our vision of others, they are always potentially dangerous.

Intensity

Intensity alludes to how strongly the stereotype is held. Based on various experiences, some stereotypes are held very strongly. Perhaps we learned them when we were young and can think of a number of experiences that support our view of the other group. This often makes it hard to notice or remember the many times when the stereotype did not hold up. It also may result in our treating others such that we encourage them to respond in stereotypical ways. Remember Gong's experience with a colleague who was sure she always ate egg rolls for lunch. Her coworker's idea of what Chinese ate made her notice any time this was the case, but not really attend to the fact that it rarely happened. However, other stereotypes are only held loosely. Perhaps we don't have much exposure to the other group or we have seen enough to know that although some things are at times the case, they are often not the case as well. In this way we are aware of the stereotype, but we consciously work at remaining open to variations in each individual case and situation.

Specificity

Specificity relates to the nature of the stereotype. Does the stereotype concern very broad and vague images, such as the other group being rude, or does it focus on very specific behaviors, such as the Japanese always bow? Generally, more specific stereotypes are easier to deal with because exceptions are more easily noted and they can be considered in very concrete terms. Vague stereotypes, such as a group being rude, are difficult to deal with because what counts as rude can vary so much. Perhaps the volume of speech or the topic of a question is seen as rude in one group, but not in another, allowing one group to feel those other people are rude even when they have good will for that other group and the other group's behavior would be seen as appropriate within their own community.

Consensus

Consensus deals with how well accepted or well known certain stereotypes are within a community. Some stereotypes have become so well known that it only takes a very indirect reference to have them come to mind and virtually everyone you talk with has heard of them. In some cases, common stereotypes can become the basis for other stereotypes. For example, one woman who had been to Mexico to sell her handiwork at various craft fairs complained on her return to the U.S., "I guess they do make beautiful things, but I hate the way those Mexicans always Jew you down." In other cases stereotypes based on personal experience may really only be held by a particular individual or family group. Stereotypes that have wide consensus in a group may be easier to see exception in, but are often very hard to really get rid of even when they are obviously misleading and inaccurate.

Accuracy

Accuracy refers to how correct a stereotype is in describing the other group. One specific type of stereotype is called a sociotype, and from a statistical standpoint these are quite accurate. It may be discovered, for example, that a certain group has a particular average level of formal education or a certain average amount of income. Thus, someone may say that such and such a group is poor or wealthy and, in a group sense, this generalization is true. Also, because different cultural communities do share certain common practices and attitudes, other broad generalizations about the group as a whole may be fairly accurate. Of course, we realize that there are always exceptions and that even quite accurate stereotypes may mislead us in regards to a particular person. However, many stereotypes are not accurate even in a general statistical sense. In addition, very broad, abstract stereotypes, such as lazy, tight, rude, and dishonest, are particularly open to inaccuracies and misunderstanding of particular practices and different ways of interpreting the world.

Everyone stereotypes. We cannot help it. Cultural differences provide a fertile field for stereotypes because these differences call out for some explanation. This book and every book on intercultural communication or, for that matter, any book about people is full of stereotypes. Any idea that we are going to eliminate stereotyping is misdirected. We need categories to function in the world, and human categories unavoidably turn into stereotypes. What is important, then, is not eliminating stereotypes, but recognizing them for what they are and managing them in productive ways. This means working hard to make our stereotypes more accurate, keeping them open to being refined, and always allowing for individual differences. We hope that this book encourages that type of openness and accuracy. Periodically we have also tried to remind you that general statements made about a group will always have exceptions. This does not negate the value that understanding general cultural tendencies has, but it does warn against a sort of complacent acceptance and application of categories as we deal with others. Stereotypes are not inherently bad, but they are inherently dangerous and must be treated with conscious care.

If someone tells you that they don't stereotype people, it simply means they don't understand what a stereotype is or they are trying to cover up that they are stereotyping. Such a cover-up is likely due to the fact that stereotypes have come to be associated with negative images of the other group. Braaten reports on a multinational banking organization's internal survey that revealed many more negative stereotypes about members of other groups than positive ones even though management had thought the multiple cultural groups were getting along quite well.[6] We will give you just a few of the examples: the Filipinos thought the Anglos were hypocritical and inconsiderate, the Anglos thought the Filipinos were petty and played favorites; the African Americans thought the Hispanics cocky and pushy and the Hispanics thought the African Americans too competitive and untrusting; the Afghans thought the Chinese did not really care about others, and the Chinese in turn thought the Afghans were bad. There were many more stereotypes reported and some were even positive, but the majority were negative. Does this mean that every group in the world is bad? No, but it is hard to find a very large group in which some people do not make foolish and sometimes bad choices. Using the reasoning of the fundamental attribution error, it is then quite easy to have "evidence" for negative stereotypes.

Reflection Question: Why are so many stereotypes negative?

In one of the classes we teach we have our students list on one day the different roles they play or groups to which they belong. The next day we put up one from each of their lists and ask the class in a general way to identify the stereotypes they are aware of regarding that role or group. There are consistently many more negative stereotypes than positive ones. Often these negative stereotypes are not so much based on wrong or bad choices by the other group, just different choices than we may be used to. If we remember that stereotypes are categories that grow out of our desire to understand *differences* that we perceive in others, this is not too surprising. Things that are different, unfamiliar, or unexpected tend to make us humans uncomfortable, and it is often easier to understand them in negative terms. However, there is another reason negative stereotypes seem so common. Although stereotypes are grounded in our human desire to understand the world, they can easily be tools in our efforts to build up our own group or community at the expense of others. Indeed, it is this destructive use of stereotypes that leads us into the next two concepts, ethnocentrism and prejudice.

ETHNOCENTRISM

Ethnocentrism has its roots in two words, *ethno*, or group, and *centrism*, or center, and it refers to assuming that one's group is the center of the world. In the original conceptualization of this concept, William Sumner went a step further and explained that ethnocentrism referred to the view that "one's own group is the center of everything, and all others are scaled and rated with reference to it."[7] Thus, ethnocentrism is not just about one's own group, but about how other groups compare to it. Sumner also used the metaphor of war to explain how ethnocentrism functions. Herein lies a major difference between stereotyping and ethnocentrism. *Stereotyping is grounded in an effort (albeit often flawed) to understand others, whereas ethnocentrism is grounded in competition and an often unconscious desire for victory.*

Although ethnocentrism often deals with cultural differences, it is, in the final analysis, based on group membership and one's own group's relative standing among other groups. Therefore, it is always competitive, always centered around feelings of superiority over others because they don't "know" as much as us or don't do things the right way. Of course, the standard for this knowledge or "right" way is one's own group, so to whatever extent other groups vary from this standard, they are automatically wrong.

This does not mean that ethnocentrism is always obvious. For example, the United States may be the only country in the world where those involved in international business do not agree on the importance of fluency in a foreign language.[8] Americans often argue that everyone speaks English and what makes a manager good in one place makes a good manager everywhere, and besides, you may wind up in different countries, so why waste your time learning a language you may not need? There is no doubt that English has become in many ways the global language of business and science, and this has certain advantages for bringing people together. At the same time it subtly creates many competitive advantages for those whose native language is English. Those who cannot speak fluent English or do not speak the "standard" dialect (meaning the dialect of those in power) of any language are often perceived and treated as somehow less intelligent than those who are fluent in English; such individuals are just as limited in their linguistic abilities and frequently even more so.[9]

Ethnocentric views are also expressed in the labels we have to refer to outsiders; for example, the implied evaluation in the terms Jew and Gentile. The Japanese refer to outsiders as *gaijin*. This term not only denotes outsider, but has a slight condescending and negative connotation to it. We hear the label foreigner often used in a slightly patronizing or negative way. When you hear the term barbarian, what does it bring to mind? Is it reliance on brute strength and uncivilized, uncouth manners and dress? The term has its origins in the Greek term *barbarikos*, and simply referred to anyone who did not speak Greek.[10] It had nothing to do with table manners, level of civilization, strength, or anything else of that nature. It was, however, a term for outsiders that had negative connotations, and although many of the connotations have changed, they still tend to be negative.

Ethnocentrism has at times been associated with positive social outcomes.[11] These include such things as a strong social identity, which may increase one's self-esteem, group loyalty, group survival, and the reduction of internal problems within a group. However, ethnocentrism also has many negative outcomes. It can prevent groups from learning new and productive knowledge that could be gained from other groups. In addition, feelings and expressions of ethnocentrism that protect a position of superiority breed increased competition, fear, anger, and hate, all of which can lead to different types of damaging conflicts.

Just as we all generalize our experiences with other groups of people through the process of categorization, thereby stereotyping them, we all carry the seeds of ethnocentrism with us as well. These seeds are our own cultural knowledge and lack of knowledge. The groups to which we belong and the ways of doing things shared by members of these groups are part of our cultural knowledge and serve as a point of reference for us to understand the world. This knowledge (of which stereotypes comprise one part) makes our social life possible. None of us is all-knowing; therefore, as we learn we typically do so by building on what knowledge we already have. If age is an important aspect of how we address other people, when we are trying to learn about how we should address members in another group we will be likely to ask questions related to how age impacts the way we should address others. It may turn out that age is not important at all in regards to personal address. Assuming that age is important may be termed by some as ethnocentric. It could also happen in reverse, such that someone from the group where age is not an important factor in addressing others doesn't even ask or worry about age when learning about address practices of the other group. Again, this person may be accused of ethnocentrism. However, we think these things are better viewed as ignorance, and we all have much about which we are culturally ignorant. Ethnocentrism sprouts from the seeds of cultural knowledge and ignorance that exist in all of us when we use this knowledge—or ignorance—to make evaluative judgments designed to demonstrate our superiority. If we decide that the other group is backward, uncivilized, thoughtless, or whatever because they either do or do not use age as a consideration in how to address others, thus demonstrating once again just how intelligent, caring, and wise our own group is, we might say that we are ethnocentric.

We are not trying to say that any evaluation of other practices is ethnocentric and should be avoided. These issues will be discussed more in Chapter 11, which deals with ethics. Taking an evaluative stance that group practices accepted by the Nazis in Germany were wrong is not what is being discussed as ethnocentrism. Ethnocentric evaluations are grounded in personal or group gain at the expense of others. However, sometimes these gains operate at an unconscious level, and it may be hard to see what type of plant our seeds of knowledge and ignorance are growing into. Charting ourselves on three continuums can help us be more aware when the weeds of ethnocentrism may be silently taking over our own personal gardens.[12]

Concern/Indifference

If we are sincerely concerned about others and their feelings and wellbeing, we are less inclined to be ethnocentric than if we are simply indifferent. One example of this that we have seen discussed throughout the United States is the issue of using names like *Redskins*, *Braves*, and *Indians* for professional sports teams. Not all Native Americans are concerned with this practice, but significant numbers are concerned with both the labels and the type of activities engaged in by some of these teams' fans. Perhaps your initial reaction is, "So what is the big deal? These names are traditional. People are supporting these groups, the labels are used to highlight positive competitive traits like strength and cunning, and besides, other groups are also labeled, for example, the *Padres*, *Saints*, and *Vikings*." These types of reactions all show a desire to justify what one group does at the expense of the other. No real concern for the Native American community is shown in these justifications. All of these justifications may be true, but it is also true that potentially damaging images are being perpetuated and large segments of the groups in question are hurt by the way these labels are used. Continued use of these labels in this way is clearly a sign of indifference. In a positive light, the University of Stanford did show concern in their name change a few years back, and also, from what we understand, the Seminoles as a tribe decided to support Florida State's use of the name Seminole.[13] Both of these examples show concern rather than indifference because the community in question was listened to.

Involvement/Avoidance

As you observe or personally participate in decisions and judgments being made about another group, consider the amount of involvement with or avoidance of the other group. Ethnocentrism is often nurtured by avoidance. If we have minimal involvement with another group, it is very easy to be ethnocentric. We have seen professional groups organize to try to assist communities in need, yet only minimally consult with the community in question. It is just assumed that these professionals know what is best for the other group. They are then often surprised and even hurt when the group in question is not brimming with gratitude for all the help being given. These reactions can even promote more avoidance of the group and more ethnocentrism; after all, who wants to spend their time trying to help a group that just won't be helped? It is difficult to avoid ethnocentrism without extensive involvement.

Enjoyment/Intolerance

We may be both concerned about another group and involved, but if we are intolerant of differences, our efforts may simply be the ethnocentric desire to turn the other group into an exact copy of our own group. If we are intolerant of differences, we will always be fertile ground for ethnocentrism. We want to note that we purposefully avoided putting tolerance at one end of the continuum. We may tolerate differences, just as we tolerate some bothersome habit of a neighbor and avoid confronting our neighbor about it, but this does not mean we don't view ourselves and our ways of doing things as superior. It is only when we can honestly enjoy differences, even when they are not what we would personally choose to do, feel, or think, that we can avoid ethnocentric attitudes.

Thinking about the need to develop our enjoyment of differences, get involved with others, and be genuinely concerned about them, we suspect you can see how in an immediate sense it is much easier just act ethnocentric, just as it is easier to let your garden go to weed. Of course, the harvest is less than desirable.

A recent example of the competitive nature of ethnocentrism and how it can incorporate indifference, avoidance, and intolerance can be found in response to the *Black Lives Matter* movement. The *Black Lives Matter* campaign is not a single organized movement; rather it is an idea that has caught hold in a wide variety of places in the United States and around the world due to the shooting deaths of a number of black individuals in the U.S. Thus, the way the *Black Lives Matter* ideas are expressed can vary widely; however, the original ideas appear to us as an expression of concern over possible indifference and prejudice. Some have responded to this call with slogans such as *All Lives Matter* or *Blue Lives Matter* (referencing the police). There is nothing wrong with the message in these alternative expressions; surely all lives do matter. However, our observations suggest that many of these are presented in a competitive manner that competes with the original slogan, thus functioning to drown out the original idea and reinforcing the idea of indifference (and at times hostility) toward what was happening. These slogans can quickly become good points that are used to compete for very ethnocentric ideas in a political arena. We are reminded of an old joke whose punch line was something along the lines of "that was no lady, that was my wife." Obviously the person could be a lady and a wife. Bringing attention to the fact that we need to remember that *Black Lives Matter* when there has been concerns raised about this in no way suggests that other lives do not matter and does not need to be responded to as if it did.

Reflection Question: Ethnocentrism is sometimes linked to patriotism; is it possible to be patriotic without being ethnocentric? Explain your answer.

PREJUDICE

The nature of prejudice as it relates to intercultural communication and why we can't just all get along is more complex than is sometimes recognized and is more widespread than we wish to admit. In its broadest sense prejudice implies a judgment made in advance of some interaction. However, this definition is too broad to be of much use. There are countless definitions of prejudice in work on this topic. However, building upon points of agreement and in talking with many people about this topic, we define prejudice as *a rigid attitude that is (1) based on group membership, and (2) predisposes an individual to feel, think, or act in a negative way toward another person or group of persons.*[14]

Poor Tetsu. He's got no idea that people dislike him and don't want his *taiyaki* [sweet bread] because he's a cremator. He goes on thinking they'll sell if he makes them tastier. That's why he only uses good quality sugar, and the very best sesame-seed oil on the griddle to give a nice smell. But people don't realize that. They just go on talking about human oil and powdered bones, saying all sorts of unkind things. He can't win—they pick on him because his *taiyaki* are so delicious, but you can bet that if they were as tasteless and dirty as they usually are, they'd only say, "Well, what do you expect from a cremator?" Poor Tetsu, he's got no idea that people dislike him and don't want his *taiyaki* because he's a cremator ...[15]

This short excerpt from the novel *River with No Bridge* illustrates the major points of the definition of prejudice. First, the people's attitude referenced in the quote is resistant to change. It doesn't really matter how good or how bad Tetsu makes his bread; the people in question will always find a reason to be suspicious of it and dislike him. Second, the key to their dislike was not Tetsu the individual, but Tetsu the *cremator*. It was his group affiliation that triggered the reaction and was the basis for their suspicion and dislike. Group membership is always important in the way prejudice is defined here. It would be possible for someone to prejudge a proposal based on a series of personal experiences with the person making the proposal, but it would only be prejudice as defined here if it was also based in part on one of the person's group memberships. Finally, the presupposition the people in the excerpt had toward Tetsu because he was a cremator was negative. There is no positive prejudice. Their negative reaction did not necessitate dramatic confrontation; instead, the snubs were indicated to be so slight and subtle that Tetsu may not even have realized what was happening. Because prejudice is a presupposition to either act, think, or feel in a negative way it is not always obvious to those who are the target of the prejudice or to those observing from a distance that prejudice is being expressed.

This definition also highlights a number of differences between stereotypes and prejudice. Although stereotypes may be resistant to change, the intensity with which they are held can vary greatly. Prejudices are always rigidly held. Although stereotypes are never completely accurate, they can vary substantially in terms of accuracy. Not only are prejudices never accurate, they always distort one's vision in such a way that they always greatly warp our view of others. Stereotypes can also be both positive and negative, whereas prejudices are always negative. Stereotypes are based on categorizing and the human desire to make sense of our world. We have to be very careful how we use stereotypes, but when not focused on what is bad about another group, consciously left open to change, and relatively accurate in terms of general group tendencies, stereotypes can play a productive role in intercultural interactions. Prejudice is based on categorization and the desire to control others in ways that demean them directly or indirectly. Prejudice is never a productive part of intercultural relations. We can never really expect to rid ourselves of stereotypes, but we can hope to rid ourselves of prejudice. Finally, stereotyping is a practice, whereas prejudice is an attitude. Therefore, stereotypes can be a tool used by those who are prejudiced to control others.

Prejudice is much more closely allied to the competitive nature of ethnocentrism, but prejudice does not necessarily imply that one feels good about one's own group and group practices. We may feel prejudice against a group to which we belong. In addition, with prejudice the differences between groups are less concerned with differences in the way groups do things (like you often find with ethnocentrism), but with the sheer fact that it is a *different* group.

The definition of prejudice we are working with is also clearly tied to the concept of discrimination as it is used in the study of intercultural communication. Discrimination in this context occurs when prejudice is put into a tangible or concrete action. If a person uses his or her prejudice to make a decision related to who to hire or what person to vote for, then that person has engaged in discrimination. When people discuss discrimination in the workplace it tends to revolve around the use of factors others than individual merit to make decisions and is seen as a symptom of prejudice that is personally held or built into the structure of an organization. Repeated discrimination creates an environment of oppression that can at times be invisible to those who have become accustomed to the environment. For example, if group A was repeatedly denied educational opportunities and then tested in comparison to group B on set criteria that is typically taught as part of the educational experience, group A's lower score would not be a sign of less intelligence, but a sign of less opportunity. Yet it would be possible for members of both group A and B to say, "We gave them the same test. Group B must be smarter and, therefore, more deserving of increased educational opportunities."

It is also worthwhile to note that this definition of prejudice also recognizes that not all negative interactions involving people of various groups are an expression of prejudice. We may be intolerant, rude, or thoughtless to others based on general feelings of frustration or a personal grievance; however, this is not prejudice unless we have a negative predisposition toward other individuals based on their group membership. It is difficult with some outward actions to determine whether they are expressions of prejudice. In particular circumstances a person may say something rude or thoughtless to a good friend. People are not perfect, and it can be unproductive to assume too quickly that a negative action or comment is prejudice. This does not mean that prejudice is not a very real concern in the world today. Sometimes people subtly express prejudice without even realizing what they are doing.

To explain prejudice and to provide a foundation from which to defend ourselves from its negative influence, we will consider three different aspects related to it. First, we will review the general forms prejudice takes when it is being expressed. Second, we will examine the types of stories people tell themselves and others to account for prejudice in their own lives. Third, we will explore the functions of prejudice in terms of what people may be said to get out of it as well as the negative consequences for both the individual and society in general.

Forms of Prejudice

Prejudice is an attitude, which suggests that it occurs within a person. However, feelings of prejudice are such a large problem because they get expressed in a variety of ways, often without people even realizing or admitting to themselves that they are expressing prejudice. The following are descriptions of five common forms of prejudice.[16]

Blatant

Blatant prejudice is the active denigration of members of an outgroup. This type of prejudice is based on the belief that the outgroup is in some way inferior to the ingroup and, therefore, not worthy of decent treatment. The Ku Klux Klan has developed a reputation as an organization based on this form of prejudice. Manifestations of the prejudice include open statements about the inferiority of the other group, desires to have them go back to where they belong, or comments and thoughts about their innate dirtiness, laziness, and general backwardness. The outgroup is often treated and referred to as a type of pollutant. The idea of contact with members of this other group is generally repugnant. Some manifestations of blatant prejudice are quite violent, such as the physical beating or terrorizing of members of the hated group. As we write this there are a number of events in the news that provide examples of this, such as the burning of churches (many of them in black communities), the beating to death of a homosexual person, and a Swastika burnt onto the lawn of a Jewish family. Other blatant expressions are relatively peaceful, such as the decision not to hire someone based on their ethnicity, false claims that there are no vacancies at an apartment complex when the person is found to be of a different race, or comments made to a friend about how another group cannot be trusted because they are all liars. Blatant expressions of prejudice are what we typically think of when we think of prejudice. They are marked by a clear and open dislike for members of the other group.

There are a variety of efforts in the United States and other places that seek through education to stop such feelings and expressions of prejudice. It is easy to see that there are still many of these problems around us, but there is some evidence that formal education does help reduce the expression of this form of prejudice.[17] Alas, the same cannot be said for the other four forms of prejudice which in their own ways can be just as damaging, although more difficult to detect.

Conceit

As with blatant prejudice, conceit is marked by a sense that the other group is inferior to one's own. Manifestations of this prejudice tend to trivialize the other group. Thus, you find comments like, "She only got the job because she is black." This type of comment implies that the other group really isn't as good as the person's own group and so requires special privileges to make up for these incompetencies. This form of prejudice often involves making fun of the other group, its values, and ways of doing things. How often have you heard people sitting around telling jokes that involve negative depictions of another group? Do we join in with our own joke, just laugh in support of these kinds of put downs, or question this practice? When questioned about this type of prejudice people may respond, "What's the big deal? We're just having fun." Although the "fun" is neither violent nor as mean-spirited as one finds in blatant expressions of prejudice, it positions the other group as second-class and trivial. This sort of prejudice creates and reinforces expectations that members of the other group are lacking in terms of professional or social abilities.

Symbolic

Those who participate in symbolic prejudice will typically deny being prejudiced at all. Manifestations of this prejudice tend to be prominent in political spheres and can be found in statements that show antagonism toward the out-group's actions in society ("Jews are getting too demanding"), resentment about so-called special treatment ("Why should Indians get rights that no one else does?"), and denial that prejudice is really a problem ("They have it too easy, and it is just breeding laziness"). Symbolic prejudice involves a concern for the status quo of existing power relationships and the fear that this other group is going to disturb it. Thus, only those who are in a position of power can engage in symbolic prejudice. This form of prejudice is also found in institutional practices that perpetuate certain advantages for the dominant group in a larger community. Often these advantages are difficult to see because we have become so used to them, such as the use of certain dialects as the "correct" way to speak or intelligence tests that use terminology that is culturally more familiar to certain groups of people. Education has much less impact on this and the other following forms of prejudice.

Tokenism

Tokenism is usually found among people who know they harbor negative feelings about the other group, but do not like to admit that to either themselves or others. Essentially tokenism involves the giving of a token, or a relatively unimportant, but positive, item while withholding more substantial or significant assistance or involvement. The giving of the token is argued to be proof that the person is not prejudiced and allows the person to avoid engaging in more meaningful acts of equality. Thus, we may whip out a couple of dollars in support of some "needy" group, but we would never really want to spend time with people from this group. At an organizational level a company may include a token minority in their advertisements, but then enact a silent glass ceiling that would make it impossible for someone of an outgroup to be promoted into substantial leadership positions.

Arm's Length

Some people will engage in positive or friendly behaviors with members of the outgroup in one setting, but not in others. Thus, it may be fine to be friendly at work or school, but you would not want to socialize with them, live next to one, or have one as a close family member. In this way you keep members of this other group at arm's length. Sometimes this form of prejudice depends not so much on the physical setting, but on the relational setting, such that it is okay to visit with a person of this group if you are alone or with a few people you don't know that well, but if one's friends from within your own group are around, you ignore the other person or try to downplay any potential friendship. This is a difficult type of prejudice to detect because those who hold it can seem quite tolerant and open to outgroup members in certain settings.

In considering the various forms through which prejudice can be expressed, it is obvious that stereotypical, blatant acts of prejudice are only one part of the problem. Blatant acts of prejudice may get more attention because of their sensational nature, but the other, more subtle forms of prejudice are perhaps even more widespread and can be just as damaging for an individual or group.

Rationalizing Narratives of Prejudice

One of the intriguing things about prejudice is that, except for a few people who have become entrenched in blatant expressions of prejudice, virtually everyone acknowledges that it is both wrong and destructive. Yet, as we look closely, we are still surrounded by it and very likely find ourselves guilty of perpetuating it in some form or another. Why, one might wonder, don't we as individuals and as a group rise up and change this? In raising this question we are not denying that many good things are done in this area, but, given the amount of consensus concerning the negative nature of prejudice, it often seems to have the powers of the ancient serpent, Hydra, who grew two heads every time one of his heads was cut off. One way of better understanding this power is to look at the way people rationalize expressions of prejudice in their own lives.

The communication scholar Walter Fisher has argued that humans are essentially *homo narrans*, or storytellers, who implicitly or explicitly make sense of their world through narrative.[18] Indeed, the quality of our lives is inseparable from the quality of our stories. In systematically analyzing 125 stories in which people talk about how they themselves have expressed prejudice as well as informally considering hundreds of others, we have found that there are basically five rationalizing narratives of prejudice that people use to make sense of prejudice in their own lives.[19] These narratives may be entitled *Morally Better, Personally Afflicted, Social Pressure, Their Turf,* and *System Abuse*.

We will review each of these narratives in the following way. First, we will overview the general storyline told from the point of view of the person who has expressed the prejudice and focus on the types of characters involved, the problems they face, the actions they take in response to these problems, and expected outcomes. Then we will give two specific examples that are directly from stories we have analyzed to give you a better feel for this form of rationalization. Of course, each example has unique aspects, but they also follow the general storyline of the narrative type in question. Finally, we will briefly consider the rationalizing reason for the prejudice conveyed by each general story type.

Morally Better

Story Line

There is this group of people out there who think they're neat stuff, but if you objectively look at their actions and self-espoused attitudes, they actually are wrongheaded. Being an open sort of person, we don't like to make a big deal about it publicly. Generally we just avoid them, but when forced into contact we tolerate them as nicely as possible. However, when we are with our own group, who understand that we are good people, we speak condescendingly about them, and frequently we share a few jokes about them just for fun. Occasionally our own behavior toward this group surprises or embarrasses us, but truly it is the other group's own fault for not acting and talking appropriately in the first place.

Examples

Prejudice is something that I pride myself on being aware of and avoiding. I try to see people as individuals and have found that there is always an exception to any stereotype. However, I found that there is a group of people with whom I have interacted that I hold a strong prejudice against. The intensity of my feelings surprised me. . . A particular incident of prejudice stands out in my mind because my feelings about it have not changed much. Several years ago I got involved with a Baptist church here in [town] because they offered sign language classes. I was just starting to take sign language classes at [the university] and wanted more practice and exposure to the language.

The group I got involved with also played volleyball as part of their parish activities. . . They had what I considered were smarmy words and overly pious sayings on their shirts. The sayings were aggressive words and phrases that were turned around so that they were religious in nature. . . . Throughout the tournament, I watched the young married men strut around with authority while their young, obedient, often pregnant, wives cared for their children. . . The roles of the women were that of demure, second-class people whose purpose seemed to be to gestate and care for children and to stand behind their husbands.

We were required to pray before and after everything that happened. The person who said the prayer would talk about God and people as if people were dirt. God was male and controlling. I stopped interacting with these people. . . I spent that tournament mentally making fun of the Baptists' ways and critiquing the things they value, such as men's dominant role. I considered their religion not as good as the one I was raised in and inferior to my current religious beliefs. My ideas of religion made them seem childish and backwards. . . The Baptists were claiming a "right" way of doing things and I felt great resentment about it. I will probably remain wary of this religion and the people that practice it even though I now understand why I felt such prejudice.

The other day my friends and I were talking outside a local bar downtown when one of our other friends, Marie, came by and introduced us to three guys. These guys had long hair, beards, and looked like they had not had a shower for about a week. She introduced them as some of her best friends. They were passing through town and staying at her house. The rest of my friends went back into the bar, but because Marie had to go get something I stayed and visited with them for a bit. I didn't want to be there. They talked about driving around from city to city playing their guitars on street corners to get money for food and gas. "Professional beggars," I thought.

When I finally got back into the bar with my friends we all started to joke about "Dead Heads" and "lost generation X." We made fun of their long hair. Later, Marie came in and invited us all to a dinner party at her house the next evening. Her "friends" would be there. I didn't say anything, but I didn't want to go. I am a pretty open guy about a lot of things and I don't want to be rude to others, but I didn't want any of their dirty hairs in my food just because they were too lazy to get a real job or clean themselves up. Besides, they seemed kind of gay and who knew what sort of disease they might be carrying.

Rationalizing Reasons

The reasons espoused in this type of narrative seem to take two sides of the same coin. On one side, the importance of maintaining appropriate behavior and beliefs and the other group's failure to do so is warrant enough for the expression of prejudice. On the other side is the sense that this is a *choice* and that the other group could be better if only they would. There is a strong sense of pride expressed in these stories.

There is one variation on the morally better stories that is worth noting here. It is when the person expressing the prejudice is also a member of the group that is being targeted for the negative feelings. The person doing this often feels they are being very objective about the whole situation, but actually they are following the same misguided reasoning as anyone else. These stories do, however, consistently include a different emotion in their telling, the feeling of embarrassment. For whatever reason they have come to accept the negative views of their group that are found around them. They are embarrassed by the negative connotations that then get attributed to them and tend to feel that they and perhaps a few others are "exceptions to the rule."

FIGURE 7.2 |

Miguel Gandert

Personally Afflicted

Story Line

Rationally we know prejudice is wrong, but in the past we or someone we loved was physically hurt or threatened by these slobs, so we can't help but feel the way we do. These people have proved themselves to be trouble starters, a threat to any peaceful and respectful society. Our past experience has caused us to fear, but mainly hate, this particular group. Generally we avoid them with a passion, but if they start anything, we hit right back vocally, physically, or any way we can.

Examples

When I was 18 I decided to go to our local junior college which was located in the city. While in high school, which was located only a mile away from the junior college, I was never exposed to the Asian population on a daily basis, but while in college I could not believe how many attended the school. Everywhere I looked there were Asians. I looked at them as I did anyone else, until I was put in a situation where I had to interact with them. One afternoon while on campus I entered a restroom alone, not noticing that I was the only white person, or what they would consider white, in the bathroom which was filled with five Asian girls. I call them Asian because I don't know whether they were Japanese, Chinese, or what. I did not think twice about being the only white person. It was not until they all began to talk in their own language, and not until they began looking and talking and laughing at me, that I finally realized I was the minority. As I went behind the stall, the talk became louder as did their laughs. As I approached the sink to wash my hands, the laughs and stares were so obviously directed at me that I became extremely uncomfortable. They just kept rambling on as they stared me up and down. My first thought was that these people have no manners as far as being considerate for other people's feelings. . . A feeling of rage came over me. I could not believe how rude these people were. From that point on I looked at every Asian person as rude and inconsiderate. . .

From that day on I have never been able to give an Asian person a fair chance to prove to me that they are not all like the girls who made fun of me. This particular incident left me with a negative feeling toward the whole Asian race. I know this incident may sound petty and insignificant to others, but it left me with a bad attitude toward the whole Asian population. This incident took place over ten years ago and I still remember it vividly.

I can remember as a child having to spend most of the day at a daycare center because both of my parents had to work. Due to the location of the school, I found that I was very much the minority with my lighter skin and blonde hair. One day I remember asking some older girls if I could play in the huge doll house with them. Their reply was that only girls with dark hair and dark skin were allowed in the doll house. I was very hurt and thought these Hispanic girls were very mean. . . When I was in sixth grade I had a bad run-in with the Mexican students known as Chicanos and Chicanas. For some reason that I did not understand I was beaten up. I was just a wimpy blonde who did not talk much unless it was necessary. I tried to stay clear from them, but the Hispanic girls wouldn't let me. In 7th grade I got to be so scared that my parents transferred me to a different school.

I recall even as a teenager walking in the mall and being called derogatory names by Hispanic teens. I was considered rich and preppy. I grew to despise the Hispanic culture. I considered them to be poor, rude, and downright uneducated. At the university I have met a lot of nice Hispanic people and I don't fear and hate them so much, but I still catch myself thinking bad thoughts about their culture and expecting them to cause problems.

Rationalizing Reasons

The most salient good reason in this narrative is that the narrator personally experienced the *rottenness* of the outgroup. A second good reason is that the narrator has experienced emotional injury as a result of the bad experience, and emotions are perceived as more powerful than rational thought. Thus, the narrator has a *right* to hate this other group.

Social Pressure

Story Line

I'm a liberal type of person with friends from many groups, including this particular outgroup. However, most, if not all, of our own group have a problem with this one outgroup. We don't want to rock the boat with our own group which we value very much, so we act in a way that denies or avoids any real or serious relationship with outgroup members. We feel really bad about this, but because our ingroup is so important to us, we don't see the situation improving anytime soon, if ever.

Examples

My most memorable experience with prejudice occurred when I was a junior at a suburban high school that had a relatively small number of blacks. Most students stayed away from the blacks, while a small percentage of the white

(continued)

(continued)

students befriended them and ignored the other prejudiced whites. I was one of those students who made friends with several black students. . . There wasn't a prejudiced bone in my body, or so I thought.

There was a young black man named John who was a senior and in my creative writing class. I'd had classes with him before and I also sat at the same lunch table where he and his friends sat. We became good friends over a period of time until I received a note from him one day in class. It was a letter professing his true feelings for me. He wanted to know if I would be his girlfriend.

I didn't know what to do after I read the letter. I quickly left class when it was over. I hid out most of the day to avoid my friend. My lunch was spent in the girls' bathroom. When I arrived home that evening, the note accidentally fell out of my pocket and my mother found it. She knew who John was and what color he was and questioned me if I was seriously considering his offer. She told me that neither she nor my father would allow it and I would be thrown out of the house if I did see John on a serious relationship level.

I feigned illness the next day, but I did attend the day after and gave my answer to John. I lied by telling him I already had a boyfriend and he politely accepted my lame excuse. We both pretended like we could still be friends, even though we knew it wouldn't happen. . . Things weren't the same between us after the incident. It was okay to socialize with John as a friend in school activities, but the thought of dating someone of a different race made me tense and nervous. This situation made me confront the fact that no matter how liberal everyone thought I was, I knew that I was prejudiced in my own way.

I don't like what happened with John. He was a very nice, sweet, and funny person and if he were white, I knew I would have gone out with him in a second. I honestly feel this incident isn't going to make things different the next time it happens. Regardless of where I'm living, I would still lose the respect of my parents and I don't want that to happen. My parents don't have me on a string, but they strongly influence me. There are a million men out in this world, but there's only one set of parents I have.

I can think of two experiences that I feel bad about, but doubt I would act any differently today. I worked at a nursery in Oregon that employed many Mexican nationals and I was friends with many of them. But our friendship did not always extend past the end of the workday. If I had invited my Mexican friends to my home for parties or down to the river for swimming and a cookout, I would have run the risk of alienating the friends in my group. So I didn't invite them, and avoided the sanctions of my friends. After I was married we moved to North Carolina. We developed some new friends named Bob and Betty. One time I remember we were in the backyard together, and we heard loud music coming from the yard down the block.

Bob said, "It's probably the blacks, they don't have any respect for anyone else. They turn their music up so loud that people five miles away could hear it."
I wanted to fit in so I said, "Yeah, no kidding."

Rationalizing Reasons

One reason for the expression of prejudice in this narrative is the fact that the person has had minimal or little contact with the other group while growing up. A second reason is that the narrator and the outgroup member are in fact different. The third and easily most pressing reason, however, is the importance of maintaining positive ingroup relations and the acceptance that a relationship with those from the outgroup will harm these ingroup relations.

Their Turf

Story Line

Actual contact with this other group is rather new to us. However, we have read and seen so much in the media about the crime and problems associated with this group that now that we are "closer" to them we are scared. They don't appear to respect the law like people we know. They all look the same and when we are on the street or some other unprotected area we fear what they may be plotting against us. We are so vulnerable. Therefore, during any interaction with them outside areas that we know to be safe or any time we are on their turf we try to do things as quickly as possible. It is too bad it has to be this way, but you never know what they might do.

Examples

I would say the strongest prejudice I have is toward black men. The reason this prejudice has developed is because I grew up in a small town with a very low percentage of blacks. Consequently I had very little interaction with them growing up. The exposure to blacks I had was through television programs and news stories. Granted the programs showed black men in both a favorable and unfavorable light, but they are seen as villains more often than good guys. That combined with watching news and seeing how much crime and violence is related to black men caused a prejudice based on fear to develop within me.

(continued)

(continued)

When I first moved to [this town] I was exposed to blacks and their culture for the first time and, although I hate to admit it, fear was there. I had stereotyped their race as being bad. . .

I have lived [here] for four years and I had hoped I would get used to seeing the basketball players that live here. I haven't. When I pass them, especially if it is a group of them, I am on my guard and somewhat afraid. I think part of it has to do with the fact that I am a small, white female and that I am in one of the most, if not the most, vulnerable groups in society in terms of violent crime.

For example, in a previous job, sometimes black men would come into the center for services. I treated them in a friendly manner, but if I see them socially, I am much more distant. At work, it is a safe situation. I am behind a desk, with many people around and there is knowledge that chances are real good nothing will occur. In that situation, I feel they are on my "turf" and, therefore, play by those rules. In a social scene that is not so and it scares me. . .

I have lumped black men into one category—that of violence, crime, bad attitudes, and the like. I realize it is wrong, but again, it is based on a very strong fear that realistically I will never get over. Actually, I hope I do not get over it because I do not want to let my guard down. I do not want to be any more vulnerable than I already feel I am.

I come from a town that has only about a 5 percent minority population. It was quite a shock to see so many Asians and black people all over the place. After some time in the city I developed a close friendship with a person from work named Pam who was of black heritage. We spent a lot of time together inside and outside of work, but it didn't change my fear of blacks. One time I was walking in downtown, when a black man yelled my name and started running after me. I began to walk much faster and tried to ignore him. He finally caught up to me and tapped me on the shoulder and I turned around scared to death, when I realized it was Pam's husband. He only wanted to ask if I needed a ride somewhere. I told him he scared me to death and he apologized. He thought I would recognize him and seemed a bit embarrassed. We all laugh about it now, but it was uncomfortable because even though I trust Pam and her husband I know I really don't trust other black people, especially when I am just out on the street.

Rationalizing Reasons

The objective sense of many media reports provides justification for the expressions of prejudice in this narrative. This is especially powerful when combined with the personal feeling of vulnerability. Finally, lack of experience is also seen as a warrant for this expression of prejudice.

System Abuse

Story Line

We are normal, competent, hardworking people and it really bothers us to see people getting unfair advantage in the system due to some accident of birth. This injustice of getting rewards based on group membership not merit makes it tough for people like us who earn our rewards to get what we actually deserve. We are, therefore, understandably angry and when talking within our own group we often refer to the outgroup in derogatory terms and tell stories of how they perpetuate injustice. We wish we could get rid of Affirmative Action and other quota systems and just concentrate on real merit. But, given the political problems of the day, it is unlikely.

Examples

I work in a bank with about 50 people with a very even distribution of black and white employees. My account has to do with my superior who is black. She is viewed by many as incompetent. To clarify, I am not saying she is incompetent because she is black. The perception I usually have is that she was given the job because she's black and the corporation had to fill a quota of minority managers. At least once a week there is a comment made regarding why she was given that job, because she is basically unskilled in management. As a result, there is a lack of respect for my superior and we make fun of the way she speaks. . .

For a time I worked outside the United States as a machinist and high-pressure welder. When I returned to the U.S. I had trouble finding a job and was always being turned down for one reason or another. Because of this I began to feel that I was being discriminated against because I am a minority. I was upset and couldn't understand how people could do this. I felt I was shielded from ever discriminating against others because of my minority status. I will explain how I found out that was not true. Deciding that eating had become a priority I swallowed my pride and found myself standing in the line at the local welfare office. I explained my situation, but because of my previous year's earnings I only qualified for 14 dollars in food stamps. Some reward for working, I thought.

Anyway, my next stop was the grocery store. I very carefully picked out 14 dollars' worth of goods and went to the shortest line. They were all quite busy because it was a government payday. An Indian woman and her three children beat me to the line. It was still the shortest line so I stayed there. The Indian woman's basket was to the point of overflowing and she struggled to push it. As the clerk began to ring up the items she turned in my direction and began to speak in an Indian dialect. At first I thought she was talking to me, but then

(continued)

(continued)

I saw an Indian man pushing one and pulling another grocery cart, both of which were overflowing.

I then heard her say in bad English, "That is my husband and we are paying with a government WIC check." This is one of the few checks issued by the Federal Government where the purchase amount is filled in by the store clerk (a blank check!?!). The clerk then asked me to let the husband through.

I couldn't believe it. I stopped short of making a scene, all the while thinking to myself, "These damn Indians have it made, no wonder I'm only getting 14 dollars." I felt the Indians were being allowed to corrupt an already unjust welfare system. After I quickly got through the line with my little amount, I saw the same Indian family loading their groceries in a brand new Chevy Van. I was fit to be tied! I couldn't wait to get with my friends and tell them about these Indians who were drunk most of the time, who cheated the rest of us out of our rights by taking advantage of the system.

Rationalizing Reasons

The major good reason espoused in these narratives is that the outgroup is unfairly taking advantage of the system. A secondary reason cited is the loss of opportunities for the storyteller and others like him or her because of the behavior of the outgroup.

Table 7.1 provides an overview of the rationalizing narratives of prejudice. We do not believe that the people who tell these rationalizing narratives are abnormal or inherently bad. They have chosen ways of viewing and coping with a challenging world that will be damaging to themselves and others, but they can learn to make better choices. The label of *prejudice* is a very damaging label in today's world, and people create life stories that make prejudice both sensible and acceptable in their specific case, while at the same time allowing them to condemn it in a general sense. This type of rationalization makes it hard to overcome prejudice. No one wants to be stigmatized as prejudiced; therefore, we tell stories to ourselves and others that prevent us from recognizing bad choices and working on making better ones.

The point here is similar to the "difference between saying 'Arthur lied to me last Tuesday,' and saying, 'Arthur is a liar.'"[20] We may all have lied at some point in our lives, but does that make each of us a *liar*? A person who cannot be trusted? The traditional ways in which prejudice is often treated and taught push people into an all-or-nothing or "liar" type of category, thus ignoring the possibility that prejudice is not so much an essential part of what a person is as a context-specific choice. It is easier for a person to make changes in something

TABLE 7.1 | Overview of rationalizing narratives of prejudice

	Morally Better	*Personally Afflicted*	*Social Pressure*	*Their Turf*	*System Abuse*
Dominant Emotion	Pride	Hate	Resignation	Fear	Anger
Narrator	Objective, Open, & Principled	Innocent Victim	Strongly Attached to Own Group	Vulnerable & Inexperienced	Hard-working & Fair-minded
The "Other"	Choosing Wrong	Mean Trouble-Starter	Nice, but Different	Dangerous, Criminal	Free-loader
Major Source	They Violate a Perceived Universal Principle	Personal Experience	Family & Friends	Media	Personal Observation & Stories
Expression of Prejudice	Avoid & Joke About Other	Avoid & "Hit Back"	Avoid & Lie	Avoid & Watch Carefully	Avoid & Complain

they do than something they are. Although this is only a subtle change in perspective, it can be very enlightening and empowering as we discover prejudice in our own lives and the lives of others.

Reflection Question: Prejudice is grounded in an emotional reaction and cannot just be gotten rid of by simply being told that it is not a good idea. What are some ways you would suggest that a person could get rid of prejudice in his or her own life?

Functions of Prejudice

Even though we understand the many ways prejudice may be expressed and how people are able to justify its occurrence in their own lives, we may still wonder why anyone would engage in it in the first place and why it appears to be such a universally prevalent problem.[21] Much like certain addictive drugs, prejudice appears to help us deal with certain challenges while simultaneously creating greater problems in the future. We will review five of the functions or transitory "helps" that prejudices seem to hold for us when we feel and express them.[22]

FIGURE 7.3 |
Miguel Gandert

Utilitarian

One reason that people hold prejudice is that it is rewarded in tangible and monetary ways. If jobs are scarce, prejudice may be a way to reduce competition for those jobs and, consequently, the valued resources they entail. Prejudice that is held by those in economically powerful positions can channel certain groups of people into socially undesirable jobs (economically and physically). Prejudice provides a justification for occupational decisions that maintain or establish certain economic advantages and disadvantages. This function seemed to be a prime motivator in much of the West Germans' feelings of prejudice in regards to the East Germans after the two countries were unified.[23] Finally, prejudice may help certain social groups maintain political power in spite of an apparently *fair* political system.

Social Status

The social status function also contains a type of reward, albeit less tangible. Prejudice may boost one's standing within one's own community or at the very least help one avoid social sanctions from those of the ingroup. One certainly does not want to be viewed as *fraternizing with the enemy* when there are obvious tensions between communities. In addition, when prejudice is being expressed it takes people who are very secure with themselves to take the social risk of naming it for what it is and encouraging others to give it up. Thus, for an English person to joke about the Irish or a French person to joke about the Belgians and Belgians to joke about the Dutch and Spanish people to make fun of the Basque are ways in which people establish themselves as right within their own community. For many people, their expressions of prejudice are simply a way of trying to build themselves up or maintain a desired social position.

Ego-Defensive

In the ego-defensive case prejudice allows people to avoid admitting certain things about themselves. If one has been unsuccessful in any kind of endeavor, blaming that lack of success on those of an outgroup can protect one's own self-esteem. If we can believe that the only reason another person got a promotion is because they are of a "privileged, but unworthy" group, we do not have to face any potential personal inadequacies. Thus, for a short time, prejudice can help people feel better about themselves. This is a common function of prejudices found within the workplace.

Value-Expressive

Prejudices can be held because they allow people to highlight certain aspects of life that they highly prize. These aspects might include basic values concerning religion, government, aesthetics, or relationships. One Japanese American student shared with me how her mother frequently taught her how to act appropriately by referring in prejudicial ways to other Asian groups. For example, her mom would say, "I never want to see you sitting like that! Only Vietnamese do that!" and the student would know what her mom meant and find it unacceptable as well. She believed that her mom did this in part to counteract the lumping of all Asians together into one big group. The United States and Poland are hardly countries that could be said to be in competition with each other or who have a relationship that would need clarifying, yet Polish jokes are common in the United States. Through the use of the negative, these jokes seem to highlight culturally important attributes. Prejudice thus ironically becomes a way to celebrate the "good" and for a person to show that he or she knows who he or she is and supports what is right.

Easy Knowledge

Prejudice also allows people to organize and structure their world in ways that make sense and are relatively convenient. Prejudice allows a person to avoid dealing with individuals on an individual level, thus making many social decisions quick and easy. Based on the other's group membership, one knows whether or not to interact with that person and how to approach that interaction if it should occur. Archie Bunker became a popular culture celebrity based on his readily organized, prejudicial view of the world. He knew immediately who was worth talking to or who to trust just by the person's group membership. Of course, problems occur because easy knowledge often proves to be faulty.

Hopefully the last two sections on rationalizing narratives and the functions of prejudice are useful in helping us to see how and why prejudice can creep into all of our lives even when we know it is destructive. Let us think about some of these less-than-desirable consequences as they relate to each of the five functions reviewed previously. At the same time that the utilitarian function economically rewards certain groups, it prevents others from receiving appropriately deserved rewards. It reminds me in principle of part of the problem with shoplifting. A shoplifter may justify his or her actions based on the idea that big stores have plenty of money and so they won't miss little items. These items add up, however, and the stores then raise prices to cover these losses, causing problems for everyone, especially those who are simply working hard to earn their paychecks and don't take advantage of anyone. Prejudice is always felt and affects someone in a negative way, even when one small act is not noticed immediately. In addition, as our society tries to be fair and deal with the effects of prejudice, laws and programs are put in place to correct these problems. Some of these programs create their own difficulties, but as long as we have prejudices directed at utilitarian benefits we will need these other compensating programs and laws. As with so many things, prejudice is a vicious cycle.

The social status, ego-defensive, and value-expressive functions are all similar in that these apparently good things (social acceptance, self-esteem, and strong values) are all built on a faulty foundation that is always under threat of crumbling. When we try to build these good things through expressions of prejudice, we try to establish our own success on the failure of others. The idea that for us to succeed others must fail is a popular misconception in the world today. This form of thinking in everyday life creates a defensive atmosphere in which persons from all groups involved have to expend considerable amounts of energy just protecting themselves. There are better ways to build positive social acceptance, self-esteem, and value adherence than through the tearing down of others. Some of these issues will be revisited in the next two chapters which deal with conflict.

Finally, easy knowledge is also a misleading function, because the type of knowledge we have is always a distortion of the way things either are or can be. Many opportunities for personal growth, solving problems, and developing uplifting relationships are lost through assumptions about other people that limit contact with them and prevent us from seeing new information that could help us in our daily lives. Although prejudice may make some decisions convenient, it does not mean that those decisions are the best ones, and the effort expended at maintaining the walls of prejudice is often more draining than just letting go of the prejudices we have. Just as our children will sometimes work incredibly hard and for many minutes to avoid doing a five-minute job, we lose more through protecting prejudice in our own life than we ever gain.

SUMMARY

In response to the question of why we can't just all get along, the answers of stereotyping, ethnocentrism, and prejudice cannot be avoided. These three concepts can be seen throughout the world and until we can understand them and deal with them in our own lives, we will always be left wondering why we all can't just get along.

We began this chapter by examining how stereotypes are a natural part of our social world. Humans need to categorize to deal with the world around them and as we categorize people, generalizing certain traits to groups of people, we stereotype. Stereotyping is a way we try to learn about our world, but unless we are very careful it can end up distorting our perceptions of the world. Stereotypes are often negative. The fundamental attribution error was discussed as representing the basic thought process that underlies much of our stereotyping. We learned that stereotypes can vary along certain dimensions such as direction, intensity, specificity, consensus, and accuracy.

After considering stereotypes, we learned about ethnocentrism. Ethnocentrism occurs when we treat our group as the center of all that is right and judge others accordingly. Of course, we all understand the world from our own limited experience and knowledge, but such understanding becomes ethnocentric when an element of competition is included. We may not always recognize our own ethnocentrism in our quest for success in life. It is often reflected in the language we speak. Ethnocentrism is especially likely when we are indifferent to others' concerns, avoid interacting with others, and find ourselves intolerant of differences.

Finally, the concept of prejudice was defined as a rigid attitude that is (1) based on group membership, and (2) predisposes an individual to feel, think, or act in a negative way toward another person or group of persons. This definition allowed us to see many different forms through which prejudice could be expressed as well as recognize that not every negative intergroup interaction is an example of prejudice. We considered some of the rationalizing narratives people tell themselves to justify prejudice in their own lives. We also reviewed five functions of prejudice. These functions may seem like benefits, but when examined more closely damaging consequences both for individuals and whole communities are revealed. Prejudice is a problem each of us can work on in our own lives.

REFLECTION QUESTIONS

1   Are stereotypes harmless or dangerous? Explain your answer. What impact do stereotypes have in your life?
2   Can we eliminate ethnocentrism in our own lives? How? Or why not?
3   A variety of forms of prejudice were covered in this chapter; can you think of any other forms not covered? Give specific examples.
4   Do you recognize any of the rationalizing narratives in your own life and in the lives of those around you? How could you change these narratives so as to avoid the negative impacts of prejudice in your own life?

ACTIVITIES

1   Imagine you have a car to sell. How would you approach selling it differently (what features highlighted, etc.) to an older gentleman, a mother with young children, a female college student, a teenage boy? How does this relate to stereotyping? Or role-play in class how you would greet a potential business client who is from Japan, Saudi Arabia, New York, California, Mexico, and so forth. How does this relate to stereotyping?
2   Select groups from around your campus, athletes, engineer majors, communication majors, art majors, fraternity and sorority members, international teaching assistants, professors, campus police, financial aid officers, and so forth. Brainstorm in a group all of the stereotypes of which you are aware related to this group. What do they tell you about the group? What sort of consequences do these stereotypes have on these people?
3   Draw a map of the world with as much detail (countries named) as possible. How well do you know where other countries are? Where is your home country placed on the page? Near the center? Ask others to do the same exercise. Do they also place their own country in the center? How does this exercise illustrate ethnocentrism?
4   Take one minute and try to list as many American heroes or important public leaders as you can. The leaders or heroes can be from any area of public life and can either be alive or dead. Now take a minute and list as many African American heroes or public leaders you can. Next list as many Native American heroes or public leaders as you can in a minute. Then do the same with Jewish Americans. Next see how many heroes or public leaders you can remember in a minute from the Hispanic/Chicano/Mexican American community. Finally, how many Asian American heroes or public leaders can you list in a minute? Now examine your lists and consider how they may relate to ethnocentrism. Does your first list have a lot of white males? Does your African American heroes list include a lot more sports

figures than the other lists? Does your Native American list include a lot of dead chiefs? Why are we aware of some of these people and not others? Do some groups just have fewer heroes and leaders?

5   Examine the rationalizing narratives of prejudice provided in the chapter. What forms and functions can you see displayed in these stories? What examples of prejudice can you find in popular culture? Discuss and compare your findings with others.

6   Write an essay about a time when you expressed prejudice, either through thoughts, feelings, or actions. Consider it in terms of the narrative types discussed in this chapter and the forms and functions of prejudice. Consider what changes you have made or would like to make in the future in reference to this prejudice.

NOTES

1   N. Cantor, W. Mischel, and J. Schwartz, "Social Knowledge," in *Cognitive Social Psychology*, ed. A. H. Hastorf and A. M. Isen (New York: Elsevier/North-Holland, 1982), 33–72.

2   L. Ross, "The Intuitive Psychologist and His Shortcoming: Distortions in the Attribution Process," in *Advances in Experimental Social Psychology*, Vol. 10, ed. L. Berkowitz (New York: Academic Press, 1977), 174–220; and T. F. Pettigrew, "The Ultimate Attribution Error: Extending Allport's Cognitive Analysis of Prejudice," *Personality and Social Psychology Bulletin* 5 (1979): 461–76.

3   B. Davies and R. Harré, "Positioning: The Discursive Production of Selves," *Journal for the Theory of Social Behavior* 20 (1990): 43–63; and B. R. Schlenker, *Impression Management* (Monterey, CA: Brooks/Cole, 1980).

4   Based on V. Vassilou, H. Triandis, G. Vassilou, and H. McGuire, "Interpersonal Contact and Stereotyping," in *The Analysis of Subjective Culture*, ed. H. Triandis (New York: John Wiley & Sons, 1972).

5   A. Tan, "The Language of Discretion," in *Language Awareness*, 6th ed., ed. P. Eschholz, A. Rosa, and V. Clark (New York: St. Martins Press, 1994), 352–9.

6   D. O. Braaten, "Banking on Diversity: Familiarity Breeds Contempt at Security First Bank," in *International Business Case Studies*, ed. R. Moran, D. O. Braaten, and J. Walsh, Jr. (Houston: Gulf, 1994), 347–63.

7   W. G. Sumner, *Folkways* (New York: Ginn, 1906), 13.

8   I. Varner and L. Beamer, *Intercultural Communication in the Global Workplace* (Boston, MA: Irwin/McGraw-Hill, 1995).

9   For a full discussion of these matters, see Y. Tsuda, *Language Inequality and Distortion in Intercultural Communication: A Critical Theory Approach* (Amsterdam, the Netherlands: John Benjamins Publishing Company, 1986).

10   W. B. Gudykunst and Y. Y. Kim, *Communicating with Strangers: An Approach to Intercultural Communication*, 3rd ed. (New York: McGraw-Hill, 1997); see also F. C. Mish, *Webster's Word Histories* (Springfield, MA: Merriam-Webster, 1989).

11   Gudykunst and Kim, *Communicating with Strangers*; and R. Brislin, *Understanding Culture's Influence on Behavior* (Fort Worth, TX: Harcourt Brace Jovanovich, 1993).

12   J. Lukens, "Ethnocentric Speech," *Ethnic Groups* 2 (1982): 35–53.

13 Brad confirmed this by calling the Seminole tribal office. He was told that the tribal chairman, James Billie, had publicly stated that he was proud to have Florida State use the tribal name. This is a very different situation than those where the Native Americans want the name changed. Each should be respected.

14 J. Duckitt, *The Social Psychology of Prejudice* (New York: Praeger, 1992); G. W. Allport, *The Nature of Prejudice* (Reading, MA: Addison-Wesley, 1954); and G. Simpson and J. M. Yinger, *Racial and Cultural Minorities*, 5th ed. (New York: Plenum Press, 1985).

15 S. Sumii, *River with No Bridge*, trans. S. Wilkinson (Rutland, VT: Charles E. Tuttle, 1990), 272.

16 Adapted from work by R. Brislin, "Prejudice in Intercultural Communication," in *Intercultural Communication: A Reader*, 6th ed., ed. L. Samovar and R. E. Porter (Belmont, CA: Wadsworth, 1991), 364–70.

17 Brislin, "Prejudice."

18 W. Fisher, "Narration as a Human Communication Paradigm: The Case of Public Moral Argument," *Communication Monographs*, 51 (1984): 1–22.

19 All of the material on rationalizing narratives of prejudice including the table is derived from B. J. Hall, "Narratives of Prejudice," *Howard Journal of Communications* 9 (1998): 137–56.

20 J. C. Condon, *Semantics and Communication*, 3rd ed. (New York: Macmillan, 1985), 78.

21 Duckitt, *Psychology of Prejudice*.

22 Adapted from work by D. Katz, "The Functional Approach to the Study of Attitudes," *Public Opinion Quarterly* 24 (1960): 164–204; J. Levin, *The Functions of Prejudice* (New York: Harper, 1975); and R. Brislin, "Prejudice in Intercultural Communication," in *Intercultural Communication: A Reader*, 4th ed., ed. L. Samovar and R. E. Porter (Belmont, CA: Wadsworth, 1985), 366–71.

23 G. Nees, *Germany: Unraveling an Enigma* (Yarmouth, ME: Intercultural Press, 1999).

Chapter 8

How Can We Manage Conflict in Intercultural Settings?

Two "True" Stories

Not too many years ago in Japan, large numbers of gangsters invaded various coastal territories causing disastrous damage, particularly to the community of Iki. The Iki fishermen were faced with a choice. They could either stand by and watch their families suffer, their material goods stolen, and their whole way of life lost, or they could stand up and fight to preserve their families, children, and way of life. They chose the latter, thus positioning themselves as heroic warriors. The beaches around the island of Iki came to be a combat zone. The battle, as expected, was a difficult one and so they decided to make a plea for help from other Japanese, via their government. This plea proved to be unsatisfactory, for, although they received some assistance in the battle being waged, the message was intercepted by outsiders. These gaijin or foreigners were attracted to the scene of trouble and, though they smiled and nodded in understanding, they began to engage in covert operations to assist the gangsters. These gaijin lacked understanding and compassion and, thus, were incapable (either by choice or ignorance) of recognizing the plight of the people of Iki or their heroic struggles. Rather, they tried to use this opportunity as a chance to impose their own will upon the fishermen and the Japanese in general.

*

There were some people who lived in the West. These Westerners were a mixed lot, but one thing in which they prided themselves was a concern for the rights and freedom of every individual. One day they heard some distressing news.

(continued)

(continued)

Some others with whom they had a friendly relationship had been cruelly and mind-lessly massacred. Now these friends were fun-loving folk and kind, and had a long history of assisting Westerners who were in trouble, so naturally the Westerners were shocked and appalled at this outrage. "What kind of people would do this kind of deed?" they wondered. Various Westerners immediately embarked on an effort to find out what had happened and what could be done to stop further blood-shed. Though disturbed, they were also partially relieved by what they found. The perpetrators of this deed were simple folk, who in their ignorance had thought the friends had done them a great wrong. "Ah," they thought, "this is a matter that can be easily cleared up." So, despite their sorrow, they rolled up their sleeves and took a close look at the problem. As it turned out the simple folk themselves were to blame. They were a gathering people, who had gotten carried away and gathered up almost all the food where they lived. Then when the friends, who were a wandering people, happened to come by picking a few items as they went by, the simple folk blamed them for the whole problem, overreacted, and killed them. The Westerners immediately set to work to teach these gatherers the errors of their ways and the means by which they could avoid the problem in the future. Much to their consternation, though, the gatherers proved to be such simpletons that they could not see the error of their ways and actually planned on continuing to kill any of the friends who came into their territory. Faced with this unsavory prospect, some Westerners engaged in daring rescue missions for trapped friends and others worked to get all the other communities they could to join with them in pressuring the gatherers to quit committing this needless crime.[1]

The above stories deal with the same series of events and are both true from the perspectives of different communities. The stories have been modified so that as you read them the first time you are able to avoid certain prejudgments and see the perspective of each community from which the story originates. The terms *gangsters* or *friends*, depending upon which version you are considering, reference dolphins. The events being described occurred in the late seventies and early eighties. The conflict reached international prominence when media coverage of dolphin killing brought worldwide attention to the island of Iki in Japan. The Iki fishermen had invited Japanese TV reporters to cover the story of dolphin slaughter, hoping that the coverage would help them raise compensation from the Nagasaki Prefectural Government for the declining local catch that was attributed to an increasing dolphin presence in local waters. However, the coverage reached around the world, and their efforts to gain public sympathy conversely resulted in shock and outrage in Western societies. After the media coverage, individual Western conservationists entered Iki island to discuss the problem and seek

FIGURE 8.1

alternative resolutions to the situation. Each visiting Westerner tried to convince the Iki fishermen that dolphins were not responsible for the declining local catch; however, none of the Westerners proposed alternative methods for dealing with the dolphins that seemed to work. Over the next decade the controversy was settled in part due to Japanese concessions at the national level, although those on the island of Iki were not pleased with the outcome of these negotiations. These events involved many factors, but part of the core of the difficulty was dealing with intercultural conflict.

The Japanese in these fishing communities (not necessarily all Japanese) saw the dolphin as an evil creature. Over the years Japanese fishermen had come to view the dolphin, who are said to gobble up large quantities of fish and squid, as direct competitors for the resources that enable life. The Japanese term for dolphin, *iruka*, is frequently replaced by terms such as enemies or gangsters in the everyday talk of the fishermen. Also, terms such as damage, steal, and threat typically co-occur with references to the dolphin by the Japanese. Dolphins are discussed as perpetrators of malicious harm and as an evil that must be tightly controlled for the well-being of the community. The fishermen's call for help to their national government brought some help, but also brought strangers, mostly Americans, to their land. These strangers were seen to have warm smiles, but devious hearts. The strangers could not feel the appropriate compassion for their plight, but instead subtly sought to hinder the islanders' fight for their own personal advantages. The dolphin was seen by the Japanese in this particular area as a truly menacing creature, for its threat was not simply to a job or source of income that can be changed, albeit inconveniently, but a threat to their very way of being (somewhat like the wolf is seen in some communities in the United States).

On the other hand, the Western view of the dolphin makes one think an entirely different referent is being considered. In Western societies dolphins are generally portrayed as intelligent and friendly mammals, deserving of special status in the animal kingdom. From early Greek society to the television show *Flipper*, in the United States the dolphin features positively in many stories. These stories tend to emphasize their friendliness, intelligence, and helpfulness to humans. At times the dolphin is referred to as the "human of the sea" and the mass killing of dolphins is seen as a particularly reprehensible act. Therefore, the problem for the Westerners was that friends were being captured and killed by a somewhat ignorant group of people. This situation called for two types of rescue missions. First, in instances where the threat was imminent, Westerners tried to go in and free this captured friend through such activities as cutting nets. The second rescue mission involved attempts to save the basically good, if somewhat simple and misguided, people of the Japanese fishing community from their ignorance. Neither of these rescue attempts was completely success-ful. However, social pressures administrated through the United Nations led to a reluctant acquiescence from the Japanese government that dolphin killing would end. The cultural differences in understanding the dolphin complicated and confused many of the efforts to deal with this situation in positive ways and helped to create an intercultural conflict.[2]

The above is just one example of intercultural conflicts that affect the lives of people throughout the world every day. Many conflicts are much more localized and may only involve two people. In this chapter, we will begin by reviewing the literature on personal and cultural approaches to conflict, and then we will define the notion of *intercultural* conflict. Based on this under-standing of intercultural conflict, we will explore and illustrate three variations of intercultural conflict. We will then consider some strategies for managing intercultural conflict in positive ways.

CULTURAL APPROACHES TO CONFLICT

There are many different approaches to the study of conflict, whether intercul-tural conflict or otherwise. One of the most common is to identify and critique five styles or approaches to conflict that individuals appear to choose.[3] Although the names may vary slightly depending upon the writers, these five approaches are *avoiding, accommodating, competing, compromising,* and *collaborating.* Sometimes these five are presented as static personality traits. However, for our purposes it is more productive to think of these as ongoing choices that people make in given circumstances. The frequency with which some of these choices are made or the way these choices are typically viewed also reflect different cultural orientations to conflict. We will review each of these five choices as they relate to individual actions and to different cultural orientations to conflict in general.

Avoiding

One way people choose to respond to a conflict situation is to avoid it as much as possible. Avoidance may be accomplished by distracting the other party involved in the conflict by bringing up other issues that change the focus of attention or by simply being silent and refusing to participate in the conflict in any active way. In the United States avoiding conflict is often viewed negatively. Wattley-Ames describes how an American manager working in Spain refused to be convinced by his Spanish secretary that open competition for a particular position where three people were to "battle" for the position was a bad idea.[4] The American felt conflict would bring out the best and avoiding it was refusing to face reality. In this case the best candidate for the position refused to be part of the confrontation and the other two became so vicious that the entire organization suffered. Spain is a country in which conflict is avoided when possible. Silence should not be taken as agreement in Spain, only an avoidance of conflict, which, when it does occur, is often very divisive.

Japan is another community in which avoidance is a culturally preferred way of approaching conflict. One Japanese student discussed with me how she had handled a conflict with a roommate from Singapore. She described how her roommate would shout or yell at her. The Japanese student was stunned and would not say anything. The woman from Singapore felt this student was emotionless and not up-front. She wanted her to yell back at her and be brutally honest. Even though the Japanese student wanted at times to tell her directly what she thought, she didn't feel right about it. She felt it was too face-threatening for all involved. She continued to practice avoidance until she just finally gave up and moved out. The Japanese have a reputation of avoiding direct conflict. The Japanese often give indirect hints about what they want. People from Western cultures sometimes assume this indirection indicates they have won the argument or that the Japanese person is in agreement with them. This can lead to surprise when the person from Japan does not then act in the way the other person assumed they would. In many cultures the ability to avoid it is seen as a sign of maturity, not weakness.

Accommodating

The accommodating approach is similar in ways to avoiding, only the focus is on finding out what the other person wants and then trying to match that without concern for your own wants or needs. Individually, many people find it easier in a particular situation to go along with what the other person wants, rather than risk conflict trying to get what they would like. The complete sense of just wanting to please the other person, without regard for one's own welfare that is implied in the accommodating approach, is seen more often in specific relationships than in large communities. However, some communities do lean toward accommodating orientations to conflict. For example, in Zimbabwe it is very common for people to try to find out what you want to hear before telling you their opinion.[5] In this way they can avoid open disagreement and can adapt their wants to fit with the other person's wants.

Thais are often accommodating in their approach to conflict, stressing consideration for the other over winning one's point.[6] Fieg gives an example of a Thai buyer purchasing more than he needs at a given moment to accommodate the needs of the other, thus diminishing potential conflicts and building positive feelings for the future.[7] When questioned about such a practice the Thai indicates "that all cannot be measured in the profit-and-loss statement." Such an example should not be understood to mean that Thais are naive in business, but rather as an indication that accommodating in conflict situations is normal and seen in a positive light.

Competing

This sort of approach, sometimes referred to as the dominating style, reflects a strong win/lose perspective to any conflict. This is an aggressive approach to conflict that sees conflict as a natural part of life and that expressed conflict is nothing to be afraid of. Rather, expressed conflict should be used in productive ways to accomplish what a person wants regardless of the needs of the other. One American sojourner talks about how when he first moved to Greece he would hear his neighbors' loud, combative tones with each other and feel bad that people had to live in such a contentious situation. Over time he discovered that these were normal, healthy relationships in Greece.[8] Greeks love to argue and public debate and conflict are typically met with enthusiasm and are natural parts of Greek life.[9]

This type of approach to conflict is also found in Israel where Shahar and Kurz report that expressed conflict is a natural part of the workplace.[10] One American manager in Israel noted that his subordinates challenged whatever he asked them to do, but that was common throughout the organization. Katriel also notes that the culture of modern-day Israel encourages direct confrontations that to many outsiders seem too harsh, but are in part a response to accommodating approaches that are attributed to many Jews before World War II.[11]

Compromising

The compromising approach to conflict is one in which a person agrees to give a little to get a little. Those who like this approach point out that it allows people to gain a middle ground in a conflict, whereas those who dislike it claim that the effort to avoid a win/lose situation merely creates a lose/lose situation because neither party gets completely what it wants. U.S. Americans like to stress the idea of equality and are often great believers in a good compromise. Richmond notes in comparing Russian and U.S. American cultures that the notion of compromise is alien to the Russian value system and is seen as a sign of weakness.[12] He also notes that the U.S. American system of law is built on the notion of compromise. Most lawyers settle cases through negotiation and most criminal cases are settled through plea bargaining. U.S. American business persons are great compromisers, always making deals. Americans, however, also have a strong desire to win, which has created the sense in other communities that American compromises mean "I've gotten everything I wanted and hopefully you at least *think* you have come away with something as well."[13]

Collaborating

The collaborating or integrating approach refers to the process of forging an agreement through the conflict. In this approach each person's goals and needs are honored and met. From this perspective, conflict should be dealt with in a joint and equal fashion. Conflict is seen as a good thing through which problems can be worked out in a win/win manner. Writings on conflict within the United States usually hold this style up (directly or indirectly) as the ideal style. In principle this style is often advocated in the United States; however, we believe in practice the mainstream culture of the United States is much more compromise-oriented.

When Brad first learned about this approach, he was told a story about two kids who were fighting over an orange. Thanks to the miracle of communication they were able to discover that one wanted it for the fruit and the other wanted it for the peel, so it could be grated and used in a recipe. Thus, the children were able to collaborate and both came out winners. Brad remembers thinking at the time, well that is fine, but what if both had wanted the fruit? There certainly are conflicts like the one with the orange that through communication can work out nicely; however, there are also conflicts in which communication only clarifies that there really are some mutually exclusive goals operating. The question is, what then?

In given circumstances each of the different approaches to conflict discussed above may be the best choice available. To assume that we either should or even can collaborate over every potential conflict is unrealistic. There are times and places where avoiding, accommodating, competing, or compromising is the best way to handle the situation. There is no quick formula that will tell you when each of these is the best, but we hope that as you read further in this chapter you will be able to see the times of value and times of danger for each approach.

We also want to stress a point noted in Chapter 1. It is easy when we read information about other cultures to generalize it in static ways to the whole community. Remember the story of a Japanese student and her conflict with her Singaporean roommate. We might read this and think all Japanese will always try to avoid conflict and all Singaporeans will be forceful in conflict situations. We have known other Japanese and Singaporean people who seem to fit just what the student described. However, we have known Japanese and Singaporean people who did not fit these generalizations at all. Sometimes these differences are due to such things as regional and ethnic cultural differences within a larger community and sometimes they are due to individual personalities or specific family characteristics. Just as people in your own culture choose various approaches to conflict based on situation and personality, so do people within every culture. Certain cultural tendencies do exist that can help us deal with conflict. However, it is important to remind ourselves to be open to variations within every culture and to use our general knowledge in helpful, not limiting, ways.

Reflection Question: Which of the five different cultural approaches to conflict is preferred by yourself and by your community? Which of the approaches do you and others in your community actually use most often?

TYPES OF INTERCULTURAL CONFLICT

We follow the lead of Hocker and Wilmot who define conflict as an expressed struggle between at least two parties who perceive incompatible goals and/or potential interference from the other party in achieving the desired goal.[14] Therefore, conflict is the *expression* of perceived incompatibility. For a conflict to be considered an *intercultural* conflict, the incompatibility must be generated, at least in part, by a difference in how meaning is produced or interpreted. After all, culture, as we learned in Chapter 1, is a shared system of making sense. When these shared (versus just personal) systems for making sense are contributing to the conflict, then we have intercultural conflict.

We suggest that there are three types of intercultural conflict: object, relationship, and priority. Object conflicts involve contrasting assumptions over what is and is not. Relationship conflicts are centered on discord between perceived rights and responsibilities. The priority conflicts involve a relative ranking of actions and a disagreement over what is good and bad. Although the general issue over which the conflict is waged differs, each of these variations of intercultural conflict involve a system incompatibility, and, therefore, a struggle over meaning. We will discuss and illustrate each of these variations of intercultural conflict.

Object Conflicts

In referring to object conflicts we use the term object in a very broad sense, referring to anything that may be perceived intellectually, be it physical or abstract. Object conflicts thus involve conscious or unconscious disagreement and misunderstanding about something. At its roots are questions of accuracy in the sense of whether something is correct or true, not in the sense of a moral judgment. These questions of right and wrong may be seen as similar to answers given on a school quiz. Whether a person can spell a particular word correctly does not tell you if the person is morally a good or bad person. In this sense these conflicts are more a matter of cultural knowledge that provides different answer keys for what at least appears to be the same test.

For example, in Wisconsin a few years ago a conflict over Native American treaty rights heated up and boiled over into open conflict at lakeside boatlandings over the tribal rights to spearfish.[15] This conflict still simmers in many areas of the state and similar ones may be found throughout the United States. This particular conflict dealt with the Anishinabe or Chippewa whose treaty rights allowed them to spearfish regardless of the time of year and the largely Anglo protest community who could not spearfish and could only fish during the official fishing season. This conflict was particularly heated during spawning season, a traditional spearfishing time for the Anishinabe and one that is illegal for others. Although there were many factors involved in this conflict, one of them was grounded in different cultural understandings of the conceptual object or term *rights*.

For the largely Anglo protest community a discussion of rights is a discussion of what individual people, such as Bob, Mary, and Pat, may or may not *do*. It is assumed that everyone has the right to engage in fair play, work hard, and achieve self-sufficiency and material well-being. These rights are viewed as essentially an individual achievement. An individual receives honor within the protest community by ostensibly cutting all strings to the community and being his or her own person (membership is then perceived as based on individual choice, not need). Material well-being is the natural and expected manifestation of self-sufficiency. This self-sufficiency or material well-being is perceived as legitimately achieved through individual hard work and the practice of fair play in societal relationships. *Fair play* implies that the actions are institutionally open to all. *Rights* is a term directed toward individual means rather than ends.

Institutions and communities are taken to play a subservient role in the case of rights. Their primary purpose is to protect the individual's ability to enact the pattern of material well-being and self-sufficiency through hard work and fair play. For the protest community, talk advocating rights inherently opposes American Indian treaties such as the one involving the Anishinabe. Treaties allow individual Americans to do things that other individual Americans cannot simply because they happen to be born into a different group (those not born into the group have no choice). Treaties are viewed by the protest community as a denial, rather than an expression, of rights.

Although the *right* to spearfish is acknowledged by the Anishinabe to have economic implications for the welfare of the tribe's immediate members, rights per se are inescapably connected with a way of life and a series of relationships. Spearfishing symbolizes the distinctive and resilient nature of the Anishinabe identity. So, even though current political law may be used in their efforts to spearfish, the right to do so is rooted in a profoundly different conception of rights.

For the Anishinabe, rights fundamentally belong to a tribe or community. Rights pertain to social relationships and responsibilities of a group member. These relationships and responsibilities pertain to all living entities upon the earth as well as the earth itself. The individual Anishinabe is positioned as a steward of the community and the earth in general. Rights are made sensible to the Anishinabe through a particular patterning of *Bimisdwin* (the balance of life), heritage, honor, and generosity. *Bimisdwin* explicitly affirms the connectedness of all things and of powers that are beyond the individual. The balance of life is maintained by carefully fitting into the place defined by one's heritage and walking a path of honor within this place.

Rights are grounded in the responsibility of people to *be* what they *are*, not purely on what they may *do*. A person may live a life out of balance, but his or her rights/responsibilities as a community member are always there calling for his or her return to them. The Anishinabe do not focus on a negotiation of rights, but on the intrinsic nature of these rights and how actions that are true and constant to one's heritage allow for a balanced life. The very idea of negotiation of rights is seen as just one more ploy to oppress and deny the Anishinabe their right to be. The *right* of spearfishing is something retained through time by virtue of one's communal identity and appropriate interaction with the world in which one resides, not something given through a negotiation process.

The term *rights* in this case functions as a *kernel image* in the conflict.[16] A *kernel image is a concept or term that both cultural communities select as important, but do not share a way of making sense of the term or concepts.* The concept of a kernel image has its roots in the literary term kernel event and in Weaver's notion of a tyrannizing image.[17] The former refers to those events that substantially change the direction of a story and give rise to the significant tensions of the story, whereas Weaver's tyrannizing image is a taken-for-granted hub or idea around which basic understandings and evaluations within a community revolve. A kernel image, therefore, is a symbol around which a particular pattern of conflict may be seen to revolve.

The kernel image is relevant to object conflicts because it functions as both common and uncommon ground within the conflict. It functions as common ground as a symbol whose meaning is thought to be clear. However, culturally two different things have been identified, therefore it functions as uncommon ground. This difference is not simply a matter of poor translation; instead it is a deeply felt way of understanding the world. This dual function results in difficulties not readily apparent to the participants. The notion of *dolphin* as discussed in our opening example is another example of a kernel image. From a cultural perspective, two very different creatures were being discussed even though the people involved all thought they were discussing the same thing. Kernel images give the illusion that everyone is talking about the same thing when in fact there is disagreement over the object or idea being discussed.

Kernel images can be detected by the following markers: members of both cultures note its importance in the conflict and have a strong reaction to it (positively or negatively); the term or concept may be found in a variety of contexts and is often surrounded by greater cultural elaboration and restrictions; it provides an explanatory bridge between other concepts; and, finally (and necessarily), the meanings associated with it are discrepant across particular cultural communities.[18]

Not all object conflicts involve clear kernel images. Hamada reports on a joint venture between a U.S. American company and a Japanese company.[19] The American company wanted to extend its market into Asia and the Japanese company wanted to expand its technology base. One of the many conflicts that arose during the early years in this venture dealt with a high rejection rate of the product in the Japanese market. Many issues surrounded this venture, but the major response to the problem from each of the two companies provides a nice example of intercultural conflict. The American company maintained that the problem was the fault of the plant manager and that he needed to be held personally responsible. They strongly urged firing him and hiring a more aggressive manager. The Japanese felt that the manager was not personally responsible and instead blamed the appearance of the product, wanting to make it more aesthetically pleasing. The Americans maintained that the aesthetics had nothing to do with how the product functioned and didn't want to spend the amount of money it would take to make the appearance changes the Japanese wanted.

In this example the object was poor sales, and the conflict centered on culturally grounded explanations for the cause of this object. The Japanese place great value on aesthetics and doing things the right way, whereas U.S. Americans are more focused on functional success. An ugly win is better than a beautiful tie any day. The Americans wanted personal accountability in their managers and wanted managers to be the best qualified individuals. The Japanese, however, placed great emphasis on seniority, both in age and tenure, and focused on the harmony of the group as a whole rather than on dynamic individual leadership. Both of the companies noted in this case had complementary goals and wanted their joint product to succeed, but in spite of these explicitly shared goals the different cultural systems involved resulted in a variety of conflicts. Many of these conflicts were focused on differing interpretations of some object with each group thinking they were right and the others wrong.

Relationship Conflicts

Relationship conflicts differ from object conflicts in that they focus on how two or more people connect with each other. Although a particular identity can be treated as an object, when the issues deal with how these identities affect and link each other together in actual, specific relationships, they may be said to be relationship conflicts. Whereas object conflicts bring attention to differences in knowledge about things, relationship conflicts often highlight the implications of human actions relative to one another. Certainly there are many relationship conflicts that have nothing to do with culture. Intercultural relationship conflicts are marked by differing views of the rights and responsibilities of each party in the conflict as framed by the different cultural systems for making sense. These rights and responsibilities are grounded in notions of identity relative to the other person or persons. What do certain behaviors indicate about a relationship, or what do the behaviors mean within the context of an established relationship? Answers to such questions can involve not only different expectations of the rights and responsibilities of yourself and others, but different perceptions of who the other person is.

Veronica Duncan's discussion of conflicts she found herself in as a young professor after becoming the first African American to join the faculty of a university illustrates how identity can become a centering point of a conflict.[20] One incident occurred after she found out that one of the older secretaries, Susan, had behind her back suggested that she was responsible for a recent theft. She knew she had not taken the items in question and was upset that she was connected in any way with the identity of a *thief*. Upset, she had written an e-mail to set up a time to meet with Susan and sent a copy of the memo to Betty, Susan's office supervisor and the department chair. She then records the following:

The next day, when it was time for our meeting, I called Susan to confirm it and find out if she was coming. She informed me that I needed to come to HER office. Who did she think she was? She obviously had her roles mixed up. I could have sworn that I was the faculty member and she was working for me. However, her perceptions of the situation seemed to be very different from mine. I told her that I would prefer it if she came to my office, to which replied that she couldn't because she had to answer the phones. I asked her if Betty could do that, and she said she wanted Betty in the meeting. Finally I told them that we could just meet in the chair's office.[21]

This conflict has many different aspects to it, but at its core were a number of relational issues. Who was Professor Duncan? Was she a thief? Was she a victim? Was she an authority figure? Was this accusation brought up because of her ethnic identity? Who was Susan? Was she racist? Was she a busybody? What is the relationship between a professor and a secretary? Who should come to whose office? Does the age difference change this? Do their different racial identifications change this? All of these questions encourage us to explore this conflict in terms of who the participants in the conflict are perceived to be and what rights and responsibilities these participants have in general and in reference to each other.

Some relationship conflicts involve threats to an established relationship. Raymonde Carroll tells of one such experience that happened between her and a woman who had been an important mentor and informant in her efforts to adjust to life in Nukuoro.

Returning to Nukuoro from France I gave my neighbor a gift: a beautiful piece of cloth of a type that one could not find in Nukuoro. This neighbor was an old woman, well known for her knowledge of traditional tales and native medicine. She had been a great help to me and I wanted to return her kindness. To me there was nothing surprising about my action; all kinds of gifts are exchanged almost every day. I will never forget, however, the way in which my gift was received on this occasion. The woman threw my beautiful piece of fabric aside and then began to literally bawl me out for having given it to her. She yelled things such as, "Why have you given me this? Is it because I told you the legend of Vave? Because I had brought you some taro?" She continued to recite a long list of what she had done for me and to wonder why I had given her this fabric she did not need.

I went back to the house shaken and close to tears. A present that I had taken such care in choosing and brought from so far was just thrown aside. I wondered what I had done. Shortly thereafter I saw the woman's daughter. She had seen the fabric at her mother's house and she asked if her mother had bawled me out. Before I replied she told me not to worry if she had, that her mother liked it very much and she was sure to wear it to church the following Sunday as proof. Relieved, but still hurt and uncertain of our relationship, I wondered why she had screamed at me.[22]

Carroll explains that over time she came to understand that by giving such a rare gift, she put herself into a position of superiority over the woman, who had been her teacher until then. By bawling her out, reminding her of the many things she had done for her and acting as if the gift were nothing and that she only accepted it to make Carroll happy, the woman reestablished the nature of the relationship they had created during her previous stays in Nukuoro. Carroll goes on to explain that such conduct was normal in the woman's culture and, although her particular actions were a bit extreme, she was perfectly within her rights to react to such a gift in that way and Carroll was responsible just to accept such a reaction to maintain the relationship. This conflict turned out to be very short-lived, as many conflicts are, but it still illustrates the nature of relationship conflicts. Our shared systems for making sense do not always agree on the rights and responsibilities associated with various relationships or with what behaviors are even sensible within certain relationships.

Priority Conflicts

Priority conflicts are distinct from the other types of conflict because they involve a judgment of the relative moral worth of certain actions. Although judgments and values play a part in the other conflicts, feelings about what is good or bad and judgments that reflect particular moral orders are at the core of priority conflicts. Priority conflicts are emotional and often reveal the different values people and communities place on both different actions and different kinds of people.

John was frustrated. He had been asked to be part of a special medical team to help care for people injured in the recent hurricane that had devastated the Virgin Islands. He had been amazed at the overwhelming destruction that had met his eyes when they had first arrived. It had filled him with gratitude for his own comparatively safe home, but it had also given him a sense of purpose and a feeling of being needed. His medical team had set up immediately. The overworked medical personnel had been happy to see them arrive. There were so many people with serious needs and medical crises. After setting up a temporary base, they had begun receiving patients. John had been part of the group assigned to triage, evaluating each patient's needs so that those with more serious and pressing needs could be treated first. From that point on it seemed like hardly anything went right. The people here just did not seem to want to be helped. Repeatedly people who had serious injuries were refusing to be seen, asking instead to wait until others were seen, and complaints were being made about the way he and those working with him were organizing triage. The language differences were not helping.

Marcus was just the latest example. He had a head wound that needed immediate attention and his hand had been severely crushed. In spite of his obvious needs and pain he was refusing to go in to see the doctors. The translator with John was saying Marcus wanted the older couple sitting in the chairs over to the side to go in before him. They were obviously suffering from some shock, but they were not in any immediate danger the way Marcus was. At first John thought they must be his parents, but the translator had indicated that was not the case and seemed just as mystified as John by all the trouble they were having.

"What is wrong with these people?" John thought, "Don't they get it? We're here to help them. If they won't let us help them, people are going to be seriously handicapped for life if not die. No wonder there is so much poverty and sickness around if they have trouble even seeing the need for medical assistance."

Again John asked the translator to reassure Marcus that they would take care of the older couple as soon as they took care of those with more serious troubles. He considered just sending the couple in, but he didn't want to be yelled at again by the doctors. He had done that already once when a woman in her thirties refused to budge until an older fellow had been sent in ahead of her. The doctors had curtly suggested that perhaps the triage operation needed some assistance. John was not about to make the same mistake again.

Just about ready to call a couple of people to help him forcibly take Marcus in to be seen, he felt a tapping on his arm. It was a young native woman. She smiled and said in perfect English, "Perhaps I can help with your problem."

"Yeah, get these people to understand we are just trying to help them and get Marcus here into the doctors' station now!" he said in exasperation.

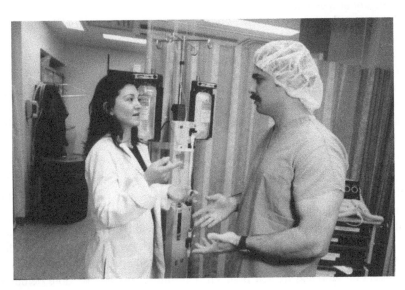

FIGURE 8.2 |
Miguel Gandert

(continued)

(continued)

"I can't do it in the way you want, but if you are willing to try a suggestion, I think everything will go much smoother."

Great! Just what he needed, another expert telling him how to do his job.

Just then a doctor barged into his area. "What is the slow-down in here?" she wanted to know.

He started to explain the problems with the patients and their refusal to be helped. The doctor wasn't pleased, but obviously shared some of John's feelings. "I know. Over half the people we are treating act like I'm a principal disciplining them rather than a doctor helping them."

"Doctor, if I may make a suggestion," again the young woman spoke out respectfully, but with a sense of concern.

"Who are you?" Doctor Braun asked, looking at her and back to John again.

"I am here visiting my family. I currently attend the University of Virginia. But I think I know what the problem here is."

John and Doctor Braun just stared at her in impatient expectation and the lines of patients continued to grow.

"My people have a great deal of respect for the elderly. I know you want to help those who have the most serious problems first and that makes sense, but here it makes more sense to help those who are elderly first. If you will do that, the others will be much more helpful and you will not have to spend all your time arguing about who goes in next."

John was about to begin his counterargument when Doctor Braun sighed loudly and said without a lot of enthusiasm, "Okay, we'll try it. This sure isn't working."

Three days later, as John was getting ready to pack up and leave, he reflected on how much easier and smoother everything had worked from that time on. Not everyone was treated in the order that should have happened, but in many cases they had saved time without all the arguing and people had seemed much happier in general about what was going on.[23]

In the case above the U.S. American medical team system for making sense of the situation demanded that people be seen in order of the seriousness of their injuries or illness. Each person was considered as worthwhile as the next and so 'seriousness of injury' appeared like a natural way to determine who was seen first. However, the cultural system working for those on the Virgin Islands demanded that elders be seen and treated first. Their position, age, and wisdom demanded respect. For younger members of the community to go ahead of them in a time of crisis was seen as extremely disrespectful. The conflict centered on efforts by each side to do what they perceived as good and morally responsible. Since the U.S. Americans were in a better position to adapt than an entire community that had just suffered great loss and were under extreme stress, it was good that they were willing to do so. Sadly, this is not always the case.

Of course, not all priority conflicts deal with what are obviously significant moral issues. Sometimes the conflicts occur over everyday sorts of concerns. For example, take the following experience between a recently married couple as told by the wife. The husband comes from Laos and the wife is from Germany.

The incident started when we received a phone call late on a Friday night. Fua was asked by his mom to bring over a check of 3,000 dollars the next day because the money was needed to purchase a new car for one of his sisters. Hettie was stunned that Fua's parents had asked them for money. They had not been married all that long and were far from rich. She'd never heard of parents asking children for money like this.

"I thought it was children who were supposed to borrow from parents and parents borrowed from banks," she grumbled to herself. Hettie became more upset the more she thought about it and later that evening laid out to Fua the options as she saw them given the situation.

"Fua, I know your family is important to you and I don't want to be a problem, but this request just isn't reasonable. I see four things that can reasonably happen. One, your sister can buy a less expensive car, one she can afford without having other people pitch in. Two, if she can't afford a car on her own, she buys one that can be bought with her own money and the money your parents feel they can give her, but not come sponging money off us, especially when we don't have much to spare. Three, if she must have that car then she goes with your parents to the bank and gets a loan. It's not like that is unheard of. Fourth, your sister could just keep the old car she has. It does still run."

Hettie didn't want to upset Fua, but she felt she had presented her points in a clear and reasonable way, even if they weren't what Fua wanted to hear.

Fua just looked at her and slightly shook his head, "None of those options are acceptable. I must give her the 3,000 dollars. It is an honor for us to pitch in and lend to family members. I would do it for yours."

"Mine wouldn't ask," Hettie replied briskly.

Fua shrugged as if he couldn't help that and explained that it is very common in his culture that family members support other family members when they are in a position to do so. Hettie continued to argue that they were not in that position and Fua continued to maintain that they were, that the 3,000 dollars in their savings was not needed at that point so they were able to spare it. After all, he maintained, his sister would reimburse it next year.

"Yeah, without interest if at all," she thought angrily to herself. She could tell Fua was going to write that check regardless of what she thought.

It is not unusual for married couples to come into conflict over money or how they relate to in-laws, but in this case it is complicated because there are cultural differences in what is good and bad and what is morally appropriate in this situation. In Germany there are strong norms against borrowing unless you absolutely have to, and then you borrow from a bank and pay it back as quickly as you can. Except for very rare occasions where a child must borrow from a parent, you would never borrow from family members, since they have enough problems of their own. In contrast, Lao borrowing norms indicate that borrowing is a natural and ongoing part of life. No one has everything they need, so everyone will need to borrow at some time. Buddha has said, "Do good and good will be done to you," so loaning is an honor. Finally, borrowing from an institution is frowned upon because you will not get a good deal and it will look like your family does not care about you.[24]

Although object, relationship, and priority conflicts are three distinct variations of intercultural conflict, they do not necessarily happen in isolation from each other. Life is often messy and does not always fit cleanly into the categories we create to help manage it better. For example, there are relationship issues that can be found in cultural conflicts over the meaning of objects; there are often disagreements about the nature of objects even when judgments of good and bad are being made in priority conflicts; and a priority of values can be found at times in those conflicts that are largely focused on the nature of a relationship. We hope that in considering the examples of conflict we have provided so far you can see how these variations in intercultural conflict can be intertwined in a given situation.

Reflection Question: To what extent do object, relationship, and priority conflicts overlap? What advantages and disadvantages come from identifying different types of conflict?

INTERGROUP CONFLICT

Another form of conflict commonly found within and across cultural communities is *intergroup* conflict. This type of conflict is so intertwined with intercultural conflict that it is difficult to consider one without considering the other. Whereas intercultural conflicts revolve around different systems of meaning, intergroup conflicts are rooted in the different group memberships. The saliency of different group memberships can result in conflict regardless of whether we share the same system for making sense of the world. Just as we may have intercultural conflicts with people who belong to a group to which we belong, so may we have intergroup conflicts with others who are culturally similar to ourselves. Cultural aspects of conflict are more about whether something is a pie or a cake or what goes with pie and how should it be served, whereas the group conflict is when we worry that the other person is trying to steal all the pie for his or herself because we know what kind of person others are and we want to make sure that our group and our interests are protected. Groups do develop different ways making sense, but often the conflict is focused more on group membership, just as Democrats and Republicans in the U.S. Senate often have conflicts that are more about supporting party lines than different ways of looking at the world. Before discussing the roots and nature of intergroup conflict, we will briefly review intergroup communication in general.

Group Membership and Communication

Intergroup communication occurs to the extent that the membership in a group category (such as male, British, Chicano, nurse, teacher, old, Lutheran, blonde, liberal, and countless others) of those communicating is salient in the interaction. In other words, intergroup communication occurs when part of why we interact with each other in the way we do is based on our awareness of their and our own group membership(s). Communication in general may be viewed as always situated somewhere on a continuum between intergroup and interpersonal communication. At one far end of the continuum is when we interact with people based solely on the unique individual characteristics they have and at the other end is interaction based purely on the other person's membership in some category or group. Communication is virtually never completely interpersonal or intergroup, but it often leans to one side of the continuum.

In intergroup communication we tend to perceive and treat others based on their group membership regardless of individual differences that may exist within their group. Members of the other group are unconsciously viewed and treated as if they were interchangeable parts in a machine. That is, we may feel that people in a particular group look alike and all seem to behave the same way. Even though we may know and acknowledge that this is not the case, we often end up acting as if it were. This form of communication also leads to a type of *self stereotyping* whereby we act and make decisions based less on what we may personally wish than on what we think is appropriate or expected of someone of our type or group membership.[25] For example, if Kristine feels that she is representing an organization, she may act in ways that support a policy that she personally disagrees with simply because she knows that is what is expected of her as a member of that group.

There are many triggers that encourage us to engage in intergroup rather than interpersonal communication. Recognizing these triggers will help us to be more sensitive to the particular challenges that this form of communication may present. Below is a list of eight common triggers of intergroup communication.

Visual Distinctiveness

One of the first things we notice about other people with whom we communicate is their appearance. If they look notably different than ourselves in terms of dress, skin color, and so forth, the likelihood of intergroup communication in nature is increased.

Oral Distinctiveness

When people speak different languages or speak with different dialects and accents than we do, our interaction gravitates toward the intergroup side of the continuum.

Assignment of Representative Role

This assignment may be a formal one, such as representing a company at a convention, or an informal one, such as when someone is asked what Americans (or any group to which they belong) feel about a particular topic. In these cases we tend to both be seen and see ourselves as somehow representing a much larger group and our interaction is typically intergroup in nature.

Large Differences in the Relative Numbers of Group Members

If a people are significantly in the minority as compared to other groups, regardless of what type of group it is, the communication directed toward that minority is often intergroup in nature. In turn, much of the minority's communication toward the majority is intergroup in nature.

Assumptions That Our Values Are Different

It does not really matter whether our values and the other group's values are in fact different. It is the assumption that our values are different that creates intergroup communication with others.

Lack of Shared Interpersonal History

Without a history of interaction together it is difficult to communicate on the interpersonal side of the continuum. When we meet people who are relative strangers, it feels safer and more comfortable to interact with them based on our knowledge of what categories they belong to.

Perceived Simplicity of Our Communication Need

The simpler our perceived needs, the more we will treat the other in terms of their group membership. Paying for gas at a service station is a simple process, and most people expect the communication to be much the same with each customer or clerk and may be frustrated if that expectation is not met.

Perceived Competition

Competition inevitably pushes communication more and more toward the intergroup side of the continuum. The minute we see things in terms of having a winner and loser or in terms of us against them, be it well intentioned or mean-spirited, we create intergroup communication.

Group Membership and Conflict

Membership in various groups is like a fertile field that in many ways encourages the growth of conflict. It functions this way because of the human tendency toward ingroup biases and a variety of common fears that may accompany communication between members of different groups.

Ingroup Bias

One of the most strongly supported ideas in the social sciences is the fact that awareness of group membership tends to result in ingroup biases.[26] Many people's opinions about Donald Trump's or Hillary Clinton's reported misdeeds during the 2016 election were grounded more in their political affiliation than on their opinion of the reported misdeed itself. To illustrate the impact of group membership we will review a study done by Brown and DeKamps that is similar to a variety of studies done around the world.[27] Their study involved three random groups of people who did not know each other and who at different times were brought to a large room to participate in the study. Each group was given the same task. Every individual in the three groups was given an amount of money and then asked to distribute that money however they wanted among the people in the room (including themselves). This distribution could be a little to everyone, varying amounts to a few, or all of it to just one person.

The crucial part of the study was the impact of perceived group membership and the way the setting was manipulated for each group. In the first group the people were all sitting as one large group and there was no effort whatsoever to group them in any way. In the second group the chairs in the room were divided so that there were visually two different groups and the researchers implicitly treated them as two groups by sometimes giving information to one side of the room and then turning and repeating the same information to the other. However, no explicit mention was made that the people were two different groups and the seating in the groups was done purely by chance as every other person entering was asked to sit on a different side. The third group was explicitly treated as two groups. Each person was asked a question about what piece of artwork they preferred before they came into the room and then they were told to go and sit with their group. Each group was given a name. Although the researchers had no real evidence for their claims, they talked about how aesthetic preferences often reflect different value systems. They did this to reinforce the participants' group membership and the perception of similarity among the two groups.

The outcomes of the money distribution task in each of the three groups were as follows. In the first group the only statistically significant finding was *self* favoritism. Individuals gave themselves most of, if not all, the money. In the second group there was again a significant self favoritism, with people still giving themselves most of the money; however, there was also a statistically significant finding of group favoritism. Not only did they give themselves money, but they gave a significant amount to the informal group that was implied in the sitting arrangement and the way the information was presented. Finally, in the third group the self favoritism finding disappeared entirely and there was only a strong finding of group favoritism. Even though the group was based purely on a single artistic choice and had only existed a short time, the researchers' explicit treatment of them as groups made their membership salient enough that they distributed the money in ways that favored the group even over their own self-interests.

FIGURE 8.3 |

Miguel Gandert

This type of research has shown that even temporary group memberships based on chance can result in group favoritism. These biases tend to creep into decisions even when we have an explicit concern for equality. Furthermore, memberships that have more history to them and have more serious conse- quences than the distribution of a little money in a research project can create very strong biases. A while back a Chinese delegation tried to establish economic and social ties with a mid-sized city in the United States. This effort resulted in a variety of intergroup conflicts, but one excerpt from a letter to the editor of the local newspaper illustrates just how strong these biases became. "Regarding the people who think we should make nice with communist Chinese, I have only one comment. Lie down with dogs, you get up with fleas."[28] These sorts of strong biases were discussed in terms of ethnocentrism and prejudice and assume an intergroup attitude of competition.

Reflection Question: Should we try to make every interaction as interpersonal as possible?

Fears Surrounding Intergroup Communication

Stephan and Stephan have identified four fears that are associated with inter- actions with members of outgroups.[29] Fear discourages interaction and helps to establish defensive attitudes that can encourage negative results when interac- tions do occur, thus functioning as a self-fulfilling prophecy. You may not feel these fears in the same way one experiences terror or immediately scary situa- tions, but we would be surprised if you cannot relate to some of them at some level as you think back on your own intergroup encounters. Often these fears are more like little anxieties that a person is barely conscious of, yet they make intergroup interactions uncomfortable, a bit risky, and something to be avoided when possible.

Tangible Harm or Loss

Faced with interaction with members of an outgroup, we often feel concern that we may be taken advantage of in some physical way. Perhaps we will be cheated out of our money, perhaps we will be physically harmed. In either case the loss or harm that we are concerned about is relative to physical items, whether mate- rial goods or our own and loved ones' bodies. For example, in the case noted above with the proposed connection between a Chinese city and an American city, many people expressed the belief that the Chinese were coming to steal technology and that American jobs would be lost because of the proposed con- nection. These people wanted no relationship with the Chinese because they feared material loss.

Negative Evaluation by Ingroup

At times interacting with members of another group can be seen as a threat to our standing in our own group. We may be worried that others within our own group will think less of us because of the interaction or as a result of an interaction with the outgroup that we are somehow perceived to have lost face. The *social pressure* narrative of prejudice discussed in Chapter 7 included an example of this type of fear about a person who did not want to be seen by members of his own group when in the company of a member of the outgroup. Gordimer writes about a pair of white South Africans who were very sociable with an Indian fellow when they were alone with him, but acted as if they did not know him when they were with friends.[30] They didn't want their friends to think poorly of them. It is hard to have very meaningful interaction with someone if we are worried about what others will say if they find out.

Negative Evaluation by Outgroup

Many may like to interact with members of other groups, but are worried that they may offend or come across looking silly to the other group. Perhaps they do not know the language all that well or they have heard about the many social differences between their own group and the other group and feel paralyzed by the thought of making a mistake. This kind of fear often stops people from any interaction or limits interaction in ways that make people appear more aloof, conceited, and uninterested than they really are. These perceptions themselves can create tensions that are easily turned into conflict.

Negative Self-Evaluation

All of us like to think well of ourselves and our communication competence, even though we may recognize that there are others better than we are. Interactions with outgroup members are potentially risky for the images we have created about ourselves. There is a level of uncertainty about such interactions, and the fear that we may turn out to not be as competent and caring as we like to believe may lead us to avoid and limit such interactions. Those who have traveled extensively and been forced to deal with many intergroup situations often find that their self-image has gone through many changes. Even though these changes may be very beneficial in the long run, they are frequently dreaded.

These fears, whether they are focused on some form of tangible damage or a threat to one's face, can create frustrations that lead to conflict and lost opportunities even in very ordinary situations. For example, one of Brad's students shared the following experience about a trip to Mexico. See if you can identify in this personal narrative all four fears we have discussed.

My family and I stayed in Cabo San Lucas, a tourist town, and we had been warned by many who had traveled there before that we needed to exercise caution because the street vendors and merchants in the city capitalized on tourists and often took advantage of them. I became determined that I wasn't going to be a naïve American. The first shop I entered in the city, I found some beautiful earrings. I asked the salesman, a soft-spoken man who spoke little English, how much for the item. He quoted me a price that in the United States would be pretty reasonable. But based on what I had heard prior to my visit to the shop, I was certain that the man was trying to cheat me, and I declined his offer. Had I been home and seen the same item, I wouldn't have thought twice about paying that much for a pair of earrings. Because of the stories I had been told and because I was unfamiliar with the man's culture, I assumed he was attempting to swindle me out of my money and I missed out on a nice souvenir.

Part of the problem was that my friends in America had very strong ideas about the Mexican people and the way they did business. Even though I wasn't with those friends when I went shopping that day, their thoughts and opinions were instilled in my head. I certainly did not want to buy those earrings and then return home to show them off to my friends only to have them ask how much I paid for them and then have them tell me that I had let the merchant cheat me. I didn't want them to think I was that inexperienced traveler they had warned me about.

I have taken Spanish classes and have worked with many Spanish-speaking families in my job. I'm not fluent, but I know many basic phrases that I often use to help me communicate with children and their families. However, once I reached Mexico, the people spoke so rapidly and fluidly that I locked up all that information. I knew I had a thick accent and while it would have been just as easy for me to say "¿Cuánto cuesta?" as I shopped, or ask the location of the baño, I didn't want to seem like an ignorant gringo or a cheesy tourist who could only say 'Sí' and 'Gracias' every other word because that was the only Spanish they knew. I didn't know any of the local people there and I probably will never see them again, but I felt out of my league and I didn't even attempt to speak Spanish because I was worried the people would think I was silly.

In addition, I did not communicate in Spanish because I was nervous that maybe I wasn't as good as I thought. Maybe those families I used Spanish with at home were just being polite and really they couldn't understand anything I said to them. I certainly didn't want to waltz into Mexico thinking I was a hot shot at the language only to learn I was mediocre at best.

Origins of Intergroup Conflict

Histories

We chose to head this section *histories* rather than *history* because it highlights the idea of multiple perspectives, and thus multiple realities, concerning any intergroup interaction.[31] The history of the American Revolution from English rule is very different depending upon whether you are learning about it in England or the United States. Was Benedict Arnold a hero or a villain? We suggest he was both and that either label depends upon your group membership. Indeed, many labels, such as freedom fighter or terrorist, often depend upon which group's history is privileged, rather than on the specific behavior of the individual.

Benjamin Broome's work on the conflict in Cyprus between the Greeks and Turks provides a classic example of these challenges.[32] He presents his research in the form of letters written by members of each group. Below are just a few of the ideas expressed in these letters to help give you a feel not only for these specific histories, but also the way different groups around the world create their own histories.

Greek View

Cyprus has been a part of the Greek world for 3,000 years. Although it has had to endure many conquerors, the worst of these were the Turks who invaded our island 400 years ago and kept us under their yoke for 300 years. In the 1900s we were a British colony, but we really wanted to join with Greece, our mother country. This became impossible because of outside pressures, but in 1960 we became an independent country. However, the constitution was drawn up by outsiders and was very unfair. It gave too much power to the Turkish Cypriots, who only make up 18 percent of the population. Although we tried to make it work, the Turkish Cypriots constantly blocked legislation, their terrorists killed Greeks and eventually the Turkish Cypriots quit the government in 1963. It was after this that Turkey started to meddle in our affairs again. They only wanted to create trouble and take control of the island, and in 1974 they invaded our island. Their army killed innocent civilians, raped the women, engaged in ethnic cleansing, and destroyed or stole many valuable resources. We were able to prevent them from taking over the entire island, but they still hold the northern part.

Turkish View

The Turkish presence in Cyprus goes back to 1571, when the island became part of the Ottoman Empire. At that time the island was ruled by Venetians who subjugated the religious freedom of the people and the residents of the island welcomed the Ottomans as liberators. Trouble started when it was decided we would no longer be a British colony. The Greeks on the island tried to force union with Greece. The British did not feel this was a good idea and, based on what happened to Turks in islands such as Crete or Rhodes when this happened, we agreed. In the ensuing fight many Turkish Cypriots were killed by the Greeks. In 1960 Cyprus achieved independence, with certain guarantees built in to keep the Turkish Cypriots from being dominated by the Greeks. The Greeks, however, still wanted to join with Greece. The Greek Cypriots even developed a plan to exterminate the Turkish Cypriots and in 1963 they kicked us out of the government. Many Turkish Cypriots had to flee their homes and band together for safety. Things got so bad over the next decade that we had to call for help from Turkey in 1974 to stop the massacres. Fortunately, they came to our rescue and allowed us to establish a separate government in the north, although many of our people from the south lost much in their escape to the north.

Consider some of the other major conflicts in the world today: Catholic versus Protestant in Northern Ireland, Arab versus Jew in the Middle-East, Serb versus Croat in old Yugoslavia, the animosity often found between Brazilians and Argentines, Chinese and Japanese, French and English Canadians, Hispanics and Native Americans in parts of the Southwest United States, or between Anglos and African Americans in the United States. Certainly not every individual in these groups is involved in conflict with those of the other group, but there are and have been enough conflicts across these various groups that there is obviously a reason for concern. We could have continued to list many more conflicts such as these, but the important thing to remember is that each of them is inescapably tied up in the histories of the groups involved. These histories cannot be ignored if we have any hope of dealing with these conflicts in ways that are productive rather than destructive.

The term history has a sense to it that is very monolithic. When we read about history there is often the unspoken assumption that "this is the way it was," and other possible interpretations are eliminated from view and legitimacy. Control of *history* is a form of power. How many times have changes in governments and rulers also meant changes in history? Often alternative histories, ones not acknowledged by the dominant or ruling group(s), are hidden, but are kept alive within their own group through stories and traditions. Uncovering and being sensitive to these hidden histories is also an important part of understanding and dealing with intergroup conflict.

Reflection Question: Explain the difference between talking about history or histories. What examples of multiple histories related to the same groups of people can you identify?

Dividing up the Pie: Competition and Power

As crucial as understanding the histories of the groups involved in the conflict is, research has shown that even groups who have a history of collaboration or who really have no history (they are made up, just for the purposes of the research) still display biases and get into conflict. To explain how this happens we will use a favorite dessert of mine, the pie.

Intercultural conflict rises out of situations in which one person orders a pie, imagining a delicious hot apple pie, but instead gets a frosty cold banana cream pie or a steak and kidney pie or something else that we may not recognize as pie at all. The mismatched meanings we have over the pie (or other objects, our priorities, and relational identities) become a source of contention because when we ordered the pie we expected that delicious apple pie, not some steak and kidney *nonsense*.

However, with intergroup conflict the incomparability is not about the meaning or variety of pie, it is about who gets what part of the pie. The pie in intergroup conflict is typically seen as a limited resource. The possibility of baking other pies is not really considered, so there is the sense that the bigger piece this other person or group gets, the smaller piece we get and, of course, vice versa. In fact, often the very existence of other groups implies that our group may not be able to get all the pie we feel we want and deserve and this creates a conflict situation. Any pie others get is pie we lose. Given this perspective, intergroup conflicts are inherently competitive in nature, regardless of the history or lack of history between the two groups.

The competitive nature of these sorts of conflicts is shown in part by who engages in them. Intergroup conflicts are always between groups that have a competitive relevance with each other. This competition is over some kind of pie (such as money, land, social privileges, people's beliefs). The examples of conflict noted earlier were things like country against country, ethnicity against ethnicity, one age group against another, and religion against religion. Baptists as a group very likely would not be in conflict against the French as a group. The only time that this may occur is if two different types of groups happen to be in conflict over the same pie.

Finally, we can see that intergroup conflicts center around issues of power in terms of establishing and maintaining control and security. Power may not always be an explicit topic, but it is always an underlying issue. After all, we want to make sure that the pie is cut as we think it should be. Of course, there are power issues involved in any conflict and power is an issue with the negotiation of meanings that is part of intercultural conflicts, but it is so in a less polarized or explosive way. Intercultural conflicts can, of course, lead to intergroup conflicts, just as intergroup conflicts can, with enough time, lead to an intercultural conflict.

Let us consider for a moment one of the conflicts we noted earlier in this chapter, the one between the Anishinabe and some of their neighbors over treaty rights.[33] We already noted how different systems of meaning surrounding the term *rights* were part of the conflict. There were, however, also signs of intergroup conflict. The largely Anglo protest community were used to a position of power. They controlled the hunting and fishing resorts (a major economic resource in that area) and many other local businesses. This power was threatened when the Anishinabe began spearfishing the lakes during spawning season and the Department of Natural Resources chose to close to regular fishing those lakes where this event happened. There was an underlying feeling in the protest community that they knew what was best for the wildlife and that it was important that the Anishinabe follow their rules. There was a sense that the Anishinabe were really not quite as intelligent or civilized as white people, represented by a number of comments decrying the lifestyle of the Anishinabe. The Anishinabe history was one that recorded many persecutions and broken promises at the hands of the Anglo community. There was a sense in the community that the power had too long been one-sided and it was time to make changes. As the conflict heated up, both sides engaged in practices that inflamed the situation. Terms such as "timber-niggers" and other intentionally derogatory names started to show up in the talk of the protest community. Heated protests at the lakes the Anishinabe were fishing were common and the local little league would no longer allow Anishinabe teams to participate. Some of the Anishinabe groups started to target certain lakes so that their spearfishing would have the greatest impact. For example, the community from which most of the protesters came had scheduled a fathers and sons fishing outing for a particular day. The Anishinabe came to that lake the night before and, using flood lights and spears, cleaned it out.

Many of the actions noted above were matters of intergroup conflict centered around power, rather than intercultural conflict centered around meaning. Suggestions given from peacemakers within each community were often rejected, not because of the ideas but because of the group from which they originated. However, there were, as noted earlier, intercultural conflicts involved as well. The combination of these two types of conflict made dealing with the situation in productive ways much more complicated. The next section of this chapter will deal with various suggestions for handling intergroup conflict, but before we go to that section we want to make a couple of observations regarding the conflict above that we believe have general application.

First, as noted, power is always a key issue in these types of conflicts, and with power comes responsibility. Too often, groups in power expect the other groups to make the first move toward better relationships, often not appreciating how difficult this is given the current distribution of power. If these conflicts are really going to be managed in positive ways for all involved, those in power must become sensitive to the power they have and make the first move toward improving relations.

Second, there were one or two other groups that had a significant impact on this conflict. The state government in the form of the Department of Natural Resources helped to create the problems by the way they reacted to the spear-fishing. Brad got the feeling as he researched this conflict that this organization was not pleased that the Anishinabe were somehow beyond their control and so they reacted in extreme ways (closing lakes and setting artificial limits) that were not necessary (the Anishinabe were engaged in a restocking program). This created problems for members of the protest community that were attributed to the Anishinabe rather than the governmental agency. Furthermore, the federal government stepped in to provide protection for the Anishinabe (which was needed as things escalated) in such a way that it created a sense of powerlessness in the protest community. Conflicts can be very complicated, and it is important in considering them that our vision encompasses more than just the two obvious groups involved. Often actions taken by third or fourth groups that may be seen as outside the direct conflict play an important role in the conflict itself.

STRATEGIES FOR MANAGING INTERCULTURAL AND INTERGROUP CONFLICT

The point of identifying variations of conflict is not so you can put a label on a conflict. Instead, it is to point out issues that need to be considered when trying to deal in productive ways with conflict. Conflicts have a way of muddying the waters in which they occur, clouding our vision and making it difficult for us to see some of the real issues involved. By thinking about the issues in terms of the three forms of intercultural conflict or in terms of the intergroup dynamics, we can get a better feel for what is happening in the conflict and how we may manage it as positively as possible. We use the term *manage* here because not all conflicts are going to be resolved or eliminated, but perhaps they can be managed in ways that eventually produce positive results. In keeping with that goal we will review some strategies for managing conflicts.

Appropriate Conditions for Successful Contact

Sometimes we like to believe that if people would just get together and talk, all conflict would be resolved and people would feel better about each other. As important as communication is, it is not some panacea for conflict, such that the more we do it, the less conflict and hard feelings there are. In fact, communication can bring to light potential conflicts that we may not even have realized existed, and sometimes the more interaction you have with members of a certain group, the more frustrated you become with them. There has been considerable research done on what sorts of conditions facilitate positive outcomes from contact with members of outgroups and what kinds of conditions hinder positive contact.[34] Based on this research, we review five of the most prominent conditions below. These conditions are especially important in intergroup conflicts.

Joint Goals

As noted, intergroup conflict feeds on competition. One of the most powerful ways to manage conflict is to develop situations in which the groups in conflict must work together to achieve some desired outcome. In many ways, joint goals help to realign the sense of group boundaries in ways that encourage inclusion rather than exclusion across groups. This subtle rethinking of group membership can have a powerful influence on reducing intergroup bias.[35] The joint goal, however, has to be significant for both groups and it is important that both groups be recognized as needed in the goal attainment. In the treaty rights conflict discussed above, the protest group and the Anishinabe had enough common interests that joint goals could have been established.

Supportive Social Climate

There are two different levels at which the social climate surrounding contact can make a difference: institutional and peer. Institutional support refers to the sentiments of the larger community and governing bodies for interaction between the groups, whereas peer support refers to the specific people a person lives and works with on a daily basis. If these two groups are supportive of efforts to interact with the other group, there is a much better chance for the interaction and conflicts to be handled in positive ways. If people have to be worried about their standing in their own community during the interaction, there is a much better chance that choices will be made that make them look good within their own community, but damage intergroup relations. Brad is reminded of when he first moved to Milwaukee, Wisconsin. He noticed that a few of the bridges seemed to go at an odd angle. After mentioning this to a longtime resident he was told that it was because many of the groups that founded the city (German, Irish, Italian, Jewish) wanted to discourage intergroup contact and so had built the roads in their areas, especially near the river, so that they did not match up with roads built by the other groups.

Equal Status

This can be a very difficult condition to meet since personal and group histories often create very unequal control of resources and social standings. There are two different kinds of status that can be equal. The first, and some research indicates the most important for intergroup conflict situations, is the group level. Do the groups to which the parties belong have relatively equal social status? When the conflict is between two nations or other types of organizations this equal social status can often be achieved; however, within a nation different ethnicities, political groups, and so on often have long histories that make any attempts at equal status coming into the interaction mere pretense. Especially in cases between unequal groups, it is important to work for the second type of equal status, individual equality. Individual equality means that people from one group are not placed in institutional positions of authority over people of another group. This can be a particular problem when problem-solving groups and so forth are chaired by people of the dominant group. If power differences exist at both the group and individual levels, it is difficult to get beyond feelings of defensiveness and futility.

Variety of Contexts

Too often we interact with members of a particular group in only one context and make assumptions about them as a group based on this interaction. We may meet members of certain Native American tribes in situations where people do not know each other that well and come to think of them as a silent and humorless people, when in fact humor is a large part of their lives and in many situations they are anything but silent. We may be introduced to some Japanese business workers at an after-hours get-together and be amazed at how informal and relaxed they are and the things they are willing to tell their supervisors. If we expect this informality to exist among the same people during a regular business day, we may be sadly disappointed. One of the best ways for stereotypes and narrow, often negative, impressions of another group to be overcome is to interact with them in many different types of settings.

Desire for Contact

This condition is focused on the feelings of the persons who are involved in the conflict rather than on the feelings of those around them. If Patricia feels forced into contact with another person, it is much less likely to result in any real understanding than if she wanted the contact. It is not always easy to get volunteers for contact during conflict situations, but if people can come to believe that the ends are worth it, they will volunteer to engage in uncomfortable means.

Recognizing Reasonableness

Often one of the most difficult things to do in a conflict situation is to recognize that the other person is also reasonable. The reasoning involved in this challenge tends to go something like this, "If everybody were being reasonable, wouldn't that mean that any conflict would be solved? Therefore, if we accept that the other person is reasonable, it must mean that we are being unreasonable, but we can think of many reasons for our own position in a given conflict, so that can't be right." The problem here is that it assumes that there can be only one truly reasonable side in a conflict. This is simply not the case, especially when we are dealing with inter*cultural* conflict. The whole idea of different cultures implies different sense-making practices. As you have read this book, we are hopeful that you can see how two individuals or groups of individuals could both be very reasonable and well intentioned and still be in conflict with each other. Of course, this is much easier to acknowledge when we are not involved in a particular conflict and acting in habitual and automatic ways, and recognition of this fact is not yet appreciation of it.

One important part of recognizing the reasonableness of the other person is to identify the *conflict identities*.[36] In any conflict we take on certain identities in relation to the other person. These identities imply who has a particular competence, who has the right to make certain decisions, who is the morally good person, who started the conflict, who has what obligation, and so forth. All people will have a view of themselves in regards to these issues, a view of the other person, and, finally, a feeling for what the other person thinks of them. This may seem complicated, but if you will take a specific conflict you have been involved in and ask yourself how you see yourself, how you see the other person, and how you think the other person sees you, you will realize that we often have answers to these three questions in a conflict situation without ever consciously thinking about it.

For example, in the conflict discussed earlier between Hettie and Fua over loaning money to family members, Hettie may realize that she sees herself as just being fair and Fua as being a pushover, too easily dominated by his family, and she may sense that Fua sees her as uncaring. These identities encourage her to react defensively to anything Fua says and to push him to stand up to his parents. However, Fua may see himself as acting honorably, view Hettie as ignorant of proper family relationships, and feel that Hettie sees him as not managing their money wisely. He also may act defensively and may try to explain issues that are not really a concern to Hettie. At the same time, Hettie's desire for him to stand up to his parents makes no sense to him, since he is honored to have been asked to help out. By considering the identities adopted in a conflict, we are better able not only to recognize the reasonableness of the other person, but really appreciate it. In addition, other people typically pick up on our new understanding and genuine desire to understand them and reciprocate with a desire to work with us rather than against us.

We also need to be very careful in the way we speak in the conflict situation or when discussing it elsewhere. Language often covers up a lot of specifics.

Simple statements, such as "_____ are rude" or "_____ are sneaky," help set a mind-set that hardens the nature of the conflict. No person or group of people are always and completely rude or sneaky. Speaking in simplistic and negative ways toward others encourages us to ignore the complexities that exist within others and allows us to treat them as objects rather than as humans like ourselves.

Often recognizing the reasonableness of the other involves some serious self-probing. This probing may include questions such as, "In what ways are we (or our group) helping to intensify this conflict?" "What might we (both your own group and the other group) lose and what might we gain from this conflict?" "What outcomes could occur that would allow both groups to come out winners (avoiding the 'one pie' mentality)?" These types of questions help us to think in terms that run counter to most thinking in conflicts, which tends to focus purely on how others are to blame and on win/lose orientations to a particular situation.

Another way to encourage a recognition of the reasonableness of the other is through the use of a mediator. The value of mediation in intercultural conflicts is being increasingly noted. Mediation allows a neutral third person to help articulate the particular concerns of each party in specific and nonjudgmental ways. This intervention often allows each person to hear and be heard in ways that encourage better understanding of the other. Mediation, however, tends to work better for intercultural conflicts than intergroup conflicts. Intergroup conflicts are often better managed through the process of arbitration. An arbitrator is different than a mediator because an arbitrator hears both sides and then actively makes a suggestion or a decision relative to the conflict, rather than encouraging the members themselves to work it out. The key with arbitration is finding a third party that both groups feel they can trust. One very successful arbitrator, U.S. Senator George Mitchell, when asked about his Northern Ireland experiences attributed much of his success to advice he received years ago, "Never ascribe to maliciousness what could be explained by incompetence."[37] Many conflicts are prolonged because we refuse to see the reasonableness of the other and attribute any felt wrongs to some unreasonable maliciousness on their part.

Factoring in Face

The concept of face refers to the public image or reputation one has. Often once a conflict has begun there is as much concern with maintaining your own or group's *face* as there is with managing the conflict. To save face is to maintain a positive position within the community and interaction. With this in mind one of the key considerations is to be aware of the *audience* for the conflict. This audience may be composed of members of the groups involved in the conflict, but our concern here is focused mainly on other groups who are only indirectly involved in the conflict. The larger the audience, the harder it is to deal with the conflict. If those involved with the conflict have to be concerned with how they are appearing to others, they are much less likely to focus on common goods and are more likely to try to make sure they win. After all, our (personal and group's) social standing is very important. Reducing the number of people in the audience when possible or framing the conflict in ways that allow both groups to save face with important audiences are important considerations when dealing with conflict.

Sometimes a person can be quite direct and still save face. Usually this is done by directly owning your feelings and perceptions rather than implying these feelings are somehow the fault of others. However, as was noted earlier in the chapter, not all communities are comfortable with explicit conflict or such individualistic communication patterns. There are, fortunately, more indirect ways to save face. Indeed, typically indirect communication patterns are more face saving than direct ones. One example of this indirect approach is storytelling. Basso discusses how storytelling among the Western Apache helps indirectly to teach people to see a conflict in a new way.[38] Griefat and Katriel also indicate that storytelling among Arabs in Israel may be one way to engage in conflict without threatening the other person's *face*.[39]

Expressing genuine concern for the other is also an important part of factoring face. Communicating this concern must take into account the other person's desires and situation. This does not mean that we can never get angry or disagree strongly with another person. It does mean that when we do so, we must also find a way to express our feelings of warmth and concern, especially after the expression of anger or disagreement.[40] In some way we must consciously look for ways to remind the other that we consider the relationship and the other to be important in themselves and not just in terms of how they serve us.

Although we won't try to give you a list of ways to show this concern (there are many), we will warn about one way this is not done. It is not done through severing the relationship and all contact. Allowing for some time alone can be a useful way to get a perspective on things, but just trying to end all contact is not the answer in the long run. Continued contact may be hard, we may feel like not having anything to do with the others involved in the conflict and become in a sense isolationists in regards to people from different cultures, but if the conflict or relationship is ever going to produce anything positive, it must be maintained, even if it is only done so with very clear boundaries for how that contact is continued.

One of the things that happens in many intercultural and intergroup conflicts is something called *gunnysacking*.[41] A gunnysack is a large bag that can hold many different things. What happens in conflicts is that we put all the perceived wrongs and misdeeds of the other group and hurts that we have felt over the years into the bag and then whenever any kind of conflict occurs between the groups we hit them over and over again with this bag of past wrongs. We are not trying to say that past hurts are not genuine. They must be recognized and dealt with in many conflicts. Indeed, an important way to help give face to another person or group is to acknowledge the legitimacy of past struggles. This recognition is particularly important for any group that is in a relative position of power. However, often a particular conflict that could be managed in a reasonable way gets out of hand because so many things from the past (many of which have probably already been addressed many times) that are unrelated to the conflict are brought up and the immediate points of concern are covered up. Groups that engage in gunnysacking tend to dig the same hole of conflict over and over, regardless of what else has happened, trapping themselves in a pit that they just continue to make deeper.

ONE FINAL POINT TO PONDER: FORGIVENESS

Conflict, be it intergroup or intercultural, has always happened and will continue to happen. The outcomes of conflict will be both good and bad, but we believe there is one other idea related to how we deal with conflict that will make a difference in our own happiness and the happiness of those with whom we interact. All of us at some point or other will find that in interacting with those of different cultures and of different groups, knowingly or not, we have made mistakes, perhaps been offensive, or created more negative feelings than good ones. The only way to prevent this from happening is to live in complete isolation from other groups. In recognition of the fact that mistakes, wrongs, and offenses will happen, we are going to need, as well as give, *forgiveness*.

To some of you the idea of forgiveness may seem simplistic, unrealistic, and an artifact from childhood teachings. In bringing up the idea of forgiveness, we do not mean to imply that individuals or groups who have done wrong to other groups should not be held accountable for their actions. Part of maturing in life comes from experiencing appropriate consequences for harm we may have inflicted. In addition, when we speak of forgiveness we do not mean pretending that nothing hurtful happened or just forgetting what has happened in the past so that it potentially keeps repeating itself in the future. Nor do we refer to a sort of pseudo forgiveness that occurs when a person or group plays the role of the martyr in a particular situation, thus providing a leverage for future conflicts. We are referring to the challenging and oftentimes lengthy process of letting go of the negative feelings toward the other person or group.

We have to be careful of the opposite of forgiveness: holding on to past hurts and wrongs. The Russian author, Dostoyevsky, insightfully warns in his novel *The Brothers Karamazov*,

> You know it is sometimes pleasant to take offense, isn't it? A man may know that ... he has ... exaggerated to make [the insult] picturesque, has caught at a word and made a mountain out of a molehill ... and will revel in his offense till he feels great pleasure in it.[42]

The character to whom this thought is addressed acknowledges it, but maintains that it is not so much a pleasure to be insulted as it is distinguished. Whether it feels pleasurable or distinguished, it never brings happiness. One of the great paradoxes of human life is that if we don't forgive, it is generally we who suffer more than the other person or group. It is true that we may exact some revenge on the other person or group, gaining some temporary satisfaction from it, but generations of experience have shown that such satisfaction does not change the wrong that was done and acts of vengeance never bring a lasting satisfaction. For whatever reason, forgiveness allows us to move past the negative feelings that may arise in conflict and get on with life in productive ways.

Most of our conflicts produce hurts that can, with a better understanding of the other culture, group, or situation, be forgiven, unless for some reason, as noted by Dostoyevsky, we want to hang onto the hurt. It is somewhat like the anger or hurt we may feel toward someone who promises to call at a specific time, but does not. If the call was very important to us, we will probably feel quite upset by their disregard of our feelings. However, if the next day we find out the person got seriously injured and was unable to call, we will quite likely no longer choose to feel angry. Sometimes as we learn about other groups and cultures we discover things that can help us forgive past wrongs. However, there are times when increased knowledge does not make the perceived wrong better; it may even make it worse. In these more serious situations it may seem that forgiveness is impossible, but it can be done. Many people, even if they are in the distinct minority, have done it in all cultures and groups for generations. Furthermore, as hard as it is to appreciate fully during or after the conflict, forgiveness in these more serious situations still improves the quality of your life.

SUMMARY

In this chapter we have tried to provide answers for how we can manage intercultural conflict in positive ways. We began by reviewing various approaches or styles that both individuals and cultural communities may prefer and adopt in a given circumstance: avoiding, accommodating, competing, compromising, and collaborating. We then focused on the nature of intercultural conflict itself. We learned that while all intercultural conflict deals with differences in sense-making patterns, three common variations of this kind of conflict deal with conflicts over the meaning of objects or kernel images, the implications and nature of human relationships, and the way values, norms, and ideals are prioritized.

We also explored another form of conflict that is distinct, but often intertwined with intercultural conflict. Group membership itself was shown to produce ingroup biases. These biases often produce a variety of fears in terms of interacting with these *outsiders*. We also reviewed how multiple histories, competition, and power are all breeding grounds for intergroup conflicts.

Attention was then given to strategies that can help us deal with both intercultural and intergroup conflicts. One way of managing these conflicts is by helping to create the right situation in which any contact is had. We discussed five important conditions for producing positive communication. We also elaborated on the importance of recognizing the reasonableness of the other person or community and suggested ways to do this. Next, it was noted how important it was to factor in the face needs of the conflicting groups and some ideas for doing this were presented. We also noted that one important element in intergroup or intercultural conflicts is the ability to forgive the other person or group. It is only when we do so that we can move past the inevitable mistakes made by others around us and on to relationships with those who are different from us that are peaceful, happy, and beneficial.

REFLECTION QUESTIONS

1 Is there is a difference between what conflict style you and others prefer and what you actually do? How would you account for this?
2 What examples of kernel images have you seen in your experience? What makes these so difficult to deal with?
3 Is it possible to avoid conflict in intergroup contact? Which situational conditions are most important in having positive intergroup contact?
4 Which of the strategies suggested for managing intercultural conflict seem most reasonable to you? Why? Does your answer have to do with your own comfort level at trying out these strategies?
5 Is the concept of forgiveness a practical one? Why or why not? Does it depend on the situation? If so, how? Does a person have to be religious for this concept to have any value?

ACTIVITIES

1 Watch a film that involves intercultural conflicts and either alone or with a small group identify the types of conflicts (object, relationship, or priority) that are depicted. Discuss the differences between these conflicts. Is one kind more difficult to deal with than another? Would certain strategies for managing intercultural conflict be more appropriate for the different types of conflict? Explain and give examples.
2 Identify a conflict you have been involved with (usually recent ones work better) and try to identify all of the expectations that you and the others had (or may have had) about what should be done, each other's identities, and what was most important. Examine these expectations and see how they

contributed to the conflict and what could be done to deal with or change or suspend them to more productively manage the conflict. Consider the many ideas for managing conflict noted in this chapter. Did you use any of them? Which ones might you want to try to use in the future?

3   We make a distinction in this chapter between intercultural and intergroup conflicts. Explain and provide examples of that difference. Select a newspaper, either for a day or a week, and make a list of all the conflicts noted in the paper. Identify which conflicts appear to be intercultural, intergroup, both, or some other kind of conflict.

4   Keep a notebook with you for a week and try to jot down all the examples of intergroup conflict that you personally see around you, your friends, and your community. It may be things you observe or things you hear said about different groups. At the end of the week, review these conflicts and identify how you think they got started and what strategies for managing them would be most effective.

5   Research a particular intergroup conflict. What and how many histories are involved? How does power play a role in the way this conflict is handled? Are there any cultural factors that further complicate this conflict? Write a paper that treats each side with respect and suggests ways to better manage the conflict.

NOTES

1   Stories taken from B. J. Hall and M. Noguchi, "Intercultural Conflict: A Case Study," *International Journal of Intercultural Relations* 17 (1993): 399–413.
2   Discussion based on work in Hall and Noguchi, "Intercultural Conflict."
3   W. W. Wilmot and J. L. Hocker, *Interpersonal Conflict*, 5th ed. (Boston, MA: McGraw-Hill, 1998).
4   H. Wattley-Ames, *Spain Is Different*, 2nd ed. (Yarmouth, ME: Intercultural Press, 1999).
5   Y. Richmond and P. Gestrin, *Into Africa: Intercultural Insights* (Yarmouth, ME: Intercultural Press, Inc., 1998).
6   J. P. Fieg, *A Common Core: Thais and Americans*, rev. E. Mortlock (Yarmouth, ME: Intercultural Press, Inc., 1989).
7   Fieg, *Common Core*, 107.
8   B. J. Broome, *Exploring the Greek Mosaic: A Guide to Intercultural Communication in Greece* (Yarmouth, ME: Intercultural Press, Inc., 1996).
9   H. Triandis, *The Analysis of Subjective Culture* (New York: John Wiley & Sons, 1972).
10   L. Shahar and D. Kurz, *Border Crossings: American Interactions with Israelis* (Yarmouth, ME: Intercultural Press, 1995).
11   T. Katriel, *Talking Straight: Dugri Speech in Israeli Sabra Culture* (Cambridge, MA: Cambridge University Press, 1986).
12   Y. Richmond, *From 'Nyet' to 'Da': Understanding the Russians*, rev. ed. (Yarmouth, ME: Intercultural Press, Inc., 1996).

13 Shahar and Kurz, *Border Crossings*, 148.

14 J. L. Hocker and W. W. Wilmot, *Interpersonal Conflict*, 2nd ed. (Dubuque, IA: Wm. C. Brown, 1985), 34.

15 B. J. Hall, "Understanding Intercultural Conflict through an Analysis of Kernel Images and Rhetorical Visions: The Case of Treaty Rights," *International Journal of Conflict Management* 5 (1994): 63–87.

16 Hall and Noguchi, "Intercultural Conflict" and Hall, "Kernel Images."

17 B. J. Hall, "Notes Toward a Theory of Intercultural Conflict" (paper presented at the Ethnography of Communication Conference, Portland, OR, 1992); for a related discussion of these ideas see also S. Ortner, "On Key Symbols," *American Anthropologist* 78 (1973): 1338–46. See also R. Weaver, *Visions of Order: The Cultural Crisis of Our Time* (Baton Rouge, LA: Louisiana State University Press, 1964).

18 Hall, "Kernel Images."

19 T. Hamada, *American Enterprise in Japan* (Albany, NY: State University of New York Press, 1991).

20 V. Duncan, "A Whole Lot of Milk with a Drop of Chocolate: An African American Woman's Story," in *Among Us: Essays on Identity, Belonging, and Intercultural Competence*, ed. M. W. Lustig and J. Koester (New York: Longman, 2000), 172–8.

21 Duncan, "Whole Lot of Milk," 174.

22 R. Carroll, *Cultural Misunderstandings*, trans. C. Volk (Chicago, IL: University of Chicago Press, 1988).

23 The idea for this example came from an experience related in a presentation by Dolores Tanno at the annual meeting of the National Communication Association in Chicago, 1999.

24 Based on material in B. Limary, "Intercultural Case Study" (paper, University of New Mexico, 1997).

25 R. Brown and J. C. Turner, "Interpersonal and Intergroup Behavior," in *Intergroup Behavior*, ed. J. C. Turner and H. Giles (Chicago: University of Chicago Press, 1981), 33–65.

26 J. C. Turner and H. Giles, eds., *Intergroup Behavior* (Chicago, IL: University of Chicago Press, 1981).

27 R. Brown and J. Deschamps, "Discrimination Entre Individus et Entre Groupes," *Bulletin de Psychologie* 34 (1980–1): 185–95.

28 B. J. Hall, *Motivations in the Global Village* (paper presented at the annual meeting of the Western States Communication Association, Vancouver, Canada, 1999).

29 C. Stephen and W. Stephen, "Reducing Intercultural Anxiety through Intercultural Contact," *International Journal of Intercultural Relations* 16 (1992): 89–106 and W. G. Stephen, "Intergroup Relations," in *Handbook of Social Psychology*, 3rd ed., vol. 2, ed. G. Lindzey and E. Aronson (New York: Random House, 1985), 599–658.

30 N. Gordimer, "The Catch," in *The Riverside Anthology of Literature*, ed. D. Hunt (Boston, MA: Houghton Mifflin Company, 1988), 472–81.

31 J. N. Martin and T. K. Nakayama, *Intercultural Communication in Contexts*, 3rd ed. (Boston, MA: McGraw-Hill Companies, Inc., 2004).

32 B. Broome, "Views from the Other Side: Perspectives on the Cyprus Conflict," in *Readings in Cultural Contexts*, ed. J. Martin, T. Nakayama, and L. Flores (Mountain View, CA: Mayfield Publishing, 1998), 422–34.

33 Hall, "Intercultural Conflict."

34 See Y. Amir, "The Role of Intergroup Contact in Change of Prejudice and Ethnic Relations," *Towards the Elimination of Racism*, ed. P. Katz (New York: Pergamon, 1976), 245–308; J. W. Jackson, "Contact Theory of Intergroup Hostility: A Review and Evaluation of the Theoretical and Empirical Literature," *International Journal of Group Tensions* 23 (1993): 43–65; and W. Stephan and C. Stephan, "Intergroup Anxiety," *Journal of Social Issues* 41 (1985): 157–76.

35 S. L. Gaertner, J. Dovido, J. Nier, C. Ward, and B. Banker, "Across Cultural Divides: The Value of Superordinate Identity," in *Cultural Divides: Understanding and Overcoming Group Conflict*, ed. D. A. Prentice and D. T. Miller (New York: Russell Sage Foundation, 1999), 173–212.

36 J. Stewart and C. Logan, *Together: Communicating Interpersonally*, 5th ed. (Boston, MA: McGraw-Hill Companies, Inc., 1998).

37 S. Hunt, "A Hope-Filled Toast to Peace in Ireland," *Denver Rocky Mountain News*, March 5, 2000, 5B.

38 K. H. Basso, "'Stalking with Stories': Names, Places and Moral Narratives among the Western Apache," in *Western Apache Language and Culture: Essays in Linguistic Anthropology*, ed. K. H. Basso (Tucson, AZ: University of Arizona Press, 1990), 99–137.

39 Y. Griefat and T. Katriel, "Life Demands *Musayara*: Communication and Culture among Arabs in Israel," in *Language, Communication and Culture: Current Directions*, ed. S. Ting-Toomey and F. Korzenny (Newbury Park, CA: Sage, 1989), 121–38.

40 D. W. Johnson, "Effects of the Order of Warmth and Anger on the Actor and Listener," *Journal of Counseling Psychology* 18 (1971): 571–8.

41 Stewart and Logan, *Together*.

42 F. Dostoyevsky, *The Brothers Karamazov*, trans. C. Garnett (New York: New American Library, 1957), 49.

Chapter 9

How Can We Succeed in Our Intercultural Travels?

With my first step on the soil of the United States I was embraced by fear. The Chinese person with whom I had flown from Beijing to Detroit was now on his way to Atlanta and I was left to make my connecting flight to Pittsburgh alone. Alone. I had never felt more alone. I still wasn't sure where I was going to live and the thought of entering an American university seemed a lot scarier now than it had a couple of months ago.

It was still summer, but I found the United States to be very cold. The temperature was hot enough, but the people, they were a different matter. Oh, the people were very friendly and always smiling, but I couldn't help feeling I was on display. And despite their nice words they were reluctant to help me. For example, I suffered a lot getting registered for my classes. My English that had seemed so good in China did not seem so good here in America. I went from person to person hardly being able to distinguish one from the other and I would go from one office to another only to return to the first office again. Finally, I got everything taken care of except for a signature from my advisor at the university.

Somewhat hesitant, I went to the department to see my advisor. She greeted me warmly, as she had my first day there, and asked how things were and without really listening asked what I needed.

I explained that I needed my form signed.

She looked at me for a moment and said, "You came from where?"

I held out my paperwork and tried to explain again.

"Oh," she chuckled, "you need your form signed."

Why was she laughing at my problems?

After signing the form, she said with a smile, "I really wanted to help you register, but you are so well organized that I didn't really think you needed my help."

I was so shocked I almost fell off my chair. She could not be sincere. Maybe I had not asked for help, but didn't she know how difficult this was for an international student? If I were in China, there would have been people to help me even if I didn't ask for help. They would have insisted on helping. There would be a sense of obligation toward the foreigner and help would be given. They would also not try to cover up their own unwillingness in meaningless compliments to the person.

Later that week, one of the graduate students I had met came up and put her hand on my shoulder. I froze and couldn't really follow what she was saying. She seemed to notice my reaction and asked, "Are you all right?"

I nodded and tried to relax. Americans always seemed to be touching everyone.

She had wanted to ask me to come to her home for dinner. I was excited and a little nervous by the idea and accepted gratefully. It turned out that I was invited to two other homes in that first month there. Each time things went pretty much the same and I left each evening feeling hungry and frustrated at myself for not being a better guest and upset that the Americans could act so nice one minute, but be so thoughtless the next. My American hosts would tell me to "help myself." I had grown up expecting the host to serve the guest by putting food directly into the guest's bowl. I felt somewhat rude doing this, but, not wanting to act like a pig and assuming that the host would serve more food to me later, I would take a very small amount. Yet the Americans never served me more food. They either never asked again or did so once quickly and when I politely replied that I was happy with what I had, they just accepted my comment and put the food away. In China a person often takes small amounts, knowing that the host will insist that the guest take more and more as the evening goes on. I felt bad for feeling so, but the Americans seemed a bit stingy with their food. Like with so many things, their words were nicer than their actions.

After a month and a half I was more than ready to go home. I talked to another Chinese student I had come to know and asked her how she had managed to live here for more than a year and explained to her some of my frustrations, such as what happened when I was invited to dinner. She indicated she knew how I felt, but told me that here in the United States I needed to "make my face thicker." To have a thin face is to be shy in China and she was telling me that I needed to speak up more. If I needed help or wanted more food, I should speak up. She said it may sound rude, but otherwise you could starve in an American home.

"Americans do not have manners, they do not know how to treat their guests properly, so you do not have to be polite with them," she explained.

"Oh, what am I going to do? This all seems so strange."[1]

FIGURE 9.1 |

Miguel Gandert

HIERARCHY OF HUMAN NEEDS

The types of feelings that this young woman from China experienced and the questions she asked are quite understandable. Were the Americans she had met being insincere? Were they really impolite, selfish individuals who had no manners and were unwilling to help? We doubt it. It is certainly possible that she did meet some people who weren't very interested in being helpful and acted in selfish and impolite ways. People in every community can act in many less than ideal ways, but chances are that many of the Americans she met were very sincere, more than willing to help if asked, and in general trying to be kind and generous, thus the dinner invitations in the first place. However, traveling from one cultural community to another and suddenly being immersed in a different way of doing things can be intimidating and often results in negative feelings toward the host community regardless of the intent of its members.

One of the reasons for these negative reactions is that many of our basic needs are either not being met or are only partially being met. Abraham Maslow identified a hierarchy of five human needs (see Figure 9.2).[2] The most basic level is physical needs that all humans have if they are to survive and continue to exist as a species: food, drink, sleep, and sex. The second level concerns items such as safety and protection. Meeting these needs allows humans to interact with each other in predictable enough ways that many fears and anxieties are overcome. The third level is human needs for belonging and social interaction. This level focuses on our needs for love, friendship, and intimacy with others around us. Fourth, we need to be valued and recognized for our achievements and contributions to society. This level allows us to develop and maintain a strong self-image, both in a personal and social sense. Fifth, and finally, the top level assumes a need for self-actualization in which a person meets her or his personal needs for growth and development.

This hierarchy is typically presented in the shape of a pyramid to emphasize the fact that each level is built upon the one below it. Humans who are able to basically meet each of these five needs are assumed to live healthy, productive lives. When we travel from one culture to another our ability to meet these needs is likely hindered or suspended for some time. The lower down the pyramid that one's needs are that are not being met, the greater the level of frustration and trouble adjusting to the new culture. Although this hierarchy itself comes out of a particular cultural viewpoint that values individualism, it still serves as a useful way to understand the challenges of moving from one culture to another.[3]

When the Chinese woman in our opening example came to the United States, she had concerns and unmet needs at virtually every level. She was unsure about her housing, about issues of food, about security, and about basic social relations.

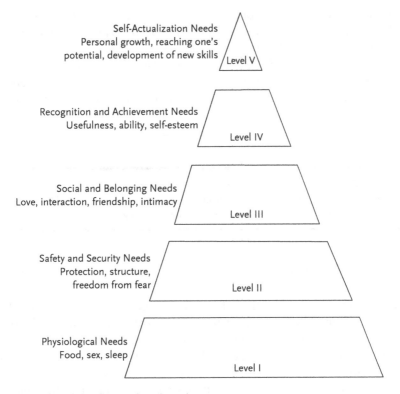

FIGURE 9.2 | Maslow's hierarchy of needs

It is likely that part of what made her advisor's compliment about her organizational skills seem so hollow was that it was directed at the fourth level of the hierarchy and she was still very much concerned with meeting the needs of the first three levels.

Iwasaki and Kishida, psychologists who help people deal with the frustrations of moving to another culture, use this pyramid of needs to help people get past some of their initial feelings of frustration, guilt, and blame.[4] The following case study is from their work and provides an example of some of the struggles Americans face in traveling to new cultures. In the example below, what levels appear to be unmet for Rachel and Richard in their assignment to Japan?

Although Rachel, a math teacher back home, keeps herself busy with ikebana and Japanese classes, she feels insecure and rather sad much of the time. Back home she enjoyed an active social life, but now she finds herself waiting for the children to come home from school and is impatient to see her husband at dinner time. Nevertheless, family dinners are less frequent these days since her husband often has to entertain business clients.

Richard is excited about doing business in Japan, but is also exhausted by it. The business opportunities clearly exist, but the differences in approach and follow-through are challenging. He would prefer to come home each evening to have time with the family, but the success of his job depends on entertaining clients most nights. He senses the move has affected Rachel, the children, and himself, but the demands of his job are such that he isn't sure what he can do to make the adjustment easier.

Reflection Question: One possible reason why intercultural travel can be difficult is because we are hindered from meeting the basic human needs identified by Maslow. Do you feel that Maslow's hierarchy of needs is applicable to other cultures? Why or why not?

ACCULTURATION

When we consider the question of how to succeed in our intercultural travels it is important to have an understanding of what is meant by *acculturation*. Acculturation refers to *the process of becoming communicatively competent in a culture we have not been raised in.* We all are raised in or *enculturated* to at least one culture and usually more. For example, a person may be raised simultaneously in national, ethnic, and religious cultures. Although these cultures are distinct, they often also share many similarities and a person learns at an early age how to manage these multiple cultures in everyday life. Acculturation, however, refers to the cultural adjustment period that accompanies travels to cultures that are different from the ones in which we were raised.

At times people will debate the value or impact of acculturation, some arguing that it is good and others arguing that it is destructive to the native cultures in which we were raised. It is true that cultures can be assimilated into other cultures and this is an area of concern, but for us to function at even a basic level and meet our needs in another culture we must become acculturated at least in part. Because we believe we live and are raised in multiple cultures, we do not think that acculturation is such a negative thing. Acculturation is not assimilation, although it is possible for that to happen over time. Acculturation is developing the ability to communicate appropriately and effectively within a cultural community in which you were not raised. This chapter is going to focus primarily on how acculturation is accomplished and what factors facilitate it. We will review four major models of acculturation. We will then consider the impact of returning to our home cultures. Finally, we will review aspects related to what it means to have intercultural communication competence.

The U-Curve Model

One of the earliest and now most well-established ways of understanding the acculturation process is through the rough visual image of a *U* (see Figure 9.3).[5] This model captures the basic idea that a person traveling to other cultures must get through some difficult times before they can get back to the same level

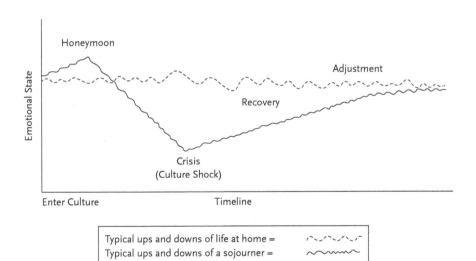

FIGURE 9.3 | The U-curve model of the acculturation process

of comfort and sense of normalcy that they felt before their travels. There are basically four stages that a person is seen to go through in this model: honeymoon, crisis, recovery, and adjustment.[6]

Honeymoon

The honeymoon stage refers to the initial exhilaration often associated with the trip. In the example presented above about Rachel and Richard's assignment to Japan, they were excited about going to Japan. They felt it provided some wonderful job and cultural opportunities and viewed their three-year assignment as a big adventure. This type of excitement is often felt when someone decides to make a career change and gets a job in a new field. There may be some initial concerns, but the newness and enthusiasm they feel about the whole move tends to outweigh any initial concerns. In this stage people are like tourists who are eagerly taking everything in and marveling at the differences they see.

> *Dear Diary: Deciding to come to London for my junior year of college was the best decision I ever made. I went to a play in the West End the other day. It was wonderful. I did have to laugh when I almost got run over by a car. I forgot to look to the right as I left the sidewalk. Of course, cars go on the other side of the street here. I have been amazed by all the museums and the sense of history around me. And the architecture here is so magnificent, it just puts me in a scholarly mood. My professors and fellow students have so much more of an international awareness about them than they did back in the U.S. My flat (a cute name for an apartment) is a bit old fashioned, but it just kind of adds to the sense of adventure I feel. Besides I just love everybody's accent.*

Crisis

The crisis stage occurs after the initial excitement wears off and the challenges of living in a different and, therefore, often difficult environment set in. Things that were perceived as funny or interesting little quirks in the way people act begin to become annoying habits. During this stage a person experiences what is called *culture shock*. The term culture shock derives from the type of shock a plant goes through when it is transplanted, often wilting before its roots take hold of the new ground and it returns to normal. Culture shock is *a feeling of disorientation and discouragement due to the buildup of stress and unmet expectations.* The hundreds of expectations we have (most without even knowing we have them) about how people should act and how we should go about daily activities are often violated in many small and perhaps a few big ways.

This creates an increasing sense of frustration that is often difficult to pinpoint to any one thing. Within our own cultural communities many of our daily activities and conversations are done without having to really think that hard about them, but when we are in a new culture we are forced by differences in language and behaviors to maintain a heightened state of awareness. This need for greater awareness often promotes a mental exhaustion at the same time that we are dealing with little things that don't quite fit our expectations. All of this together results in what is called culture shock. It is very common during this stage for people to feel tired all the time and to actually feel sick even though there is no specific illness that a doctor can identify. People also typically feel very negative toward members of the other culture, blaming them for their problems, feeling like people are just out to get them and that this new culture is nowhere near as good as their own home culture. It is during this period that high numbers of international students, international business people, and other travelers abroad cut their stay short and return home.

Dear Diary: It has been almost three months since I arrived here, but it seems like more than three years. I was going to stay here through the Christmas break, but now I think I will try to scrounge up the thousand dollars or so it will take to go back home for the break. I wonder if I should even come back. My flat is cold and miserable. The Brits are like fifty years behind the United States in terms of just about every modern convenience. The houses around here are all stuck together and look like they have a few hundred years of soot on them. I wish I had a car here so I could get out and travel more, but then the roads aren't real safe here. My classes are a joke, all lecture, lecture, lecture. No one wants to get into a real dialogue and when I do try to talk about things with my English classmates all they can do is run the United States down. Sometimes I wish we wouldn't have helped them out in the last two world wars, then maybe they wouldn't be so uppity. I mean, they can't even spell right over here and if I see one more steak and kidney pie, I think I'm going to puke.

Recovery

The third or recovery stage occurs when people are able to weather the storms of the second stage and continue to try to operate in the new culture. It is during this stage that a person can again start to see some positive aspects about the people and community in which they now live. People may still yearn for home, but unmet expectations are becoming increasingly fewer. In this stage people are starting to understand, emotionally as well as intellectually, that people are different and thus they are able to adjust their expectations to fit their new knowledge.

Dear Diary: I'm glad I didn't go home for the Christmas break. It would have been hard to come back. I was surprised to read the other day about all the problems the President is having. Sometimes Americans can be even sillier than Brits. It has been real interesting here lately since the vote of no confidence in the Prime Minister. They are going to have new elections in a fortnight. Wow, that is quick. I'm not sure that gives people enough time to get to know the issues, but it will really cut down on the kind of never-ending campaigning that goes on back home. Still, it seems odd to me that people don't even vote directly for the Prime Minister. They just vote for their local official and then the Prime Minister comes out of whatever party wins the most seats in parliament. I still wish my flat had a better heating system, but one thing I'll miss is the blokes at the open market where I get my lunch every day. They know me by name and they are so friendly, we always have a good time teasing each other.

Adjustment

Finally, a person reaches the adjustment stage. In this stage the person has adjusted to life in the new culture. Just as they could at home, they are now able to see and accept that they are surrounded by good and bad things. People have their normal variations in moods, but overall they are able to cope with life in much the same way they were able to when they lived in their home culture. There may still be little differences that they find uncomfortable, but there is often a redeeming feeling of satisfaction that comes from having *insider* information and understanding about the host culture and an ability to help other outsiders coming to this culture. They are able to again perform many of life's activities without a large amount of conscious thought.

Dear Diary: England in the springtime is a beautiful place. It was funny, I went with some mates to Hyde Park and this obviously American couple stopped to ask some questions and then they asked me if I'd always lived in London or if I had moved here from the country! As funny as that was, it felt even better the other day when this English bloke asked me if I knew where Blackheath Close was. It was nice being able to help an Englishman find some place in London. I do feel quite comfortable here now. I don't know why I ever wanted a car. It is so easy to get anywhere you want by bus, train, or the tube. My classes turned out much better this semester, but I still like the American system a bit better I think.

As useful as this model has been, there are some concerns about it. First, not everyone enters a new culture with a sense of excitement. Many people feel forced to move to a new culture because of political, economic, religious, or social pressures. Second, some people do not seem to go through each of these stages and some seem to go through them more than once. Of course, part of this could be that people may often go home before they would have moved into one of the later stages. Finally, the time that people take in each of these stages varies dramatically. Some people take more than a year to go through all four stages and others may feel that they have gone through all four in barely over a week.

The Hero's Journey: Osland's Model of Working Abroad

This model comes from the meeting of Joseph Campbell's work on mythic heroes and Joyce Osland's own dissatisfaction with the literature she read about the expatriate experience.[7] Osland felt that her experience as an expatriate (anyone living in a different country than the one in which they were raised) and the experiences of many others that had been shared with her were not well described in the academic writings about these cultural transitions and so decided to develop her own model of them. Based on numerous interviews and observations, she found many similarities between the expatriate acculturation experience and Campbell's work on mythic heroes. She describes a six-part journey: *the call to adventure, the belly of the whale, the magical friend, the road of trials, the ultimate boon,* and *the return.* Her model is one that can happen, but is not meant to be a description of what will happen for everyone. People may opt out of the hero's journey anywhere along the path.

Call to Adventure

The call to adventure is the opportunity to go abroad and experience a new way of living in a new world. Most of these expatriates are seen as eager to go abroad. It is something they have always wanted to do or seen as a great career opportunity. Often the decision to accept the call is immediate and, even if it has to be weighed out very carefully, it is still an experience to be seized and lived to the fullest. Osland does note that some people may accept the call to go abroad without accepting the call to adventure and for these people the hero's journey does not really apply, as they often insulate themselves from exposure to the new culture and return home without really experiencing an adventure.

In the Belly of the Whale

Entering the belly of the whale refers to one entering an unknown culture. It is like crossing a threshold from one's past life into a totally different life.

Often crossing this threshold is made difficult by factors that seem to be guarding the threshold into the new life. These guardians include such things as culturally inappropriate constraints put on the expatriates by headquarters, a deep distrust of the hero as a stranger by the members of the new culture, a lack of language ability, and an expatriate community that severely restricts interaction with members of the host community, such as a *golden ghetto* (a place heavily populated by Americans or other expatriates that tends to be economically very well off). If the expatriate is not careful or is willing to succumb to these guardians, she or he will not be able to finish the hero's journey. Stepping into the unknown is challenging and just because one is cast in the role of hero it does not mean that things will go smoothly or that the person will handle everything competently.

> *The first day we got to Japan, well, first of all they lost our bags, which was typical. But I told my wife, who was staying at a hotel in Tokyo, "Take the train out to the bus and get on the bus and our stop is like the ninth stop and the house is right there," because I had bought the house and she had never seen it. So she got to the train station, had enough money to get onto the train. She got off the train at the right place and went down to get the bus. She got to the bus, went to get on the bus and then ran out of money, change. So she went into a Pachinko parlor [where a game is played with steel balls] and asked for change and they pointed to a machine and she put a thousand yen into a machine, and got a big plastic bucket of Pachinko balls. And she thought that they were tokens for the bus ... We kept it [bucket of balls] with the thought in mind that anytime you felt stupid about something you did—just drag those babies out.*[8]

The Magical Friend

Regardless of the mistakes one may make and challenges that one may face in this new land, one seems to eventually find a magical friend or a cultural mentor. This mentor may be found through information seeking efforts on the hero's part or by a recognition of the hero's need by someone else who has traveled a similar path in the past. The mentor is often a member of the new culture, but can also be another well-seasoned expatriate. These mentors serve as guides during the hero's initial journeys, helping with language concerns, living accommodations, social contacts, and advice for greater work effectiveness. During this stage it is helpful for the hero to remember to never complain about the other culture, regardless of what the other person says. Complaints have a way of slowing down the process of finding these mentors, especially among members of the new culture itself.

Road of Trials (Paradoxes)

Even with a magical friend to serve as mentor, the hero must eventually go down his or her own road of trials. These trials take the form of various paradoxes that, to truly deal with them, must be experienced, although mentors can help during this process. Paradoxes are the *seemingly contradictory, but equally true ideas* that emerge as one tries to mediate between two cultures. Osland discusses many different paradoxes that the hero may face. We will briefly review five of these.

Seeing as valid the general stereotype about the local culture, but also realizing that many host-country nationals do not fit that stereotype. Experience in another culture encourages one to see how certain communal tendencies create stereotypes that can help a person understand and deal with members of the new culture. However, at the same time that one gains this better understanding of the general culture, one discovers more and more individuals who do not really fit the stereotype, forcing one to be aware of individuals, rather than just cultural membership.

Feeling at ease anywhere, but belonging nowhere. The hero's journey may help develop a person's ability to feel at home in a variety of places and situations, yet the person still might not fit in. For example, we know a person who lived for almost 20 years in Japan and, although he was well acculturated, he was never really accepted as Japanese. A certain feeling of marginality often exists even upon returning home, as the hero and his community have both changed during the journey.

Feeling caught between the contradictory demands of headquarters on one hand and the demands of the host-country nationals and the local situation on the other. A person who is abroad on an organizational assignment will often find that their home organization wants things done within a certain time period or information sought in a certain way, yet this timing or method of garnering information may be virtually impossible within the cultural context in which the person is working. The person must act as a translator for both groups, trying to convey the point of view of the home office to those in the new culture without losing their trust and explaining what can effectively be done in the new culture to the home office without being accused of going native and being brought home before the journey is completed.

Giving up some of one's American [or any other home community] *cultural ideas and behaviors to be accepted and successful in the other culture while at the same time finding some of one's core American values becoming even stronger as a result of exposure to another culture.* The hero soon learns that to be effective and to avoid standing out in negative ways he or she must make some changes in attitude and behavior. Differences often exist in areas such as perceived work ethic, the level of formality expected in certain situations, how differences in social class are dealt with, and a wide variety of verbal and non-verbal communicative practices. Many practices and attitudes that seem like the one and only right way to do something in one's home culture become just one of many possibilities in another community. Osland reports on one expatriate who had actively protested against the government when he lived in the United States and was surprised by the strong feelings of patriotism he experienced after living abroad for some time. It may not always be people's feeling toward their homeland that emerges, but often certain core values and attitudes come to be held more intensely at the same time that others are changing dramatically.

Becoming more and more "world-minded" as a result of exposure to different values and conflicting loyalties, but becoming more idiosyncratic in putting together one's own value system and views of life. Osland notes that her interviewees felt that this was the most significant of the paradoxes they faced. A hero tends to recreate her or his identity in very unique ways even as she or he is more aware and accepting of many different identities. This paradox involves a macro/micro tension that is very open and inclusive toward others, but very exclusive and firm in terms of personal beliefs.

Ultimate Boon and Return

The next part of the journey is the ultimate boon or the transformation of the self. The "boons" that Osland refers to can come in many different and unexpected forms such as the one Miranda describes in the following story:

In her early 30s, Miranda moved to a small, rural town in Mexico where she lived for three years. She moved from Chicago, leaving a successful career in a law firm to start her own business. The business was successful, but not in financial terms as she had anticipated. Instead, the success Miranda experienced was about how she viewed life. Through her hero's journey, she came to realize the importance of family, of relaxation, and the peace available through connection with the environment and natural world. During her first weeks in Mexico, Miranda became used to sleeping in a hammock at night. It became her favorite feeling. The natural and easy sway of the hammock that supported her body and gently rocked. In fact, Miranda accumulated a few hammocks during her time in Mexico. They were handmade around fires in the jungle and had a distinctive smell that also became comforting to Miranda. One hammock was for sleeping at night, one was for relaxing indoors strung across the living room, and one was for outside where she could feel the sun and breeze.

After three years, Miranda returned to the United States and settled in New Mexico. She had never been to that state, but chose New Mexico because she thought that location would best support her love of the Hispanic culture formed during her time living in Mexico. Before leaving her adopted town in Mexico,

Miranda recalls she was laying in her hammock one day and consciously told herself that when she returned to the United States she must remember to be still and do nothing at some point during the day. She wondered where she would find to hang her hammocks in the United States, and she promised herself that she would always remember the wisdom of the natural world that would guide her if only she paused to listen.

Osland describes the successful hero as one who has learned to sacrifice for the good of others, yet has developed a self-sufficiency and inner power that allows for the accomplishment of seemingly impossible tasks. Finding ways to deal with the trials of the road results in an empowered person: a person who recognizes that he or she has grown and matured and feels better because of it; a person with a broader perspective on the world and a greater appreciation of differences; a person who not only has better work skills, but also can better lead others in accomplishing important goals; a person with a much wider base of knowledge and understanding; and, finally, a person who has developed closer, more rich personal and family relationships.

On the hero's return he or she often finds that things have changed. Perhaps certain things were idealized, but they may no longer have the same elevated status. Other people have changed and often are not that interested in the many stories the hero has to tell. Of course, Osland emphasizes that not everyone who has lived abroad travels the hero's journey, but those who do reap immense rewards and, regardless of their reception upon their return, have benefitted from the journey. Based on her *hero* interviews she synthesizes a variety of tips for people either beginning or ending such a journey. These are shown in Table 9.1.

Surprise and Sense-Making Model

Meryl Louis's sense-making model was formulated to better understand the acculturation process as it applies to moving from one organizational culture to another, but it is applicable to any cultural transition.[9] Figure 9.4 gives a broad overview of the model. However, it is important to remember that this is not a traditional stage model in which a person is assumed to basically be in one stage at a given point in time. Instead, people are likely to be involved with almost every part of the model simultaneously. We may at any given time be feeling the contrasts between the two cultures, be seeking information with which to make sense of some other contrast, attributing meaning to another separate point of surprise, and updating our expectations about a fourth issue. The sense-making process is a continually overlapping process that people new to a culture experience as they upgrade their cognitive maps to deal with the new culture. We will explain each of the key elements in the model using the opening example of the Chinese student coming to the United States to study.

TABLE 9.1 | Osland's tips for beginning or ending a journey overseas

Inform yourself about the culture and office beforehand.

Find a cultural mentor.

Get eight hours of sleep in the first weeks to help you deal with stimulus overload.

Avoid negative people.

Get yourself and the family settled in before you go to work.

Choose a neighborhood that will easily accept you and where you will feel at home.

Go slow at work, and get the lay of the land before making big changes.

Expect to undergo culture shock and accept that the first six to eight months may be difficult.

Find substitutes for what you enjoyed in the previous country.

Be adaptable and flexible.

Expect a certain degree of marginality.

Don't make negative attributions about the locals.

Try to understand why people behave as they do.

Don't make negative comparisons with the previous country; accept each for what it is.

Focus on the positive and overlook the negative.

Maintain a positive attitude; try not to complain.

Take advantage of what the country has to offer.

Get involved as quickly as possible.

Be humble (neither an Ugly American nor an arrogant internationalist).

Expect a testing period before you are more fully accepted at work or in the neighborhood.

Expect logistics to be annoying in the beginning.

Beware of failed expectations; if something is not what you expected and cannot be remedied, try to get over it quickly.

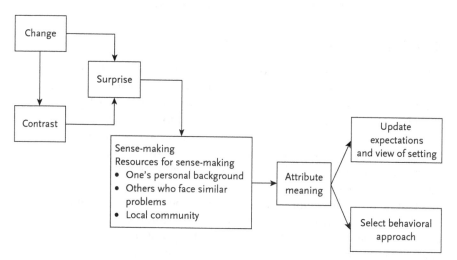

FIGURE 9.4 | Adapted from Louis's sense-making model

Change

Change deals with the differences between the old culture and the new culture that are obvious or can be seen with some consideration. These are differences that almost anyone could notice. These types of differences can be taught in a training program for someone entering a new culture. They may deal with things like dress, language, nonverbal cues, social organization, and all the other factors we have discussed so far in this book. Thus, a person can be prepared, mentally if not emotionally, for many of these changes. In the case of the Chinese graduate student, she knew beforehand that English was spoken in the United States. She was probably told that Americans are very independent and concerned with individual freedom. As she lived here she learned that many social situations are handled differently, whether that be in the classroom or when visiting someone's home for dinner. Americans often allow and expect a guest to serve themselves the food they want. In addition, anyone could notice that Americans do not offer to help a newcomer as often as do the Chinese, and when they do make an offer to help they do not insist that their help be accepted as much as you would find in China.

Contrast

Contrast refers to those things that the individual person notices, things that really cannot be taught in advance. Contrasts are personal, generally emotional, reactions to the changes that anyone could see. You may know that time or interpersonal space are viewed differently in the culture, but you do not know how a person arriving a half-hour late without a word of apology or concern expressed, or someone standing very close and gently rubbing your arm as you chat, is going to affect you until it happens. These contrasts may be a refreshing change, no big deal, or a point of serious discomfort and even anger. Although contrasts stem out of general observable changes across the cultures involved, they have a very personal dimension to them. A husband and wife, two siblings, or two exchange students from the same culture may have very different reactions to the same changes. These very personal reactions and observations are the contrasts depicted in the model. The personal reactions of the Chinese student in our example may be quite different from those of some other Chinese students, and even when they are similar there are always personal history factors that make one's observations and reactions unique in some way, even if our language does not allow for a complete expression of these unique aspects.

Surprise

Surprise is an inevitable outcome of both the changes and contrasts people experience. Even though we may have been told what to expect in the new culture, we will still experience varying degrees of surprise in response to these changes and contrasts. Although cultural sensitivity training may be very helpful, it does not eliminate surprise. We may be surprised about general changes or cultural differences; for example, the American student in London found that most homes were attached to other homes, rather than standing alone like they typically do in the United States. We may also be surprised about our own reactions to those differences; like the expatriate discussed in the earlier section who did not think he was patriotic at all, but discovered a great love for his country after living abroad. Living in a new culture results in many ongoing surprises, both large and small. The Chinese student was surprised at the words of her advisor, who said she would have liked to help, but that the student had seemed so organized that there was no need. She was surprised by her fellow graduate students, whom she hardly knew, touching her in casual conversation. She was also surprised that the dinner hosts left her to fend for herself and did not insist that she take more food. In each of these cases her expectations for what would happen were violated, resulting in surprise.

Sense-Making

The surprises lead naturally into a sense-making situation. Since what happened was not expected, the situation virtually demands attention and some effort at sense-making. In general, there appear to be three major inputs to this sense-making process: one's background, others who are concerned with similar surprises, and local interpretations. A person's background includes one's own personal experiences, presuppositions, and cultural knowledge. The Chinese student has her own Chinese culture to use in making sense of her new experiences as well as a variety of past personal experiences that may help her understand what is going on. We also may turn to other people who have faced similar challenges either by talking directly to them, such as the Chinese student did in talking with another Chinese student who had been in the United States longer than she, or by going to published material, such as a book or website, describing the situations with which we are concerned. Finally, a person may seek out local interpretations through observations, asking questions, or seeking out information generated from native members of the local community. The Chinese student could have asked an American how she should make sense of some these surprising behaviors or watch carefully how Americans reacted as invited guests or when touched on the shoulder, and so forth.

Attribute Meaning

The various strategies that one chooses for sense-making all result in some sort of attributed meaning. For example, using her own cultural knowledge the

Chinese student felt the advisor was insincere in her comments about being willing to help. However, if she had read a book about American culture, she may have read about how Americans are very careful not to do things that may take away someone else's independence and often wait to help until asked. Based on this she may have decided the advisor was trying to show concern and respect to her. In regards to her dinner hosts' lack of insistence on her eating, the Chinese student talked with another person who had faced this kind of surprise. The meaning or interpretation she learned was that Americans have no manners, so you don't have to use any when eating with them. She could just as easily have been told by someone with more experience that the Americans were trying to be good hosts by allowing their guest to decide on her own how much food she would eat. The meanings that people get through this sense-making process may be more or less accurate, more or less useful, and arrived at almost instantaneously or after much thought, but they do come.

Update Expectations

Based on the meanings that a person accepts for what is going on around them in the new culture, he or she will change his or her expectations of the situation and the appropriate actions in the situation. Depending upon how deeply these expectations are held by a person it may take repeated surprises before a person is no longer surprised by certain changes. The Chinese person may at first feel that just specific people are insincere or rude, or she may believe that there is something unique about this situation, such as the Americans only act this way toward foreigners. However, more experiences of surprise may lead her to believe that these actions are what it means to be polite in the United States. Of course, all this depends on the nature of the surprises and the results of the information seeking processes chosen in the sense-making stage. It is possible that future interactions only confirm initial judgments.

Select Behavioral Approach

Also based on the meanings that people attribute to the points of surprise, they will select certain behavioral responses. The Chinese student may decide to avoid as much as possible further contact with Americans, she may decide she has to explicitly ask for help when she wants it, she may decide to take bigger first helpings of food at dinners she attends in the future or to eat before she goes to eat out, she may decide to ask people to keep their hands to themselves, or she may decide to touch back. Whatever the decision, she will then be in a new situation that may result in further surprise and the process begins all over again.

Louis's model of sense-making thus helps a person deal with the acculturation process, not by becoming so well prepared that no surprises will occur,

FIGURE 9.5 |

but by acknowledging that the unexpected *will* occur. The key is how we deal with the unexpected. Indeed, much of this sense-making process is grounded in particular communication strategies. The model also recognizes that people's transitions from one culture to another are not just about going to a new culture, but also about leaving an old one.

Kim's Adaptation Model

Kim has written extensively on the acculturation process.[10] Her work assumes a human need to adapt to and grow in a new culture, and highlights both the dynamic nature of acculturation and the role of communication in this process. Her model is very broad-based and applies to both the immigrant and temporary sojourners. In addition, she argues that acculturation necessitates a certain degree of deculturation or a loss of certain cultural ways of seeing or doing things. This loss is depicted as part of the natural change that occurs during growth. This perspective reminds us of an account by a Mexican American whose family had come to the United States when he was quite young. He felt that his education had separated him from his culture, so one summer he took a manual labor job similar to what his father did for a living because he wanted to experience some of the culture of his father and feel what his father and others like him had felt coming to the United States from Mexico. In regards to his experience he wrote the following:

That summer I worked in the sun may have made me physically indistinguishable from the Mexicans working nearby. But I was not one of "los pobres." What made me different from them was an attitude of mind, my imagination of myself ... I will never know what he [his father] felt at his last factory job. If tomorrow I worked at some kind of factory, it would go differently for me. My long education would favor me. I could act as a public person—able to defend my interests, to unionize, to petition, to speak up—to challenge and demand. I will never know what the Mexicans knew, gathering their shovels and ladders and saws.[11]

His education and experiences in a new culture had changed him so that he could not experience a way of looking at the world that had once been part of his family's culture. However, deculturation does not mean that one loses all of one's culture or that one cannot continue to share many important cultural practices and values with others from that home culture. Kim's model recognizes a certain amount of deculturation, but emphasizes that acculturation is a process of growth. Although a person's ways of looking at the world may be forever changed, this change can be additive in ways that expand both the quality and quantity of a person's relationships. The basic idea of Kim's model is depicted in Figure 9.6, which shows how stress and adaptation promote growth over time in a continual process of adjustment.[12]

Kim's model is similar to the previous models reviewed in that it assumes there will be challenges to the acculturation process, whether they take the form of crises, trials, or surprises. These challenges inevitably result in stress.

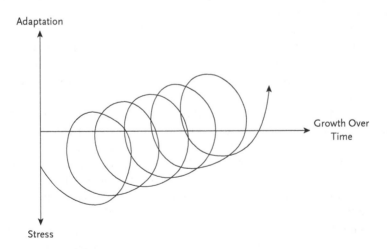

FIGURE 9.6 | Stress–adaptation–growth dynamics of the process of intercultural transformation

This stress creates a need for change. This change may be one of growth and expanded relational abilities or it may be one in which the person draws tighter into themselves in what we would call an attempt to culturally hibernate during their life in another culture. Kim does not discuss much the more negative *cultural hibernation* reaction to the stress of living in a new culture, but it is implied in her discussion of structural factors that facilitate positive growth or acculturation and those that do not. These factors influence the acculturation process in ways which promote either hibernation or growth, and Kim organizes them around four broad aspects of the acculturation process: personal communication, predisposition, environment, and social communication practices.

Personal Communication

Personal communication refers to the individual's abilities at a *cognitive, affective,* and *behavioral* level to communicate competently in the host culture. Personal communication in Kim's model is both a means and an end in terms of acculturation. Development and change in the three types of personal communication serve as a means to acculturate and the host communication competence that is developed through these three areas is a sign of acculturation.

The cognitive factor refers to the ability to recognize and understand the different practices of those in the host community. This ability can be increased through both culture-specific education and the education process in general. The culture-specific information is the amount of familiarity one has with the other culture by gathering information about it both before and after arriving in the other community. The general education process relates to a person's ability to perceive many different ways of looking at any situation, an ability often connected with increased levels of formal education. The more familiar one is with the new or host culture and the more one is able to see many legitimate reasons for others' behaviors, the greater the tendency for growth rather than hibernation.

The affective component of personal communication involves things such as a person's motivation for going to the host culture and their self-image. If the move is voluntary and something we want to do, we are more likely to acculturate quickly. If our image of ourselves is flexible we are more likely to acculturate quickly. The behavioral or operational factor involves how capable the person is in terms of physically matching what those in the host community are doing. Although this may involve a wide range of physical abilities, the most important is the ability to speak the language. Obviously, these three factors are closely connected to each other and taken together they are a measure of the host communication competence that a given person has.

Predisposition

Predisposition refers to what the stranger brings to the acculturation experience. Some aspects covered in this part of Kim's model are closely connected to items also touched on in the personal communication area, but we will focus on aspects that go beyond those discussed in relationship to personal communication. The three main factors within this area include the stranger's *preparation for change*, *ethnic proximity*, and *adaptive personality*.

Although one's preparedness for change could include many things, one of the most important indicators of this is prior cross-cultural experiences. The more experience that a person has had dealing with a variety of different cultural communities, the more prepared that person is to deal with the changes involved with the most recent move. Ethnic proximity refers to the compatibility and relative similarity that one's home culture has with the host culture. The more compatible or similar these are, the easier the acculturation. An adaptive personality involves aspects of openness, strength, and positivity. Openness, in terms of being open to new ideas and meeting new people, provides a foundation for activities that promote acculturation. Strength in personality means that a person has a secure and positive enough self-image that he or she is willing to take risks and is not as defensive or self-absorbed as those with a weak self-image. Without a strong self-image it is easy for a person to withdraw from difficult situations and the acculturation process is slowed down. Positivity involves a perspective that is optimistic and believes that, come what may, things will work out okay.

Environment

The environment is what the host culture brings to the acculturation experience and includes such things as *host receptivity*, *host conformity pressure*, and the relative *ethnic group strength* of the stranger's home community within the host community. Host receptivity encompasses the hosts' attitudes toward the stranger and thus the potential for interaction. A host community that is open to the stranger and encourages the stranger to interact with its members will facilitate acculturation at a quicker pace. The next factor to consider related to the host environment is the demand for conformity or how much pressure exists within a community for a stranger to acculturate. The greater the demand, the greater the acculturation. Ethnic group strength refers to the amount of social power one is perceived to hold because of the status of the group one comes from. Kim's model suggests that the greater the status of the stranger's home community, the easier it is to get things done without having to acculturate and the more likely that the stranger will focus on finding a group of expatriates to hang out with, further slowing down the acculturation process.

Social Communication

Kim emphasizes two main types of communication in her model: *mass communication* and *interpersonal communication*. The access to and active use of both mass and interpersonal channels of communication will help someone acculturate much quicker than would otherwise happen. Mass communication allows a person to practice language skills and pick up community knowledge in a relatively stress free situation. Interpersonal communication is typically much more stressful. Kim notes that interpersonal communication itself is often seen as a mark of acculturation and is perhaps the most crucial factor in the process that we have considered.[13] There are two major considerations relevant to interpersonal communication. One is the sheer number of interpersonal contacts and the other is the existence of a high degree of intimacy in at least one of these contacts. By intimacy we refer to the ability to share with each other serious concerns in a supportive and honest manner.

In addition, Kim discusses two different types of mass and interpersonal communication based on whether the communication is with ethnic or host sources. The positive influence of communication noted above is specifically in reference to communication with host members and host media. However, after the stranger moves to the host community she or he can also focus their communication, at both the mass and interpersonal levels, with members of their own ethnic or native community. There are a variety of television and radio stations, magazines, and social groups within a community that are run by and target minority ethnic groups. Thus, if we attend a university in another country, we still may be able to find a radio station that speaks our native tongue and be able to associate with on a social level only others who have our same cultural background. This sort of ethnic communication may provide some initial help with sense-making for the new stranger, but Kim's work suggests that if ethnic communication stays or becomes the primary form of communication, the acculturation process will be hindered.

Intercultural Transformation

Kim also stresses that the acculturation process typically involves a transformation in terms of functional behaviors, psychological health, and intercultural identity. Thus, a person who acculturates will develop the functional skills to be able to act appropriately and effectively in the new culture, will be able to feel satisfied and comfortable with their life in that new culture, and will develop an identity that is simultaneously inclusive in its attitude toward others and yet recognizes the legitimacy of differences.

Reflection Question: We have reviewed four different models of acculturation: the U-curve model, the hero's journey model, the surprise and sense-making model, and the stress, adaptation, growth model. Which of these best reflects your personal experiences? Why?

RETURNING HOME: READAPTING TO OUR OWN CULTURAL COMMUNITY

One element of living in a different culture for an extended time that has received more and more attention recently is what happens when you return home.[14] It is easy for people to forget that the return home is also a cultural transition and for many people it is just as difficult, if not more so, than their initial adjustment to living in a new culture. Typically the longer one has spent abroad, the more challenging the return. When Brad returned to the United States after having lived for more than two years in England, he experienced a greater sense of loss than when he had left the U.S. to go there. Gullahorn and Gullahorn extended the idea of the U-curve model discussed earlier to a *W* to highlight that a person tends to go through stages of euphoria, frustration, and readjustment before again returning to a normal functioning mode on their reentry to their home culture just as they do when they initially move abroad (see Figure 9.7).[15]

Reverse Culture Shock

While culture shock is experienced when a person visits a new environment, shifts to a social context unfamiliar to them, or transitions to a new lifestyle (i.e., when people retire from their jobs at the end of a career), a counterpart disorientation exists. This disorientation is most commonly known as "reverse culture shock" but associated terms include "reentry shock" or "own culture shock." Reverse culture shock may be experienced when persons return to their own home culture after having gotten habituated to a new one. For example, missionaries conducting church work in a foreign country, soldiers stationed overseas, students earning college degrees in countries foreign to them, Peace Corps volunteers, or business managers assigned to foreign posts—all of these groups of people may experience reverse culture shock when they return home. In reverse culture shock, returning persons may experience effects similar to those

FIGURE 9.7 | W-curve model

of culture shock—disorientation, stress, distress, frustration, and loneliness— as they find that life, people, and interpersonal relationships in their original environments have changed. And, importantly because re-entrants have undergone many changes themselves (i.e., examining their beliefs, values, ideas, opinions, and feelings), they now have to figure out how to reintegrate into their home communities given their many internal changes and those surrounding them. It is not unusual for re-entrants to find it more difficult to deal with reverse culture shock than with culture shock perhaps because they were not expecting the changes that occurred in their communities during their absence. Re-entrants find that they simply cannot pick up where they left off.

Raquel, a former student of Patricia's, recalls her experience with reverse culture shock and the ambiguity she felt going through it.

After two years of living as a college student in the U.S., I returned to Brazil and faced the uncomfortable reality of feeling like a foreigner at home. I felt disconnected from my friends who had no idea what living and studying abroad entailed. And my acquired straightforward way of speaking sounded rude to my family, as my mother sharply admonished me when I said, "Mom, there are too many things stored here. Let's clean it up and donate some of it" instead of a more acceptable, "Wow, Mom, look at all of these different things. Do you think we need all of that? Maybe we can sort it out and donate some of it?" Mom turned to me and said, "Do you have to talk like that?" and I saw she was hurt by the remark and later told me I was being rude. In addition to being considered rude, I was all of a sudden incapable of asking a question without adding, "I'm asking you" to the sentence. It seemed that getting used to switching subject with verb when asking questions made me unused to raising my intonation at the end of a sentence when asking questions in Portuguese. So people thought I was making statements instead of asking questions. I said to my sister once, "você vai para casa" and without the right intonation in Portuguese, such a sentence can either mean, "You are going home" or "Are you going home? [você vai para casa?]." My sister had a puzzled look on her face, so I added, "I'm asking you if you are going home."

But not everything I experienced upon returning home was negative. I also felt relief about being in familiar territory, and enjoyment in being able understand jokes and sarcasm again. I was glad to have explicit tools built into the Portuguese language for speaking about my male and female relations, like cousins (primos/primas) and not have to add the odd, "My male/female cousin" to the sentence, so that I could feel I properly conveyed my thoughts to people. But in the end of the day, I couldn't help longing for the life I'd created for myself in the U.S. I longed for the feeling of independence and for a culture that had less of a touchy-feely component among strangers (instead of the hugs and kisses on the cheek of Brazil). I longed for that certainty of self, that sense of "I know who I am" that was so clear in the U.S., but not so much in Brazil, where I felt like "I don't know who I am here."

Change in Self and Others

Based on a variety of literature, personal conversations, and personal experience, we will review three main reasons why this return can be so difficult or frustrating. First and foremost, *there has been actual change both in oneself and in others during a person's sojourn.* People who have lived abroad consistently refer to it as life-changing. Based either on your own experiences or the readings so far in this chapter, we hope you realize that spending time in another culture is going to change you. Smith reports the following observation from a person returning from abroad:

> *I think from the moment I left, there was no way to ever go back to what I was. Certain things that I remember about myself I know I'm not anymore ... had I not gone away, I would have continued along a different path. But my whole life now revolves around having been abroad.*[16]

The process of acculturation is one of personal change. How people see themselves and others is different than it was before they left to live in a new culture. Developing communication competence in another culture involves the need to negotiate mutually acceptable identities in interactions. Learning about other ways to identify people and what expectations are associated with those identities is basic to developing the ability to communicate in appropriate and effective ways within other cultural communities. These identity changes are not merely superficial changes in the way we do certain things. They affect us deeply, in the way we act, think, and feel. One sojourner, who had lived in Taiwan, explained how something that would not have been given a second thought while in Taiwan was viewed very differently upon returning home.

> *In Taiwan, if I was talking to someone in his office, I'd shake his hand and he'd show me the door. And I'd say, "No, you don't need to show me the door," but he'd show me to the door anyway. I was in a situation recently in a man's office here in Minneapolis and he was showing me the door and I said, "Ahhh, you don't need to show me to the door, I know my way out." He just stopped ... I had to open the door myself. And I thought to myself, "What a rude guy! Where does he come off?" Then I thought, "But you told him ..." But it still left a sour taste in my mouth.*[17]

One of the reasons that just knowing about acculturation challenges, whether going abroad or returning home, is not enough to eliminate the struggles one faces is because of the emotional aspect. Emotional reactions that resonate with members of the other community are one indication that a person has become or is becoming acculturated. We have discussed acculturation as the development of communication competence in another culture, but it may be argued that there is a difference between communication competence in intercultural settings and cultural competence in different cultural settings.[18] The difference is at the level of emotion. People have communication competence when they can act appropriately and effectively within a community. However, just because we can greet people correctly, avoid offensive nonverbal gestures, or learn to speak in ways that allow us to accomplish our goals does not mean that we *feel* about things the way members of another culture do. One develops cultural competence within another culture when one also shares the appropriate feelings about things. This type of acculturation involves a change in identity and is much deeper than the kind that is simply the strategic use of another community's ways of doing things. This emotional aspect is the reason that simply knowing about all the acculturation challenges is not enough to eliminate all the potential struggles involved. Knowledge of the other community and the process we are experiencing is helpful because it assists us in making sense of our experiences in positive ways, but educating our feelings requires certain experiences. It is the difference between knowing something and knowing about something. However, even if one severely limits that identity change by opting for choices that encourage hibernation rather than intercultural growth, the person will be experiencing things that will change them in some way.

In addition, at the same time change is happening to the sojourner change is also happening at home. The amount of change that is going on all around us is often overlooked and it is only when we have been gone for a time that we really notice these changes. The people you knew will have changed and developed new relationships, even when the people involved appear to be the same. The concerns of the community and the issues of importance will often have changed. Sometimes these changes are just the furthering of paths already begun before the person steps aside to follow a different path. When they return, the returnee may fail to recognize the nature of these changes and feel frustrated that everything isn't just the same as it was.

This issue of change is also true at a cultural level. Cultural communities do not stay static, but also move on. Radha Hegde explains that many immigrant groups seek to *freeze* their culture in time when they move to a new community to try to protect it and their own identities in a foreign land.[19] A native of India now living in the United States, she tells of how she took a visitor from India to a gathering of other Indian immigrants to the United States. The visitor expressed surprise that, "You immigrants are more into 'Indian stuff' than we are in India."

In a similar sense Wong (Lau) records the following comments from a young immigrant from Hong Kong who recently arrived in the United States:

> [American-born Chinese] *are so old fashioned. You are young, but it is like you live in old Chinese history books ... You celebrate August Moon festival. You know how to make wonton and potstickers. You have no money but you order white rice in fancy restaurants. How embarrassing! I can't believe you are Chinese. Chinese are supposed to be "tight," you know, good dressers, good in business, "tight" cars, go out to eat all the time, cell phones.*[20]

She further describes an interview from 1994 with a Greek who had recently immigrated to the United States:

> *Greeks in Greece are currently interested in disco and fashions from Milan. There is a new form of music called urban music, which is like traditional Greek music and disco. I think Greek Americans whose ancestors immigrated to America generations ago are usually quite shocked when they get there.*[21]

Indeed, people returning to their home culture after considerable time abroad often discover that their culture has changed. The issue here is not whose culture is authentic Indian, Chinese, or Greek. Instead, we need to recognize that cultures are always changing in usually slow and sometimes speedy ways. These changes mean that when a sojourner goes abroad and returns to her or his home cultural community, s/he may find that it has changed in many ways.

Unrealistic Expectations

This realization leads to the second reason why returning home is so difficult. *People who are away from their home community often develop very unrealistic expectations about life "back home."* For one thing they may expect everything to be the same and that returning home will be easy. Indeed, the idea that it is going to be easy when they return home and that they will somehow just slip back into the normal routine often leads people not to bother to prepare for their return home in the way they may have prepared for their journey abroad. This lack of preparation often leaves one with a general sense of agitation and trying to deal with unexpected challenges without adequate resources.

Also related to these unrealistic expectations is something sometimes referred to as the *Rebecca Myth*, after a classic film in which a past wife is idealized after her death. People often idealize their home culture, creating in their minds a version of the warmth, openness, hospitality, efficiency, and general goodness of their own culture. This type of idealization often happens when one is experiencing difficult times in adjusting to the new culture and provides a way for the person to justify their difficulties. The idea of returning home and again experiencing all the good foods, sensible ways of doing things, and the many respectful people may make people very anxious to get home. Alas, these idealizations were not really true even before people left and arise out of the many initial frustrations people feel during the acculturation process. It is not too surprising that real life back home has a difficult time living up to the wonderful expectations created while the sojourner is abroad. This process is illustrated in the two quotes below:

> *As I shivered in Quebec's minus 35° winter, I remembered Los Angeles' blue sky and sunshine, driving to the beach on a warm January morning ... I didn't remember skies opaque with smog, freeways so clogged with cars that driving anywhere was impossible, nor did I remember my car being broken into while parked at the beach.*

> *In Venezuela, getting things done was a hassle ... and we said, "In the U.S.A. it would be so easy." When we came home, everything was delayed and frustrating. Here in the United States! The U.S.A. was a continual Venezuela story ... and we had always said, "This will never happen at home." HA!*[22]

Lack of Appreciation in Home Community

A third reason these returns home can be so difficult is that *other people are rarely as interested in what you have gone through as you wish, making it difficult to really express or share the growth you have experienced.* One person after returning from working abroad for years expressed his frustration upon returning home this way:

> *They don't want to hear about it* [his experience abroad] *though you think you've gone through something unique. They'll listen for 30 seconds and tell you what the pro football team did in your absence. The feeling is that you can't hold their interest long enough to talk about it ... They think* [your experience abroad] *was like a vacation, so don't tell them about any problems because they're convinced you were really on vacation. And don't tell them any good things because that's boring, too. That goes for family too—they're just more polite about it.*[23]

One of the most frequent complaints and frustrations for people returning from other cultures is that people just do not seem very interested in what they have to tell about their experiences or are only interested in what is exotic or *strange*. Most people feel fortunate to have even limited chances to share their experiences. Thus, the person feels they have much more to give than they are allowed to share. Their experience in a new culture left them with many new insights and stories to tell, yet they often find that people are busy with their own lives and don't have the time or interest to listen to these stories. Those who return from time abroad may find that questions about their trip are similar to general questions about how one is feeling. The only answer that is really wanted is a simple "fine." When these travels abroad are business related, those who return home often feel that not only is their new knowledge and expertise ignored, but they have to almost prove themselves all over again within the company setting.

Returnees deal with the struggles they face in a variety of ways. Research by Nancy Adler characterized three strategies that people choose when dealing with this challenging time: alienation, resocialization, and proactivity.[24] These three strategies do not refer to types of persons, but to adaptive attitudes that people adopt as they try to cope with their reentry into their home culture. These three approaches are distinguished by people's attitudes toward the culture they experienced abroad and their home culture.

The alienated approach happens when someone comes to assimilate the values and lifestyle of the culture in which they lived in such a way that they reject their home culture. Alienated returnees often isolate themselves or seek out a few other people with similar experiences. They develop defensive and judgmental attitudes toward those from their own culture, especially those who have not lived abroad. Those who have traveled related to business often find themselves leaving their company upon returning home. Adler's research indicates that this approach is most common among spouses who have traveled with their spouse on a business assignment and those who have been abroad on volunteer stays, such as with the Peace Corps.

The resocialized approach is almost the exact opposite of the alienated approach. The person typically carries with them negative images of the other culture and their time abroad and is very anxious to be home. In this approach the returnee sheds as quickly as possible any influence the trip to the other culture has had on them. In a sense the person works to cleanse themselves of their overseas experience, thus negating all the benefits that could have been derived from that experience. Often people who choose this type of approach also kept themselves as distant as possible from the other culture even when they were living there. Adler's research indicates that this approach is most common among people who had worked for a corporation in the other community.

The proactive approach is the one recommended by Adler and it maintains a positive attitude toward both the culture one visited and one's own culture. This approach requires an active effort to integrate both cultures and to look for ways in which the different ways of doing things they have experienced can be productive in both one's own life and one's work. Those who take this approach are able to see tradeoffs between the two cultures with each having aspects that are both better and worse than the other. She reports that those who make this effort are much more satisfied with their experience both abroad and upon returning home. Adler offers two suggestions that can help in developing a proactive stance. First is the importance of communication during one's stay abroad. This includes the importance of actively seeking out communication with members of the other culture as well as keeping the communication lines back home (with family, friends, and organizational colleagues) as open as possible. This helps one acculturate, yet also allows one to be aware of changes happening at home as well as abroad. Second is the issue of validation or recognition of the changes and worth of those changes that have occurred abroad. Certainly returnees can help facilitate this validation and some of it may come from personal reflection, but a large part of this is influenced by the reactions of those who have stayed at home. She argues that organizations that arrange for stays abroad for their members need to remember that a big part of the benefits that can occur from these stays abroad depends upon how the sojourner is received upon their return.

FINAL THOUGHTS ON CULTURAL TRANSITIONS

Hopefully as we have reviewed the different models of acculturation, related to both going to and returning from life in another culture, you have been able to make connections with your own experiences. There are a couple of final points that we want to emphasize about our efforts to be successful during cultural transitions.

First, as you have read this chapter you may have felt that cultural transitions occur only when a person goes through a major move. This is misleading. As transportation and communication abilities have increased we may find the need and opportunity to adapt to new cultures all around us. A person may move to a different neighborhood in the same city or take on a new job that involves a cultural transition, thus requiring that person to experience much of the acculturation process discussed in this chapter. Even without people moving their permanent residence, situations arise that create a need for cultural transition. Understanding the process and form that these transitions take can help us deal with them wherever and whenever they may occur.

The second point we wish to consider deals with the emotional aspect of these transitions. Sometimes as we learn about another culture or attend intercultural training we may pick up a silent, but dangerous assumption: that our knowledge or training will eliminate the feelings of discomfort that typically arise during these transitions. We have talked with more than one person who was very disappointed that this was *not* the case. When we experience living in a culturally unfamiliar environment or interacting in other intercultural situations we will often still experience discomfort and frustration, even when we have been *prepared* for it. You may wonder, "Why bother with intercultural training if we are still going to experience these emotional struggles?" The reason is simple: even though this type of preparation does not eliminate such feelings, it does give us resources for making sense of these experiences in positive, patient ways rather than with the negative, condemning reaction that so often happens. We may not feel comfortable with someone who stands what we consider too close to me, but if we understand that it is a part of their natural, cultural behavior, we can deal with this discomfort in ways that don't turn negative. And, with time, our feelings will also likely change, so that the behaviors that we felt so uncomfortable with no longer bother us and may even become what we prefer.

SUMMARY

In this chapter we have considered how to be successful in our intercultural travels. We began by considering the hierarchy of human needs proposed by Maslow and how our ability to meet these needs is changed when we travel to a new culture. The process of moving to a new culture is referred to as acculturation. Acculturation may be viewed as developing communication competence in the new or host culture.

We then reviewed four different models of acculturation. First, the U-curve model was discussed. It is a general model that charts the sojourner's experiences of excitement, crisis, and readjustment to normal life. The second model was the hero's journey. In this model the sojourner is portrayed as a mythic hero who accepts the call of adventure and enters a new and strange world where she or he faces many trials, but with the help of a mentor the hero is able to succeed and reap extraordinary rewards. Not everyone who travels to a new culture is able to successfully finish this journey.

Third, we considered the surprise and sense-making model, in which surprise is positioned as inevitable. The key is how a newcomer seeks information for making sense of these surprises and the way he or she updates his or her cognitive map and behavioral choices. Fourth, we reviewed a comprehensive model of stress, adaptation, and growth. In this model stress was seen as natural, rather than as a failure to cope. Based on a variety of contextual issues and choices in one's personal communication practices, the stranger's predisposition, the host environment, and the social communication practices one could either experience growth or hibernation as described in the model. The internet has become a useful tool for getting specific information about a place you plan to travel to, as well as understanding the transition process. You may want to explore two useful sites: www.iagora.com and www.transitionsabroad.com.

Attention was then turned to the return home of the traveler. The return home often proved more problematic than the original intercultural trip. Three reasons for this are: The inherent personal and cultural changes that occurred during the sojourner's time away, the development of unrealistic expectations about one's home culture, and a general lack of interest in the experience by those who remained home.

Finally, we noted that these cultural transitions can happen even when we do not make a major move to another community, and that, although our preparation for these cultural transitions may not eliminate all our feelings of discomfort, they do help us deal with these discomforts in positive ways.

REFLECTION QUESTIONS

1   This chapter takes a fairly positive attitude toward acculturation. Do you feel this is justified? Why? What about when a person or community is assimilated into another culture, losing their native culture? How does a person acculturate without assimilating?

2   Osland's model of acculturation involves a *hero* on a journey. How may mentally using this metaphor help and/or hinder a person's acculturation experience? Osland's model also identifies many paradoxes that sojourner's may face in their intercultural travels. What intercultural paradoxes have you experienced?

3   We discuss the possible difference between being communicatively competent in many cultures and being culturally competent in many cultures. What was the key difference between these two perspectives? Do you feel this distinction is a valid or useful one? Why?

4   In this chapter it is argued that returning to your own culture can be just as difficult as going to a new culture in the first place. Do you really believe this? Why or why not? What experiences have you had or observed that support your position?

ACTIVITIES

1   Compare the four models of acculturation reviewed in this chapter through one of the following means:

> Interview international students or other intercultural sojourners about their experiences.
>
> Reflect on your own past experiences in this area.
>
> Read a novel depicting this type of cultural transition.
>
> Watch a movie that deals with the challenges of intercultural travel.

Each of these four resources should provide examples that can be used to assess the value of the four models.

2   Using Kim's model, create profiles of what a successful and an unsuccessful intercultural traveler would look like. Use this information to either make sense of what went on in your experience or to better prepare yourself for the future.

3   Keep a journal during a cultural transition experience (even if it is just moving to a new city or neighborhood to go to the university or becoming involved with a group culturally different from what you are used to for a semester). This is a good practice to do with each cultural transition in your life. These journals become great sources of enlightenment, strength, and enjoyment over time.

4   Talk with members of your family (grandparents can be particularly good resources) about your own family history in terms of moves and cultural transitions. Why were the moves made? What differences in the way people thought or did things were noticed? How did your family maintain a connection to the culture from which they moved? What were the challenges and hardships associated with the move? What were the benefits?

5   Interview a person from your own culture who has spent considerable time living in other cultures. Find out about their experiences in both going from and returning to your own culture. What did they learn about themselves and their home culture?

NOTES

1   J. Yin, "Comparing Cultures: China and the United States" (paper, University of New Mexico, 1999).

2   A. H. Maslow, *Motivation and Personality*, 2nd ed. (New York: Harper & Row, 1970).

3   For example see J. Iwasaki and A. Kishida, "Needs Called Key to Culture Shock," *The Japan Times*, October 27, 1994, 15.

4   Iwasaki and Kishida, "Needs Called Key," 15.

5   S. Lysgaard, "Adjustment in a Foreign Society: Norwegian Fulbright Grantees Visiting the United States," *International Social Science Bulletin*, 7 (1955): 45–51; and K. Oberg, "Culture Shock: Adjustment to New Cultural Environments," *Practical Anthropology* 7 (1960): 177–82.

6   Oberg, "Culture Shock."

7   The information relating to this model comes from J. S. Osland, *The Adventure of Working Abroad: Hero Tales from the Global Frontier* (San Francisco, CA: Jossey-Bass, 1995).

8   Osland, *The Adventure*, 82.

9   M. R. Louis, "Surprise and Sense-Making: What Newcomers Experience in Entering Unfamiliar Organizational Settings," *Administrative Science Quarterly* 25 (1980): 226–51.

10 Material for this model is derived from these works by Kim: Y. Y. Kim, *Becoming International* (Thousand Oaks, CA: Sage Publications, 2001); Y. Y. Kim, "Adapting to a New Culture," in *Intercultural Communication: A Reader*, 8th ed., ed. L. Samovar and R. Porter (Belmont, CA: Wadsworth Publishing, 1997), 404–17; Y. Y. Kim, *Communication and Cross-Cultural Adaptation* (Clevedon, UK: Multilingual Matters, 1988); and Y. Y. Kim and B. Ruben, "Intercultural Communication: A System's Theory," in *Theories in Intercultural Communication*, ed. W. B. Gudykunst and Y. Y. Kim (Newbury Park, CA: Sage, 1988), 299–322.

11 R. Rodríguez, *Hunger of Memory: The Education of Richard Rodriguez* (Toronto, Canada: Bantam, 1982).

12 Kim and Ruben, "Intercultural Communication."

13 See Kim, "Becoming International."

14 J. N. Martin, "The Intercultural Reentry: Conceptualizations and Directions for Future Research," *International Journal of Intercultural Relations* 8 (1984): 115–34; and S. L. Smith, "Identity and Intercultural Communication Competence in Reentry," in *Reading in Cultural Contexts*, ed. J. N. Martin, T. K. Nakayama, and L. A. Flores (Mountain View, CA: Mayfield, 1998), 304–14.

15 J. T. Gullahorn and J. E. Gullahorn, "Extension of the U-Curve Hypothesis," *Journal of Social Issues* 19 (1963): 33–47.

16 Smith, "Identity in Reentry," 308.

17 Smith, "Identity in Reentry," 307.

18 R. Scruton, "The Significance of Common Culture," *Philosophy* 54 (1979): 51–70.

19 R. S. Hegde, "Translated Enactments: The Relational Configurations of the Asian Indian Immigrant Experience," in *Reading in Cultural Contexts*, ed. J. N. Martin, T. K. Nakayama, and L. A. Flores (Mountain View, CA: Mayfield, 1998), 315–22.

20 K. Wong (Lau), "Migration across Generations: Whose Identity Is Authentic?" in *Reading in Cultural Contexts*, ed. J. N. Martin, T. K. Nakayama, and L. A. Flores (Mountain View, CA: Mayfield, 1998), 304–14.

21 Wong (Lau), "Migration," 128.

22 N. J. Adler, *International Dimensions of Organizational Behavior* (Boston, MA: Kent, 1986).

23 Osland, *The Adventure*, 178.

24 Adler, *International Dimensions*.

Chapter 10

How Does Culture Impact Applied Contexts?

Emma was involved in a significant car accident a number of years ago. She had a good friend as a passenger in her car when they were struck by another car at high speed. The accident seemed to happen in slow motion to Emma, and it seemed strange to her friend that just before the cars collided Emma said in a very calm voice, "I think we're about to get hit."

Throughout the entire incident Emma remained completely calm. She made sure her friend was alright, talked with the police officers who appeared on the scene, recorded the appropriate insurance information, etc. She went home and went about her daily activities that day and it seemed as though she had really escaped a harrowing incident without much harm. But as the days passed, Emma had a difficult time sleeping, and she was overly sensitive and emotional about things that otherwise would not bother her. She even started to prefer to stay home and be alone rather than socialize with her friends. One of her friends who knew of the car accident noticed her changed behavior. This particular friend, Gloria, had started training as a curandera recently and suggested that Emma visit Gloria's teacher. Gloria was training to become a sobadora, a curandera who specializes in massage for relief of ailments, but her teacher had more experience as a curandera and a deeper understanding of the connections between the mind, body, spirit, and environment so integral to this approach to healing.

Emma agreed to visit the teacher, not necessarily knowing why or what might happen. She hoped the teacher could help her sleep better so she would stop being so overly emotional. In talking with the teacher, Emma cried (as she had begun to do regularly) and related the story of the car accident even though the incident had not entered her conscious thoughts since it occurred

(continued)

(continued)

FIGURE 10.1

over two weeks earlier. The curandera/teacher listened and asked questions. When it appeared Emma had finished talking about physical, emotional, and social areas of her life, the curandera/teacher told Emma that she believed she suffered from susto.

Emma learned that susto translates as a fright that could lead to soul loss. It is a cultural belief that physical illness is a manifestation of a spiritual condition that results from a tragic or shocking incident.[1] As a result of the shock, a piece of the soul goes into hiding as a protective measure. To regain the hiding piece of soul, the curandera performs a ceremony to retrieve the missing piece and allow the soul to heal itself and become whole again.

Emma agreed to the treatment prescribed by the curandera. The ceremony included smudging to purify with sage, many prayers uttered by the curandera and Emma, along with other cleansing and soothing words and practices. At the end of the ceremony, the curandera told Emma to go home and relax. She asked her to stay calm and peaceful for the rest of the day, and take that day off before continuing her everyday activities. Emma followed the directions and her sleeplessness ceased and she began to enjoy spending time with her friends again. Emma also felt less sensitive and emotional at the slightest provocation. While Emma had no prior knowledge of susto or ceremony as holistic healing practices, Emma remains to this day a firm believer that there are many physical ailments that have causes and cures that are inexplicable by scientific means.

Emma's experience touches on two of the applied areas we will cover in this chapter: health communication, environmental communication, and leadership communication. Her experience with what may be considered in the mainstream United States as an "alternative" health practice that was culturally unfamiliar has implications for our discussion of the connection between health communication and culture. It also has implications for our discussion of environmental communication. For example, *curanderismo* emphasizes the idea that the body, spirit, and environment are intertwined and inseparable, and so what happens to the body impacts the spirit and vice versa. Likewise, the environment affects body and spirit, and thus one's connections with the environment in which one lives affects one's relationship to nature. This more holistic approach to medicine will be discussed further later in this chapter as we cover health communication and applications of cultural consideration in medicine.

In this chapter we will talk about three different applications of intercultural communication. We begin with a discussion of environmental communication and how it both informs and is informed by considerations of culture. We then discuss intercultural applications in health and medicine. Leadership is the final area of applied cultural communication we discuss. We include explicit leadership approaches that are mentioned in the sections on environment and health. Although these are three very different areas of communication, they serve as useful samples of fields of study that are impacted by intercultural communication in everyday human life. We hope you will explore the areas that interest you the most and find the points of connection where you can apply your cultural knowledge. In the meantime, we offer some ideas to get you started.

ENVIRONMENTAL COMMUNICATION

A wide and quickly growing global conversation deals with communication about the environment for the purpose of not only understanding human–nature relations, but also finding solutions to urgent environmental concerns. These numerous and diverse concerns include:

- climate change and global warming;
- water, air, light, soil, and noise pollution; clean vs. dirty energy with attention to petroleum, biofuels, coal, offshore drilling, and the controversial practice known as 'fracking' (hydraulic fracturing);
- the control of radiation from space program-related projects;
- the protection of animals and their habitats or ecosystems;
- the production and consumption of healthful vs. unsafe food.

Environmental Communication as a Symbolic Resource for Making Sense of Our World

The goal of environmental communication scholars and practitioners is to stress the idea that humans use symbolic resources—verbal and nonverbal—to shape our connection and interactions with the natural world. These connections and interactions occur communicatively in individual, societal, cultural, and/or institutional contexts. Moreover, as Cox notes, environmental communication as a symbolic means serves both a pragmatic and a constitutive function.[2] The pragmatic function or "communication-in-action," as he calls it, enables people to talk about nature, to educate about it, or to persuade one another about how to interact productively with nature. Examples of the pragmatic function would be when car manufacturers buy ads using words and images to oppose higher fuel standards or when environmental groups use online forums to dialogue and rally support for the protection of a natural forest or an animal preserve. The constitutive function makes up or composes representations of nature by actively influencing our awareness and perceptions through the symbols we use to talk about nature. How our attitudes and ideologies about nature get formed by the particular communication choices we make would be examples of the constitutive function. For example, the particular words chosen in a press release about a new dam can orient our understanding of and attitudes about the dam, if let us say, the dam is framed as "menacing to life" or as "fundamental to more plentiful communities." The words chosen and the images they conjure themselves point us to how the senders of the message want us to think about the dam. Or, for example, if insecticides are presented as destroyers of insects that cause malaria vs. destroyers of entire sectors of natural ecological systems, the specific language used is constitutive of our thoughts; that is, the language used shapes our viewpoint about what and how we think about pesticides, and the relationship between humans and nature. In the former approach humans, through their uses of human-made pesticides, can be seen as tamers of nature, while in the latter viewpoint nature is suggested as being capable of regulating itself.

Elizabeth Dickinson, a scholar of environmental communication, shared with us a personal example of how she is actively trying to affect the ways future generations think about nature by changing her communication about it:

As a researcher who studies environmental communication from a cultural perspective, when my daughter was born, helping her see nature differently was important to me. I worry she'll fall into the same traps that disconnect many of us from nature, myself included. But shedding our cultural lenses is difficult.

For example, we often walk in nearby, beautiful forests—"walks with the forest," as we call them. Many people approach nature from a Western, rational, disconnected perspective, which I attempt to avoid. Trying to deemphasize talking so that we can better connect and slow down, for instance, as we walk, I tell my daughter, "Shh, let's not talk. Let's listen instead." But she starts speaking and asking questions, and I find myself responding. The silence and slowing down get pushed to the backburner.

But we are sometimes able to do things differently. I often deemphasize a focus on intellectual naming, something Western cultures do too much of (learning names and quickly moving to the next thing, not emotionally connecting and learning little else). My daughter sees a millipede and asks, "What is it, Mama?" Instead of telling her "a millipede," I say, "First, let's just spend time with it." In silence, we squat by the millipede. I say, "What do you think it is? What does it look like? Hold it in your hand. Does it smell?" When she asks the name, I ask, "What name would you give it?" This causes us to relax down and connect—both with nature and with each other.

Environmental Communication as a Place of Conflict

Since Rachel Carson's 1962 publication of *Silent Spring*, there have been many examples of how communication about our environment is tied to competing interests and perspectives about the natural world.[3] Carson was a marine biologist who advanced the global environmental movement. She was the first to describe the catastrophic consequences for humans and nature caused by the spraying of agricultural pesticides such as DDT. Another example of an interested perspective is the spotted owl controversy. In the Pacific Northwest during the 1980s and 1990s, a species of owl known as the northern spotted owl became the center of very heated debate between owl supporters and the loggers and mill workers whose livelihoods depended on the trees which served as the owl's habitat. For the loggers and mill workers, the trees represented a multi-billion dollar industry that provided profit as well as subsistence for many families. For environmental activists, the trees represented dwindling forests and declining numbers of spotted owls. To add to the controversy, some of the trees were located on federal lands, bringing the U.S. Fish and Wildlife Service into the dispute. In 1986, an environmentalist group petitioned the U.S. government to list the owl as an "endangered species," thereby barring the timber industry from particular lands. In June 1990, following much wrangling, negotiation, and litigation between the government, environmentalists, and the timber industry, the northern spotted owl was officially declared a threatened species. Since that time, other species of animal life have served as foci for debate between environmentalist and business interests including, whales, dolphins, desert tortoises, and snail darters. In all cases, defining the human to other-than-human problem, responding to it by articulating costs and benefits, and working out resolutions fundamentally has relied and continues to rely on communication. Discussions related to the environment inevitably draw on a wide variety of interests.[4] In other words, regardless of whether communication occurs verbally, nonverbally, in public or interpersonal contexts, face-to-face, or via mediated channels, it is influenced by social, economic, and political contexts and interests. Moreover, these interests often clash, as there is often disagreement about how to balance economic development and environmental well-being. Balancing, working out, talking through, or negotiating competing interests then becomes a communication activity. Discussions over things like endangered species or climate change or any other environmental issues highlight a wide variety of different interests and values within and across cultural communities.

The very way we communicate about nature can reveal our attitudes about it and can itself be a point of conflict. As you may have noticed from some of the examples above, nature has been treated with what some people would describe as human-like qualities: owls have rights, nature can talk, and whales can speak. There are writers who point out that there are dangers in *anthropomorphizing* nature; that is, of attributing human qualities to nature. For example, in La Fontaine's fables, animals can do all sort of human things including speaking to each other in similar fashion to how humans would.[5] Some environmentalists have tried to bring attention to contemporary struggles between human–nature relations by using theatrical representations. In some of these performances trees, for example, may be endowed with human attributes such as the ability to speak and have familial relationships with one another.[6] May (2007) cautions that dramatizing nature through an anthropomorphic lens maintains the focus on humans, and, thus, is a "reflection of human power and privilege, [where] the Other [is] transformed in a performance of human desire."[7] So, is it really nature speaking or is it humans speaking using nature as medium? The quandary is, then, how to talk about nature without granting to it human-like traits.

Environmental Communication as Gendered

Environmental communication as "gendered" promotes the assumption that the human to other-than-human connection is not gender neutral. This means that gender is a cultural lens through which we see environmental matters. Not only can different gendered groups experience and have different relationships with the environment, but humans also talk about environmental ideas in gendered ways. The assumption that gender is a key element in environmental relations has received vigorous support and activism from women worldwide for several decades, and this area is known as "ecofeminism." According to Braidotti, one of the reasons why women have been at the forefront of environmental-political activism is because women "are more directly exposed to the negative effects of environmental degradation in developing countries."[8]

Gendered perspectives about the environment were first brought to public awareness at the First World Conference on Women held in Mexico City, Mexico, in 1975. At that meeting Indian physicist, Dr. Vandana Shiva, introduced the issue of Himalayan women's struggle to protect their woodlands against the commercialization that had long threatened the community's sources of nutrition, house-building materials, and other goods.[9] Since that time she has advanced the global Green Movement by supporting grassroots activism in Africa, Asia, Austria, Ireland, Switzerland, and various countries in Latin America.

Since 1975, women throughout the world have been strongly active in international movements aimed at protecting the environment from pollution and hazardous-scale technical projects (i.e., dams and nuclear energy constructions), defending land ownership by women, preserving subsistence economies, and maintaining the cultural identities and integrity of communities. Some of women's efforts have received high praise in global contexts. For example, in 1992, Rigoberta Menchú Tum, who has dedicated her life to improving the lives of indigenous peoples in her native Guatemala, was awarded the Nobel Peace Prize. As activist and politician her extensive work throughout the world includes protesting environmentally destructive tar sand pipelines and promoting a clean energy economies. And, in 2004, Dr. Wangari Maathai, founder of The Green Belt Movement, was awarded the Nobel Peace Prize for her 30 years of work with combatting deforestation in her native Kenya. As rhetor and African peace-building leader, she was a "strong voice speaking for the best forces in Africa to promote peace."[10]

From a communication perspective, Milstein and Dickinson have argued that our everyday talk about environmental issues contains terminology and behaviors that appear to favor a feminine perspective but instead actually privilege masculine standpoints.[11] On the surface, we seem to honor feminine-based perspectives, such as through terms like "mother nature" and "mother Earth," and through communal, emotional, and sensory perspectives. By using "mother" terms we presumably honor the Earth by attributing feminizing cultural ideas about life-giving and nurturance. But, while this view exists, it is overshadowed by masculine ways of looking at nature, where nature is seen as something to conquer. So, while we may say and think we connect with, honor, and protect nature, human actions in fact reveal that we ultimately objectify and abuse it and sometimes disregard the common good.

Environmental Communication in the Context of Ecotourism

Since the 1980s "ecotourism," sometimes called "sustainable tourism," has become a key area of attention for scholars and practitioners of environmental communication. Ecotourism is a type of tourism that involves visiting relatively undisturbed, remote, pristine, fragile places around the globe for a variety of purposes including educating travelers about biodiversity, raising funds for conservation projects, and encouraging respect for local peoples, their cultures, and their human rights. Ecotourism differs from conventional tourism in its emphasis on social responsibility by minimizing the possible negative aspects of outside interventions such as distressing local environments, cultures, and peoples. Or, as The International Ecotourism Society (TIES) defined the term in 1990, ecotourism is: "Responsible travel to natural areas that conserves the environment and improves the well-being of local people."[12] Ecotourists, then, actively seek educational and environmental advocacy opportunities. Their travels take them to rainforests, coral reefs, cave dwellings, wildlife preserves, deserts, and volcanoes. And their activities may include camping, fishing, wildlife watching, hiking, trekking, cycling, volcano and rock climbing, cave exploration, rafting, surfing, and scuba diving.

Within the field of communication, Sowards has studied the ways that ecotourism activities are shaped by communicative practices before, during, and following the travel experience, and how these practices can affect conservation efforts around the globe.[13] She says that communication comes into play in the materials people read and watch preparing for travel, such as websites, brochures, magazines, guidebooks, and television shows dedicated to nature-based travel. During travel, ecotourists visit information centers, read local materials, participate in guided tours, and converse with fellow travelers and people they meet along the way. Following travel, ecotourists continue to shape their experiences by talking about them with friends, by sharing photographs and postcards, and perhaps by journaling. And, so, given that ecotourism

FIGURE 10.2 |

activities are fundamentally constructed and experienced within communication, she argues that understanding the communication strategies people use to anticipate, experience, and remember ecotourism activities ultimately can be used for improving conservation efforts, tourists' self-awareness, and social interactions with all involved in the ecotourism industry.

Sowards says that it is important for ecotourists to make conscious their expectations and assumptions about the environments they plan to visit and the people inhabiting those environments.[14] This consciousness or self-awareness about the role of the presence of outsiders, she believes, can influence a greater environmental and cultural awareness. Further, she believes that this enhanced awareness of the cultures and the people inhabiting ecotourism locations ultimately can lead to productive communication strategies that involve local peoples in decision-making and policy-setting processes that directly benefit them as well as their environments. Of her journey into this type of self-awareness, she says:

A few years ago, I traveled to Kayan Mentarang National Park, located in the province of East Kalimantan, Indonesia, and along the border with Malaysia. Along with three of my students and approximately 10 others, we took a small wooden boat up river for two days (camping on the side of the river overnight) to reach the small village of Long Punjungan, with approximately 400 inhabitants. I had learned about this national park and this village from the WWF office in Indonesia. Very few tourists had ever visited this area, and as a researcher and academic, I was interested in how it might be promoted as an ecotourism destination. In reviewing their logbook, we saw that only a handful of foreigners had visited this area over the previous 10 years.

Ecotourists often think about opportunities for hiking, rafting, birding, and wildlife watching, but another aspect of ecotourism is interaction with local people. The people in Long Punjungan and Kayan Mentarang National Park are known as Kenyah Dayaks, an indigenous group on the island of Borneo. WWF posters and brochures advertising Kayan Mentarang National Park emphasized how tourists would be able to interact with indigenous people and participate in local activities. Given my own interest in how difference is created, exaggerated, and emphasized, the focus on the "exotic other" is one of the selling points of ecotourism. While riding the wooden boat up the river to reach Long Punjungan, we discovered that we were also traveling with the camat (district head), his wife, and his daughter, our first encounters with people from Kayan Mentarang National Park.

Once we arrived in Long Punjungan, we were invited to stay in the camat's house, where we stayed for approximately the next 10 days. Over those days, we found out that in the celebration of Indonesian independence

(continued)

(continued)

day, there was a cultural festival for the Kenyah, who would be competing in traditional dances and music competitions as well as karaoke. Each night, we attended the festivities from 7 p.m. to 12 a.m., watching performances by everyone in the village and those who had come from other villages for the competition. On the last night, we were invited to do our own performances of the dances we had seen. The camat urged us to don the head pieces and clothing for the competition and perform to the best of our ability in front of 300 or 400 people, who had also been competitors. That moment of being asked to participate in something that these folks took great pride in, but at the same time thinking about cultural appropriation of something that did not come from our own cultural background, was disconcerting. I still wonder today about that moment. In performances that were meant for the Kenyah themselves, what role did we play in our presence and through our own performances of Kenyah traditional dances? Given the loud guffaws from the audience as we interpreted the dances, we clearly provided a lot of entertainment. The search for the "exotic other" is a problematic aspect of ecotourism, but not one that was felt in the same way by our hosts as felt by us. That moment still causes me to reflect on my own ethnic background, privilege, class status, and gender, and how that plays out in ecotourism experiences. This experience also demonstrates the importance of cultural adaptation and critical reflection on our roles as ecotourists. Knowing about the Kenyah Dayaks and their connection to place and home in tropical rainforests also reflects the importance of conservation efforts, for both local people and for everyone else.[15]

Environmental Communication as Inherently Cultural

How humans view the natural world has been studied from diverse theoretical and applied perspectives. In communication, environmental concerns have been studied using environmental theory, ecolinguistics, media theory, rhetorical theory, social movement theory, pop-culture theory, and cultural theory.

Using cultural theory, the work of Carbaugh brought attention to the ways that Blackfeet people established human–nature relations in and through "listening" vs. "speaking."[16] In the case of the particular Blackfeet community, humans and other-than-humans were represented as co-participants in a way of life that engaged them in a "highly reflective and revelatory mode of communication." Via the nonverbal resources of "listening" to nature, people could open themselves up to the mysteries of unity between the physical and the spiritual, to the relationships between human and natural forms, and to the links between places and persons. An interesting aspect of this line of work is that it explores not only human communicative processes, but also communicative aspects of nature.[17] In other words, this approach showcases a key assumption held by particular communities that humans communicate with nature and that nature communicates with humans, similar to the *curandera* perspective noted in the beginning narrative of this chapter.

The idea that communication extends beyond human discourse and should embrace nonhuman communication is a theme echoed by researchers studying other communities. Milstein, who studies communities involved with whales and whale tourisms, offers such an example.[18] Studying nature tourism as cultural expression, she addressed the social and environmental struggles within the largest concentration of whale watching operations in the world. This area is located in transnational waters in the North Pacific off the coasts of Canada and the United States. Milstein's work claimed that the local tourism industry was privileged over the best interests of other-than-humans; in this case, a community of endangered orcas (*orcinus orca*) or killer whales. She argued that companies who valued and were motivated by profit-making, who at the time drew some 500,000 tourists annually, threatened the whales and their habitat through tourist boat engine noise and exhaust, and other stresses. To illustrate issues of communication as mediator in human–nature relations she identified various themes from her ethnographic observations of human–whale interactions. Among those themes is one she labels: "whales speak for themselves." That whales speak for themselves means that in that particular society the very communicative presence of the whales served as means for interesting people, not only in whales but also in nature more broadly. This interest, she argued, made it possible for people to "be in touch" with whales, to inspire people to learn more about whales, and ultimately to motivate humans to protect whale habitats so as to avert the animals' worldwide extinction.[19]

The work of Valladolid and Apffel-Marglin, two *campesino* [peasant farmer] scholars from the Peruvian Andes, offer a perspective of the nature–human relation as a multi-voiced conversation and describe it as their community's "cosmovision."[20] In this worldview, the connection between nature and humans is seen as reciprocally constant, wherein the environment and humans are seen as collaborators in the creation and nurturance of biodiversity. From this perspective, communication is not necessarily perceived as words or language but, rather, as a type of communication that transcends Western understandings of dialogue. In this perspective nature and humans are part of a unity that is not dependent on words, and that is larger than an earthly world.

Environmental culture also can express something powerful about a person's individual identity as José's experience illustrates. *In this case a cultural move valuing the diminishing or elimination of waste is at the heart of how he views himself:*

Waiting in line to pay my groceries, I realized I had forgotten to bring my reusable bag. Sometimes I give myself a hard time for being so careless in my contribution to saving the planet. But most of the time, I indulge myself by comparing my attempt to use less plastic or paper bags with the big environmental problems around the world. Thus, I label my effort helpless, and my guilt subsides.

I am next in line. While I put my stuff on the counter I noticed that all my food is "certified organic." This is easy to see because the certificate is a central part of the product's presentation, along with a bucolic depiction of the place where the product comes from. What am I saying about myself with my bags full of organic, farmer-style vegetables? "One or two bags?" the cashier asks.

"One," I said, hoping to contribute to the elimination of waste at the supermarket.

In the parking lot I found Chris, my neighbor. He had one little bag in his hand. "Where are you going?" I asked, noticing he was walking toward his car. "Back home," he replied. "Did you use your car to come here? It's only five blocks!" I said in a tone mixed with irony and disappointment. He smiled. I turned around and walked to my bike. "It is one gallon of gas less," I thought. Then, I smiled too.

In the area of cultural approaches to environmental communication, much work remains to be accomplished with regard to understanding similar and dissimilar ways for viewing and valuing natural life and for understanding the identities we adopt within a cultural community.

HEALTHCARE AND INTERCULTURAL COMMUNICATION

Differing Cultural Expectations

Differing viewpoints on what may seem obvious to members of a particular culture in relation to health issues are also very common. Take for example this simple yet intense example shared by one of our students who spent time in Italy.

My American roommate, Laura, and I had invited several Italian friends over to dinner at our apartment one evening. As an act of appreciation, my Italian friend, Valentina, had made her favorite dessert to share with everyone. When she uncovered the dish and started passing portions around the table, Laura and I did our best to seem thrilled and eager to take the first bite. However, we were very alarmed that Valentina's dessert was covered in raw eggs, something which we consider extremely bad for a person's health in our culture. We were afraid to eat the dessert for fear of getting poisoned from the raw eggs, but everyone else was digging in, so we did our best. Even our best attempt, however, could not hide the screaming nonverbal language that we were displaying, prompting Valentina to ask us what was wrong. Eventually, we explained the taboo of eating raw egg in America since there have been numerous accounts of salmonella linked to ingesting raw eggs. Thus our verbal and nonverbal communication did not match. This led to an interesting conversation about health and food in the United States and Italy.

Different ideas about food choices mirror the diverse ways people talk about healthcare both across and within national boundaries. For example, in the story above we are aware of some groups in the United States that have no problems eating raw eggs. The healthcare field itself encompasses a multitude of culturally different ways of viewing what is appropriate healthcare, as Kris's experience exemplifies.

Many years ago I worked at a medical school in an administrative position. I was also taking graduate courses toward a master's degree in communication. My area of interest centered on spirituality within medical settings. I was interested in learning how patients and providers (together and separately) navigated the varying concepts, beliefs, and occurrences of spirit or non-logic within the medical field. During that time a guest speaker was brought to the university's medical school for three days of seminars and lectures. There was one large public lecture that anyone could attend. The speaker was Dr. Andrew Weil. He has since become widely recognized as the founder and chief proponent of Integrative Medicine, also referred to as Complementary and Alternative Medicine (CAM).

Dr. Weil advocated the use of an integrative approach to medicine that combines modern approaches of Western medicine with more traditional use of plants, nutritional knowledge of foods with healing properties, and other non-invasive treatments such as yoga, breathing techniques, massage, exercise, and meditation. He talked about his research which had discovered that humans more easily assimilated organic substances than those that are synthetically produced. He emphasized nutrition, exercise, and stress reduction to maintain the body's natural healing abilities. He also spoke of his medical training at Harvard and supported the use of conventional medicine when needed to intervene in health crises.

(continued)

(continued)

I was one of the very few non-medical personnel who attended the public lecture that day. Dr. Weil presented his research, talked about Integrative Medicine, and answered questions. He was abundantly respectful of those in attendance, including the physicians' opinions, questions, and the various comments among the audience members. I heard the following types of comments from physicians and other medical personnel around me in the audience: "I can't see how this would be practical." "Nah, it'll never work," and "maybe, but how do we decide what approach to take?" Most of the audience members went on to the luncheon that was set up after the lecture, talking about various work-related matters. I was left speechless. I thought the ideas Dr. Weil presented were amazing and revolutionary. His research intuitively made sense to me, and the connection to my research on spirituality in medicine was obvious. His way of communicating about health was more holistic with an approach that combined attention to body, mind, and spirit for overall health, but his approach did not adhere to the model of logic so ingrained in traditional medicine at that time.

Roughly 15 years after I attended that public lecture given by Dr. Weil, Integrative Medicine became more popular than ever. By 2012 approximately 50 percent of all hospitals in the United States offered nonconventional medical services, and overall around 35 percent of adults living in the United States used alternative treatments to medical conditions.[21] Those statistics only represent reported medical data within the United States which is somewhat of a late bloomer when it comes to more "natural" health beliefs and practices. However, discussing health in terms of indigenous healers and holistic has quickly become more culturally sensible within the United States and numerous other countries who have used integrative approaches to health and healing for a very long time.

As Integrative Medicine becomes more accepted in the United States, there are other dimensions of culture within the healthcare field that are complex and slow to evolve. Some of the issues associated with understanding how culture intersects with healthcare include dynamics intrinsic to medicine like various areas of specialization, length of time in practice, and relative status of medical specialization and/or individual practitioner. Kreps used the term "professional prejudice" to name the inherent rank and prestige awarded to some medical specialties and associated roles within the medical profession.[22] *Status* is one level of distinction that defines the medical culture. For example, a scrub nurse does not hold as much power as a physician. Within a subspecialty, there are also levels of prestige and power. In general, surgeons are most highly regarded with orthopedic surgeons viewed as the elite among this already elite group of physicians. This type of internal pecking order contributes to decision-making, values, and norms that are inherent in the world of medical providers. While the distinctions in status are inherently recognized within medical culture and among medical professionals, the differentiations are largely unknown for patients, families, and caregivers.

In addition, choices of treatment and patient care can vary widely depending on the provider's medical training and background. Understandably, a patient without the awareness of inherent differences among providers would question why one physician made a referral to a chiropractor or acupuncturist while another prescribed medication for what seems like the same set of symptoms. Given the complexity of patients and providers with a myriad of cultural backgrounds, it makes sense that most patients and medical providers lack the cultural knowledge base and awareness to communicate among and with each other using cultural sensitivity. There are ways that intercultural communication can increase understanding among patients and providers. The next section describes how communication skills can be applied for beneficial health outcomes.

Specific Applications of Cultural Communication in Healthcare

Kris has conducted extensive research with physicians who work together in the operating room. Initially her primary goal was to improve communication between anesthesiologists and surgeons. What she learned over the course of a decade of research was that an approach hoping to find universals in healthcare was not applicable. There was not a predictable pattern to communication styles of physicians in the operating room. To best offer ways to improve communication among the physicians, it was important to create training sessions that were adaptable to the participants, their individual experiences, and the cultural backgrounds of those involved. Kris developed communication training programs that offered a broad array of communication skills for all operating room physicians regardless of whether they were anesthesiologists, general surgeons, obstetricians, or other surgically specialized physicians. What emerged as most important was to provide training sessions as a venue for the various specialties to learn about communication together with multicultural participation.

Much of the variation in perspective arose from inherent norms ingrained in each cultural group. Picture in your imagination what you know about a patient undergoing surgery in an operating room. During most surgical procedures, the patient lies prone on an operating table. An anesthesiology team congregates at the head of the patient, while the surgical team concentrates on the larger landscape of the body to "repair" the problem area. What you may not know is that a screen and extensive draping are used to separate the patient's head from the rest of the body. This physical layout gives rise to interesting communication patterns because there is an actual barrier between groups of physicians. The use of surgical masks that cover all but the eyes, limiting some facial cues, adds an additional communication hurdle that must be overcome. At the head of the patient, anesthesiologists administer multiple medications to anesthetize the patient, and also maintain blood pressure, breathing, and blood flow within the parameters necessary to perform the surgical procedure. On the other side of the draping a much different dynamic occurs. Surgeons work rapidly to repair the physical "problem" with a tight focus on the area of concern and a desire to complete the procedure and reconnect body tissues as soon as possible. While anesthesiologists concentrate on an overall systemic functioning of the patient, surgeons focus on a specific location in the body with speed as a motivating factor.

Ideally the surgeons are able to "get in and get out" with a removal or repair of the damaged body part. However, surgeons must pause or stop if the anesthesiologist notifies them that the patient's blood pressure or oxygen level changes in such a way that compromises the patient's health. While both teams have an overall goal to help the patient, the inherent values and norms are different for each. It is not uncommon that the anesthetic team will want the surgeons to stop while they get the vitals (blood pressure, oxygen saturation, etc.) back to optimal levels. The surgeons on the other hand often believe they can finish the procedure and then the anesthesia team can work to resume normal levels of blood pressure and breathing functionality.

The anesthesiologist's goal of maintaining and the surgeon's goal of fixing are both deeply ingrained. The values held by each member of the surgical team reflect norms that have been passed on through multiple generations of medical practitioners. The inherent conflict that arises with these disparate goals is unfortunately also a norm among surgical physicians. As is the case in many areas of cultural conflict, it is difficult to determine if one is right and the other is wrong. They are merely different perspectives based on different viewpoints and values. The training sessions that Kris conducted gave the physicians an opportunity to recognize the cultural values that underlie the different preferences and realize there was merit in both. Individual physicians also realized that variation in communication choices among them was based on inherent medical culture. Once norms and values unique to each specialization were explored, the training sessions then provided opportunities for the physicians to practice newly acquired communication skills based on similar goals of saving or healing patients as a well-integrated team with consideration for the different perspectives and approaches.

One example helps demonstrate how the training sessions increased understanding and improved communication among the physicians. A total of four physicians were involved in this example, as was the case in all training sessions.

A team of two anesthesiologists and two obstetricians did not successfully save a mother and child during a complex emergency procedure that was conducted in a high-fidelity simulation lab. During a debriefing session after "the patient died," the four physicians talked about what happened. The anesthesiologists were physically located at the head of the patient and separated by a drape from the obstetricians who were focused on the mother's lower abdominal area. While the anesthesiologists worked to maintain vitals that kept the mother alive, the obstetricians worked to save the life of the baby. Each pair had a primary purpose to save the life of a different person (mother or baby) based on values and norms inherent in each specialty. What was unique about this case and all obstetrical cases conducted during training was that the patient was both mother AND child. The two were inseparable. However, the overall goal of the anesthesia team was to maintain health functions of the mother (blood pressure, oxygen levels, etc.) who was experiencing difficulty, while the obstetrical team worked as rapidly as possible to deliver the baby since the child's life was also in jeopardy. Because of the different norms associates with each team, the obstetrical surgeons' primary concern was the infant and assuring the delivery of a healthy child, while the anesthesiologists' primary concern was the mother and the maintenance of her essential vitals to keep her alive.

Neither team was right or wrong. The two surgical teams merely had different perspectives on area of need based on values and goals inherent in their own medical cultures. Communication played a large part in the failed procedure because none of the values and norms were verbally expressed. Since neither team had prior knowledge of the others' cultural foundations, and points of urgent attention, the lack of communication to explain the driving forces behind their actions during the procedure limited the knowledge base of all concerned. In effect, the four physicians were simultaneously performing two separate surgical procedures rather than working as a team to save the lives of both mother and child.

The discussion that occurred during the debrief session was eye-opening for all four participants as they realized the importance of communicating as a team. Each pair had specified values and norms of procedure that conflicted with the other half of the four-person team. By talking about the goals and perspectives each team member held as intrinsic to the surgical procedure, the group of four physicians experienced a group "lightbulb moment." They all realized that they had worked at cross-purposes without consideration of the other pair who were as critically important to a successful outcome. As a group of four, they discussed areas of different perspective. The anesthesiologists explained that they strive to maintain the health of the mother for easier delivery of the child, and

(continued)

(continued)

as often occurs, that goal conflicted with the surgeons' aim to deliver the child as quickly as possible, with the belief that the mother can be rehabilitated later. These two different ways of approaching the same situation were completely unknown to the other members of the surgical team. Both perspectives and associated goals had value, and awareness of the different cultural values enabled the entire surgical team to agree on better communication practices to help save patient lives in the future. Specifically the four agreed to verbally express concerns and desired outcomes as the case unfolded rather than assume the other team knew what the justifications were for slowing or rushing procedures.

The four-person team then had another opportunity to practice new communication abilities with a different simulated patient case. During the second scenario all four verbally communicated what was occurring on their end of the patient, while checking to see how the others were progressing. All four discussed concerns and helped stabilize vital functions of the "complete patient." During this second case, both mother and child lived, and the physicians operated as a four-person team, with collaborative communication based on their newly acquired respect for values and associated procedures inherent in each cultural group.

The example of the four physicians highlights how inherent and subconscious values and norms can be within medical culture. It also provides one example of how awareness of the goals and values of other cultural groups can provide new lenses and new practices with which medicine can integrate culture and communication to improve patient outcomes and save lives.

Sensitivity to Cultural Communication Considerations in Healthcare

So far, most of our discussion has focused on medical culture within groups of physicians. We have not yet considered other cultural affiliations of medical providers, nor have we discussed patient cultural values, goals, and beliefs. Intercultural diversity and complexity in health communication expands exponentially with these other cultural considerations. Our text has noted numerous times that there is variation among members within any nation state or other cultural group. The diversity in healthcare is further compounded by cultural complexity among patients in addition to providers. Generalization or simplification according to cultural group with these multi-layers of diversity results in misunderstanding and confusion at best, and tragic health outcomes at worst.

Verbal and Nonverbal Communication in Healthcare

Cultural values, goals, and beliefs are often reflected in language. As one of the building blocks of communication, language includes both verbal and nonverbal forms. Many of the intercultural terms covered in Chapters 5 and 6 earlier in the text have application in healthcare. Do you recall how we discussed the intricate ways verbal and nonverbal communication are intertwined? In discussions of healthcare, sensitivity to both verbal and nonverbal communication is necessary to convey and comprehend health information among patients and medical providers. An ideal healthcare setting integrates sensitivity to both forms of communication for understanding dissemination of information among families, caregivers of patients, and all medical staff.

Census figures from 2014 in the United States reveal demographic information that influences verbal communication in healthcare. These are merely one country's demographic data, but they exemplify discrepancies that challenge accurate uses of verbal communication in healthcare. In the 2014 census, individuals who identified as Hispanic or Latino comprised approximately 17.4 percent of the overall population, with 20.7 percent reporting languages other than English spoken at home.[23] While it is quite likely that persons who identify languages other than English spoken at home also have exceptional proficiency in English, it is also possible that some nuances can be lost in discussions that surround healthcare.

Part of the discrepancy is that healthcare providers are not as ethnically diverse as patient populations reflected in the census data. Instead, the majority of medical practitioners identify as white, non-Hispanic, with a growing number of healthcare providers who identify as Asian American. The inherent language barrier that is created with this verbal communication discrepancy can be detrimental to positive health outcomes. It is critical that patients understand what the medical providers tell them, as much as medical personnel completely comprehend what the patient tells them for all to collaborate on the best care possible.

One approach to help bridge the language barrier in healthcare is translation or interpretation. Unfortunately the majority of translations in medical encounters use a family member or staff person who is not medically trained and/or culturally sensitive enough to capture the necessary language nuances needed for accurate understanding of the medical issues and treatment procedures. Although translations from family members or other medical staff may be better than a complete lack of communicated understanding between patient and medical provider, the problems associated with these forms of translation are abundant.

When family members serve as interpreters, the burden often falls to young children. The younger generation is more likely to be exposed to English in schools, and is therefore usually selected to converse in English with the medical providers.[24] While the literal translation of words may not be problematic, the interpretation of the information may be compromised. Younger family members are less likely to have a framework of knowledge to support important health information that does not translate easily from one language to another. In addition, children may become frightened of the information conveyed by medical providers, especially when family members are gravely ill, or the subject of the conversation is considered an unspeakable topic. Terminal illness and sexual health matters are two examples of problematic health conversations that children are asked to interpret for older family members. Imagine how difficult it would be for a 16-year-old son to translate for his mother who is being seen by her obstetrician. Best-case scenario, the mother is healthy and the son can happily assure his mother that all is well. But what if the mother has stage-three uterine cancer? Would the 16-year-old have enough medical background to convey the seriousness to his mother? What about the emotional implications for the young son who realizes his mother's life is in jeopardy? Yes, the 16-year-old has a firm grasp on English, but is his role as interpreter healthy for him or his mother?

Individuals with English as a second language are not the only ones who struggle to communicate with healthcare professionals. For most people living in the United States, healthcare jargon, abbreviations, and the intricacies of medical terminology are difficult to understand. A significant amount of current consideration and research is directed toward improved communication and comprehension of medical information. Research conducted in this area informs the emerging industry of health literacy, which is another growing field of intercultural health communication.

Nonverbal communication is equally important in healthcare communication. To complicate matters further for both patients and providers, nonverbal communication norms vary greatly across and within cultural communities. For example, as noted in Chapter 6, eye contact and facial expression are not normative communication behaviors for all persons and cultural affiliations. For some individuals, the interpretation of direct eye contact indicates that the conversational partner is attentive and able to understand the information. Lack of eye contact would indicate the opposite. However, for many cultures, direct eye contact is considered rude and indicative of an affront to authority. For those whose cultural framework teaches deference to authority within a hierarchical worldview, the use of direct eye contact would be considered insulting when used during communication with a medical provider.

Facial expression also varies in interpretation among cultural communities. For some a smile represents affinity, and perhaps sympathy or understanding. For others a smile is a politeness gesture that is not meant to convey a sense of understanding, affiliation, or anything other than a very impersonal acknowledgment of another person. In other cultural groups a smile indicates discomfort or unease in regard to the situation or topic of conversation. These are all very different interpretations that require cultural sensitivity to navigate the nuances of communication meaning that occur in the emotional contexts of healthcare.

Consider also the differences in interpretation of touch discussed in Chapter 6. Now consider how integral touch can be in many, if not most, healthcare settings. Touch does not have a universal interpretation. For some patients and family members, touch of a shoulder or hand from a medical provider conveys empathy and compassion. However, for others, that same touch is considered invasive and could be interpreted as threatening or insulting.

In many Arabic cultures, women maintain modesty though complete coverage of body parts. Islamic medical ethics dictate that women receive care from female medical providers. An observant Muslim woman may receive care from a male physician only if a mahram male accompanies her. Mahram men are those related by blood or marriage, for example husbands, sons, brothers, and fathers. Since a prophetic tradition states that when a non-mahram woman and man are alone together, Satan is the third among them, Islamic law prohibits any type of proximity to adultery.[25] This modesty extends to touch in that both men and women believe it is forbidden to touch a member of the opposite sex who is not mahram. Shaking hands or a light touch on the shoulder to reassure are as taboo as a physical examination by a medical provider who is a member of the opposite sex.

This example from Islamic culture is only one example. There are multiple cultural distinctions that are part of deeply ingrained belief systems that influence the dynamics of nonverbal communication in healthcare. How can these cultural nuances be navigated for the best? In attempts to be culturally sensitive, medical providers often fail in nonverbal communication competence. Jennifer's story can help illustrate how awareness of nonverbal communication across cultures can help in healthcare.

Jennifer recalls accompanying her friend Jin-Ae to the doctor for an annual physical. The exam began in the usual manner with Jin-Ae responding to questions that covered her medical history. As the physician made small talk and asked about medical issues at the same time, Jin-Ae kept her eyes on her hands that were clasped in her lap. The physician repeatedly asked Jin-Ae if she was ok, to which Jin-Ae continuously responded, "yes." As the history-taking concluded, the physician had become brusque with the questions, and stopped trying to form a personal connection with Jin-Ae, merely asking the questions in rapid-fire format. Jennifer could not figure out what had happened to alter the dynamic so readily until she noticed that Jin-Ae never once lifted her gaze to meet the physician's. While Jin-Ae was showing deference out of respect, the physician did not realize that his status was being nonverbally acknowledged. Instead he assumed Jin-Ae was disinterested in the procedure and therefore matched her assumed indifference with diminished attempts at personal connection.

The burden of understanding nonverbal communication cues and behaviors usually falls to medical providers who are not educated in nonverbal intricacies or norms of a variety of cultural communities. Rather than receive this type of knowledge during their medical training, most providers acquire cultural knowledge from personal experiences or individual backgrounds that have experience in multiple cultures. Medical schools and training programs may one day address verbal and nonverbal communication issues, but in the interim, patients may need to help providers better understand appropriate communication behaviors.

The different attitudes toward health within the healthcare industry and various cultural groups illustrate the challenges that can come from working within a multicultural organization. The third context we would like to consider in terms of culture is how leadership within various organizational settings is influenced by culture. How do different cultures understand effective leadership and what can we do to be more sensitive to intercultural differences within a given organizational environment?

ORGANIZATIONAL LEADERSHIP AND INTERCULTURAL COMMUNICATION

One of the growing areas of interest in intercultural communication is the concept of leadership or cross-cultural management. We live in a world where intercultural connections involving business, health and humanitarian organizations, and various political alliances are quite common. Understanding leadership in global or intercultural organizational settings is, therefore, becoming increasingly important. There are two major approaches in the field as it relates to understanding leadership in intercultural settings. One is tied to the social-scientific approach and the other to the interpretive approach. We will provide an overview of some key findings from each of these approaches.

Social-Scientific Approach: Dimensions of Intercultural Leadership Success

One of the largest efforts to understand leadership in multicultural settings is a project known as GLOBE (Global Leadership and Organizational Behavior Effectiveness). The GLOBE project has involved surveys and interviews with many thousands of subjects across at least 24 countries.[26] This project has primarily focused around two broad issues: developing a culturally endorsed theory of leadership and then assessing CEO leadership behavior and effectiveness in multicultural settings. We will give you a feel for what they have focused on related to these two issues and highlight some of the key findings from this line of research.

FIGURE 10.3

The development of culturally endorsed leadership has been focused on identifying certain dimensions (similar to attributes) that are perceived by various cultural communities (identified as nation states or regions of the world) to be important in terms of leadership qualities. After a long winnowing process, their research identified six leadership dimensions: charismatic/ value-based, team-oriented, participative, humane-oriented, autonomous, and self-protective.[27] These dimensions are similar to the worldviews we discussed in Chapter 2 as they may be seen to reside on continuums which different communities would emphasize to different degrees.

- The charismatic/value-based leadership style is focused on the degree to which communities stress the importance of an inspirational leader that has a clear vision, is decisive, and is seen to have integrity and a performance orientation.
- Team-based leadership is centered on issues related to collaboration, diplomacy, and the ability to integrate and administrate well.
- The participative leadership dimension revolves around how much a leader involves others in decision-making and the way decisions are implemented.
- The humane-orientation dimension focuses on the modesty, compassion, and generosity of the leader.
- Autonomous leadership is centered on how independent and individualistic a leader should be.
- The self-protective dimension involves status, face-saving concerns, the relative importance of internal competition in the organization and an emphasis on procedures.

The six dimensions noted above are proposed as an etic framework intended to capture leadership styles within any given community.

Efforts to identify culturally endorsed styles of leadership also led to an examination of potential universal leadership preferences. The most universally valued dimensions were charismatic/value-based and team-oriented leadership. Issues related to having a clear vision, integrity, and the ability to integrate different groups and individuals into a cohesive whole were consistently noted as important across the different cultural communities. These dimensions were seen as particularly important in countries like the United States and Brazil, but all countries identified these as very important. This research suggests that, although there may be important cultural differences in how one community values internal competition, the importance of status, participation, autonomy, and a humane orientation, and the ability to have a clear vision, inspire others, act with integrity, and integrate various parties into the team are valued in virtually all cultural settings.

The rest of the dimensions revealed more cultural differences in terms of preferred leadership styles. For example, the participative dimension was still seen as very important in countries like the United States, Brazil, and Germany. This was seen as much less important in countries like Russia, Taiwan, India, and Mexico. One explanation is that, although these latter countries may be collectivist in nature and appreciate the ability to work together as a team, they also are more hierarchal in terms of expectations and expect their leader to make the decisions. In contrast, on the humane-orientation scale countries like Taiwan, India, and Nigeria are very strong, whereas countries in Eastern Europe, as well as Germany and Spain, tend to not see this as having the same importance. The respondents from the United States saw this as an important dimension, but not as important as the other dimensions we have covered. In what may be surprising for some, the United States scored relatively low on the autonomous dimension. In spite of being quite an individualistic nation that is known for the self-confidence that is part of this dimension, leaders who act entirely independently are not seen to be as desirable as those with a team-orientation. Perhaps this is due to a history that emphasizes checks and balances in government. Brazil and Guatemala scored even lower in terms of the autonomous dimension, whereas countries such as Egypt, Russia, and Germany scored relatively high in this area. Finally, in terms of the self-protection dimension the countries that scored the highest were Egypt, Guatemala, and China. Countries scoring near the bottom of this dimension were the United States and Germany. It should also be noted that none of the scores in this final dimension were as high as even the lowest scores in the more universal dimensions of charismatic/value-based and team-orientation. So, although there appear to be clear cultural differences in how self-protective actions are taken, these differences are not as strong as the universal values, such as integrity, vision, and team integration skills.

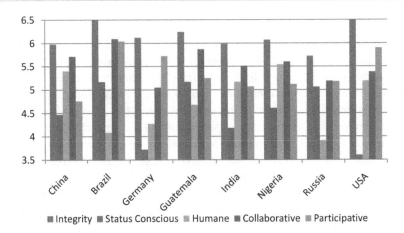

FIGURE 10.4 | Desirable leadership qualities

Source: Adapted from work by R. House, P. Dorfman, M. Javidan, P. Hanges, and M. Sully de Luque published in *Leadership Across Cultures: The GLOBE Study of CEO Leadership Behavior and Effectiveness in 24 Countries*, 2014

This leads us to the second issue covered by this research, which focused on the behavior reported on CEOs and the effectiveness of these leaders. As noted above, certain qualities were consistently marked as important across each community, whereas others varied by nationality. For example, in Figure 10.4 we highlight the scores (on a seven-point scale) that seven representative countries had for five leadership factors that were used in developing the dimensions we have discussed.[28]

The research conducted by the GLOBE team stresses the importance of matching performance with the culturally endorsed expectations. Thus an effective leader is one who can act in a way that meets the expectations of the cultural community in which the leader resides. In addition, understanding different cultural expectations for leadership provides information that can be used to help someone become a more effective leader in multicultural settings. This type of research is designed to be able to predict what behaviors will be the most effective so that the leader can have more control of a situation. For example consider the case of "Alan" reported in the *Harvard Business Review*:

When Alan, a rising star at a U.S.-based manufacturer, arrived in Beijing to take a position as the general manager for consumer products in China, he was energized and excited. He'd been charged with leading the firm's expansion in what

(continued)

(continued)

his bosses kept telling him was the fastest-growing market in the world. Though his predecessor had warned him that some internal tensions were interfering with the company's growth efforts in the country—in particular, that marketing and sales were making promises that the operations and distribution groups couldn't meet—it seemed like a relatively easy problem to resolve. All Alan had to do, he figured, was to better integrate the different parts of the organization in China.

He'd read that the Chinese tended to be collectivist in their thinking, inclined to prioritize group interests. So he decided to urge his direct reports to focus more closely on the overall good of the company and tackle problems together. In his first meeting with his function heads, he emphasized the need for better cooperation and established a cross-functional team to get marketing and operations on the same page. The new team expressed hearty support for its mandate, which was to identify the reasons for the lack of coordination and develop recommendations for how to remedy it. The members met at least once a week and made all the right noises about their plans for change.

But 60 days into the effort, coordination remained poor. The team members had agreed on some general goals but had never committed to any specific action or target or held one another accountable for improvements. Instead, in respectful exchanges, they constantly reminded one another that while cross-functional coordination was important, each function also had to deliver against its own objectives. To Alan's chagrin, turf protection in China was stronger than anything he had ever seen back home. And before long his enthusiasm began to give way to frustration. Alan essentially withdrew, both in the office and at home. He lost interest in the Chinese culture. He took a dislike to the local food and preferred to frequent Western restaurants and clubs. Even though he'd far exceeded expectations in his previous roles back home, he started to question his competence. He was failing at a highly coveted assignment—one that was fairly straightforward and was supposed to do so much for his development. Sure enough, Alan was soon called back to the States, and he has since given up his global ambitions for good.[29]

In short, it can be argued that, although Alan may have been an effective learner in his home country, he was not prepared to have success in an intercultural setting. An offshoot of the GLOBE work identifies three important criteria in considering one's preparedness for taking on a leadership role in an intercultural setting: intellectual capital, psychological capital, and social capital.[30] Intellectual capital in this context deals with your knowledge of how industry works worldwide, your interest in learning about foreign lands, and your ability to make connections and sense across a wide variety of options. Psychological capital deals with one's desire to explore the world, take risks, and experience new things, as well

For each question below rate yourself on a scale of 1–5 with 1 equaling not at all and 5 equaling to a very large extent.

All nine questions begin with "To what extent do you . . . "

Area One:

1   Know about the history, geography, and the important business and cultural leaders of several countries?

2   Know about the major religions of the world and their impact on society?

3   Discuss the economic and political ramifications of world events with friends and colleagues?

Area Two:

4   Enjoy exploring different parts of the world?

5   Challenge yourself in new and different ways?

6   Feel comfortable even though you are not in control of a situation?

Area Three:

7   Work effectively with people who are very different than you?

8   Understand the nonverbal expressions of people from several different cultures?

9   Willingly coordinate your activities with people who are culturally different than you?

The three areas correspond to the three types of capital. If you average 4 or above in an area this area is seen as a strength. If you average below 3 in an area it is seen as an area that needs work.

FIGURE 10.5 | Self-test: three forms of capital

as one's ability to accept and even enjoy uncertainty in life. Social capital implies the ability to build bridges between those with diverse opinions, to be concerned with listening more than getting your own point across, and to empathize with people from very different backgrounds than your own. Figure 10.5 provides an informal sample test for you to take to give you a feel for this work. These are not the actual questions used in the research. Remember, though, that regardless of where you score on such a test, the real key to success is desire. These skills can be grown if the desire is there and this type of analysis is mainly useful in guiding your own efforts to grow your intercultural ability.

Interpretive Approach: Leadership and Sense-Making in Intercultural Settings

In contrast to the approach of identifying cultural dimensions or worldviews that can be used to predict and explain how to be an effective cross-cultural leader, another approach is focused on how people make sense of the actions taken by leaders, the meanings that are created in intercultural contexts requiring leadership, and understanding leadership more in terms of a lived experience rather than a compilation of answers to pre-set questions. Meaning becomes the central point in this approach. Two people may both agree that respecting others, demonstrating integrity, and being team-oriented are each important. However, do they mean the same thing when they talk about showing respect, having integrity, or being a team player? These are questions that need consideration at the level of specific cases.

Case Studies

An example of different ways that people make sense or create meaning is reflected in work on meetings by Sprain and Boromisza-Habashi.[31] They give an example of a U.S. American running a meeting in Nicaragua related to developing strategies for fermenting coffee. The meeting starts off well as the U.S. American explains some possible strategies and a couple of the Nicaraguan participants chime in with comments and ideas. However, early on the U.S. American makes a perfunctory agreement to a comment and asks quickly if others have questions. The style in which this is done quickly shuts down the meeting in terms of participation and the U.S. American is left wondering what went wrong. Further analysis of the case indicates that for the Nicaraguans this meeting was a time to share ideas and discuss issues among relative equals, but the U.S. American treated the meeting as if she were the expert and the others were there just to gather her knowledge. Each party in this misunderstanding had a different image of what meetings like this should be like and what roles each person was to play. Each party would agree that they wanted a participative meeting (one of the dimensions discussed above), but what that meant in terms of specific practices was quite different.

Chevrier reported on a specific case involving a Franco-Vietnamese development project that was struggling. Her work analyzes a French non-governmental organization that was working on projects related to a variety of issues, such as improving infant health, micro-financing, and aiding agricultural endeavors in Vietnam.[32] Based on her work, one could imagine these contrasting responses from an interview with two participants in the project:

French participant: The funny thing is that we are just here to serve the needs of the Vietnamese community. Yet, the Vietnamese are always waiting for us to take the lead. I wish they would do more to take the initiative. We are here to empower them. I want to inspire them to feel a sense of pride and responsibility in making these economic and healthcare changes, to act courageously in changing the norm. I hope to see them take the lead in making these changes so they can make sure that what is right is done, even if that means standing up to family pressures. I hate the feeling of betrayal when those helping with the project fail to stand up to local leaders or when resources we help to generate are not made available to all, but only benefit close family members. We have had to monitor closely some activities to make sure things are done appropriately. The other thing I wish is that in our meetings we could have a real discussion about the pros and cons of different implementation options. What is the point of meeting if everything is already settled?

Vietnamese participant: I appreciate what the French are trying to do, but I wish they would spend more time in the community helping us do things rather than sitting in some office telling us what to do. They do not seem to understand the family obligations that exist in a community. They do not understand the importance of respect in dealing with local authorities. They spend so little time in the community that they often end up insulting people with how they address them. Their meetings are awkward and almost ask for people to act disrespectfully. Then when I show deference and flexibility, they act like I betrayed them in some way. The French are great people, but really they need to get out in the community more.

The challenges expressed by these hypothetical interviewees (based on Chevrier's compilation of research findings) are grounded in differences of making meaning. We suspect that both groups may agree in terms of what is perceived as ideal attributes for a leader that were noted earlier, such as having a vision, having integrity, and being able to integrate a diverse team, but the question becomes: what do these mean in practice? The research noted that the French felt betrayed by actions that the Vietnamese felt were just showing appropriate deference. The Vietnamese wanted to see the French more involved and out of the office, and the French felt they were empowering the Vietnamese by directing things from within the office. So one of the things we learn is how important it is to discover what actions mean in specific cases.

In another case study of a multinational organization we can see how looking for ways to bridge differences across meaning can prove effective. Clausen reports on a Danish audio-visual (AV) company that had important subsidiary partners in Japan.[33] We will review two meaning-making issues that were troublesome for this business alliance. The Danish company's vision statement was "Courage to constantly question the ordinary in search of surprising long lasting experiences." This statement was seen by Danish management as a powerful and important guide, but managers in Tokyo felt that questioning the ordinary did not promote a desirable image in the Japanese community, in which the ability to fit in with others and blend with what exists is valued. Some of the marketing problems this statement created were remedied by focusing on a cultural value that both the Danes and the Japanese agreed upon: simplicity. The ongoing questioning was able to be reframed as a search for greater simplicity, something both communities agreed upon.

Another problem arose in terms of the way the organization was structured. Danish cultural traditions tend to be egalitarian and focused on role (functional) responsibilities, whereas the Japanese tradition tends to be more hierarchical in nature, highlighting a person's status within an organization. For the Japanese employees knowing where one fit in the hierarchy improved one's commitment to the organization and created a firm foundation on which to build expectations. Initially, the organization only used an organizational chart that showed a matrix of responsibilities and the connections between everyday tasks; it did not show the "chain of command" or who reported to whom. This chart was seen as problematic by the Japanese employees, so a second chart showing the formalized hierarchy was developed and both were displayed in the official publications of the organization. This allowed each group to use the chart that best helped them make sense of the organization.

Case Study "Take-away" Messages

These last two cases were part of a larger research project focused on understanding the lived experience of leadership in intercultural settings.[34] The organizers of this work (Primecz, Romani, and Sackmann) identified a variety of what they deemed practical suggestions for someone in an intercultural leadership role. We will highlight a few of these. **First**, one should expect differences. This may seem obvious, but generally people expect similarities; after all, their way of doing things and the meanings they associate with certain actions are just common sense, right? **Second**, one should work to understand the relevant frames for making sense that each community is using. Just because gender or hierarchy is vitally important in interpreting actions in one community does not mean that it is the key for understanding another situation. Sometimes we want to make sense of others in terms of our own lens, so that they always come up lacking whatever we deem to be important. Use of culturally relevant lenses suggests a type of listening and research that looks for the important criteria and frames for the other community. In this way it is an emic approach, rather than an etic approach that already assumes that certain dimensions are most important for explaining some action. **Third**, one should seek to act as an interpreter and mediator of meaning in a way that shows respect for each perspective. In the example between the Danish and Japanese firms noted above, the importance of each perspective was acknowledged and adaptations were made, rather than there being a winner or a loser in terms of what was the "right" organizational chart. **Fourth**, one needs to search for and build on common ground. This includes a willingness to learn about others and have a willingness to come together in developing a common vision or goal. Sometimes the idea of culture can be used as a resource to create division in strategic ways. Ailon reports on an Israeli–USA cooperative project where culture was used as a means to gain power or control over one's work environment.[35] Exaggerating differences was a useful tool to an end. This type of approach was also reported on by Mahadevan who discussed how German engineers in a company that had branches in India initially dismissed cultural differences focusing on the shared knowledge of the engineering field, but later became worried about their jobs and changed the way they spoke to create a distance between themselves and their Indian colleagues.[36] As noted in Chapter 8, fears associated with another group often lead to intergroup conflict and a splintering of relationships. This is the opposite of the effort to learn about and appreciate differences in ways that seek common ground and connection.

SUMMARY

In this chapter we have looked at how culture impacts communication in three applied contexts, including environmental communication, healthcare, and leadership within organizational settings. Specifically we looked at how communication serves as a resource for mediating relations between humans and nature. We also looked at some cultural approaches to the study and practice of environmental communication. We then took a very specific industry, the healthcare industry, and examined how intercultural communication impacts work in this context. Finally, we explored two different ways of looking at the role of culture within organizational settings. One adopted a social-scientific approach and tried to identify universal characteristics that would mark good leadership in multicultural settings. A second approach focused on the community-specific meanings associated with leadership within various cultures.

REFLECTION QUESTIONS

1   How can we talk about nature—trees, animals, mountains, water—without attributing human-like characteristics (i.e., age, gender, the ability to speak, and the capacity to express emotions such as love and hate) to nonhuman entities?
2   Do you think that nature tourism such as whale-watching tours enhances or damages our connection with nature?
3   Imagine that the city where you were born loses its access to potable water, clean air, or uncontaminated soil. What would be the consequences for your country?
4   Which approach to understanding leadership in intercultural setting do you believe would work best: trying to identify common attributes that would be valued in any culture or trying to discover the specific meanings associated with leadership in specific communities?

ACTIVITIES

1   Have you received non-allopathic medical treatment? If so, what was it? What was your experience? What kind of outcome did you experience? Would you choose that type of treatment again? Why or why not? Share your answers with another or within a small group.

2   What do you think the future of healthcare will bring in terms of practices that involve multiple cultural communities?

3   Have you, a close friend, or family member experienced a healthcare situation that was extremely positive or negative? Was there a communication component to it? What suggestions would you make to change the outcome of what was experienced? Is there a way you might "train" others (physicians, patients, family members) to respond in a similar situation? What kind of training would you develop? Develop the training sessions in as much detail as possible and share your ideas with another person or within a small group. Be sure to ask for feedback or how you might improve your ideas.

4   In a small group, brainstorm what qualities go into effective leadership. Which worldviews from Chapter 2 do these correspond to? If you can, interview individuals from a different cultural background and compare the perceived qualities of effective leaders.

NOTES

1   L. Willies-Jacobo, "Susto: Acknowledging Patients' Beliefs about Illness," *Virtual Mentor* 9 (8) (2007): 532–6.
2   R. Cox, *Environmental Communication and the Public Square*, 2nd ed. (Thousand Oaks, CA: Sage Publications, Inc, 2010).
3   R. Carson, *The Silent Spring* (Boston, MA: Houghton Mifflin, 1962).
4   R. Carson, *The Silent Spring*.
5   J. de La Fontaine, *The Fables of Jean de La Fontaine: Bilingual Edition: English-French*, introduction by Sarah E. Holroyd (Sleeping Cat Press: http://sleeping catpress.com/, 2013).
6   D. Eshelman, "Voice of an Angry Tree: Trees Hate Us on the Arkansas Radio Theatre," *Liminalities: A Journal of Performance Studies* 9 (3) (2013): 1–10.
7   T. J. May, "Beyond Bambi: Toward a Dangerous Ecocriticism in Theatre Studies," *Theatre Topics* 17 (2) (2007): 95–110.
8   R. Braidotti, "Towards Sustainable Subjectivity: A View from Feminist Philosophy," in *Sustainability and the Social Sciences: A Cross-Disciplinary Approach to Integrating Environmental Considerations into Theoretical Reorientation*, ed. E. Becker and T. Jahn (Paris/Frankfurt a.M./London: Zed Books, 1999), 74–95.
9   C. Chelala, "Environmental Degradation's Heavy Toll on Women and Children," http://www.counterpunch.org/2016/02/19/environmental-degradations-heavy-toll-on-women-and-children/ (CounterPunch, February 19, 2016).

10 The Green Belt Movement. Wangari Maathai. http://www.greenbeltmovement.org/wangari-maathai/the-nobel-peace-prize.
11 T. Milstein and E. Dickinson, "Gynocentric Greenwashing: The Discursive Gendering of Nature," *Communication, Culture & Critique* 5 (4) (2012): 510–32.
12 The International Ecotourism Society (TIES), http://www.ecotourism.org/ties-overview (1990).
13 S. K. Sowards, "Expectations, Experiences, and Memories: Ecotourism and the Possibilities for Transformations" *Environmental Communication* 6 (2) (2012): 175–92.
14 Sowards, "Expectations."
15 Sowards, "Expectations."
16 D. Carbaugh, "'Just Listen': 'Listening' and Landscape among the Blackfeet," *Western Journal of Communication* 63 (3) (1999): 250–70.
17 Carbaugh, "Just Listen."
18 T. Milstein, "When Whales 'Speak for Themselves': Communication as a Mediating Force in Wildlife Tourism," *Environmental Communication: A Journal of Nature and Culture* 2 (2008): 173–92.
19 Milstein, "When Whales."
20 J. Valladolid and F. Apffel-Marglin, "Andean Cosmovision and the Nurturing of Biodiversity," in *Indigenous Traditions and Ecology: The Interbeing of Cosmology and Community*, ed. J. A. Grim (Cambridge, MA: Harvard University Press, 2001), 639–70.
21 T. C. Clarke, L. I. Black, B. J. Stussman, P. M. Barnes, and R. L. Nahin, "Trends in the Use of Complementary Health Approaches among Adults: United States, 2002–2012," *National Health Statistics Reports*; Number 79 (Hyattsville, MD: National Center for Health Statistics, 2015).
22 G. L. Kreps, "Applied Health Communication Research," in *Applied Communication Theory and Research*, ed. D. O'Hair and G. L. Kreps (Hillsdale, NJ: Lawrence Erlbaum, 1990), 313–30.
23 United States Department of Commerce, Census Bureau, 2014, http://www.census.gov/en.html.
24 A. duPre, *Communicating about Health: Current Issues and Perspectives* (New York: Oxford University Press, 2014).
25 A. Padela and P. Rodriguez del Pozo, "Muslim Patients and Cross-Gender Interactions in Medicine: An Islamic Bioethical Perspective," *Journal of Medical Ethics* 37 (2011): 40–4.
26 R. House, P. Dorfman, M. Javidan, P. Hanges, and M. Sully de Luque, *Strategic Leadership Across Cultures: The GLOBE Study of CEO Leadership Behavior and Effectiveness in 24 Countries* (Los Angeles: Sage Publications, 2014).
27 House et al., *Strategic Leadership.*
28 House et al., *Strategic Leadership* (pp. 239–44).
29 M. Javidan, M. Teagarden, and D. Bowen, "Managing Yourself: Making It Overseas," *Harvard Business Review*, April 2010.
30 I. Tamer, B. Dereli, and M. Saglam, "Unorthodox Forms of Capital In Organizations: Positive Psychological Capital, Intellectual Capital, and Social Capital," *Procedia-Social and Behavioral Sciences* 152 (2014): 963–72.
31 L. Sprain and D. Boromisza-Habashi, "Meetings: A Cultural Perspective," *Journal of Multicultural Discourses*, iFirst article (2012): 1–11.
32 S. Chevrier, "Exploring the Cultural Context of Franco-Vietnamese Development Projects: Using an Interpretative Approach to Improve the Cooperation Process,"

in *Cross-Cultural Management in Practice: Culture and Negotiated Meanings*, ed. H. Primecz, L. Romani, and S. Sackmann (Cheltenham, UK: Edward Elgar Publishing, 2011), 41–52.

33 L. Clausen, "Corporate Communication Across Cultures: A Multilevel Approach," in *Cross-Cultural Management in Practice: Culture and Negotiated Meanings*, ed. H. Primecz, L. Romani, and S. Sackmann (Cheltenham, UK: Edward Elgar Publishing, 2011), 77–88.

34 H. Primecz, L. Romani, and S. Sackmann, *Cross-Cultural Management in Practice: Culture and Negotiated Meanings* (Cheltenham, UK: Edward Elgar Publishing, 2011).

35 G. Ailon, *Global Ambitions and Local Identities: An Israeli-American High-Tech Merger* (New York: Berghahn Books, 2007).

36 J. Mahadevan, "Engineering Culture(s) across Sites: Implications for Cross-Cultural Management of Emic Meanings," in *Cross-Cultural Management in Practice: Culture and Negotiated Meanings*, ed. H. Primecz, L. Romani, and S. Sackmann (Cheltenham, UK: Edward Elgar Publishing, 2011), 89–100.

Chapter 11

What Diversity Exists in the Study of Intercultural Communication?

A Parable; A Dream

 I lay one lazy afternoon in my youth by the side of a meandering stream. I closed my eyes but for a moment, when it seemed to me that three gentlemen emerged from my very being. One old fellow, looking very much like a wandering minstrel with a harp slung over his shoulder, addressed me first. "You look like a reasonable fellow; come along this path of culture and together we will seek enlightenment."

 "Where does this path of culture go?" I wondered.

 "Oh, many places," he replied with an innocent grin. "It is a path of discovery. A path of understanding and knowledge."

 "I don't know," I hesitated, "it sounds like an intriguing journey, but what is at the end of such a path?"

 "Oh, don't worry about the end, young man, it is the means, the path itself that is important. The path does not take each person to the same places. Sometimes it leads to far-off places you have dreamed of, sometimes to places you have not yet dreamed of, and sometimes it simply takes you home. But these are not ends, they are just more means."

 "So you're a musician," I noted, glancing again at his harp.

 He chuckled lightly and whispered as if thinking of other places, "Not really. I simply like to learn the music within those I meet, so I can share it with others I meet. You too will learn to resonate with the lives and songs of those we meet. To learn people's songs, even your own song, is what enlightenment really is. This ethnographic harp is just one way I interpret these songs and stories."

(continued)

(continued)

This all seemed just a tad mystical to me, but at that moment I was distracted by the loud rhythmic sound of the second fellow marching in to my line of sight.

"Hello there, young person," he called out. "Time to be off, battles to be fought, the war waits for no one."

Taken aback, I stated flatly, "I don't know what war you speak of, and please don't mistake me for some kind of mercenary soldier."

"Mercenary?" he exclaimed indignantly. "I'm no mercenary and I want no mercenaries. I don't engage in battle for money. No, indeed. The war I speak of is all around us and the battles I fight are for the oppressed and downtrodden among us."

"I'm sorry, I didn't mean to be offensive," I explained. "I just didn't even know there was a war going on."

"Not surprising. Lots of people are blind to the battles they face every day." Jerking his thumb at the old minstrel, he continued, "That culture he speaks of is no path leading to understanding. It is a battlefield, a place of struggle for those masses of marginalized people everywhere. I urge haste because many of these oppressed people don't even realize that they are oppressed. We need to help them recognize what is being done to them."

"But if they don't realize they are in a battle, how do you know they are in one?"

Pointing to some of the weapons he carried, he nodded and said quietly, "These help me to detect oppression everywhere. Sometimes even the oppressors don't know they are doing it, poor fools. This hegemonic lantern and ambivalence blaster are never wrong, though."

"Well," I hesitated, "I am not really armed for conflict right now."

He put his arm around me confidentially, and shared, "We are all weak when compared to the hidden structures of power that surround us, but that cannot stop us from engaging the enemy. The power to resist is the power that matters. With time and training, you too will learn to recognize and expose the subtle abuses that surround us all. Then you too can fight the good fight."

Before I could pursue my questions about the nature of this "good fight," I was hailed by the third old fellow who had sprung out on me. He had on a jaunty pair of trousers and was standing next to a golf cart looking handsome and confident. "Hop aboard, son," he called. "You can finish the rest of the round with me."

He seemed quite different from the old soldier with whom I had just been visiting and I was a bit unsure how to respond.

"Well, hurry up now. Others are going to want to play through. Can't stand there all day. After all, this culture course is one of the most challenging courses there is to play. It is becoming more and more popular."

"But I thought culture was a battleground for the oppressed?"

"Oppressed?" he smiled. "The biggest oppression is not knowing how to play right, how to predict the lay of the greens and the depth of the rough. My lad, I can

tell you need a few tips on how to play the game. I can show you how to be a winner, the right grip, which club to use when, and how to approach each challenge on the course. For example, when you get to the sandtrap on the Japan hole, make sure you start off with your driver marked 'bow.' Or when you get to the pond on the American hole, you need to play aggressively and have clear objectives."

He noticed that I seemed quite dazed by it all, and smiled knowingly. "Don't worry, I understand the theory behind the game and I can empower anyone with the power to succeed."

The hand on my shoulder was the old minstrel's. "A game of golf won't satisfy your thirst for knowledge. Success is not to be found in perfecting technique or in a score. Tips for a better swing are all very nice, but it can never teach you the specific songs of the heart in those with whom you interact. You must walk the path of culture to learn to understand as others understand."

Laughing, the old golfer winked and said, "Never you mind him, son. I occasionally pick up a few tips about the next hole from such as he, but nothing that can be relied on without replication and theoretical testing. The poor fellow doesn't even really know why he walks around with that harp. You can't hit a hole-in-one with that. You have to practice with a club many times to learn how far it carries the ball and if it is any good. And that is important if you are going to beat your own personal best, meet your goals, be a winner."

"Pst. Pst. Over here." I turned and walked toward the old soldier who was waving to me from behind a tree.

"Watch out for that fellow. He is just the type to unwittingly lead you into battle for the oppressors. All his fancy talk of winning. Who do you think he's beating? Who do you think had to slave all day make his clubs, eh?"

"Don't let him distract you," volunteered the minstrel. "The old golfer may be simplistic, but that old soldier is so quick to judge others that he can only see what he wants to see. The battle cry he sings is never-ending and is just a reproduction of his own pet peeves."

"What nonsense," countered the old soldier. "Poor old poet has been living in the lofty towers of his mind so long he doesn't know what is really happening on the cultural battlegrounds of life. Poor old, innocent fool. I haven't given up on him yet, but sometimes his innocence amazes me."

The old golfer drove up in his cart. "Son, don't worry about the fleeting songs and unsubstantiated conspiracy theories of these two. It's time to test out a new club."

I turned away from them all, confused and amazed by all they had to say. What I need, I thought, is a break today. So I got up and got away to the Golden Arches where I could get two all-beef patties, special sauce, lettuce, cheese, pickles, and onions on a sesame seed bun. Ah, just the way I want it. Good to the last drop. Now this is the real thing, after all.

FIGURE 11.1 |

The narrative above may seem strange to you on first reading, but we are hopeful that it will help you remember and think about some key differences between three major perspectives on the concept of culture that exist within the field of intercultural communication. One of the benefits of studying intercultural communication and of education in general is that we learn to look at things from different perspectives. Now that you have some understanding of culture and its impact on communication, we want to broaden that understanding by considering some different perspectives about what culture means and how it might impact our lives.

Culture has been discussed in this text as a system of sense-making practices. Different communities develop different sense-making patterns that are shared in ways that allow members of these communities to interact with each other in meaningful ways. However, when members of different cultural communities interact, things that seem like common sense to members of one community may appear inappropriate or ineffective to members of other communities. Throughout this text we have reviewed a variety of examples and contexts in which different systems for making sense create different expectations. This can lead to misunderstandings, frustrations, and conflict. We have tried to demonstrate how these different systems of sense-making are inescapably tied up with how we believe the world works, how we view ourselves and others, the way we interact (verbally or nonverbally) with others, and the way we manage and adjust to living with those with different cultural backgrounds.

Each of the issues discussed in this text, from worldviews to identities and conflict to acculturation, has been largely explored through a particular perspective. This perspective is generally referred to as *interpretive* in nature. It is referred to as interpretive for many reasons. One of these is because people are assumed to socially construct or interpret what is meaningful in their interactions with others.

This interpretive approach to culture and intercultural interactions is not the only one advocated within the communication discipline. We noted briefly when reviewing the history of the study of intercultural communication that one way this field of study is categorized is by three broad research perspectives: *interpretive, critical,* and *social scientific.* The divisions between these three perspectives are not always clear cut and, although this text is largely written from an interpretive perspective, there are elements within the text that overlap with the other perspectives. We considered when writing this text trying to approach each topic from all three perspectives, but opted against it for two main reasons. One, we worried that trying to deal with each perspective for each topic would become cumbersome and limit the depth of the text. Two, efforts at combining all three of these perspectives tend to end up doing a disservice to one or more of the perspectives, so although there may be an explicit effort to treat each one fairly, there are built in subtle biases that often mislead the reader.

So why bring up the three perspectives now? As noted above, one of the great benefits of education is learning to understand multiple perspectives. This seems particularly important for those interested in culture and communication. This text is intended to introduce you to important concepts and ideas in the area of intercultural communication. Having at least some understanding of the different ways culture is approached is an important part of that introduction. Our hope in introducing you to these other perspectives is that you, your instructor, and your fellow students can engage in a dialogue that deepens and broadens your understanding of culture.

Our review of these various perspectives will of necessity involve a certain amount of simplification. Indeed, within each of these three broad perspectives there exists considerable variety. We cannot do justice to all these differences in this chapter. Instead, we will focus on some key differences in attitude and approach that were suggested in the opening narrative. After reviewing, contrasting, and comparing some general differences across the three perspectives, we will introduce you to pervasive types of culture and communication not yet discussed in this text: popular culture and media in general. These expressions or forms of culture impact virtually everyone's life and provide a nice discussion point for extending our understanding of the two perspectives not adopted generally in this text.

MAJOR PERSPECTIVES IN INTERCULTURAL COMMUNICATION

Interpretive Perspective

From the interpretive perspective culture is a way of making sense of things around us.[1] *Sense-making* becomes a centering concept around which other concepts revolve. The goal of someone working within the interpretive perspective is to be able to explain what sense certain acts make and how people are able to create shared meaning and coordinate their actions. Culture, then, as a system of sense-making, constitutes a path toward greater knowledge and understanding of the human condition. Knowledge and understanding are sufficient goals in and of themselves.

One of the typical ways researchers gain this knowledge is through the practice of ethnography. Ethnography encompasses a series of activities that are meant to help a researcher learn what and how things mean what they do from a member's perspective. Thus, the emic knowledge we discussed in Chapter 3 plays a pivotal role for an ethnographer. The interpretive ethnographer wants to understand the practices of another community from a "native" perspective. One way of sharing this knowledge is through narratives. This book takes a narrative approach because narratives are a basic form of humans' sense-making, and learning others' narratives is a great way to increase our knowledge in ways that resonate with other communities.

Interpretive research is not so worried about being able to predict exactly what someone will do when, but more what consequences these actions have in terms of relationships and what is understood between people. This understanding comes from a very careful exploration of the member's discourse and must resonate with the understanding displayed by members of the community in question. This kind of understanding does not prevent a person from making comparisons across groups; in fact it encourages it. However, it also creates an assumption of reasonableness that encourages a very cautious approach to judgments based on those comparisons. A concept such as power, for example, is not denied, but it is seen as important to the extent that it is an issue within the perspectives and ideas of the community being studied.

Thus, this book is written from a perspective that assumes that members of different communities believe themselves to be acting in reasonable ways. As you look back on the last nine chapters or as you read the final chapter you will be able to detect this perspective. Even when we deal with items that we, personally, and people generally believe are wrong, such as prejudice, we do so in a way that highlights the reasoning behind the prejudice. We do this not to excuse or advocate prejudice, as we think will be even more obvious in the chapter on ethics, but because understanding the reasoning that makes sense of our actions empowers us to make better choices. The interpretive perspective that we followed in this text is represented by the old minstrel in the opening narrative and to think of culture primarily as a pathway to understanding that members of a given community traverse with one another.

Critical Perspective

The critical perspective in the opening narrative is represented by the old soldier.[2] This representation is not because critical researchers have a fondness for the military; in fact many would likely argue that the military is one of the great oppressive structures in a society. However, the discourse of those writing and working within this perspective is filled with terms and metaphors that suggest they are in the middle of a battle or a struggle. Things that can be seen as oppressive in some way are seen as the enemy. This would include anything that limits alternatives or creates roles for people not of their own choosing or that positions people as secondary in some way. Knowledge and understanding are all well and good, but what is more important is using knowledge to expose the inequities of life. By exposing how power imbalances are created and maintained, these scholars provide a critique of society. These critiques are typically directed toward some kind of liberation. This liberation could be physical, emotional, or psychological.

In addition, this perspective highlights the importance of large-scale political, economic, and historical forces. Individuals and community members always find themselves positioned in historical, economic, and political ways that go beyond any of their specific desires or choices. These historical, economic, and political forces have a lot of power. Groups of people that have historically had a lot of power in political and economic senses are inherently positioned in oppressive stances, whereas groups that may be said to be more marginal or lower on the social ladder are inherently positioned as oppressed. These positions do not depend upon the active intentions or perceptions of the individual members of these groups. While it may be interesting to know what people think, it is much more important to know how people are positioned in society. Someone in an oppressive position may not even realize this or intend to be oppressive, and someone who is being oppressed may not actively recognize this oppression. Just because someone does not intend to oppress others and others do not perceive this oppression does not mean that no oppression exists.

The centering term in the critical perspective is that of *power*. All other concepts may be seen to revolve around the power relations that are created in the relative positioning and interactions between communities. For critical scholars, perspectives that do not explicitly focus on these power differences in all of human life are viewed as somewhat naive and simplistic. As powerful as these societal structures are, however, there is still room for resistance. A corporation may have a lot of money and influence on what we think is important or popular, but ultimately it does not cause us to act in a given way. As with the interpretive perspective, there is an important role for human agency in this perspective. Bringing to light the hidden ways corporations and other groups in power manipulate things to their advantage is one of the key goals of this perspective. By bringing these often unnoticed powers to light, people are better able to resist them and make their own choices.

As with most aspects related to this perspective, resistance is often not a simple process. For example, groups that are oppressed in some way often have ambivalent feelings toward those who oppress them.[3] A Native American community may desire to fit in and acquire some of the goods of the dominant U.S. culture while at the same time wanting to resist much of what that culture stands for and emphasize their own traditional values. The complexities involved with resistance in a world saturated by oppressive structures make any effort to make predictions based on straightforward causal relations nonsensical. The world and its many cultures are constantly being struggled over and created through the tensions created by these competing powers. Although the interpretive perspective also emphasizes the social construction of meaning, the critical perspective feels that the bigger, structural forces impinging on this social construction of meaning are ignored in the interpretive perspective. Any group or thing that influences culture or our way of life is powerful. Culture, from the critical perspective, is a point of conflict or struggle and a very important battleground. Winning the culture wars is essential to maintaining the kind of liberty and opportunities that critical researchers believe should be held by all groups who have historically been placed in second-class positions.

Social-Scientific Perspective

The social-scientific perspective is grounded in very practical aspirations.[4] Like the old golfer, those working within this perspective want to help people be more effective in whatever sphere of life they find themselves. Much of the research in this area carries with it the aroma of a recipe for winning. Although examples of winning in terms of business negotiations and other competitive settings are easy to find in this literature, there are also many working within this perspective that are concerned with winning in ways that are not competitive with other people per se. Just like a golfer who is trying to better her or his score, regardless of how well the others in the party are playing, a social-scientific researcher is often focused on improving effectiveness for everyone.

The key to winning or to having the recipe work out right is predictability. *Predictability* is the centering concept within this perspective. Typically, quantitative methods are used in this research. These are designed to be able to predict the typical behaviors of those who fit within various categories. When a person can predict how and what people will do, in the face of various stimuli, then people with this knowledge can make sure to create the stimuli that produces the outcomes they desire. This perspective is patterned after the research model found in the natural sciences. Understanding basic things like the law of gravity or principles of leverage provides someone with knowledge that can be used to accomplish many tasks. Researchers within this perspective strive to come up with laws and principles (theories) that explain why humans act the way they do and allow other humans to predict what will happen in the future. The notion of stimuli and response or causal relationships is the basic building block to theoretical work within this perspective.

Culture may be seen as a particular golf course that must be played in the game of life. Just as knowing how the ball will roll on certain greens or what effects a rough will have on play is vital for someone who wishes to win at the game of golf, so knowing how people from different groups will do business or handle conflict can be vital for winning the game of life. Power in this perspective is how we can accomplish our various goals and how we empower others to accomplish their goals by verifying certain causal relationships. Thus, if you know a person is from a high-context culture, you can predict how she is likely to respond to conflict and engage in behaviors that will result in success. In addition, sense-making is not a central concern because it is so subjective and can be so specific to only small groups of individuals. The social-scientific perspective seeks to generalize and predict behavior to larger groups than the interpretive perspective. Social-scientific scholars believe it is better to focus on concepts that can be clearly measured, tested, and replicated for generalizability.

Scholars using this perspective follow a pattern of thought that resonates with the monolithic force perspective discussed in Chapter 2. Variables, such as group membership (a key criterion in determining one's cultural background), different worldviews, and values, are assumed to have consistent enough relationships with certain types of behaviors that we can use these manifestations of culture to predict what will happen with a high level of certainty. Thus knowing what group people come from can reduce our uncertainty in a wide variety of situations, allowing us to be more confident and successful.

Much more can and has been written about these different perspectives. Certainly each of these perspectives can produce worthwhile results. Fighting for those who are disadvantaged in some way, working to gain more control of our own lives so we can reach our goals, and learning to really understand others on their own terms are all useful endeavors. How successful and useful each of these perspectives is in accomplishing these goals is open for discussion and debate. However, what is not in question is that these different perspectives bring different types of foci and insight to any given topic. In line with our effort to use this chapter to broaden our understanding of culture and how we may view it and its influence in our lives, we are going to turn to a specific application. Our point of application is popular culture and the media with which it is typically associated. Since the book as a whole is written from an interpretive perspective, we will more explicitly use the critical and social-scientific perspectives in considering implications related to the media and popular culture. But first let us turn our attention to the general concept of popular culture.

POPULAR CULTURE

One of the most prevalent manifestations of culture in today's world is what is commonly referred to as popular culture. According to Nachbar and Lause, popular culture refers to the *"products of human work and thought which are (or have been) accepted and approved of by a large community or population."*[5] Admittedly this definition is quite broad and there is room for debate on just how large is large and what counts as being accepted and approved. Nachbar and Lause discuss a number of characteristics of popular culture to help clarify their definition. We will review four of these.

Easily Accessed

Popular culture owes much of its significance in the world today to our increasing ability to quickly communicate with masses of people. Popular culture is inherently tied to the mass media: television, film, books, magazines, newspapers, radio, the Internet, and specifically social media. It is found in advertisements, on clothing, and in our homes, businesses, and schools. Although it is not impossible, it is hard to live out a day without being exposed to some form of popular culture. Although the United States is the chief producer of popular culture, it is found throughout the world. The fact that popular culture surrounds us does not mean that we must always like it or appreciate it. A popular culture fad as we write is a new *Pokémon* app for the cell phone. It reminded Brad of how *Pokémon* was initially met in his household in very different ways. His son accepted it fully, watching the show, collecting the cards, playing the video games, and reading about *Pokémon* on the Internet. His daughters, however, despised it, constantly put anything to do with it down and reported with disgust on its popularity at school. Popular culture surrounds us and access to it is so easy that it is difficult to avoid; however, our reactions to it are not uniform and are often far from positive. Indeed, as the *I Hate Madonna Handbook* illustrates, mass negative reactions to popular culture can in turn become part of the popular culture.

Commercial

Popular culture, as we know it today, is an economic creation. Regardless of original intent, whatever has achieved popular culture status is tied to money. You can be assured that if it is an example of popular culture, it is making somebody money. Even if a rock band, for example, decries materialism and the making of money, the songs and other items, T-shirts, posters, and so forth of the group are in fact all generating money. Even aspects of popular culture we may not initially think of as money oriented, such as the news, are tied to money-generating activities. If no money was generated, the band would never achieve popular culture status. It is the making of money that serves as the stamp of acceptance and approval noted in the definition given, not necessarily that a majority of people like it. The more successful a particular artifact of popular culture is in making money, the more likely it will be imitated. A successful show often generates many spin-offs and sequels, as people try to replicate its success. The aspect of monetary profit involved with popular culture has led many to decry the leading role played by the United States in the production of popular culture as American imperialism. The popular culture products of the United States have had a much more controlling impact on the lives of people in other countries than its political government. Many worry that this impact is serving to homogenize the world's cultures in negative ways.

What We Believe and What We Should Believe

Tied to the commercial aspect of popular culture is the effort to give people whatever they want. Producers of popular culture will spend vast amounts of time, effort, and money in market analysis. They want to find out what the people want and what they believe so that they can better produce and sell the artifacts of popular culture to the masses. Popular culture thus becomes a wonderful window to the beliefs and desires of the people who embrace it. Lause examined 10 top box-office hit films for the prominent beliefs they espoused. He found such things as support of individual freedom, technology as a protector and savior, violence as a legitimate means of obtaining justice outside of the law, and the celebration of youth.[6] Within the United States these beliefs are held by many; however, not everyone within or beyond the United States agrees with these beliefs.

Popular culture not only reflects held beliefs, but it also challenges them and encourages people to adopt new beliefs. We not only learn how to satisfy our wants through popular culture; we learn what those wants are and should be. Popular culture always presents a view of the world: what is good, desirable, and right. The views espoused in popular culture may well challenge views within a community and often become vehicles for change. Some of these changes may be desirable, such as the use of popular culture to educate people on issues of health and other social issues.[7] Change, however, is not always positive and many believe popular culture erodes traditional cultural values in ways that damage society. One thing that can be said about change is that it is almost always controversial. Hence popular culture will almost always be controversial. As popular culture reflects and directs the views of society, it also provides a forum for discussion of these beliefs. Discussions of issues dealing with intimate relationships, difficult moral choices, and other sensitive items may be hard to initiate, but when they are raised in social media, a popular television show, or in the lyrics of a popular song, they are often addressed at work, school, and home among friends and family in ways that otherwise would not happen. By elevating these issues to points of public debate, conflict and change are quickened and increased.

Who We Are and Who We Should Be

"Advertising shapes egos, influences our sense of self-worth."[8] The same could be said about popular culture in general. We are constantly exposed to ideas about what the ideal identities are and what expectations are associated with them. Popular culture provides role models or prototypes of a wide range of identities, thus subtly providing standards by which we learn to judge ourselves and others. Often without any direct, personal contact we know through film and other popular culture outlets what it means to be a lawyer, a detective, or many other relational identities, as well as communal identities such as a Mexican or an Arabian. We may feel we have learned what it means to be Greek by watching *My Big Fat Greek Wedding*, or what life is like in Mexico by watching *Once Upon a Time in Mexico*. Through exposure to pop culture people assume that they know about other people, places, and things that they will never visit or personally see.

There is an urban legend that we have heard various versions of which tells the tale of a woman who was in Las Vegas gambling. She had done particularly well one evening and decided to take her winnings and return to her room while she was still so far ahead. She gathered all her winnings and went to the elevator to return to her room. As people left the elevator and she got in she noticed that she was left alone with two black men. All of a sudden she was very nervous. Clutching her purse tightly she said a silent prayer and stared straight ahead. As the elevator started to rise she heard one of the men say, "Hit the floor," and she didn't realize that he was asking his friend to push the appropriate floor button. She immediately dropped to the floor, fearing for her life. There was silence for a moment and then the two men started to laugh uncontrollably. The next morning she found a huge bouquet of flowers at her hotel door with a note that said, "Sorry if we scared you, but that is the best laugh we have had in years," signed by Eddie Murphy and Michael Jordan. Obviously the woman in the story had a negative set of expectations for African American men. What we find particularly intriguing is what the identities of these two black men turned out to be, a sports hero and a comedian. The pictures presented of African American men for many years in popular culture have been sports heroes, comedians, and criminals. This story captures all three. Popular culture is always giving us a picture of cultural others in the ways these groups of people are presented (or in the lack of presentation).

Even when we have had direct personal contact with the identities portrayed in popular culture, we are still learning about how these roles may be enacted or what to expect from them. Popular culture characters become role models for many people. It is sometimes surprising to us to find out how many people are loyal fans of certain popular culture characters. Brad had a student a few years ago who just adored Rosie O'Donnell. She bought products Rosie advocated and didn't buy ones that Rosie expressed disfavor toward. She never missed Rosie's show. She even went out to New York for a week to try to get into the show. For her, Rosie was a prototype of what a person should be. The Rosie she knew, however, was a popular culture creation. The outcomes of this type of learning via popular culture can be both positive and negative, but the important thing for us at the moment is to remember that this learning is happening.

Reflection Question: Can you find examples of how popular culture has influenced your friends, family, or yourself?

Many of us may feel like we are not all that influenced by popular culture. After all, *we* don't fall for all the advertising hype or try to act like a movie star. However, given the number and volume of messages, as well as the acceptance popular culture artifacts have as indicated by how much money is spent on them, we suspect that we as well as others are more influenced than we care to admit. The type of people we should be, the way we dress, what we eat, and what we think is funny, sad, noble, and so on are more connected to popular culture than we may realize. We may not all be as obviously obsessed with a popular culture figure as the student was with Rosie O'Donnell, but we are still learning about who we are and who we should be in the countless popular culture messages we are exposed to every day.

Popular Cultural Artifacts

The basic manifestations or artifacts of popular culture are the objects and people that come to be readily recognized and known by the masses. For example,

TABLE 11.1 | Real and imaginary icons and celebrities

Type of Artifact	Real	Imaginary
Icon	Harley-Davidson Motorcycle	Light Saber
	Tattoos	Captain America's Shield
	Skateboard	Harry Potter's Wand
	Visa	James Bond's Car
	Cell Phone	Lone Ranger's Silver Bullet
Celebrity	Tayler Swift	Mickey Mouse
	Harrison Ford	Pokémon
	LeBron James	Spiderman
	Kate Upton	Calvin & Hobbes
	Bill Gates	Cinderella

more children in the U.S. can recognize Ronald McDonald than can recognize the president of the United States. We suspect this type of phenomenon is true in many other countries as well. Nachbar and Lause refer to these objects and people as icons and celebrities.[9] Icons and celebrities come in two types: real and imagined (see Table 11.1). We will discuss each of these four types of artifacts in terms of how they may be used to help someone make sense of their world and their role in it.

Real Icons

There are well over 10 million skateboarders in the United States alone. The skateboard is a physical item that has come to represent much more in society than just a short board with four polyurethane wheels that provides a form of transportation.[10] Skateboards provide not only transportation, but a way to accomplish feats of daring and skill. Skateboards have come to represent individual freedom and a defiance of institutional control. We have seen numerous signs prohibiting skateboarding in various public places. With almost equal frequency we have seen skateboarders honing their skills in these same public places. What does it mean to be a skateboarder? That question was brought home one day after Brad's son had purchased a skateboard. His friend and neighbor came over on his roller blades (another real icon), and he overheard him ask, "So you gonna be a *boarder* now?" My son just shrugged and his friend continued to discuss the pros and cons of being either a *blader* or a *boarder*. Skateboards are an object, an icon, but they also represent an identity, both to the skateboarder and to those who see him or her. In this way, popular culture may be seen to provide new ways to express certain identities and new identities in general.

FIGURE 11.2 | Is popular culture colonizing or convenient in nature?

Imagined Icons

Although we have no *data* [pun intended] to support our claim, we are confident that more people in the world are familiar with the name of an imaginary spacecraft of the future that is supposed to go where no one has gone before than are familiar with the names of either the first real spaceship to travel around the world or the one to first convey humans to the moon. The Starship Enterprise (not the *Mir* or *Apollo 9*) has for decades represented that which is best about human technology. It represents a hope for the future, one in which humans have overcome their own internal warfare and are going forth to discover new worlds and life forms. Although its original crew and the one of the *next generation* are explicitly multicultural, the messages of individualism and exploring new frontiers are very American.[11] Yet this imaginary ship represents to *trekkies* throughout the world, of all different levels of dedication, a place of hope, a place where personal identity is reverenced over communal identities. Thus, the ship is an icon that explicitly acknowledges the value of all levels of identity, yet subtly gives preference to personal identities in resolving problems created by identities associated with the relational and communal levels discussed earlier.

Real Celebrities

We use the term celebrity here in a very broad way. Any character whose fame allows them to be considered part of popular culture may be said to be a celebrity. The connection between celebrities and identity is easier to see. From the "I wanna be like Mike" ads to the historical tale of Abraham Lincoln's rise from a small log cabin to the White House, people learn to identify with particular people such as Michael Jordan and President Lincoln. These are real people who have what we want. They become a standard to shoot for. Reactions to the standard created by the public persona of this celebrity may vary, but celebrities still influence how we see ourselves and those around us.

One television show has given rise to a number of celebrities. *Modern Family* debuted in 2009 and portrays an extended family that is significantly different from the traditional extended family based on the grandparents, parents, grandchildren pattern. The more current representation of family dynamics found in *Modern Family* shows a family living in Los Angeles that includes a "patriarch," Jay Pritchett, living with his second wife, their child, and his stepson. Jay's second wife, Gloria, is played by Sofía Vergara who became one of the most widely recognized Spanish-speaking female celebrities. Sofía brought the warmth of the spotlight to the fierce independence combined with loyalty to family and quick humor of Hispanic women. Through her celebrity status, she brought Latina values into the consciousness of hundreds of thousands of individuals.

Jay's two adult children also figure prominently in the series. His adult son, Mitchell, is portrayed by Jesse Tyler Ferguson who also brought current values into the mainstream. Mitchell and his male partner adopt children, marry, and maintain their bond as an integral part of the extended modern family. Like Sofía Vergara, Jesse Tyler Ferguson in many ways legitimized same-sex male couples and associated the values of warmth, humor, and love with these relationships.

These are brief descriptions of two characters of the 10 main characters on the *Modern Family* series. Other family characteristics and values that are representative of the wider variety of families found across the world are likewise represented in the series. The celebrities who play these characters have helped cast positive light on values of less represented cultural groups and helped start dialogues that may lead to wider acceptance across the spectrum of humanity.

Imaginary Celebrities

There are long lists of imaginary celebrities, from Superman to Darth Vader to Bart Simpson, all of which present a picture of the ideal, although the particular *ideal*, the way it is presented, and the identities affected by that ideal are often quite different. Sometimes the line between imaginary and real celebrities gets very fuzzy. Take, for instance, Paul Hogan (real), also known as Crocodile Dundee (imaginary). Was it Paul Hogan or Crocodile Dundee who was the spokesperson for Subaru cars? Celebrities can also be part of a group, such as the imaginary celebrities Chandler, Rachael, Phoebe, Ross, Monica, and Joey from the popular television show *Friends*. In the show six people share laughter, love, lust, life, and most importantly friendship. Two of them are brother and sister and engage in some traditional sibling rivalry, and later two become married, but in general they are all just a bunch of friends. The show and the celebrities who populate it have become the standard for what it means to be friends for millions of viewers. These friends live the good life. Like many imaginary celebrities, they live a charmed life where things work out, in spite of ups and downs faced in the show. They appear to be living a life that many would love to have. As with all identities portrayed in popular culture, one may wonder to what extent their enactment of this identity is a reflection of society or a shaper of society.

At one level these icons and celebrities provide important resources for people to make sense of their lives, and understanding how this happens can help us understand the potential impact of popular culture in our own lives. These types of concerns would be appropriate within the interpretive perspective. However, the interpretive perspective would also be interested in other connections between popular culture and culture in general. For example, Donal Carbaugh studied the American talk show host Phil Donahue's effort to take his show on the road to Russia.[12] Many of the basic practices, such as the public discussion of problems and revelations of personal problems that are so successful in the United States, were unable to be generated in Russia because they simply did not make the same kind of sense. However, we want to move away from interpretive types of issues to issues that would be focused on in the critical and social-scientific perspectives.

CRITICAL PERSPECTIVES ON POPULAR CULTURE AND THE MEDIA

One of the most basic concepts within the critical perspective is the notion of hegemony.[13] Hegemony deals with the dominance and subordination of various groups, particularly as this relates to various ways of thinking or ideologies. Thus, a hegemonic relationship is one that involves the dominance of one group over another. Certainly dominance may be manifest in many different ways, economic, political, and so forth. However, the dominance that is primarily focused on within this perspective is in terms of how one thinks and interprets the world. This ideological focus can be traced to the Italian intellectual, Antonio

Gramsci, who wrote about how ruling elites used the mass media to perpetuate their power and their way of viewing the world. One of Gramsci's major contributions in terms our understanding of hegemony was his observation that the dominant ideologies of those in power came to be seen and accepted by the general public as simply the way the world is.[14] This naturalization of dominant ways maintains the power of the dominant groups in a society. Part of what makes a hegemonic relationship is the unwitting acceptance by the subordinated group of the assumptions and perspectives of the dominant group. This form of hegemony is even more powerful than hegemonic relationships based purely on physical dominance because this acceptance is typically unnoticed by the subordinate group so it may be harder to resist. The naturalization of the ruling classes' assumptions provides boundaries for looking at the world that support the types of inequitable social relations that exist. Thus, the range of alternatives from which one may choose are limited.

The mainstream media and particularly popular culture are powerful tools in the creation and maintenance of hegemonic relationships. Corporations and commercials do not simply respond to audience demands, they help create them. Often the creation of these demands is reinforced through multiple media sources. For example, commercials on TV, films, toys, fast-food chain promotions, songs from popular musicians, and so forth all may work together to sell a product. However, as powerful as these marketing forces are, there is still not a simplistic one-to-one causal connection between these messages and what people do. Because part of a hegemonic relationship is the acceptance by the subordinate group of dominant philosophies, goals, and wants, there is room for resistance.

This resistance happens in part because people and communities are different and do not all respond in the same way to efforts to get our attention and support. Sometimes, in fact, resistance to popular culture inadvertently becomes part of the popular culture. A music band may start out as explicitly rebelling against past popular culture images and become popular because of this explicit rebellion. Or a minority group may develop a type of music that connects to their specific community and departs radically from other forms of music in the dominant culture. However, as these efforts at resistance grow they end up being co-opted by organizations and media outlets and typically attract an increasing range of consumers. Thus, it may become *cool* to be *uncool* or *good* to be *bad*.

We suspect that you can quickly think of examples where it is obvious that organizations that stand to earn a lot of money and maintain a position of power engage in advertisements and promotions that reinforce behaviors that maintain their position of power. If you come to accept a certain ideal in terms of how one should look, then those marketing that look will benefit. However, critical theorists tend to look at more subtle forms of oppression. Often messages are sent out that reinforce stereotypes and power positions with limited or no conscious effort by the advertisers. For example, Seiter discusses how white babies and children are positioned in commercials in very active ways and in ways that reinforce a wide range of potential careers, whereas black and other minority children tend to either be ignored or shown in more passive positions or in positions that are very stereotyped.[15] When asked about systematic differences in the portrayal between white and minority groups, those in control of the media tend to say they are not thinking about these things at all, they are just responding to marketing demands.

In a similar way, roles for members of minority groups have often been very limited and stereotyped over the years. Angharad Valdivia uses the example of Rosie Perez to show how many Latinos are forced into playing a limited range of stereotypical parts. This very narrow range of character possibilities contrasts sharply with the wide variety of parts available for white actors and actresses and helps promote a feeling in the general public that this is just the way "all those people" are. Sometimes the alternative to stereotypical roles is just to be virtually ignored. Navita James writes about how difficult it was growing up when Mrs. America could only be white.[16] In a similar vein, Rona Halualani also talks about how difficult it was for her when the only faces she saw growing up on television that really looked like her family were the evil "Japs" in old World War II movies.[17]

Although there have been improvements in these subtle forms of oppression over the years, many argue the changes are not as big and significant as we like to believe.[18] Often the members of the dominant communities perceive that there has been a much greater change than what is seen by members of minority groups. Critical theorists would typically account for this difference by pointing out that dominant groups are blind to the oppressed positions others are forced to live in relative to their own privileged position. This type of blindness is captured in the work of Peggy McIntosh on white and male privilege. She presents close to 50 statements that if you can say they are true of you then you are enjoying the type of hidden privileges she identifies. A sampling of these statements include:

- I can if I wish arrange to be in the company of people of my race most of the time.
- If I need to move, I can be pretty sure of renting or purchasing housing in an area which I can afford and in which I would want to live.
- I can do well in a challenging situation without being called a credit to my race.
- I can worry about racism without being seen as self-interested or self-seeking.
- I can take a job with an affirmative action employer without having my co-workers on the job suspect that I got it because of my race.[19]

Reflection Question: What is the ethnic make-up of the stars in the shows you enjoy? What range of roles are played by different ethnicities on a given night on mainstream television?

I lived most of my childhood in front of the television. . . . I was utterly fascinated with the "tube." Watching the domestic bliss and everyday ease of family shows such as the Brady Bunch *and the* Partridge Family *provided me with a false sense of what life is like, of what life in "American" society is like.*

It never really hit me that I was "different" from other people until I was about eight. I remember watching reruns of That Girl *on TV. I, a scrawny kid with buck teeth, reddish hair, and eyes that took up most of my face, wanted to look exactly like Marlo Thomas—the flipped hairdo. I would try to brush down and up in a curl everyday just so that I could be like, "That Girl." But, of course, the thickness and frizziness of my hair from my Hawaiian heritage never allowed for the "do." This routine would continue until my mother would yell, "Sista, time for school." Suddenly, I would drop the brush, unlock the door (I would be devastated if anyone found out), and run to school. At school everyone knew me as "girl with the really long and yet cool last name." I would smile when kids used to call my older brother Michael "H," short for "Halualani." I would just laugh when both teachers and students asked if I could dance hula or if I ate lots of pineapples and coconuts. After all, I was only eight. Life was carefree and fun.*[20]

Although popular culture is connected to generating consumers, the knowledge it produces through the news and other media outlets goes well beyond the obvious consumption of goods. Popular culture narratives are often found in the news and a wide range of media outlets. These narratives tell us what to think about various groups and people. What most people in the United States know about Muslims comes from portrayals in the news, but if we have ever seen ourselves or groups we are personally involved in depicted in the news, we know that the depictions can be very limited and often misleading. Even with this knowledge it is very easy to just accept what is found in the news about other groups and even some large groups to which we belong as just the way it is. An example of how certain stories can be naturalized through the media and popular culture is the "model minority" narrative. Do you know what group in the United States is seen as the model minority? Is it African Americans, Asian Americans, Latinos, or Native Americans? This narrative is popular enough that we suspect you knew that Asian Americans are typically viewed as model minorities.

In the model minority narrative Asian Americans are seen as especially hard-working and intelligent. Asian immigrants are portrayed as generally respectful and very successful in terms of education and jobs. This may seem like a very positive narrative, but Yuko Kawai describes in detail how such a vision subtly works to recreate oppressive positions within the United States.[21]

For example, she explains that the narrative relies on the contrast between being a model minority and minorities that are seen as less successful. Expressions of this narrative use comparisons with a number of other "minorities," but especially African Americans. These comparisons suggest that Asians are law abiding and industrious with strong family units, whereas African Americans are characterized as being more prone to single-parent homes, wanting to get something for nothing and frequently in trouble with the law. Thus, the narrative positions minority groups against each other even though there is no need for this.

To make this comparison more legitimate, those espousing this narrative often point out how Asians at different times have been discriminated against in keys ways, such as the Japanese concentration camps during World War II or the lack of social opportunities for the Chinese railroad workers. These comparisons are made in ways that highlight comparisons with other minority groups, not in ways that bring attention to the dominant white society that is depicted as neutral in all this. The implication for other "minority" groups is that something is wrong with them. It cannot be American society. There must be some inherent flaw in these other groups of people. After all, look at the Asians.

In keeping with the critical perspective, this narrative can be looked at historically as well. It originated back in the 1960s during a time of heavy civil unrest in the United States and was adopted as a rhetorical tool to justify the American way of life. This narrative fits well in American society because it reinforces the notion that American society is color blind and, like the old Horatio Alger stories, a person can raise themselves up from the very lowest position in society to the highest simply by hard work and diligence. Kawai argues that anecdotes and statistics used to support this narrative are often misleading and taken out of context. She, along with others, argues that this narrative is not an accurate picture of what is going on in American society.[22] Instead, she says the color blind idea becomes a way of ignoring real differences and problems that are rooted in historical injustices. The model minority discourse indicating that all you need to do is work hard to reach the *American Dream* and that *color* is not a real factor serves to blind people to what was really going on. Critical theorists argue that such a dream is designed to keep oppressed people working toward something that never will be, while allowing people in power to ignore and to continue to benefit from the injustices of the American social system.

Kawai also maintains that the model minority narrative puts unrealistic expectations on a large group of people. For example, it does not recognize important differences in the nature of immigration, such as those between the relative economic poverty of the Hmong compared with many of the Japanese who have come to the United States. And even though it may seem positive for Asians, it can have a variety of backlash consequences that make life more difficult. Brad recently had one Asian student relate to him in a class how he always hated math, both because he was not very good at it and especially because everyone expected him to be good at it and acted like he was lying or avoiding helping them when he indicated that he didn't know how to do a particular math problem. Halualani, who we quoted earlier, remembers being told, "It figures you're a TA, all Asians are the superbrains."[23] This type of comment seemed to her to set her off from other graduate students in ways that did not feel right or comfortable.

SOCIAL-SCIENTIFIC PERSPECTIVES ON POPULAR CULTURE AND THE MEDIA

Scholars from the social-scientific perspective look at popular culture and the relationship between the media and culture in terms of causal types of connections. Discovering these connections enables a researcher to better predict and control what will happen in the future, providing the basis for a winning game, whatever that game may be. There are three main types of connections that we will discuss from this perspective. First is the direct impact that the media has on various cultural aspects of our lives, such as values, identification, acculturation, and our understanding of other cultural groups. Second is the reverse of the first type of connection. It examines the relationship between culture and the production and use of media. Third is the use of culture as an intervening variable between media sources and various desired outcomes. In each of these connections all mass media may be seen as a form of popular culture and culture is essentially equated with group membership, especially in terms of nationality, ethnicity, or race.

Impact of the Media on Culture

In some ways this is similar to issues raised in the critical perspective. Researchers focused on these types of questions are often interested in what effects the media is having on different cultural groups in the United States or what impact the media produced in the United States is having on people in other countries. Stephen Chaffee reports on a series of studies that reflect this perspective.[24] One of these reports suggests that Chinese women who were exposed to media programming from the United States developed more individualistic attitudes than those who only watched media produced in China. However, these kinds of effects are not always substantiated. For example, another study found that, although media in general had an impact on various values in adolescents in Argentina and Taiwan, exposure to media produced in the United States did not have an impact on the cultural values of either group.[25]

Another one of these reports by Chaffee describes how different forms of the media produce different effects on adolescents in Belize. In this case, greater exposure to U.S.-produced television inspires Belize youth to immigrate to the United States, whereas exposure to news magazines has the opposite effect. Another of these studies found that exposure to popular culture may help Korean women acculturate to the United States. However, Young Kim in her work on acculturation suggests that the type of media may again be important.[26] She indicates that documentary or news-style programs may be more effective than sit-coms or other popular entertainment shows.

Individuals who watch popular entertainment shows can develop distorted views of other people with whom they have not interacted. This may be because they do not recognize in what ways popular media departs from everyday life in a community. For example, one team of researchers studied how international students perceived Americans before and after they actually encountered them.[27] All of the international students involved in this study were categorized as medium to high users of U.S. media (watching on an average 15 hours of television or film a week) before coming to the United States. Images that came to mind before actual interaction were things such as friendly, independent, beautiful, fast paced, optimistic, and living a dangerous life. After living in the United States both groups of students interviewed felt the Americans were more conservative and pessimistic, less good looking and promiscuous, slower paced, not as smart, and more easily persuaded than earlier imagined. Perhaps this sounds like their impressions became largely negative, but really it was just a tempering of unrealistic expectations. Even after living in the U.S. students felt they had gained some insights about Americans from the media. It was just that some things had been exaggerated in ways that created unrealistic expectations and concerns. The exact same process happens for many Americans when they watch Hollywood versions of life in far-off countries to which they have never been.

Impact of Culture on the Media

The working assumption behind this idea is that membership within different groups and the differences that implies will create differences in what becomes popular culture and in what and how media outlets produce. News sources controlled by African Americans tend to provide a fuller picture of African American participation in local communities and are willing to address issues that impact minorities in more detail than can be found in mainstream media.[28] Spanish language radio and television are also outlets for some forms of popular culture that connect a wide variety of Hispanic audiences to music and entertainment that would otherwise not be available in the United States.[29]

One group of researchers studied the nature and content of television newscasts across eight different countries.[30] A variety of differences was found, such as the fact that the United States, Italy, and Japan took a much more sensationalistic approach, focusing much more on disasters and crime compared to countries like China, Russia, and Germany that spent more time on issues related to economics and science and technology. The United States frequently produced coverage that was critical or questioning of political leaders and decisions, whereas China avoided any negative reports. However, there were also many similarities. All of the countries focused heavily on political issues, although how this was done varied. In spite of the differences found, the researchers concluded their report by stating that "the strongest impression generated by the study is that the concept of 'what is new' was in fact fairly consistent across these eight countries."[31]

Culture as an Intervening Variable

The key idea here is trying to understand culture so as to make the impact of popular culture and media ever greater. Knowing if a group is individualistic or collectivistic in nature may help a person design more effective advertisements. Marieke de Mooij, for example, has mapped out the buying motives for things like automobiles, personal products, and insurance across 25 countries based on how the countries score on various worldview-type dimensions, such as individualism/collectivism.[32] Thus, consumers in Spain are more interested in style and design, whereas a Danish consumer is focused on safety. This kind of information is designed to help the advertiser to produce more effective messages to sell their products.

Not all forms of this research are focused on winning by getting different cultural groups to buy a particular product. Often what counts as winning are behavioral outcomes that are taken as a universal good. This type of work can be seen in what is known as *entertainment-education*. Entertainment-education typically refer to radio and television shows, often in soap opera format, that are designed to be both popular and to encourage a specific set of behaviors that are seen as healthier or more socially beneficial. One such radio soap opera produced in India was *Tinka Tinka Sukh* which centered around the daily lives of a dozen main characters and focused on issues such as domestic abuse, family planning, female equality, HIV prevention, and child marriage.[33] This program generated widespread interest and the radio station that produced *Tinka Tinka Sukh* received over 150,000 letters in response. The vast majority were very supportive and many, such as the following, described how the characters had changed their lives.

Nandini is my favorite character. She is my role model and my inspiration. The women of the world should unite with the motto that we will not tolerate abuse nor will we be abusive towards other women. Once we women take this stand, men will have to toe the line. Poonam's suicide, Kussum's death at child-birth, Sushma's struggle to stand on her own two feet, and Rukhsana's life and problems have shaken up my world and filled my heart with emotions. Nandini has taught me to stick to my ideals and fight against injustice, Champa has inspired me to realize my inner potential, and Suraj has taught me to be proud of my heritage and culture. I can relate completely to Champa since my family life is very similar to hers. I had decided to quit school, but after listening to the soap opera, I have started school again.[34]

(p. 174)

Although this program was specifically focused on what may be seen as women's issues, it also attracted a lot of male listeners as over half of the letters to the station were from males. Knowing what is offensive or acceptable in the various communities and countries in which these are produced is an important part of the success of these types of programs. Programs advocating pro-social norms are also found in the United States.

Thinking about specific cultural aspects before preparing messages is exemplified in much of the work related to health communication. Referring to work done within this perspective, Witte notes, "In sum, the existing literature has enabled us to determine many of the Hispanic men's salient beliefs and referents about using condoms to prevent AIDS."[35] She goes on to discuss how certain cultural values, such as *respeto, simpatía, personalismo*, and *machismo*, are able to be used in health campaigns to promote behavior change.[36] The goal in this form of research is to learn predictable cultural responses so as to better win whatever game one might be playing, whether that be promoting one's business or encouraging a healthy lifestyle.

In spite of the many differences between the critical and social-scientific perspectives, there are also similarities. Both have some form of change in mind. Although the goals of social-scientific research are quite diverse, many of them are concerned with persuading people of all cultures to engage in specific health and social practices that are taken to be universal goods. The critical perspective scholars would shy away from *universal* goods, though any form of oppression would clearly be for them an underlying universal bad. Even so, the critical perspective still wants change and is dedicated to revealing the hidden ways that social inequities reproduce themselves. Both perspectives also privilege the researcher's perceptions, based either on statistical measurement or researcher insight to subtleties, over the perceptions of the members of communities under study. These similarities contrast with the interpretive perspective that is typically not looking to change what is happening in the communities under study and places member perceptions on a more equal footing as those of researchers.

The critical, social-scientific, and interpretive perspectives provide different lenses through which to view the world and the role of culture in it. The critical perspective sees the world as a dangerous place full of war crimes that need to be exposed. Culture is one of the crucial battlefields upon which a struggle for freedom is fought. People need protection. The social-scientific perspective sees a world of opportunities and challenges. Culture is both. In order to win in the game of life one will do well to learn with certainty what causes lead to what outcomes. People need direction. The interpretive perspective views the world much more like uncharted waters that need to be explored and understood for their own particular peculiarities. People need understanding. It may well be argued that at different times we all need protection, direction, and understanding. So, the fact that the three perspectives provide various insights that at times complement and at other times conflict with each other is not a bad thing.

SUMMARY

In this chapter we have reviewed three different theoretical perspectives in the field of intercultural communication: interpretive, critical, and social scientific. The interpretive perspective that is largely adopted throughout this textbook is primarily focused on culture as different ways of understanding. This focus leads us to explore the many possible ways different cultural communities create understanding with other members, but often create misunderstanding when interacting interculturally. The critical perspective focuses on culture as largely a point of struggle and thus directs us to see life in terms of a struggle for power and control. The social-scientific perspective views culture as a variable that must be considered in accomplishing the goals of life. This variable may be identified as group membership, but this membership is associated with set values and specific forms of action that need to be considered in interacting successfully with others.

We discussed these perspectives in terms of research on popular culture and the media, with particular attention paid to the critical and social-scientific perspectives. We first discussed that popular culture is easily accessed, commercial, and a reflection of who we are and what we believe, as well as a force in changing those beliefs and views of ourselves and others. We also explained how popular culture is made visible through icons and celebrities, all of which carry implications for who we and others are. We then illustrated how from a critical perspective one can see subtle ways that minority groups are positioned in ways that disempower them. Finally, we reviewed work from a social-scientific perspective that demonstrates how media and popular culture can either be used or overcome in efforts to achieve certain social goals. All perspectives were seen to have advantages and disadvantages in understanding our world.

REFLECTION QUESTIONS

1 What are the advantages and disadvantages of each of the major perspectives on culture reviewed in this chapter?
2 What impact do you think popular culture is having in your own community and around the world? What can or should be done about this?
3 What are your assumptions about the way the world works? Which of the three perspectives, interpretive, critical, and social scientific, seems to fit best with your view? Why?
4 What impact is the media having on your own culture? Is this a good thing? Is the media helping other cultures to get along better? Why or why not?

ACTIVITIES

1 Brainstorm individually or in a group about what you know (or believe) about another country and its people that you have never visited. Take each of the items you identified and try to determine where this belief came from. To what extent has the mass media shaped your understanding of what this other country and its people are like?
2 Take a specific intercultural interaction or relationship and analyze it in terms of the three theoretical perspectives discussed in the chapter. What sorts of things would the perspective lead you to pay attention to? What sorts of things might be missed? What other sorts of information would you want if you were going to further study this type of interaction or relationship in more detail from this perspective? Of what use or importance would the different kinds of knowledge gained by looking through a particular theoretical lens be?
3 Select an example of popular culture, such as a commercial or a popular song. Analyze it using the narrative framework discussed in Chapter 3, answering questions such as: who are the main characters (what identities are important for them), what problems do they face, how do they react to those problems, and what are the results? What sorts of things are being taught explicitly and implicitly in your example of popular culture? What does your example say about relationships? What is presented as good or bad?
4 Select a cultural community different from your own that interests you and try to find three to five movies that involve members from this group. Watch them and explore what you learn about this group just from what is depicted in the movies. If possible, find a person from that community, show them what you found, and talk to them about their reactions to these findings.

NOTES

1 One good compilation of interpretive research is D. Carbaugh, *Cultural Communication and Intercultural Contact* (Hillsdale, NJ: Lawrence Erlbaum Associates, 1990); a review of this perspective in comparison with the other major perspectives can be found in B. J. Hall, "Theories of Culture and Communication," *Communication Theory* 1 (1992), 50–70; and J. N. Martin and T. K. Nakayama, *Intercultural Communication in Contexts*, 3rd ed. (Boston, MA: McGraw-Hill Companies, Inc., 2004).

2 A good compilation of critical research is *Transforming Communication about Culture*, ed. M. J. Collier (Thousand Oaks, CA: Sage Publications, 2001); also, for a comparison review, see Hall, "Theories of Culture"; and Martin and Nakayama, *Intercultural Communication*.

3 H. K. Bhabha, *The Location of Culture* (Oxford, UK: Clarendon Press, 1994).

4 A good compilation of social-scientific theories is W. B. Gudykunst, "Intercultural Communication Theories," in *Handbook of International and Intercultural Communication*, 2nd ed., ed. W. B. Gudykunst and B. Mody (Thousand Oaks, CA: Sage, 2002); also, for a comparison review see Hall, "Theories of Culture"; and Martin and Nakayama, *Intercultural Communication*.

5 J. Nachbar and K. Lause, "An Introduction to the Study of Popular Culture: What Is This Stuff That Dreams Are Made Of?" in *Popular Culture*, ed. J. Nachbar and K. Lause (Bowling Green, OH: Bowling Green State University Popular Press, 1992), 1–36.

6 K. Lause, "Seeing What We've Said: The Top Ten American Box-Office Hits Taken Seriously," in *Popular Culture*, ed. J. Nachbar and K. Lause (Bowling Green, OH: Bowling Green State University Popular Press, 1992), 39–54.

7 A. Singhal and E. M. Rogers, *Entertainment–Education: A Communication Strategy for Social Change* (Mahwah, NJ: Lawrence Erlbaum Associates, 2000).

8 C. Moog, *Are They Selling Her Lips? Advertising and Identity* (New York: Morrow, 1990), 222.

9 Nachbar and Lause, *Popular Culture*.

10 Nachbar and Lause, *Popular Culture*.

11 Nachbar and Lause, *Popular Culture*.

12 D. Carbaugh, "*Soul* and *Self:* Soviet and American Cultures in Conversation," *Quarterly Journal of Speech*, 79 (1993): 182–200.

13 J. Lull, *Media, Communication, Culture: A Global Approach*, 2nd ed. (New York: Columbia University Press, 2000).

14 Lull, *Media, Communication, Culture*.

15 E. Seiter, "Different Children, Different Dreams: Racial Representation in Advertising," in *Readings in Cultural Contexts*, ed. J. N. Martin, T. K. Nakayama, and L. A. Flores (Mountain View, CA: Mayfield, 1998), 304–14.

16 N. C. James, "When Miss America Was Always White," in *Our Voices: Essays in Culture, Ethnicity, and Communication*, 3rd ed., ed. A. González, M. Houston, and V. Chen (Los Angeles, CA: Roxbury Publishing Company, 2000), 46–51.

17 R. T. Halualani, "Seeing through the Screen: A Struggle of 'Culture'," in *Readings in Cultural Contexts*, ed. J. N. Martin, T. K. Nakayama, and L. A. Flores (Mountain View, CA: Mayfield, 1998), 264–75.

18 S. Cottle, "Media Research and Ethnic Minorities: Mapping the Field," in *Ethnic Minorities and the Media*, ed. S. Cottle (Buckingham, UK: Open University Press, 2000), 1–30.

19 P. McInstosh, "White Privilege and Male Privilege," in *Critical White Studies: Looking Back Behind the Mirror*, ed. R. Delgardo and J. Stefancic (Philadelphia: Temple University Press, 1997), 291–9. Questions taken from pages 293–4.

20 Halualani, "Seeing through the Screen," 266.

21 Y. Kawai, "Revisiting the 1966 Model Minority Myth: A Narrative Criticism of Its Textual Origins," *Kaleidoscope* 2 (2003): 1–31.

22 See for example F. Wu, *Yellow: Race in America beyond Black and White* (New York: Basic Books, 2002); and N. Gotanda, "Re-producing the Model Minority Stereotype: Judge Joyce Karlin's Sentencing Colloquy in *People v. Soon Ja Du*," in *Reviewing Asian America: Locating Diversity*, ed. W. L. Ng, S. Chin, J. S. Moy, and G. Okihiro (Pullman, WA: Washington State University Press, 1995), 87–106.

23 Halualani, "Seeing through the Screen," 269.

24 S. H. Chaffee, "Search for Change: Survey Studies of International Media Effects," in *Mass Media Effects across Cultures*, ed. F. Korzenny, S. Ting-Toomey, and E. Schiff (Newbury Park, CA: Sage Publications, 1992), 35–54.

25 M. Morgan and J. Shanahan, "Comparative Cultivation Analysis: Television and Adolescents in Argentina and Taiwan," in *Mass Media Effects across Cultures*, ed. F. Korzenny, S. Ting-Toomey, and E. Schiff (Newbury Park, CA: Sage Publications, 1992), 173–97.

26 Y. Y. Kim, *Becoming Intercultural: An Integrative Theory of Communication and Cross-Cultural Adaptation* (Thousand Oaks, CA: Sage Publications, 2001).

27 D. Ekachai, N. S. Greer, and M. Hinchcliff-Pelias, "International Students' Perceptions of Americans Via U.S. Mass Media," in *Civic Discourse: Intercultural, International, and Global Media, Vol. 2*, ed. M. Prosser and K. S. Sitaram (Stamford, CT: Ablex, 1999), 145–56.

28 A. A. Tait and R. L. Perry, "African Americans in Television: An Afrocentric Analysis," in *Afrocentric Visions: Studies in Culture and Communication*, ed. J. D. Hamlet (Thousand Oaks, CA: Sage Publications, 1998), 195–206.

29 M. Romero and M. Habell-Pallan, "Introduction," in *Latino/a Popular Culture*, ed. M. Habell-Pallan and M. Romero (New York: New York University Press, 2002), 1–21.

30 J. D. Straubhaar, C. Heeter, B. S. Greenberg, L. Ferrira, R. Wicks, and T. Lau, "What Makes News: Western, Socialist, and Third-World Television Newscasts Compared in Eight Countries," in *Mass Media Effects across Cultures*, ed. F. Korzenny, S. Ting-Toomey, and E. Schiff (Newbury Park, CA: Sage Publications, 1992), 89–109.

31 Straubhaar et al., "What Makes News," 106.

32 M. de Mooij, "Mapping Cultural Values for Global Marketing and Advertising," in *International Advertising: Realities and Myths*, ed. J. P. Jones (Thousand Oaks, CA: Sage Publications, 2000), 77–102.

33 Singhal and Rogers, *Entertainment-Education*.

34 Singhal and Rogers, *Entertainment-Education*, 174.

35 K. Witte, "Preventing AIDS through Persuasive Communications: A Framework for Constructing Effective, Culturally-Specific Health Messages," in *Mass Media Effects across Cultures*, ed. F. Korzenny, S. Ting-Toomey, and E. Schiff (Newbury Park, CA: Sage Publications, 1992), 67–88. See page 80.

36 Witte, "Preventing AIDS," 81.

Chapter 12

Can Judgments of Right and Wrong Be Made When Dealing with Other Cultures?

Frank was feeling tense and frustrated when Cindy came at noon to pick him up.

"Try to relax dear, it will be okay. They'll love you I'm sure and you'll love them too." The "they" she was referring to was an American Indian family in the pueblo [similar to a tribe] that had adopted Cindy after she had helped them at her social service office. She attended all the ritual dances and feasts at the pueblo with her adopted family and wanted to share this part of her life with Frank now that they were getting more serious.

"It's not that," he mumbled, though, in fact, it was that, more than he cared to admit.

"I had a really bad day at work again." He went on, "Those Japanese, sometimes I wonder why they hired me in the first place? I'm beginning to think taking this job was a mistake."

Cindy had heard this before. Frank had worked with Fukon Corporation for five months now. Fukon was new to the U.S. market and their representatives had indicated they wanted an American perspective as part of their management team. Cindy and Frank both loved to travel and they had been excited about the career opportunities this position promised. They both had done some reading about Japan and Cindy knew Frank was trying to be flexible in this new work environment, but it seemed like something was always happening that caught him off guard.

"What are they doing to you now?" asked Cindy. Some of the stories Frank had told her had also made her wonder why the Japanese had hired Frank or any American for that matter.

"They really just don't give two cents for what I have to say. We had a meeting today on the new expansion proposal. I had a ton of good ideas, ideas that could make a difference. But they don't even listen." Frank's voice changed into a bad imitation of a Japanese person speaking English. "That could be difficult," he mimicked and then grunted in disgust, "I was so mad I went to Mr. Yamashita and told him just what I thought. He just hummed and hawed around as usual. I got the feeling the decision had already been made before the meeting even began and he acted like all my hard work was just causing unnecessary problems."

"I'm sorry. Let's try to think of more pleasant things," Cindy said, hoping Frank would calm down before they got to the pueblo. She really loved her adopted family and wanted everything to be perfect.

Frank stared out the window. "Consensus!" he blurted out with a fake laugh. "Consensus is supposed to be so important for them, but they won't even talk through the issues so a decent consensus can be formed." He looked back at Cindy and shook his head, "I really wanted this to work. I don't know what I'm doing there."

If Frank only knew several of his fellow managers were wondering the same thing. They had wanted to get an American perspective, not turn their company into an American company. Frank's tendency to spring new ideas and plans on them in a meeting and his constant debating as if he had to win every little discussion seemed to them very immature and they were questioning the wisdom of their hire.

Nearly before Frank knew it they had crossed the one-lane wooden bridge that separated the pueblo from highway 44. They parked the car and got out to stretch. The first thing Frank saw as he looked around at the pueblo was the aggressive movement of a tribal member toward a nearby tourist who had just taken a shot of the front of the small church that stood at the center of the dirt

FIGURE 12.1

(continued)

(continued)

plaza. Without speaking the Indian man grabbed the camera from the tourist, opened it, removed the film, and handed the camera back.

"No pictures," he said and walked away toward the row of ancient adobe houses.

Frank wanted to go home. He'd had a rough morning at work and all of a sudden this seemed like very hostile territory and he wanted no part of it. Cindy could see his anxiety growing.

"Give it a chance, okay?"

Frank turned and walked with Cindy toward the house she identified as belonging to "her family." He knew Cindy loved spending time with her newly adopted family, but he still felt a deep desire to turn and flee. Suddenly the screen door creaked open and slammed shut and Frank watched as a very tiny old woman came to Cindy and hugged her with more vigor than her frame would have suggested possible. Then she turned to him.

"You must be Frank. Come in. Come in."

She seemed very nice and Frank was starting to relax, but when he went inside his eyes were drawn toward Jimmy. Jimmy was at least six-feet-five. He had a big round pot belly, long coal black hair and fierce eyes. He was an intimidating sight. Jimmy mumbled a hello and immediately left the room. Frank was sure it was because he was there and that Jimmy wasn't too excited about having some white guy at his house. Frank felt awkward. Inside all kinds of emotions, hurt, fear, and anger, were swirling around. He had better things to do with his time than drive eighty miles to be blown off by this guy. About the only thing Frank did not feel right then was happy and Cindy could see that in his eyes.

"Give it time," she whispered. "Okay?"

Oh well, he was already there. For her he would give it time. He would give Jimmy and the whole situation another chance. A bit later everyone walked outside to see the dances. As they walked from the house to the center of the plaza where the dances were to begin, Frank was intrigued. The costumes were beautiful. The women all wore headdresses that were covered with symbols. Jimmy stood watching. Frank saw what he thought would be a chance to make conversation and get past the bad start they had had earlier by showing interest in Jimmy's culture.

"What do the symbols on the headdress mean?" Frank asked.

"The stars or something," Jimmy mumbled quickly and walked away.

Now Frank had really had it with this guy. Forget him and all of these Indians. He would hang around for Cindy's sake, but he would not participate or try to be friendly. He knew where he wasn't wanted. For the rest of that day and for the next few visits Frank kept quiet. This was hardest when he and Cindy had gone out to eat with her adopted family. After the meal Frank noticed that they hadn't tipped and when he asked indirectly about it, he felt it was just sort of blown off. As the others left the restaurant he had gone back, not caring who saw him, actually he hoped they all noticed, and had put down a generous tip. It reminded him of the first time he had gone out with some of his Japanese coworkers and some of them had acted almost offended at the idea of tipping. What is wrong with people nowadays, he wondered.

About the sixth or seventh time Cindy and Frank went to visit the pueblo was around Christmas time. Frank was sitting in the living room and observing what he considered the assimilation of the Indian culture into the Anglo culture. The children in their dancing costumes were all playing with their Pokémon toys. All of a sudden a voice came from behind him.

"Good morning, Merry Christmas. It's a nice day, isn't it?"

It was Jimmy. Frank could not believe his ears. Not only was Jimmy speaking to him, but as he did so he was actually changing before his eyes. Jimmy's fierceness was replaced by a painful shyness. This man who had seemed so intimidating suddenly seemed very welcoming and very fragile. Frank felt a sense of shame and embarrassment coming over him. He knew he really hadn't done too much to build any bridges between them.

"Yes, it is a nice day."

"The food is ready, please come and eat with us."

For Frank and Jimmy that simple conversation was the beginning of a very important friendship.[1]

George Eliot commented in her novel *Middlemarch*, "Sane people did what their neighbors did, so that if any lunatics were at large, one might know and avoid them."[2] Alas, in today's world we may seem surrounded by lunatics. As the world has continued to evolve into a global village, our neighbors not only differ from us, but they differ from each other as well. These differences make it easy to conclude that our neighbors are tricky, insensitive, and improper. Indeed, such consistent problems may suggest that our neighbors are worse than insane; they may be downright unethical. How are we to deal with such a situation? Although the strategies of avoidance and name calling referred to by Eliot are still popular responses, there seems to be a growing awareness that in the long run these do not result in the type of community we enjoy living in. The experiences related above provide a number of examples that deal with the question that begins this chapter, the idea of ethics it implies, and the potential for intercultural communities that are so needed in today's world. Some of these include:

- The meetings in which the decisions were essentially already made through a process of Japanese decision-making called *Nemawashi*[3] before the meeting was held. This process of decision-making that involves confirming feelings and working through any problems before a more public meeting is generally viewed as inappropriate in many American settings. I have seen more than one school board or city council be accused of unethical behavior for just a hint of this behind-the-scenes conferring.

- The judgments made by both Frank (and perhaps Cindy) and some of the Japanese management team about each other and the appropriateness of each other's behavior are clearly based on ethical standards and at the same time may themselves be evaluated as to their appropriateness.
- Questions of how one treats another group's sacred or religious traditions are raised both in the tourist's picture-taking that was stopped abruptly by the Native American gentleman and Frank's casual questioning of the meaning of the symbols on the headdress. It also raises the issue of how one responds to other people's violations of things that are sacred to you.
- Ethical issues related to intercultural contact and the cultural change this may lead to are also raised. The Native American children were playing with Pokémon. This was perceived as moving from their Native American culture to a U.S. Anglo culture. Of course, the Pokémon toys originate from Japan, so in this case perhaps one may better view the Native American children as being assimilated to Japanese culture. However, the issue over assimilation or the loss of one culture through the dominance of another is raised regardless of the cultures in question.
- Finally, the tipping incident raises issues of when and in what context certain practices are appropriate or ethical. Although there is variation across the many American Indian cultures, tipping is not a common practice in many of these and this has led to more than one negative stereotype. Tipping is also not appropriate in Japan. Yet for most people in the United States tipping is not only appropriate, but to fail to tip is considered virtually unethical.

This chapter will focus on the idea of ethics in intercultural settings, including the types of issues raised above. First, a general discussion of ethics and six general approaches to making ethical decisions will be considered. Second, we will consider the nature of the connection between communication and ethics. We will then review the relationship between ethics and culture as it is revealed in the universalism/relativism debate. Finally, we will suggest three ethical principles that we believe will help us develop intercultural relationships that can improve the quality of life for everyone involved.

ETHICS

General Perspective

Ethics refers to the means or moral standards by which actions may be judged good or bad, right or wrong. They are the rules of conduct that govern our lives. Sometimes people who love freedom and the diversity of action and thought that different cultures suggest bristle at the very idea of introducing ethics into intercultural interactions. They fear that this will simply become a way for one culture to dominate others. However, ethics exist in every group we are aware of, be they professional, social, religious, political, or kinship groups, and it is important that we consider this issue if we really want to understand the development of intercultural relationships. There is, has been, and will continue to be an enormous amount of discussion related to ethics and there is no way we can do complete justice to this vast literature.[4] We will try to review a few of the approaches frequently discussed in hopes that this brief overview will provoke you to think about and discuss with others these basic, but important, concepts.

Six Golden Approaches

We will review the six *golden* approaches to ethics or the standards by which we decide what is good and bad, right and wrong for ourselves and others: the golden purse, the golden mean, the golden public, the golden law, the golden consequence, and the golden rule.

To aid this discussion we will briefly review the situation Sarah Streed faced in Morocco that was presented in detail in Chapter 4.[5] As a peace corps volunteer she was teaching English in a Moroccan school. One of her students, Hamid, the son of the richest man in the town, did work over the course of a semester that deserved a below-passing grade. When this was made known he asked that he be given just a couple of extra points so that it would be a passing grade. She refused and he and his friends continued to plead for the change, noting his high status in the community as a reason for the change to be made. Streed also received pressure from others within the community and school. One of her fellow teachers came to her as an official representative of the young man's father to request the change. Indeed, most of the Moroccans she talked with concerning this issue indicated that the grade should be changed (one Moroccan was identified as backing her stance). Streed was teaching in a culturally different school system. Should she follow the ethics of teaching she had been raised with or should she follow the norms advocated in the community in which she now lived and worked?

Golden Purse

The golden purse may be understood by the somewhat humorous saying that spun off of the golden rule. *He who has the gold rules*. This perspective is based on the notions of power and personal advantage. Power, of course, can be manifest in many ways, such as wealth, quick wits, or physical strength, for example. Brad has a cousin, let's call him Ned, who used to tell him that there were only two things in life, "Things that please Ned and things that don't." Backed with sufficient power, this saying could be seen as an ultimate ethic from the golden purse perspective, for in short this perspective encourages each person to seek their own benefit to the extent they have the power to do so. When they do not have the power they should make choices in accordance with the desires of those who do have the power. As Hamid's teacher, Streed had the power simply to say, "I am the teacher and I will give you the grade I think you deserve and that is final." However, given the greater power and status of Hamid's father, Streed may realize that her very job is in jeopardy and thus decide to give Hamid the extra points.

We do not know many people who really advocate such an ethic expressed in its most blatant forms, yet it does get expressed more subtly and followed in everyday life. Sometimes without thinking too deeply about it people maintain positions that in essence say, "It is her or his own money, s/he ought to be able to do with it what s/he wants," in regards to situations where other people may be hurt through no choice of their own. Or people quickly make decisions that are solely in their own personal (or group's) best interest without any real consideration of others, and as long as these decisions work out well for themselves or their group (evidence that they have the power), all is considered to be right. A review of the history of virtually any group of people will reveal more than one example of this approach to decision-making. As long as that person or group is still in power, these types of decisions will often be portrayed as good or right, but as soon as there is a change in power those decisions tend to be viewed as bad and wrong. This is in part because an ethic grounded in power and personal advantage will always change with time. Some may feel that this is hardly an ethic at all because, in contrast, all the other approaches to ethics maintain that for an action to be ethical it must go beyond personal considerations. However, this form of reasoning does provide a way of deciding what is best in a given situation and is commonly used in intercultural settings. Still, it provides an extremely unstable foundation upon which to build mutually beneficial intercultural communities.

Golden Mean

The golden mean may be traced back to Aristotle's teachings from the fourth century in which he argued that virtue may be seen to lie between two extremes or vices.[6] Aristotle identifies a number of virtue ethics such as justice, liberality, gentleness, wisdom, and more, all of which are positioned as existing between two vices that are the extremes. Thus justice may be found between extreme harshness and a complete lack of accountability. One of the most common examples of this ethic at work focuses on the opposing vices of cowardice and foolhardiness with courage as the golden mean in-between these extremes. These virtues are all related to our human interactions, yet virtue itself is viewed as grounded in the character of the individual. Thus, virtuous characters will act in virtuous ways even though their actions are not the same. Patterson and Wilkins provide a nice example of this in relation to the courage virtue.[7] Suppose there are two onlookers to a potential drowning. One of them does not know how to swim, but is a very fast runner. In this case it would be foolhardy for the person to attempt to jump into the water and try to save the person and it would be cowardly to do nothing, so the courageous thing to do is to run as quickly as possible to get help. The second person, however, is a good swimmer, so in this case either doing nothing or taking the time to run for help would be either cowardly or foolhardy and jumping in to try to save the person would be courageous. In this perspective, ethics has a very rational and functional element. Some would argue that this approach allows too many rationalizations and excuses and undermines the ability to take a strong position.

The idea of avoiding extremes has some similarities to Taoist ideas of the *yin* and the *yang*, in which both sides are inescapably involved, decisions must seek a blending of opposites, and what is right is only understood in relation to what is wrong.[8] Obviously, Taoist and Aristotelian philosophies have many differences, but the idea of a golden mean or happy medium that holistically takes into account all sides and comes up with a choice that is most ethical is another approach for dealing with the ethical issues that arise in intercultural encounters. Although there are not set actions that are demanded from every person from this perspective, the situation Streed faced in Morocco would need to be approached in a way that avoided extremes. Thus, neither judging the Moroccans to be a corrupt community and just flatly refusing Hamid nor just saying, "When in Rome do as the Romans," and giving him the couple of extra points would be likely to be the most ethical choice. She may need to talk with Hamid about her standards and provide an opportunity to redo some of his work and she would most likely want to discuss her expectations with her students early on in the semester.

Golden Public

When Brad first accepted the position of department chair, one of the administrators he worked with suggested that if he was unsure if a particular course of action was appropriate, he should imagine how it would look to his peers if the criteria for his choice of action were part of the next day's headlines. This "headline test" was focused on the idea of whether you would be embarrassed to have your actions known publicly. The potential for shame becomes the guiding force in this form of ethical reasoning. If you are comfortable with having all those who may be influenced by your actions know why you made the decisions you did, you may be said to be acting ethically. The challenge for this ethic in intercultural settings is that it is grounded in one's own community or peer groups, so it has the potential to be blind to alternative ways of viewing the world.

A variation of this ethic is sometimes referred to as a *professional ethic* because it rests on the idea that we should only act in a way that we would feel comfortable explaining before our own peers. In this case the golden public is your professional peer group and the key is whether you would be embarrassed to have them know how and why you have acted in the way you have. In the case of Streed, the question centers not on what is inherently right, not on what the outcome for the students will be, not on finding the middle ground, or even on whether she can do it; it is grounded in what it will look like to others, particularly her peer group if everyone knows she did this. If she refuses to change the grade, will she look fair and equitable or unbending and ethnocentric? If she changes the grade, will she look culturally sensitive and adaptable or like she plays favorites and has no real standards? Only by assessing this public reaction can she know what the ethical thing to do is.

Golden Law

The golden law focuses on the goodness or badness of particular acts in and of themselves. Kant's discussion of categorical imperatives is a typical example of this form of ethical reasoning.[9] Kant emphasizes that people should be treated as an end in themselves and not as a means to some other end. Before making a particular decision, people working from this perspective should ask themselves whether it would be right for their choices to become universal laws that would apply equally to everyone. Unlike the golden mean, which may encourage different behaviors for different people, with the golden law what is right for one person is also right for any other person. It is the law or the action in accordance with the law that is inherently ethical, regardless of who performs the action or what the outcome of the action is. Obviously, positive outcomes are hoped for, but it is the means, not the end, that are important.

These universally ethical means are described by Kant as certain types of duties that every human shares. The most important of these duties tend to be what he calls the *strict* duties that are typically presented as negatives, such as do not lie, do not murder, do not steal, and so forth. A second type of duty, *meritorious* duties, are phrased in positive ways, such as give aid to needy others or show gratitude. These laws are assumed to be internalized in all humans in the form of a conscience that tells people that what they are doing is right or wrong. The challenge that arises in intercultural settings, as well as others, with this perspective is that the idea focuses on the assumption of universality in regards to certain duties. Is there ever a time when it is okay to break a promise or to refuse to give aid? According to the golden law, the answer is no. Using this ethic, Streed may look at her situation as one that demands that she not change Hamid's grade because, in a sense, this would be lying. This *strict* duty would typically take priority over any conflicting *meritorious* duty, such as to be generous. However, regardless of the decision made, Streed would need to apply this to everyone equally, such that she always (or never) would be willing to give these extra points and give them to all of her students regardless of their social standing. In addition, she should act the same at a Moroccan school as she would at a school in the United States.

Golden Consequence

The golden consequence is grounded in the outcome or ends that will be accomplished through a particular act. The right or wrong of a particular action must be considered in light of the consequences of that action. Mill's discussion of utilitarianism is a classic example of this way of thinking.[10] Utilitarianism may be summarized roughly as advocating the greatest good for the greatest number. No one person is seen as more important than any other person. This sort of perspective is often popular in types of societies in which each person is seen as equally important and having a voice in what should be done. Decisions are made based on what will bring the most good to the greatest number of people, regardless of whether the person holds some prominent position or is you. The nature of the actions that lead to this good is not significant in and of itself. Thus, some sorts of actions that people may consider to be unethical in a general sense, such as lying, breaking a promise, or even killing another individual, may in fact be the right thing to do because of the greater good the action accomplishes. This sort of argument often advocates that it is the spirit of the law (or the end purpose for which the law was given) that is important, not the letter. Thus, if a law must be violated to achieve a good, so be it.

In Streed's situation it would be possible to either change or not change the grade based on this form of ethical reasoning. One could easily look around at all the people who want her to change this grade and decide that no real harm will come of changing the grade and that many people will be very happy and better off because of the change and, therefore, she should go ahead and make the change. On the other hand, one may feel that the example set and stringent standards enforced by not changing the grade will be beneficial to many people who are aware of this situation and that really only Hamid and his family have a very temporary benefit from its change, so she should not make the change. This ability to go either way using this reasoning points us toward one of the concerns raised about this approach. Humans don't really know what the consequences of certain actions will be. Perhaps by changing the grade Streed will find greater acceptance in the community and have a positive influence on the lives of many as well as helping to build better U.S./Moroccan relations. Or perhaps the change will suggest to many that they really don't have to learn the material she is teaching and later down the road they will wish they had. Or by not changing the grade U.S./Moroccan relations may be spoiled, especially if

Hamid rises to a position of power and remembers the experience negatively. Or he may come to respect Streed for her decision and learn lessons about life that will help him and others in the future. We have touched very lightly on some of the possible consequences, but the point is that humans are not very good at predicting all the outcomes. Will a broken promise help a friend face and recover from a drug addiction or will it spoil a friendship and just cause someone to withdraw even more? Because of human limitations, decisions based on the golden consequence have a tendency to be focused on short-term outcomes and benefits, which are clearer and easier to predict than long-term ones.

Golden Rule

The golden rule states that we should act toward others as we would have others act toward us. This is an ethical guide based on the assumption that even though people may dislike themselves and what they do in certain circumstances, they still, deep down, want good things for themselves. Some may argue that the golden rule is just one particular duty within the golden law perspective; however, the *rule* in this case is more general in nature, and therefore more flexible in its application, than are ethical duties that are found within the golden law perspective. For example, Patricia may decide to break a promise not to tell someone about a problem because it is the only way she can see to get help to that person, and if she were in that position, she would really want help, even if she claimed that she didn't want the person to tell about her problem.

The general or abstract nature of this rule also helps to clarify a frequent, but misguided, critique of the golden rule in many intercultural texts. This critique assumes that when people follow the golden rule they will automatically treat others based on their own culturally specific desires. Thus, if Kristine's culture values directness in a given situation, she will always be direct, even when it may be more respectful in certain cultures to be indirect in that type of situation. Bennett proposed the *platinum rule* to replace the golden rule, which states in effect that people should do unto others as the others would have done unto them.[11] The idea is that we need to focus on the other culture's perspective as well as our own. If the wording of the platinum rule helps you to take into account the other culture's perspective, then we think that is a positive thing, but actually we think there is no real need for it. If we take the golden rule in the same specific, concrete way that creates a problem at the cultural level, it also creates a problem at the individual level within a culture. For example, Brad doesn't, as unusual as it is, particularly like chocolate, which would mean that he would never give his wife chocolates even though she loves them. However, if he remembers the abstract nature of this rule, then he won't get caught up in the particular behaviors or specific actions. Instead, Brad will know that he does like to get a tasty treat now and then, so he will try to find things that his wife would feel are tasty treats and get them for her, including chocolate, even though he doesn't like it. This would be true with general concepts such as respect, politeness, kindness, and so forth. At the cultural level we know that there is more than one way to show respect to others.[12] If we want respect shown to us, we should find appropriate ways to show respect to others and not just assume that everyone is exactly like we are. Certainly we don't want people to make that assumption about us. Of course, this still leaves the challenge of learning and understanding these different ways to act to show respect and so forth, and we must be careful to avoid ego or ethnocentrism in this process.

In regards to the situation faced by Streed, if we were to apply the platinum rule, the decision would be fairly clear. Give Hamid the extra points and the grade because that is what he and his community express a desire for. For some this may raise a question about the platinum rule since it may be possible for people to want something given to them that may not be appropriate. Following the golden rule would require more thought. It would mean a

TABLE 12.1 | Golden rule articulations from different religious cultures[13]

Religious Culture	Golden Rule Articulation	Source
Buddhism	"Hurt not others in ways that you yourself would find hurtful."	Udana-Virga, 5: 8
Christianity	"All things whatsoever ye would that men should do to you, do ye even so to them."	Matthew, 7: 2
Confucianism	"Do not do unto others what you would not have them do unto you."	Analect, 15:23
Hinduism	"This is the sum of duty: do naught unto others which would cause you pain if done to you."	Mahabharata, 5:1517
Islam	"No one of you is a believer until he desires for his brother that which he desires for himself."	Sunnah
Jainism	"In happiness and suffering, in joy and grief, we should regard all creatures as we regard our own self."	Lord Mahavira, 24th Tirthankara
Judaism	"What is hateful to you, do not to your fellow man. That is the law: all the rest is commentary."	Talmud, Shabbat, 31 a
Native American	"Respect for all life is the foundation."	The Great Law of Peace
Zoroastrianism	"That nature only is good when it shall not do unto another whatever is not good for its own self."	Oadistan-I-Dinik, 94:5

Source: Compiled by the Temple of Understanding, a global interfaith organization.

careful consideration of whether you would really want at a deep level for someone to just give you those points and it would require that you study some basic beliefs and values from the Moroccan culture. There was, after all, one Moroccan who told Streed she supported her stance. Such consideration may result in the discovery that there are certain values within the Moroccan culture that conflict with the idea of just giving the grade to this person, regardless of their high social position, and, somewhat similar to the golden mean, in this case there may be some other options available besides simply giving or refusing to give the points necessary for the change of grade.

Reflection Question: What are the benefits or weaknesses of the six *golden* ethical approaches? Which do you feel is the best approach for intercultural interactions? Why?

ETHICS AND COMMUNICATION

Constraint

Ethics tends to be viewed in terms of systematic constraints on what actions are acceptable, appropriate, and worthy of approbation. Certainly ethics form a series of constraints on human communication. The ethical constraints on communication within a culture function as a form of quality control for the community. Those who wish to be members in good standing within a community and receive all the rewards that such full fellowship implies must interact in ways that are supported by that community's system of ethics. However, this focus on constraints may overshadow another important consequence of ethical systems: empowerment.

For example, Cronen, Chen, and Pearce describe and analyze a conversation that occurred around a Chinese family's dinner table (including the father, mother, teenage daughter, and her uncle and aunt).[14] The particular episode in question involves a statement by the uncle about youth with which everyone knows the teenager disagrees. At the end of his statement the uncle makes eye contact with the teenager. She returns it, smiles slightly, and looks away. Her father then responds to the uncle, while the teenage daughter continues to remain silent.

This episode is then contrasted with a hypothetical one involving similar participants, but in a North American home. In this case it is supposed that the teenager would respond directly to her uncle's challenge, thus appearing to be less constrained than her Chinese counterpart. However, Cronen et al. go on to explain how the Western teenager is in fact very constrained in her options. They illustrate how the uncle's comment is likely to convey either a challenge to the teenager's individuality or her personal identity and that she must somehow respond in a way that both defends herself and shows respect for the adult at the same time. They argue that these conflicting demands put the Western niece in a bind and constrain rather than free her communicative choices. Cronen et al. evaluate such a situation negatively because they maintain that the highest goal for communication, that of liberation, is not being met.

Empowerment

Although a cultural system of values may be shown to constrain the choices of the individual if they wish to maintain a positive identity and membership within the community, what is often not seen in cases such as those discussed above is that the individual is also empowered at the same time that he or she is constrained. The North American teenager is allowed to express her feelings out loud and perhaps work through and make sense of those feelings in an active exchange with adults. The outcomes of this exchange may be either positive or negative, but she is empowered by her culture to engage in the process in ways that are mutually understood and accepted by those around her. Similar things could be said about the Chinese teenager. She may also be portrayed as being dominated by the adults and put into a position of relative weakness. Yet, as Cronen et al. point out, the teenage girl's silence shows respect for her position in the family while not denying her stance on the issue under discussion. Her silence also prevents the uncle from being able to explicitly argue with her about the subject and it gets dropped. It is the cultural system of which she is a participating member that allows for this mutual respect and understanding.

Edmund Burke captured this paradoxical relationship in writing about the French revolution when he argued that rights and responsibilities could never be realistically separated.[15] Liberation or empowerment requires not unlimited choices and freedom, but a system of constraint that allows for productive action and interaction. Just as traffic laws not only constrain us, but make relatively safe travel possible, ethical systems must be recognized as essentially both constraining and empowering. Part of being culturally competent is knowing what you can do because of the particular pattern of constraints on meaning that exists within a community.

That culture implies ethics and that ethics serve not only to constrain, but to empower individuals in their social lives serves as an important foundation in dealing with the question of whether we can make ethical judgments in multicultural settings. It changes ethics from some sort of anchor, weighing down intercultural interactions, to an important part of the beautiful intercultural tapestry we call our world.

Values/norms are recognized as resources for communication, for making sense, for creating community, and for establishing one's personal and social identities. This relationship can be further understood by considering in more detail the metaphor through which our lives are viewed as a piece of tapestry in the making. When tapestry is woven on a loom it is done so through the use of two types of fiber. One is called the warp and the other is termed the weft. The warp fiber is attached to the loom and then the weft fiber is put on a shuttle and interwoven in and around the warp. Although it is typically the weft fiber that is seen and is what creates the design within the fabric, the warp fiber provides a base or resource without which the weft fiber would quickly unravel and fall as a tangled mess upon the floor. Communication may be said to be the weft fiber of our lives, whereas ethical systems are the warp fiber. Both types of fibers are necessary to create a beautiful and sturdy cloth. Without the warp, the weft would lie in confusion on the floor, yet it is the weft fiber that forms the patterns (relationships) of our lives and makes the warp meaningful in terms of use. Like all metaphors, this one can be stretched to the point of distortion. We hope, however, that it helps the reader to grasp the vital, interdependent nature of the relationship between communication and ethics.

ETHICS AND CULTURE

Culture, as a system of sense, necessarily implies ethics. Important as this implication is, much of the debate surrounding culture and ethics is focused on the question of whether ethics implies culture (community-specific systems of common sense) or whether ethics goes beyond the reach of culture. There are two strongly held opinions on this question. On one hand, there is what is frequently referred to as the universalist position, which strongly supports the idea that ethics goes beyond culture and, on the other hand, there is the relativist position that firmly maintains that all ethical systems are culture bound. The debate between universalist and relativist stands has marked the discussion of ethics and culture since at least Plato's time[16] and has probably been part of the discussion for as long as there has been one. Extreme formulations of these two positions have been used by those in opposition as straw men set up to demonstrate the correctness of one's own side. Because of the history and impact these positions have held, it is worth taking a bit of time to review each of these stands and some of their implications. We have no pretensions that this discussion will resolve this long-debated controversy, but we hope it will help clarify some of the implications of each position and establish a foundation for productive discussion and the opportunity for you to form your own opinion.

Universalism

The *universalist* position maintains that ethics is something that goes beyond the cultural limitations of any one cultural system and therefore does not necessarily imply culture. In its strongest form the universalist position maintains that there is a single set of values and standards of action that is applicable to all cultures AND that there are correct and incorrect ways for these values to be enacted. Such a stance becomes problematic when we consider such experiences as the story of Wanida, a Thai student studying in the United States, which we told to begin Chapter 2. Wanida was put into a difficult spot by a well-intentioned student from the United States who volunteered her in front of the class to do some coding for the professor. Wanida could not do the coding, but did not want to be disrespectful to the professor and tell her no in front of the whole class, so she nodded in agreement, but did not make the scheduled meeting. Later the American student was upset by what she felt was Wanida's lack of respect in not telling everyone about her scheduling conflict. The problem this type of incident creates for the strong universal position is that Wanida's behavior could be perceived to be both disrespectful and respectful. Yet if there is truly one right way of doing things, this cannot be. For the American student, volunteering Wanida to help out and then backing her up when she expressed doubts was a sign of respect, whereas Wanida's lack of straightforwardness about a timing conflict was a sign of disrespect. For Wanida, respect was shown to the professor by avoiding a direct refusal to a request, especially in public, and it was the American student's eager volunteering of another person's time that was inappropriate. Given the different cultural systems operating, two very different sets of behaviors may rightly be seen as being both respectful and disrespectful.

Furthermore, being completely straightforward and honest is not always a sign of respect in American society. A coworker, Dave, may have had a very discouraging week and, in an effort to lift his spirits, gets a new haircut. It would not generally be seen as a sign of respect to blatantly tell him that the haircut really doesn't look good even though you may sincerely believe that it doesn't. Those favoring a relativist position use such situations as these to show how mistaken it is to assume that there is somehow one right way for all people to do something. Assuming that there is universally one right way to do things is the cornerstone of ethnocentrism and a key element in many devastating conflicts around the world.

Relativism

The polar opposite to such a universal stand is complete *cultural relativism*. We use the term cultural relativism here to highlight that we are dealing with a community rather than an individual system of ethical relativism. We do this in part because the focus of this book is on cultural, rather than individual, issues and also because even those who have written in favor of relativism note that the existence of a completely individual ethics system must by definition destroy human society.[17] There must be some shared understanding of what is right and wrong across individuals for a community to exist.

The strong relativistic (culturally based) position, then, is simply that each cultural group has its own value system and can only be judged and evaluated from an insider position. In support of the relativist position and in opposition to a universalist perspective, Howell maintained that: "The concept of universal ethics, standards of goodness that apply to everyone, everywhere, and at all times, is the sort of myth people struggle to hold onto."[18] Strongly stated, there is no cross-cultural or universal basis that can be used to evaluate a community different from one's own.

There are two common responses to this relativistic position. One is that by its very definition a completely relativistic stance is impossible. The reasoning behind this is revealed in Howell's use of the word *myth* in regards to those who do not share his relativistic view of the world. His use of the word implies a belief that any community that disagrees with his stance is wrong. Such a stance indicates a belief in a universal social reality that goes beyond specific cultures, thus implying an objective base from which the intelligence and insight of one community may be compared to another. Howell's very use of the term myth is condescending toward other cultures. Carbaugh noted a cultural dilemma of a similar nature in his work on cultural norms revealed in the popular Donahue talk show.[19] An explicit social rule for the communication on that show was that, regardless of how controversial, any *personal* opinion was acceptable. Donahue would defend this right for any and all. However, at the same time there was another informal rule that one could not acceptably hold an opinion that implied that others should also hold it. Thus, a person's opinion could only be valid so long as that person did not assume it should hold for others. Such an exception, of course, allows for the rejection of many personal opinions and implicitly demands conformity in the way opinions may rightfully be expressed. In a similar manner, universalists would argue that absolute relativism is a vicious cycle that continually denies its own basis for existence.

A second common response is to point out the social dangers of a relativist position. Universalists typically point toward such communities as the Nazis of Germany or certain white communities in South Africa, both of which developed cultural beliefs that supported persecution and discrimination in such extreme forms that the world in general has agreed in its condemnation of these communities. If we were truly and completely relativistic in our outlook, we would have to agree that these communities and their beliefs were just as valid as any other cultural community and their beliefs. Such a stand is as potentially dangerous and untenable as the strong universalist stance noted above. Herskovits, a strong advocate of relativism, rejects the notion that cultural relativism is a doctrine of ethical indifference and that all things should be tolerated.[20] However, he does not go into detail on what criteria he would use in deciding what to tolerate and what to try to change. Even if one refuses to discuss or think about what this basis is, there is some standard being used when the Nazis or some other cultural community are evaluated either negatively or positively by people outside of the specific community.

In recent years more and more writers who maintain a relativistic outlook still identify some value or ideal upon which communities may be judged. For example, Cronen et al. note that all cultures are incommensurable, yet they advocate cultural critique based on the notion that all communication should be liberating.[21] Kale and Hatch both argue for a relativistic perspective that is grounded in the universal need to respect the worth and dignity of humans.[22] Steiner's work "rejects ethical schemas that could or would justify acts that increase the oppression of women."[23] We suspect that one would not have to look long to find cultures whose ethical systems could be argued to oppress women. Whatever the basis for the judgments made, these relativistic approaches are no longer *only* community specific. From a universalist's perspective, a relativistic stance simply allows people to blame others for having biases while subtly nurturing some of their own. Certainly both relativism and universalism may become tools to use in condemning others.

CRITIQUE

Based on this brief review of relativistic and universalistic philosophies, three points seem worth noting. First, behaviors do not have meanings inherent in them, but rather particular meanings are dependent upon specific systems of shared sense-making. Thus, the meaning and/or correctness of a behavior cannot be known or judged without understanding the culture from which it stems. It is important that behavior should not be confused with action. By behavior we refer to the sheer motion and physical movements engaged in by humans, whereas action is behavior that has been infused with meaning.[24] A single behavior may in fact constitute multiple actions. Thus Wanida's nod of agreement to the professor may be respectful or disrespectful depending upon which cultural system one is applying.

Second, there are values that are appropriate in determining the worth of actions across cultures. These values, however, have an open texture to them and are not necessarily connected to particular behaviors. Again, the distinction between action and behavior is crucial here. Meaning cannot be separated from culture. Therefore, we can only determine the worth of actions, not behaviors.

Finally, universalism and relativism are not dichotomous. Indeed, ethics may be viewed as a compound of universalism and relativism. All ethical systems involve a tension between what is universal and what is relative. It is this tension that both enables and constrains creativity and stability in human societies. Like the tree limb that can bend in the wind, together they are both flexible and strong, but in isolation they are both rigid and weak. The challenge, then, is to understand the nature of this compound and its implications in intercultural settings.

These positions may be seen as the two extremes of excess and deficiency noted in the golden mean perspective, but considered from a real desire to promote intercultural relations, they can be seen as opposing tensions that help us think through the dilemmas that arise in our multicultural world. There are many different attempts to find the balance these two extremes address. We will briefly review two of these to give a feel for the types of things brought to the fore in these efforts and then we will discuss three ethical principles that we believe are crucial for developing intercultural relations that are productive for all involved.

Reflection Question: Do you feel more comfortable with the universalistic or relativistic approach to cultures and ethics? On what basis, if any, would you make judgments about the worth of culturally accepted practices? Does how well you know the culture or whether you are a member of it make a difference? How and why?

EFFORTS TO FIND UNIVERSAL ETHICS THAT ACKNOWLEDGE THE RELATIVISTIC NATURE OF CULTURES

Jensen reviewed the teachings of various religions in an effort to find common ethical admonitions in regards to communication.[25] His effort is of interest for our purposes for two reasons. First, it is focused specifically on communication and what it means to be an ethical communicator. Second, many of the sharpest cultural differences can also be linked to different religious traditions, and Jensen has drawn from a fairly wide variety of religious backgrounds including Buddhism, Christianity, Confucianism, Hinduism, Islam, Judaism, and Taoism in his search for common communication ethics. Although the exact wording may vary in the different religious texts, he presents five common ethical admonitions for communicators:

1 Tell the truth; avoid deception.
2 Do not slander other people.
3 Do not blaspheme God or other sacred figures or objects.
4 Avoid speech that demeans others and life in general (includes things like flattery, silly, glib, or vain speech).
5 Earn the trust of others by matching one's actions with one's speech.

Another effort at discovering universal values and communication ethics is found in research compiled by Christians and Traber.[26] They draw on work done in a variety of geographically diverse entities, including Africa, Asia, South,

Central, and North America, as well as parts of Eastern Europe and the Middle East. Based on this work they claim three universal ethics that they call *prot-onorms*. The first protonorm is truthfulness. They maintain that society is not possible without a tacit assumption that people are generally speaking truthfully. The second universal ethic stresses respect for another person's dignity. They argue that, although the way human dignity is affirmed may vary across cultures, humans have a *sacred status* in all cultures. The third and final protonorm they espouse is that innocents should not be harmed. Although the specifics may vary, they maintain that it is a universal ethic to protect the powerless. All such efforts are open to critiques and questioning in light of specific cultures. Often such critiques paint the work in too narrow a way, making it easier to find fault. Our purpose here is not to evaluate these efforts, but to bring them to your attention for your information and consideration.

ETHICAL PRINCIPLES FOR INTERCULTURAL RELATIONS

As we have written this text and considered these issues in the past, we have felt strongly about three principles which we believe can guide the process of making ethical judgments within intercultural settings. These three principles are not specific behavioral norms that eliminate creativity and diversity, but they do provide a reasonably clear resource for approaching ethical questions as they arise and promoting intercultural communication competence in general. Often intercultural competence is thought of in terms of three levels: thought, action, and feeling. The three ethical principles that we discuss highlight these three levels and include an effort to understand (thought), peaceful disagreement (action), and loving relationships (feeling).

Effort to Understand

Teachable Attitude

An effort to understand implies a teachable attitude, one that allows a person to learn and eventually helps others to open up to learning about you and your community. Without this willingness to learn from others, our efforts to build positive relationships and serve others may fail. Such an instance occurred recently in Kenya.[27] A Non-Government Organization (NGO) decided that a certain village there could use windmills to provide water for the community. The community, however, did not want the towering structures. The NGO were surprised by the resistance and felt the people should have been grateful for their help. The windmills were eventually built, but the people were not taught how to use or repair them and they now sit dormant in the village, an ugly memorial to patronizing attitudes and a silent testimony that an unwillingness to learn or understand turns even well-intentioned interactions into negative outcomes.

Mutual Legitimacy

Although there is a lot involved in establishing understanding, one of the key principles is captured in the idea that we each need first to focus on understanding others before we worry about making sure we have been fully understood. There are many ways in which we may incorporate the principle of first seeking to understand others into our lives, but we want first to consider an international incident that largely promoted misunderstanding rather than understanding. Consider the two terrorist attacks targeting *Charlie Hebdo*, the satirical French weekly magazine in Paris. The 2011 and 2015 attacks were both presumed to be responses to the controversial cartoons it published about the Islamic prophet, Muhammad. The second attack claimed the lives of 12 people including the publishing director. In non-Islamic communities there were people who on one hand expressed shock and general condemnation of this lack of respect for freedom of speech, and, on the other hand, those who attempted a culturally sensitive reaction, declaring that we could not impose our standards on others and that under Islamic law the death sentence could be justified. The difficulty of this situation was that there were different ethical standards and cultural misunderstanding,

FIGURE 12.2

including intergroup dynamics and concerns over identity. However, dialogue and an effort to understand was never really seriously considered by either side in this ethical conflict.

Dialogue

One of the most influential advocates of dialogue is Martin Buber who maintains that it is only through this form of communication that we truly become human.[28] To engage in dialogue we accept that each person's reality is influenced by personal experiences, and we try to imagine as best we can the perspective of the other without ignoring the legitimacy of our own experience. This process involves a real effort to empathize *with* others rather than sympathize *for* them. We may sympathize or feel bad for a person without any effort at understanding or feeling as they may feel. Johannesen has synthesized many of Buber's ideas and the ideas of others discussing the importance of dialogue into what may be viewed as six characteristics of ethical communication.[29]

1　*Authenticity*. Although humans need not say everything about themselves or what is on their minds, their communication should be genuine and allow the other to see into who the person really is.
2　*Inclusion*. The other's understanding of the world should be treated as just as important as one's own. The ethical communicator makes the effort to include and respect others' perspectives in the dialogue.
3　*Confirmation*. We need to recognize actively the worth of the other person, thus confirming the other's existence and our mutual importance in the dialogue. To engage in dialogue is to engage in a type of communication that truly values the other person.
4　*Presentness*. We resist the temptation to maintain a distance from the other person or to be distracted by internal or external concerns. Instead, at that present time the other person and the dialogue between us become our top priorities.
5　*Spirit of mutual equality*. This idea is just the opposite of one person dominating the other person or conversation. Instead, an awareness of mutual legitimacy allows all involved to speak freely and openly.
6　*Supportive climate*. A supportive climate is one that encourages everyone involved to participate and suspends judgments that position one person over another with the right to evaluate the worth of the other person.

Reflection Question: Do you think dialogue, as discussed in this chapter, is a reasonable expectation? Are there times when it is more reasonable than others? When? Have you experienced this kind of communication with others? If so, when? If not, why not?

Considering Context

Some of these six principles overlap, but taken together they provide a way to assess our own communication in terms of its ethical appropriateness as we struggle with intercultural differences. Not recognizing that there are many mutually legitimate, albeit seemingly incompatible, behaviors that constitute ethical behavior prevents us from engaging in dialogue and establishing true understanding. It takes a sincere effort for us to see beyond the reasonableness of our own perspective. Some of this may be clearer as we compare two examples of how ethical dimensions are interwoven into the cultural tapestry of everyday life in mutually legitimate, yet contradictory, ways. To do this we will use Basso's discussion of a form of joking among Western Apache, in which someone pretends to be a *whiteman*, and the second example examines Fitch's research on leave-taking at large Colombian social gatherings.[30]

One of the examples of joking that Basso elaborates is the following exchange that occurs at L and K's home after L responds to a knock at the door from J:

> J: *Hello, my friend! How are you doing? How are you feeling, L? You feeling good?*
> *[J now turns in the direction of K and addresses her.]*
>
> J: *Look who here, everybody! Look who just come in. Sure, it's my Indian friend, L. Pretty good all right!*
> *[J slaps L on the shoulder and looking him directly in the eyes, seizes his hand and pumps it wildly up and down.]*
>
> J: *Sit down! Sit right down! Take your loads off your ass. You hungry? You want some beer? Maybe you want some wine? You want crackers? Bread? You want some sandwich? How 'bout it? You hungry? I don't know. Maybe you get sick. Maybe you don't eat again long time.*
> *[K has stopped washing dishes and is looking on with amusement. L has seated himself and has a look of bemused resignation on his face.]*
>
> J: *You sure looking good to me, L. You looking pretty fat! Pretty good all right! You got new boots? Where you buy them? Sure pretty good boots! I glad . . .*
> *[At this point, J breaks into laughter. K joins in. L shakes his head and smiles. The joke is over.]*
>
> K: *indaa? dogoyaada! ('Whitemen are stupid!').*[31]

Let us consider for a moment what turns the above into a humorous exchange. Certainly there is exaggeration in the above joking sequence, but more important than that for our purposes is that many of the things that are either nonsensical or wrong and, therefore, seen as legitimately laughable are perfectly sensible and socially correct within the whiteman culture being referenced. Take, for example, the systems of sense surrounding the use of a person's first name. J's frequent use of L's name is inappropriate among the Western Apache who view one's name as personal property and refrain from "borrowing" that property too often. In contrast, the whiteman often uses the first name as a sign of interest in and concern for the other person. We have seen advertisements for more than one business that tout the fact that they know their customers by name and promise to use that first name every time you do business there, thus capitalizing on this cultural understanding of first-name use.

Furthermore, the Western Apache prefer to come and go from social groups unobtrusively, whereas in many communities in the U.S. that would be considered rude. You might ask yourself, if you arrived at a party and the host did not make a point of greeting you and introducing you to those already there or when someone left your party they did so without going the rounds in saying goodbye, what you would think? In the example given there are also the questions about L's health and if the guest would like something to eat or drink. Such questions and comments are frequent, expected, and appropriate in many other communities. The list could go on, but the point here is that the joking in this case not only makes use of violations of common sense (good manners) among the Western Apache, it reinforces the guidelines for future behavior if one does not want to come across badly or as a marginal member of a community. These social *Dos and Don'ts* are but outcroppings on the deeply felt and deeply patterned cultural landscape of the Western Apache. They reflect and constitute standards that are used to evaluate the worth of actions. These standards constrain what can be seen and understood when one is asked about one's health or called by her or his personal name repeatedly (is this polite and caring or intrusive and stupid?).

Standards and values such as those just noted are not always expressed in direct opposition to other cultural communities, but they are most noticeable when a multicultural contrast is possible. Fitch's discussion of her experiences at large Colombian social gatherings provides a nice contrast to the ideas about leave-taking among the Western Apache. She noted that when someone attempts to leave such a gathering, the Colombian hosts inevitably performed what she came to call the *salsipuede* (or leave if you can) ritual. The hosts would ask why the guest had to go and then upon hearing the reason come up with some way to discount that reason and convince the guest to stay (quite different from the Western Apache approach). Through ethnographic research Fitch discovered that this practice reflected and honored the importance of interpersonal connections (not the specific relationship, but interpersonal ties in general) among the Colombians. Indeed, after convincing the guest to stay the host may not even directly interact with that person again until they finally manage to leave. Still, for either the host to respond to the guest's announced intention of leaving by saying, "Well, thanks for coming. We were so happy to have you and we'll see you later," or for the guest to refuse to stay at least a little bit longer, would be very rude and have serious social consequences. For the Colombians this way of taking leave is simply common sense and, like all common senses, is infused with ethical standards for what is important or unimportant, right or wrong, good or bad.

The leave-taking actions of both the Western Apache and the Colombians in the settings described above require very different behaviors for the individuals involved to act in appropriate ways and not be seen as violating basic social standards. However, at a more abstract level both the Colombians and the Western Apache are treating each other with respect and thoughtfulness. The vast majority of everyday ethical conflicts can be traced to problems at the level of performance, rather than differences in relational intent. An important question to ask when we find ourselves making negative judgments about other communities based on our own ethical standards for behavior is, "Why must it be done this way?" If we are open and honest in our questioning, we believe we will realize that both ways are legitimate. We do not have to reject either our own or the other community's ways of doing things; instead, we need to accept that both are legitimate and act in ways that are appropriate to the situation in which we find ourselves.

This, of course, is often much easier to see when looking at an example from a social distance and it is easier said than done. It is easy to forget that we are personally part of any such discussion. We were again reminded of this during a recent graduate seminar when one of our international students became quite incensed at the presentation of another student. The presenting student had done an analysis of an educational entertainment program designed to help encourage family planning and combat the HIV and AIDS epidemic occurring in Tanzania. The presenter had raised some concerns about the effect of some of the content of the program on Tanzanian culture. The program encourages a modern versus a traditional approach, which involves some common Western practices, such as encouraging women not to be stuck at home with the children all day, but to go out and develop financial independence.[32] In addition, she also presented some evidence that Tanzanians actually perceived the spread of the AIDS virus to be less pressing than a variety of other social concerns and suggested that some of these pressing problems need to be dealt with first. The objecting graduate student, who is part of a research team involved with the entertainment education project being evaluated, just could not believe that anyone could be critical in any way with what was being done with the program. She proclaimed, "We are saving lives here." She stressed that regardless of how important the native people saw it, AIDS prevention is the most important issue facing that country today and it is time people recognized just how important it is.

Our point in considering this instance is not to determine the relative importance of AIDS prevention, the worth of women with young children working outside the home, or even the worth of entertainment education. Indeed, this particular project has included many efforts to make its pro-social messages and presentation resonate with Tanzanian culture. Instead, we want to focus for a moment on the graduate student's reaction. We believe that the strength of her reaction was due to a perceived threat to her identity. She is an international student with an intercultural focus, engaged in helping on an intercultural project. To suggest that this project, in which she is involved and supports, may in some way not be 100 percent culturally pure and sensitive threatens her self-image. In this case, the student strongly identifies with the goals of the project, thus encouraging a more explicit and emotional response. However, even when there is no specific project identification involved, we believe that one of the complicating factors that emerges in any discussion of cultures and ethics is that people's identities are intertwined with the outcomes of these discussions. Thus, it is often easier to see the mutual legitimacy of ethical standards when we are quite distant from it than when we are personally involved in the interactions in question.

The attitudes reflected in both the strong universalistic and relativistic perspectives can also close off dialogue that can lead to establishing real understanding. We are reminded of a colleague from India who recently told us about a loan officer who had asked him when he was applying for his loan to come to study in the United States what the loan was worth to him. This was after months of frustrating and unsuccessful efforts at obtaining the loan. In discussing this situation he noted that, although he was very well qualified for the loan, it was common practice to give the loan officer some funds on the side to obtain the needed loan. Thus, the clear implication of the officer's statement to him was, "You'll get the loan when and if you're willing to pay me enough on the side."

Let us just consider this situation as if we were coming at it from either a universalistic or relativistic standpoint. From a universalistic viewpoint one might immediately assume that the loan officer's comment reflects a corrupt practice. As such, it should be exposed, condemned, and corrected. A somewhat more laissez-faire approach might be to nod and note how interesting such a practice is, but silently maintain that no matter what one says, it is simply still a bribe and like the proverbial rose it will always smell just the same, regardless of what you call it. In either case, though, further discussion and discovery is preempted by the fact that one *already knows* what act such behavior constitutes.

From a relativistic position we would respond by quickly and fully accepting that giving money to the loan officer to get the loan is perfectly fine because it is a common and generally accepted practice in India. After all, such a practice does not physically damage another human, so it is just as valid as any other practice.

We may then go to my intercultural class and teach them that in India it is okay and perfectly normal to pay a loan officer money on the side to get a loan. By doing so we may even create the impression that it is even seen as unethical if we don't do that. This may appear to be a more culturally sensitive response, but it also oversimplifies the situation and still discourages discovery and discussion by positioning any attempt to question or explore the worth of such an action as ethnocentric.

In the example noted above, our Indian colleague did not pay the loan officer anything. Even though he knew that such a practice was appropriate in one sense, it still seemed unethical to him and he did not want to get his loan that way. In a personal e-mail correspondence with another person from India this feeling of my colleague that, although a *bribe* may be common and accepted, it is still seen by many as unethical was also supported. Our colleague eventually got his loan after his mother talked to an uncle who was a high-ranking bank officer. Our colleague did not know that this discussion had occurred until quite some time after because his mother knew that he had wanted to do this strictly on his own.

Now, both the relativist and universalist could twist the above information to say, "See, I'm right," but this would miss the point. The point is that either extreme encourages one to ignore the subtleties of other cultures and limits discussion and understanding. On one hand, you have an often unconscious smugness from the feeling that you and your group are the only ones that really see what is going on, thereby eliminating any need for true dialogue. On the other hand, you may patronize that culture, automatically treating any discussions related to the relative worth of actions accepted within another culture as threatening and avoid them. Whether one takes a completely universalistic or relativistic stance, the need for a detailed dialogue and discovery process is often covered up and replaced by a type of simplification that distorts our understanding of culture and leads to misunderstanding and unnecessary conflict. Anthropologist Edward Hall warns of the dangers in missing the subtleties within other cultures.[33] Too often discussions surrounding ethics and culture do just that and the opportunity to understand each other is lost.

As we conclude this section, we think it is worth noting that our efforts to establish understanding should be of an additive rather than replacement nature when possible. Sometimes when people first really understand that there are other legitimate ways to look at the world, they start to reject their own culture. In this way people still reject the idea of mutual legitimacy and miss out on many of the advantages of a multicultural perspective, even while telling themselves how cosmopolitan they are. In addition, as people within a culture watch this rejection happen, they often become afraid of intercultural contact and seek to build bigger walls, rather than bridges. Isolationism is not a productive path in today's increasingly global village. Hegde writes about the need for people who are sailing in new cultural waters to develop cultural anchors which help people (especially children) maintain a sense of who they are culturally.[34] The challenge is to build and use those anchors in ways that do not create a fear of leaving our own cultural harbor. Thus, it is as we are able to establish a balance between our own and others' cultures that the type of understanding we are talking about is gained, an understanding that comes through dialogue, empathy, an assumption of mutual legitimacy, a teachable attitude, and paying attention to the context which gives actions their meaning.

Peaceful Disagreement

Perhaps one of the most obvious implications of a multicultural world is that there will be disagreements about what, how, when, where, and why things should be done, as well as who should do them. The differences reflected in many of these disagreements involve ethical considerations of what is right and wrong and what is good and bad. These disagreements often lead to conflict, which can in turn lead to various kinds of violence being inflicted on one person or group from another person or group. Violence is not just physical. It can be engaged in verbally and can be structured into the social situation. In any case violence is always focused on efforts to dominate, control, and harm the other. To follow the notion of peaceful disagreement we must be aware of the power inherent in situations and relationships and try to make the situation safe for all those involved.

Nonviolence

The principle of peaceful disagreement suggests that to be ethical these disagreements and conflicts, as discussed in detail in Chapters 8 and 9, must be approached with peaceful rather than violent actions. This is true even in the face of injustice as is illustrated in the personal account of a lawyer, educated in England, but working in South Africa. His narrative picks up with him traveling in first-class accommodation on a train bound for Pretoria.

A white man entered the compartment and looked me up and down. He saw that I was a "colored" man. This disturbed him. Out he went and came in with one or two officials. They all kept quiet, when another official came to me and said, "Come along, you must go to the van [third-class] compartment."

"But I have a first-class ticket," said I.

"That doesn't matter," rejoined the other. "I tell you, you must go to the van compartment."

(continued)

(continued)

"I tell you, I was permitted to travel in this compartment at Durban and I insist on going on in it."

"No you won't," said the official. "You must leave this compartment or else I shall have to call a police constable to push you out."

"Yes, you may. I refuse to get out voluntarily."

The constable came. He took me by the hand and pushed me out. My luggage also was taken out. . . and the train steamed away.[35]

The lawyer was left to spend a cold winter's night at a deserted railway station without his overcoat or his luggage, both of which had disappeared with the officials. That night the lawyer pondered many things, such as seeking revenge or fleeing such a country and returning to his homeland. He chose neither extreme, but instead decided that he would never yield to force and never use force to win his position. Although his philosophy on life and his belief about how to deal with unethical situations continued to develop for many years, the lawyer, Mahatma Gandhi, cited this night as the most creative incident of his life.

In many ways Mahatma Gandhi exemplifies the principle of peaceful disagreement. Kale argues that peace is the fundamental human ethic and that we can only achieve optimal peace when we take others' goals as seriously as our own—not more seriously, just as seriously.[36] Gandhi certainly took into account many different religions (Hinduism, Christianity, Islam, Buddhism, and more we suspect) and secular writings, such as Henry David Thoreau's writing on civil disobedience, as he developed his ideas on nonviolence.[37]

Although Gandhi himself said, "I have nothing new to teach the world. Truth and nonviolence are as old as the hills,"[38] we believe there is much to learn from both his teachings and his example as it relates to this basic human ethic. Many may assume that nonviolence or peaceful disagreement is a stand taken by those who are weak and passive. Gandhi claimed that his "creed of nonviolence is an extremely active force. It has no room for cowardice or even weakness. There is hope for a violent man to be some day nonviolent, but there is none for a coward."[39] Peaceful disagreement does not mean that we don't get involved in conflicts or that we just give in to others, but it does mean that our actions, both verbal and nonverbal, are nonviolent in nature.

According to Gandhi these nonviolent actions should not stem from anger or the desire to embarrass and gain vengeance, but from a desire to get in touch with the heart of the other person and to discover and do that which is right. Gandhi, of course, would have freely admitted that he did not live a perfect life, but we have always been impressed that he stayed true to this ethic even in the later part of India's struggle against British control when it seemed he could have used some violence to more quickly free the Indian people (a worthy goal). Instead, if he heard of Indians using violence in the struggle for what was right, he would withdraw his own participation until the people were again willing to engage only in peaceful disagreement.

Of course, as noted above, the idea of nonviolence or peaceful disagreement is not new or unique to Gandhi. For example, history indicates that Muhammad, the founder of Islam, had more than one opportunity to take vengeance on those who had severely persecuted and abused him, but he refused to do so.[40] Jesus Christ, the cornerstone of Christianity, taught that we should turn the other cheek to those who would smite us.[41] Indeed, when Christ was about to be taken prisoner he rebuked his follower who attempted a violent resistance[42] and when he died he prayed that his Father would forgive those who had crucified him.[43] The Greek philosopher Socrates is attributed as claiming that retaliation is never justified.[44] The basic idea in all of these teachings is that violence only results in more violence and problems, regardless of the intent or goal. A close look at the lives of those who have followed these nonviolent ideas shows a firmness and strength of mind that is sometimes misunderstood when peaceful disagreement is advocated. Indeed, many who come after such leaders and claim to follow them often forget about the need for peaceful disagreement.

The principle of peaceful disagreement is in many ways at odds with much of what would be considered realistic, sophisticated, or practical in today's world. A person who adopts such a stance is often seen as naive; not very smart or realistic. Gandhi argued that his stance was very practical and, if you look at the overall impact the lives of those who have advocated such an approach have had, creating worldwide religions, freeing huge countries, and so forth, it is hard to argue that such an approach has no practical benefits. It is interesting to us to note that a holiday established in the United States is in honor of a man, Martin Luther King Junior, who strove to follow this principle. Similarly, César Chávez, another follower of Gandhi's nonviolent protest method, had his birthday, March 31, become a state holiday in California, Colorado, and Texas. Regardless of what some of their detractors may say about them, their practice of peaceful disagreement paid great dividends not only for the black and Latino communities in the United States, but for all people.

Truth and Openness

Sissela Bok, a prominent writer on ethics and peace, maintains that being peaceful involves more than nonviolence but also an avoidance of secrecy and various types of deception in our communication with others.[45] Her inclusion of deception and secrecy as practices to be avoided is consistent with Gandhi's constant watchwords, *satya* and *ahimsa*, which mean truth and nonviolence.[46] Without trust in the truthfulness of another's word it is difficult to have a real sense of peace. This can be difficult at times because our lack of understanding of a given situation may make us feel that another is dishonest when that is not the case. For example, the Thai student we discussed earlier who did not directly tell the professor that she could not come to the coding session may be accused of dishonesty. However, we believe she felt she acted in a true and respectful way. One ethic grounded in these concerns is the idea that one does not do or say what one would not want to have known to a wide audience. In this case we believe the Thai student would have been more ashamed to have many people (including those she admired) know that she had publicly refused her professor than to have them know that she had been indirect and not stringently honest in her comments. Public knowledge of our actions provides the type of check on our behavior that is suggested in the truth often associated with peace. When the truth of an oppressive situation is made known to a wide audience, those who have been powerless are often liberated and more able to live in peace.

M. Scott Peck seems to be getting at the idea of this principle when he talks about the importance of fighting gracefully if we are to experience community with those different from ourselves.[47] He argues that the traditional wisdom that we will be able to develop community only after we are able to resolve our conflicts is misleading. He suggests that it is only after we achieve community that we can resolve our conflicts. The third and final principle we will consider is essential for such a community.

Loving Relationships

To us intercultural communication is inherently an emotional experience, so it is this principle based in emotion that serves as the keystone of ethical behavior (see Figure 12.3). The keystone is what allows an arch to stand firm, without which the other stones, no matter how good or strong, will crumble. The principle of loving relationships is potentially quite vague. The details and nuances associated with the concept of love, for example, tend to be varied within a given culture, let alone across cultures. We do not want to eliminate all of this openness because we think some of it is essential to the concept, but we will try to explain some of the key features we have in mind when we advocate this ethical principle.

In focusing on loving relationships we are explicitly recognizing the interconnection that we as humans have with each other. We cannot practice this ethical principle in isolation from others. If we are to follow this principle, we must extend ourselves beyond usual comfort zones and communicate and connect with others who may be culturally different from ourselves. Of course, the expectations and desires associated with various relationships may vary across cultures. We have seen examples of that throughout this text.

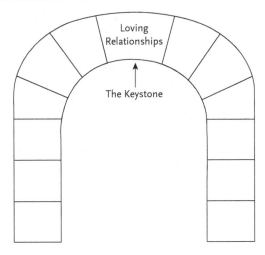

FIGURE 12.3 | Loving relationships as the keystone of ethical intercultural interactions

In advocating loving relationships we are not trying to say that there is only one way to do this. The more we learn about different culturally appropriate ways to engage in relationships, the better we are able to act ethically in our relationships with others.

Intercultural Marriage Microcosm

One way of better understanding how one develops these loving relationships is by looking at what has worked in other intercultural relationships. Of course, there are many possible places to look for these kinds of relationships, but one area that is a likely resource is intercultural marriages. We chose marriage because it is a relationship that carries with it many expectations in all cultures with which we are familiar and one in which the participants are typically forced to deal with each other either for good or bad. It appears, therefore, that most of the problems that threaten various types of relationships would also be faced in some way in this relationship.

Romano interviewed hundreds of intercultural couples, some with very good marriages and some with bad ones, and derived ten factors for success.[48] We will review these to help give a feel for typical characteristics associated with loving relationships.

Good Motives for the Marriage

In Romano's opinion this motive was love and genuine concern for the other person and the relationship. If we are engaging in the relationship simply as a way to escape a negative situation or accomplish a selfish end outside of the relationship itself, it is likely to end in problems. Considering our motives in any kind of relationship is important. If we are simply using the other person to gain prestige, further our career, or avoid negative situations, it is virtually impossible to have a loving relationship. Aristotle taught that to speak well a person must be basically good.[49] Certain Christian and Hindu teachings indicate that one's motives need to be pure for the outcome to be acceptable, such that a gift given unwillingly may just as well have been retained for all the good it does.[50] This should not be taken as an excuse to engage in poor or unethical behavior. It is possible to teach ourselves appropriate motives through loving actions. Indeed, as we act toward others with love, we often find that our emotions have followed our explicit lead.

Common Goals

Romano notes that those who either initially shared or over time established common goals that they could work on interdependently had stronger marriages. The same would seem true of any relationship. It is important to take the time to develop or discover these goals. Although we would argue that one may have very different goals than someone with whom that person has a loving relationship, we suspect that the bond that comes from having and recognizing these goals certainly facilitates such a relationship.

Sensitivity to Each Other's Needs

Whether it is an inter- or intracultural relationship, different people will have different needs. If the relationship is to work, people must pay attention to and honor as best they can the needs of the other. A relationship that is one-sided in terms of needs met is not a loving relationship. However, as with the process of establishing understanding, people tend to have more success with this factor if they first try to give to the other and meet their needs rather than first trying to make sure their needs are met or keep a mental score sheet to make sure they do not fall too far behind in terms of needs met.

A Liking for the Other's Culture

Romano provides two contrasting examples, one in which each couple enjoys (but does not prefer) the other's culture and finds ways to express this; and one in which the couple each constantly complained about the other's culture. Romano reports, "Carol knew her country was less than perfect, but it was hers to criticize, hers to hate at times, *not his!* She took his criticisms personally, as criticisms of herself."[51] If a person feels threatened, it is hard to build a loving relationship. As with Carol, we may not appreciate all or even a lot of our own cultural heritage, but criticism from the outside is rarely appreciated and often feels like a personal attack. You may not like all aspects of another's culture, but from a relational standpoint it is important to find and focus on those aspects you do like as you interact with your partner.

Flexibility

A relationship that is marked by flexibility tends to avoid the negative and vindictive conflicts that can ruin or end a relationship. Flexibility implies the strength of the tree limbs that bend with the wind or the weight of a heavy snow. Sometimes being flexible involves taking turns, sometimes it involves an active negotiation of how to handle certain situations, but it always allows for the positive acceptance of unexpected frustrations.

Solid, Positive Self-Image

Romano discusses this factor as a personal foundation that allows individuals to deal with the many challenges of an intercultural marriage. She notes that most people in her interviews saw themselves as special or unique in some way and were comfortable with this uniqueness. When people are comfortable with themselves, they are more easily able to quit worrying about themselves and focus on the relationship. This is true regardless of the relationship type. Those with poor self-images often become dependent in negative ways on others in a relationship and seek to control the other person so they will meet their deficiencies. Although at one level it may sound like a recipe for selfishness, a good self-image is a basic part of a loving relationship.

Spirit of Adventure

The people in successful intercultural marriages expressed a sense of adventure or a desire to do and experience new things. People vary in terms of how much they like to experiment with new places, people, and ways of doing things. There is nothing wrong with variety in this desire for adventure, but loving intercultural relationships require a bit more of a risk than do intracultural relationships. At some point we need to be willing to move beyond what is comfortable, to interact with others that we don't culturally *know*. Some time back there was a study done of interracial friendships in high schools in the United States. The most significant finding we remember was that of reciprocity. Both partners reported that the other person seemed to want to be their friend. To develop these types of relationships we have to show to the other person our desire for this kind of contact with them.

Ability to Communicate

Really this whole book has been dedicated to this particular finding and factor in successful relationships. The communication that Romano describes among some of these cultures is at times anything but calm and harmonious. However, they keep communicating and eventually are able to work out their differences and get the messages that are important across to each other. An important part of this communication is being clear in your own mind about what is important and what needs to be expressed. Communication has the power to both help and harm relationships and we need to be careful that even in times of upset or disagreement we try to communicate in ways that confirm the importance of the other person in our lives.

Commitment to the Relationship

Perhaps one of the most important aspects of loving relationships is the commitment that each party feels to the relationship. Most relationships have good times and bad. The key to loving relationships is the commitment that gets them through the bad times. Intercultural relationships are often marked by times where one person is somehow offensive or feels foolish or is nervous about even maintaining contact with the other. The commitment to the relationship that doesn't let us just give up or avoid further contact is a sign that people love or value each other enough to make it through the hard times. In addition, these relationships need to involve enough commitment to overcome the outside pressures that often arise from other people.

Sense of Humor

The use of humor in intercultural settings is often risky and can often create more tension than it ever reduces. However, the sense of humor in which a person refuses to take themselves and their problems too seriously can be an important adaptive tool for successful relationships. As the relationships mature, the ability to use and appreciate appropriate humor grows. The ability to laugh together (or share other emotions) creates a positive, loving connection. The kind of humor that promotes loving relationships is the kind that both can share in and enjoy, rather than the type in which one person suffers for the sake of the other's wit.

Romano notes that virtually no couple seems to have all ten of these factors operating completely in their own lives, yet the more of them they have, the more happy and fulfilling their relationship. Although these were derived with the marriage relationship in mind, we feel they are quite applicable to many different types of relationships and we have tried to make that clear in our review of them.

Nature of Love

The form of love that we are emphasizing in this principle here is defined by Peck as the "will to extend one's self for the purpose of nurturing [a person's] spiritual growth."[52] We use this definition because it is active in nature and implies a type of emotion and communicative action that can be chosen regardless of what others may be choosing. Some may get concerned with the use of terms like spiritual and growth and the potential cultural baggage that goes along with them. Indeed, academic research sometimes avoids notions such as loving relationships and spiritual growth, and you may wonder if this is really appropriate for a textbook. We believe it is part of real life and that, in fact, it would be misleading and disrespectful to not share about these issues that we take to be so important in our intercultural relationships and the ethical quandaries that arise because of them.

Buddha taught, "When one person hates another, it is the hater who falls ill—physically, emotionally, spiritually. When [a person] loves, it is [that person] who becomes whole. Hatred kills. Love heals."[53] Jesus Christ charged his disciples to *love one another*.[54] Regardless of a person's beliefs, we argue that this is sound intercultural advice. Mistakes may be made as one tries to promote loving relationships, but if people accept this definition fully, they will openly acknowledge these mistakes without retreating to the strategies of hate, avoidance, and name calling. Love is no guarantee that there won't be problems, only a guarantee that genuine efforts to deal positively with these problems won't cease. Without this form of love, the best we can hope for is a manipulative form of negotiation in which our only concern for the other is grounded in how the relationship might better serve us. However, when this form of love exists, many of the perceived threats to and concerns over identity fade away. A person or group who has this love or feels that the others have this love for them is by definition engaged in a type of communication that produces understanding and finds ways to weave the different common senses together in mutually satisfying, even joyful ways.

SUMMARY

In this chapter we have asked if there is any way possible for us to judge those of another culture. To answer this question, we explored the idea of ethics. Ethics in general deals with standards of right and wrong, good and bad and is a part of every cultural community. We detailed six different *golden* approaches to ethical decision-making: the golden purse, golden mean, golden public, golden law, golden consequence, and golden rule. Each of these provides a rationale that people may use in evaluating their interactions with others.

We then focused on the relationship of ethics with both communication and culture in general. In terms of communication, we were able to see how ethics both constrain and enable our communication. The idea was captured by the realization that rights and responsibilities are really inseparable. The culture and ethics connection is often dominated by the debate between universalism and relativism. We proposed that strong stances in either of these two camps discourage cultural sensitivity and competence. Universalism and relativism do not have to be name-calling dichotomies, but rather are two ends of an ongoing tension that makes human choice meaningful.

We then briefly noted some attempts to identify a cross-cultural or universal ethic. We then turned our attention to three ethical principles that we believe are crucial to intercultural communication contexts. The first was an effort to understand that requires a stance of mutual legitimacy, genuine dialogue, a teachable attitude, and consideration of contexts. The second principle was peaceful disagreement, which incorporated nonviolent actions and choices that promoted truth and a safe environment for all involved, not just the powerful. Third was loving relationships, which involved a committed effort to help others and the relationship grow in positive ways. These three principles are much easier to write about than to live and it is acknowledged that they are guides to help us live among cultures in truly joyful ways.

As we conclude this book, we wish to share with you a short stanza from T. S. Eliot's poem "Little Gidding":

> We will not cease from exploration
> And the end of all our exploring
> Will be to arrive where we started
> And to know the place for the first time

It is our hope that the exploring engaged in through reading this book has not only helped you to understand other cultures, but has helped you to understand yourself and your own culture in a new and beneficial way.

REFLECTION QUESTIONS

1   We argue in the text that ethics both constrain and empower an individual's communication. Do you agree with this? What examples in your own life support both the constraining and empowering functions of ethics?

2   What should be our attitude toward people who act and think differently from ourselves? Does it make any difference whether they are living in our cultural community or we are living in theirs? Should we try to blend in

with their way of doing things, demand they conform to ours, or just do our own thing and tolerate them doing theirs?

3   The United States and other governments often put political pressure on outer communities to adhere to what most Americans feel is ethical behavior in areas of human rights and so on (such as the economic boycotts of South Africa). Is this kind of pressure appropriate? What sorts of factors does your answer depend on?

4   The three ethical principles discussed at the end of this chapter sound good to many people, but are often difficult to put into practice. Why? Is it worth even thinking about these sorts of things if we don't seem to be able to really put them into practice? How could one better put these principles into practice?

ACTIVITIES

1   Think of an ethical dilemma or question, ideally one with which you have been faced, but it could also be one you have heard about or be one of the group that led off this chapter. Then apply the six *golden* approaches discussed in this book to the problem. What answers or actions does each approach suggest? Do some of the *golden* approaches seem more ethical or better suited for intercultural interactions? Which of these approaches seems to be used most often in your community or in intercultural interactions of which you are aware?

2   Find a one-on-one conversation partner from another culture and actively try to put into practice the ideas discussed in the chapter about having a real dialogue with others. This will likely take more than one or two conversations.

3   Identify five different types of relationships you have with people (hopefully at least one will be intercultural) and then, using the list of ten factors that go into successful intercultural marriages according to Romano, give your relationship (regardless of the type) a score of 4 if your relationship fully illustrates this point, 3 if your relationship is pretty good in this area but can still use work, 2 if the relationship only occasionally fits the factor discussed and definitely needs work in this area, and 0 if your relationship simply lacks this factor completely. Add up the scores and then compare them and consider your general level of satisfaction with each of these different relationships. Hopefully this process will help you realize how you can help your relationships become even better and stronger than they already are.

4   Find a newspaper or magazine that deals with world news. How many different intercultural, ethical problems can you find? Discuss with a group of your peers or other friends how these problems could be dealt with in positive ways given the concepts discussed in class.

5   Do your own research on ethical universals. Interview people from at least five different cultures and ask what they feel are the most important ethical standards that people in general should follow. Perhaps give them an example of an intercultural ethical dilemma and get their reaction. Based on these answers, see if there are certain standards that are consistently viewed as more important than others. Write a paper in which you defend certain standards as universal or a paper in which you defend the claim that there are no universal ethical standards.

NOTES

1   This story is based on a compilation of experiences told to Brad by past students. The name Fukon Corporation is not the real name of the company in question.
2   G. Eliot, *Middlemarch* (New York: W. W. Norton, 1977), 3.
3   M. Saito, "*Nemawashi*: A Japanese Form of Interpersonal Communication," *Et cetera* 39 (1982): 205–13.
4   A few examples of more extensive discussion of ethics related to communication include F. L. Casmir, ed., *Ethics in Intercultural and International Communication* (Hillsdale, NJ: Lawrence Erlbaum Associates, 1997); J. V. Jensen, *Ethical Issues in the Communication Process* (Mahwah, NJ: Lawrence Erlbaum Associates, 1997); and T. Nilsen, *Ethics of Speech Communication* (New York: Bobbs-Merrill Company, 1966).
5   S. Streed, "A Moroccan Memoir," in *The House on Via Gombito*, 2nd ed., ed. M. Sprengnether, and C. W. Truesdale (Minneapolis, MN: New Rivers Press, 1997), 63–99.
6   Aristotle, *Nicomachean Ethics*, trans. H. Rackham (Cambridge, MA: Harvard University Press, 1934).
7   P. Patterson and L. Wilkins, *Media Ethics: Issues and Cases* (Dubuque, IA: Wm. C. Brown Publishers, 1991).
8   T. Wei-Ming, *Confucian Thought: Selfhood as Creative Transformation* (Albany, NY: State University of New York Press, 1985).
9   I. Kant, *Lectures on Ethics*, trans. L. Infield (London: Methuen, 1979).
10 J. S. Mill, *Mill's Ethical Writings*, ed. J. Scheenwind (New York: Collier Books, 1965).
11 M. Bennett, "Overcoming the Golden Rule: Sympathy and Empathy," in *Basic Concepts of Intercultural Communication: Selected Readings*, ed. M. J. Bennett (Yarmouth, ME: Intercultural Press, 1998), 191–214.
12 P. Covarrubias, "*Respeto* [Respect] in Disrespect: Clashing Cultural Themes within the Context of Immigration," in *The Handbook of Communication in Cross-Cultural Perspective: International Communication Association Series*, ed. D. Carbaugh (London: Routledge, 2017), 208–21.
13 Found in J. D. Beversluis, *Sourcebook of the World's Religions*, 3rd ed. (Novato, CA: New World Library, 2000), 172–3.
14 V. E. Cronen, V. Chen, and W. B. Pearce, "Coordinated Management of Meaning: A Critical Theory," in *Theories in Intercultural Communication*, ed. Y. Y. Kim and W. B. Gudykunst (Newbury Park, CA: Sage, 1988), 66–98.
15 E. Burke, *Reflections on the Revolution in France* (New York: Liberal Arts Press, 1955).

16 S. Fleischacker, *The Ethics of Culture* (Ithaca, NY: Cornell University Press, 1994).
17 S. Hauerwas, *The Peaceable Kingdom* (South Bend, IN: University of Notre Dame Press, 1983); and D. W. Kale, "Ethics in Intercultural Communication," in *Intercultural Communication: A Reader*, 6th ed., ed. L. Samovar and R. Porter (Belmont, CA: Wadsworth, 1991), 421–6.
18 W. S. Howell, *The Empathic Communicator* (Belmont, CA: Wadsworth, 1982), 187.
19 D. Carbaugh, *Talking American: Cultural Discourses on Donahue* (Norwood, NJ: Ablex, 1988).
20 M. Herskovits, *Cultural Relativism: Perspectives in Cultural Pluralism* (New York: Vintage Books, 1973).
21 Cronen, Chen, and Pearce, "Management of Meaning."
22 Kale, "Ethics"; and E. Hatch, *Culture and Morality: The Relativity of Values in Anthropology* (New York: Columbia University Press, 1983).
23 L. Steiner, "A Feminist Schema for Ethical Analyses of Intercultural Dilemmas," in *Ethics in Intercultural and International Communication*, ed. F. L. Casmir (Hillsdale, NJ: Lawrence Erlbaum Associates, 1997), 59–88.
24 K. Burke, *A Grammar of Motives* (Berkeley, CA: University of California Press, 1969).
25 J. V. Jensen, *Ethical Issues in the Communication Process* (Mahwah, NJ: Lawrence Erlbaum Associates, 1997).
26 C. Christians and M. Traber, "Introduction," in *Communication Ethics and Universal Values*, ed. C. Christians and M. Traber (Thousand Oaks, CA: Sage, 1997), 1–18.
27 K. Speakman, "Considering Kernal Images" (paper, University of New Mexico, 1997).
28 M. Buber, *I and Thou*, trans. W. Kaufmann (New York: Scribner's, 1970).
29 R. L. Johannesen, *Ethics in Human Communication*, 4th ed. (Prospect Heights, IL: Waveland Press, 1996).
30 The information for these two examples comes from K. Basso, *Joking as a "Whiteman" among the Western Apache* (Cambridge, MA: Cambridge University Press, 1979); and K. Fitch, "A Ritual for Attempting Leave-Taking in Colombia," *Research on Language and Social Interaction* 24 (1990/1): 209–24.
31 Basso, *Joking as a "Whiteman,"* 46–7.
32 R. Swalehe, E. M. Rogers, M. J. Gilboard, K. Alford, and R. Montoya, *A Content Analysis of the Entertainment-Education Radio Soap Opera "Twende Na Wakati" (Let's Go with the Times) in Tanzania* (Albuquerque, NM: University of New Mexico, Department of Communication and Journalism, 1995); and Arusha, Tanzania, *POFLEP Research Report*.
33 E. T. Hall, *The Dance of Life: The Other Dimension of Time* (Garden City, NY: Anchor Books/Doubleday, 1983).
34 R. S. Hegde, "Translated Enactments: The Relational Configurations of the Asian Indian Immigrant Experience," in *Readings in Cultural Contexts*, ed. J. N. Martin, T. K. Nakayama, and L. A. Flores (Mountain View, CA: Mayfield Publishing, 1998), 315–22.
35 L. Fisher, *The Essential Gandhi: His Life, Work and Ideas: An Anthology* (New York: Vintage Books, 1962).
36 Kale, "Ethics."
37 Fisher, *Essential Gandhi*; and J. A. Black, N. Harvey, and L. Robertson, eds., *Gandhi the Man* (based on the perspective of E. Easwaran) (San Francisco, CA: Glide Publications, 1972).
38 Black, Harvey, and Robertson, *Gandhi the Man*, 142.

39 Black, Harvey, and Robertson, *Gandhi the Man*, 87.
40 H. Smith, *The Religions of Man* (New York: Harper and Row, 1958).
41 Smith, *Religions of Man*.
42 *The Holy Bible: Authorized King James Version* (Matthew 26:52) (Salt Lake City, UT: Church of Jesus Christ of Latter-Day Saints).
43 *The Holy Bible* (Luke 23:34).
44 G. Vlastos, *Socrates, Ironist and Moral Philosopher* (Ithaca, NY: Cornell University Press, 1991).
45 S. Bok, *A Strategy for Peace: Human Values and the Threat of War* (New York: Vintage Books, 1990).
46 Black, Harvey, and Robertson, *Gandhi the Man*.
47 M. S. Peck, *The Different Drum: Community Making and Peace* (New York: Simon & Schuster, 1987).
48 D. Romano, *Intercultural Marriage: Promises and Pitfalls* (Yarmouth, ME: Intercultural Press, 1988).
49 Aristotle, *Rhetoric*, trans. G. Kennedy (New York: Oxford University Press, 1991).
50 Smith, *Religions of Man*.
51 Romano, *Intercultural Marriage*, 81.
52 M. S. Peck, *The Road Less Traveled* (New York: Simon & Schuster, 1978).
53 Black, Harvey, and Robertson, *Gandhi the Man*, 53.
54 *The Holy Bible* (John 13:34).

Index